ugly feelings

ugly feelings

SIANNE NGAI

HARVARD UNIVERSITY PRESS

Cambridge, Massachusetts · London, England

First Harvard University Press paperback edition, 2007

Library of Congress Cataloging-in-Publication Data
Ngai, Sianne.
Ugly feelings / Sianne Ngai.
p. cm.
Includes bibliographical references (p.   ) and index.
ISBN-13 978-0-674-01536-4 (cloth: alk. paper)
ISBN-10 0-674-01536-3 (cloth: alk. paper)
ISBN-13 978-0-674-02409-0 (pbk.)
ISBN-10 0-674-02409-5 (pbk.)
1. American literature—History and criticism.
2. Emotions in literature.
3. Psychological fiction, American—History and criticism.
4. Negativism in literature.   5. Sex role in literature.
6. Race in literature.   I. Title.
PS169.E48N45 2004
810.9'353—dc22   2004051133

To my parents

acknowledgments

I have been waiting a long time to thank Keith and Rosmarie Waldrop, who, long before I deserved it, first took me seriously as a writer and intellectual. Their encouragement set me down on the circuitous path that eventually led to the writing of this book.

Barbara Johnson, Stanley Cavell, and Lawrence Buell have been sources of inspiration during and well beyond the years in which my ideas first took shape. In different ways, each has been a model for the kind of critic I aspire to be. It was Larry Buell who first brought my work to the attention to Lindsay Waters, a small act of thoughtfulness on his part with significant consequences for me. Without Lindsay's energy and dedication to matters of affect and aesthetics, this book simply would not exist.

I feel lucky to have been read closely (at times unnervingly so) by some especially sharp colleagues. Specific chapters in this book owe a great deal to the critical insights of Rebecca Walkowitz, Douglas Mao, Steve Evans, Rob Halpern, Thalia Field, Gopal Balakrishnan, Barrett Watten, and my anonymous readers at Harvard University Press.

A very special thanks to Jay Fliegelman, friend to all books and to this one in particular. I am also grateful to my department chair Rob Polhemus, both for his camaraderie and commitment to supporting the scholarship of Stanford's junior faculty in English. Other Stanford colleagues—Roland Greene, Franco Moretti, Terry Castle, Rob Kaufman, Paula Moya, and Alex Woloch—caringly took time away from their own work to read mine.

Artist Marcel Dzama generously allowed me to use his drawing on the jacket. Thanks also to Maria Ascher for her editing, and to

Seagan Ngai, Justin Klein, and Matthew Jockers for their heroic assistance with technical matters. Kia Ling Ngai and Linsen Ngai were the first to show me what a passionate engagement with ideas looks like. I wish to thank them, as well as Dan Farrell, Aviva Briefel, and Monica Miller, for the simple but meaningful act of standing by me during the years I spent writing this book.

I owe the most to Mark McGurl, my toughest critic and most caring reader, for helping me discover what this book was actually about.

Financial support for the project was given in the form of research grants from Stanford University, and a Stanford Humanities Center Fellowship in 2002–2003. Early versions of some of the chapters appeared in *American Literature, Camera Obscura, Differences, Postmodern Culture*, and *Qui Parle*. I am grateful to Duke University Press, Johns Hopkins University Press, and the editors of *Qui Parle* for permission to republish these essays here.

contents

introduction

This book presents a series of studies in the aesthetics of negative emotions, examining their politically ambiguous work in a range of cultural artifacts produced in what T. W. Adorno calls the fully "administered world" of late modernity.[1] This is the world already depicted by Herman Melville with startling clarity in "Bartleby, the Scrivener: A Story of Wall Street" (1853)—a fiction in which the interpretive problems posed by an American office worker's *affective* equivocality seem pointedly directed at the *political* equivocality of his unnervingly passive form of dissent. What, if anything, is this inexpressive character feeling? Is Bartleby's unyielding passivity, even in the polemical act of withholding his labor ("I prefer not to"), radical or reactionary? Should we read his inertness as part of a volitional strategy that anticipates styles of nonviolent political activism to come, or merely as a sign of what we now call depression? In Melvillean fashion, the following chapters dwell on affective gaps and illegibilities, dysphoric feelings, and other sites of emotional negativity in literature, film, and theoretical writing, to explore similarly ambivalent situations of suspended agency. They thus draw together two seemingly disparate philosophical definitions—Hannah Arendt's claim that "what makes man a political being is his faculty of action" and Baruch Spinoza's description of emotions as "waverings of the mind" that can either increase or diminish one's power to act—and attend to the aesthetics of the ugly feelings that index these suspensions.[2]

Recalling the corner of the office in which Melville's scrivener is wedged and cordoned off by a screen, we might think of this book's project as Bartlebyan in a more reflexive sense, in that it privileges the circumscribed standpoint of the literary to examine problems whose greatest import arguably lies beyond the sphere of the aesthetic per se. For Bartleby's powerful powerlessness can also be thought of as exemplified by literature or art itself, as a relatively autonomous, more or less cordoned-off domain in an increasingly specialized and differentiated society. As Adorno's analysis of the historical origins of this aesthetic autonomy suggests, the separateness from "empirical society" which art gains as a consequence of the bourgeois revolution ironically coincides with its growing awareness of its inability to significantly change that society—a powerlessness that then becomes the privileged object of the newly autonomous art's "guilty" self-reflection (*AT,* 225). Yet one could argue that bourgeois art's reflexive preoccupation with its *own* "powerlessness and superfluity in the empirical world" is precisely what makes it capable of theorizing social powerlessness in a manner unrivaled by other forms of cultural praxis (104). In this manner, the discussion of aesthetic autonomy in *Aesthetic Theory* suggests that literature may in fact be the ideal space to investigate ugly feelings that obviously ramify beyond the domain of the aesthetic proper, since the situation of restricted agency from which all of them ensue is one that describes art's own position in a highly differentiated and totally commodified society.

Each of the feelings explored in the following chapters—envy, anxiety, paranoia, irritation, a racialized affect I call "animatedness," and a strange amalgamation of shock and boredom I call "stuplimity"—can thus be thought of as a mediation between the aesthetic and the political in a nontrivial way. As a whole, the book approaches emotions as unusually knotted or condensed "interpretations of predicaments"—that is, signs that not only render visible different registers of problem (formal, ideological, sociohistorical) but conjoin these problems in a distinctive manner.[3] My exclusive focus, however, is on the negative affects that read the predicaments posed by a general state of obstructed agency with respect to other human actors or to the social as such—a dilemma I take as charged with political meaning regardless of whether the obstruction is actual or fantasized, or whether the agency obstructed is individual or collective. These situations of passivity, as uniquely disclosed and interpreted by ignoble feelings like envy (of the disempowered for the powerful) or paranoia (about one's perceived status as a small subject in a "total system"), can also be thought of as allegories for an autonomous or bourgeois art's increasingly resigned and pessimistic understanding of its *own* relationship to political action. At the core of *Ugly Feelings,* then, is a very old predicament—the question of relevance—that has often haunted the discipline of literary and cultural criticism. The evidence here would suggest that the very effort of thinking the aesthetic and political together—a task whose urgency seems to increase in proportion to its difficulty in a increasingly anti-utopian and functionally differentiated society—is a prime occasion for ugly feelings.

Yet I want immediately to emphasize the deeply equivocal status of the ugly feelings featured in this study. For although dysphoric affects often seem to be the psychic fuel on which capitalist society runs, envy, paranoia, and all the emotional idioms I examine are marked by an ambivalence that will enable them to resist, on the one hand, their reduction to mere expressions of class *ressentiment,* and on the other, their counter-valorization as therapeutic "solutions" to the problems they highlight and condense. Admittedly it is part of this book's agenda to recuperate several of these negative affects for their *critical* productivity, but no one warns us better about the danger of romanticizing them than Paolo Virno, for whom the classic "sentiments of disenchantment" that once marked positions of radical alienation from the system of wage labor—anxiety, distraction, and cynicism—are now perversely integrated, from the factory to the office, into contemporary capitalist production itself: "Fears of particular dangers, if only virtual ones, haunt the workday like a mood that cannot be escaped. This fear, however, is transformed into *an operational requirement,* a special tool of the trade. Insecurity about one's place during periodic innovation, fear of losing recently gained privileges, and anxiety over being 'left behind' translate into flexibility, adaptability, and a readiness to reconfigure oneself."[4] Here we see how capitalism's classic affects of disaffection (and thus of potential social conflict and political antagonism) are neatly reabsorbed by the wage system and reconfigured into professional ideals. Nothing could be further from Fredric Jameson's more widely known thesis about the "waning" of negative affect in our contemporary moment.[5] Instead, Virno shows how central and perversely *functional* such affective attitudes and dispositions have become, as the very lubricants of the economic system which they originally came into being to oppose.[6] Yet while irreversibly integrated into the contemporary, post-Fordist organization of labor, these ugly feelings remain, for Virno, "open to radically conflicting developments" ("AD," 26). For example, while there is nothing redeeming about the "eager" disposition of opportunism, its "'truth' . . . what might be called its neutral kernel, resides in the fact that our relation with the world tends to articulate itself primarily through possibilities, opportunities, and chances, instead of according to linear and univocal directions." As Virno points out, "This modality of experience, even if it nourishes opportunism, does not necessarily result in it" (25). For other kinds of behavior, and even kinds diametrically opposed to opportunism, "might also be inscribed within an experience fundamentally structured by these same possibilities and fleeting opportunities. We can discern such radical and transformative behavior, however, only by tracing in the opportunism so widespread today the specific modality of experience to which this behavior might indeed be correlated, even if in a completely different way" (25). Indeed, one could extrapolate from Virno's claims to argue that in the transnational stage of capitalism that defines our contemporary moment, our emotions no longer link up as securely as they once did with the models of social action and transformation theorized by Aristotle, Thomas Hobbes, and others under the signs of relatively unambiguous emotions like anger or fear. In other words, the nature of the sociopolitical itself has changed in a manner that both calls forth and calls upon a new set of feelings—ones less powerful than the classical political passions, though perhaps more suited, in their ambient, Bartlebyan, but still diagnostic nature, for models of subjectivity, collectivity, and agency not entirely foreseen by past theorists of the commonwealth. This is why, for Virno, even an unattractive feeling like opportunism can provide the "kernel" from which to shape "transforative behavior." For all its pettiness, the feeling calls attention to a real social experience and a certain kind of historical truth.

While this book makes a similar if more modest claim for the social significance of its own fundamentally ambivalent "sentiments of disenchantment" (an ambivalence demonstrated by the fact that all are mobilized as easily by the political right as by the left, as the histories of disgust and paranoia illustrate so well), it is useful to recall that with notable exceptions like Hobbes or Niccolò Machiavelli, who made fear central to their theories of modern sovereignty and the state, it is the discourse of philosophical aesthetics, rather than that of political philosophy or economy, in which emotions have traditionally played the most pivotal role—from Longinus to Immanuel Kant on the sublime (perhaps the first "ugly" or explicitly nonbeautiful feeling appearing in theories of aesthetic judgment), to the twentieth-century mutation of this affect I describe in my chapter on stuplimity. Or, to trace another exemplary arc, from the seventeenth-century "Affect Theorists" who tried to systematize the correlation of musical forms and genres to specific emotions, to Susanne Langer's analysis of music as a "tonal analogue of emotive life" in *Philosophy in a New Key,* to my own attempt to re-animate the concept of literary "tone" by means of the atonal but no less musical concept of noise. The investigation of how new theories of affect might expand the discourse of aesthetics thus continues a long-standing intellectual project, even as it sets this book apart from cultural histories of specific emotions (as, for instance, *American Nervousness, 1903: An Anecdotal History,* by Tom Lutz; *Anatomy of Disgust,* by William Ian Miller; and *Cato's Tears and the Making of Anglo-American Emotion,* by Julie Ellison), as well as from new philosophies of emotion that inquire into what feeling is (*Parables for the Virtual,* by Brian Massumi; *Feeling in Theory,* by Rei Terada; and *The Vehement Passions,* by Philip Fisher). In a sense, the book's turn to ugly feelings to reanimate aesthetics is simply the flip side of its privileging of the aesthetic domain as the ideal site to examine the politically ambiguous work of negative emotions.

More specifically, this book turns to ugly feelings to expand and transform the category of "aesthetic emotions," or feelings unique to our encounters with artworks—a concept whose oldest and best-known example is Aristotle's discussion of catharsis in *Poetics.* Yet this particular aesthetic emotion, the arousal and eventual purgation of pity and fear made possible by the genre of tragic drama, actually serves as a useful foil for the studies that follow. For in keeping with the spirit of a book in which minor and generally unprestigious feelings are deliberately favored over grander passions like anger and fear (cornerstones of the philosophical discourse of emotions, from Aristotle to the present), as well as over potentially ennobling or morally beatific states like sympathy, melancholia, and shame (the emotions given the most attention in literary criticism's recent turn to ethics), the feelings I examine here are explicitly *a*moral and *non*cathartic, offering no satisfactions of virtue, however oblique, nor any therapeutic or purifying release. In fact, most of these feelings tend to interfere with the outpouring of other emotions. Moods like irritation and anxiety, for instance, are defined by a flatness or ongoingness entirely opposed to the "suddenness" on which Aristotle's aesthetics of fear depends.[7] And unlike rage, which cannot be sustained indefinitely, less dramatic feelings like envy and paranoia have a remarkable capacity for duration. If *Ugly Feelings* is a bestiary of affects, in other words, it is one filled with rats and possums rather than lions, its categories of feeling generally being, well, weaker and nastier.

This weakness and nastiness notwithstanding, most of the negative affects in this study have managed to endure in a way that other feelings once widely in circulation (like the nineteenth-century feelings of "neurasthenia" and "amativeness") have not, acquiring a colloquial status that broadens the range of sociohistorical dilemmas they can be used to interpret. Each ugly feeling will thus be examined in a cultural context where it seems particularly charged or at stake, ranging from contemporary feminist debates over the perceived problem of aggression between feminists (a context in which the antagonistic as well as pejoratively feminized feeling of "envy" becomes especially problematic) to an American cultural discourse that from the antebellum period forward has found it compelling to imagine the racialized subject as an excessively emotional and expressive subject (a situation in which the affect I call "animatedness" becomes especially problematic). Envy and animatedness could thus be described as affective ideologemes, in the sense of being "historically determinate conceptual or semic complex[es] which can project [themselves] in the form of a 'value system,'" but also, more simply, as concepts that become the site and stake of various kinds of symbolic struggle.[8] While this book pays close attention to the conditions under which these struggles unfold, and singles out specific contexts in which they become particularly intense, it is not a history of feelings. Its overarching project is rather a theoretical one, calling for a more fluid reading across forms, genres, and periods than is the prevailing norm in academic criticism today. Hence, texts are frequently read in what may seem like jarring juxtapositions: Alfred Hitchcock's *Vertigo* and Martin Heidegger's analysis of anxiety in *Being and Time* read with Melville's *Pierre,* for instance, in my analysis of anxiety's curious elevation to a place of prominence in Western intellectual life. In the tradition of Barbara Johnson's book *The Feminist Difference,* this method of disjunctive alignment is intended to allow the texts to become "readable in new ways" and thus generate fresh examinations of historically tenacious problems.[9]

In this manner, the strength of this book resides not in the historical detail it will supply, but in the theoretical groundwork it will construct. In fact, by not just analyzing but mobilizing affective concepts to investigate a wide range of dilemmas, the book makes arguments that provide motivation for further historical research by explaining why these feelings might be interesting enough to merit attention in the first place. It also demonstrates how feeling can be used to expand the project of criticism and theory. Just as one chapter mobilizes envy to disclose the unusual difficulty feminine aggression has posed for an otherwise versatile and capacious psychoanalytic theory on which feminist film criticism has strongly relied, another invokes the affect I call "stuplimity" to highlight certain limitations in classic theories of the sublime that prevent it from adequately accounting for the experience of boredom increasingly intertwined with contemporary experiences of aesthetic awe. Marshaling its minor affects to investigate impasses in contemporary theory and criticism that might otherwise remain unseen, the book attempts to demonstrate how emotion might be recuperated for critical praxis in general, shedding new light on the intimate relationship between negative affect and "negative thinking," Herbert Marcuse's shorthand for ideology critique in the dialectical tradition.[10] In general, like a vaudeville show or revue film (where Max Horkheimer and Adorno find "the negative" to "glimmer for a few moments" in their otherwise unhesitating indictment of the culture industry), this book spotlights a large and transatlantic ensemble of texts by authors across genres and periods.[11]

Despite an array that may seem idiosyncratic, the selection of texts by these authors—Sigmund Freud, Ralph Ellison, Silvan Tomkins, Harriet Beecher Stowe, Gertrude Stein, Nella Larsen, John Yau, and Melanie Klein, among others—has been determined by the *kinds* of negative feeling I have chosen to emphasize. In this I follow the lead of Hobbes. In his discussion in *Leviathan,* for instance, of the role played by fear in securing the covenants upon which social order in the commonwealth depends, Hobbes argues that the human fear of "invisible spirits" (which, prior to the time of civil society, superseded our fear of the power of other humans) gave rise to a specific form or genre: the oath. Hobbes defines this as "a form of speech, added to a promise, by which he that promiseth, signifieth, that unless he perform, he renounceth the mercy of his God." "And this," he adds, "that the fear of breaking faith might be the greater."[12] Specific kinds of emotion thus could be said to determine specific "literary kinds"—and, in Hobbes's example, one that will strategically intensify the very emotion at its origin (Fisher, *VP,* 8). In a similar vein, the noncathartic feelings in this book could be said to give rise to a noncathartic aesthetic: art that produces and foregrounds a failure of emotional release (another form of suspended "action") and does so as a kind of politics. Such a politics is of a Bartlebyan sort—very different, say, from the direct activism supposedly incited, according to what has now become American folklore, by Harriet Beecher Stowe's poetics of sympathy and the genre of sentimental literature as a whole.[13] Just as one can study fear through the specific forms to which it gives rise, such as the oath, the alibi, or complex genres like the horror film, my book examines the synthesis of boredom and shock I call "stuplimity" through a literature of exhausting repetitions and permutations, paranoia through a transcription-based poetry that continually raises the question of whether writing comes from inside or outside its author, and the racialized affect of animatedness through the screen genre of animated cartoons.

The equivocality of the Bartlebyan aesthetic suggests that there is a special relationship between ugly feelings and irony, a rhetorical attitude with a decidedly affective dimension, if not a "feeling" per se. For the morally degraded and seemingly unjustifiable status of these feelings tends to produce an unpleasurable feeling *about* the feeling (a reflexive response taking the form of "I feel ashamed about feeling envious" or "I feel anxious about my enviousness") that significantly parallels the doubleness on which irony, as an evaluative stance hinging on a relationship between the said and the unsaid, fundamentally depends.[14] In their tendency to promote what Susan Feagin calls "meta-responses" (since it is hard to feel envy without feeling that one should *not* be feeling envy, reinforcing the negativity of the original emotion), there is a sense in which ugly feelings can be described as conducive to producing ironic distance in a way that the grander and more prestigious passions, or even the moral emotions associated with sentimental literature, do not.[15] This is why the aesthetic examples in this book tend *not* to be drawn from the more recognizably "emotional" genres—such as melodrama, sentimental fiction, tales of supernatural horror, or lyric poetry—to which literary critics interested in such matters have traditionally turned. While the ironic as well as the non-cathartic aspect of ugly feelings drives this book's preference for "constructivist" rather than "expressivist" forms as ideal sites for examining the social and symbolic productivity of emotion in general, it is another key aspect of these negative feelings—that of being noticeably weaker in intensity than what Philip Fisher calls the "vehement passions" underwriting canonically major forms and genres like Homeric epic and Shakespearean tragedy—which informs its preference for texts that even seem oddly impassive: texts that, like "Bartleby," foreground the absence of a strong emotion where we are led to expect one, or turn entirely on the interpretive problems posed by an emotional illegibility. The fact that this book reads the tonally ambiguous *Confidence-Man* rather than the rage-driven epic *Moby-Dick,* Nella Larsen's superficially "irritated" *Quicksand* but not the melodrama of jealousy that is *Passing,* and Beckett's exhausting poetry of permutations and combinations as opposed to the Romantic lyric, proceeds directly from its emphasis on the ignoble cousins of the philosophically canonical emotions featured in Fisher's study. With the turn to the ambiguous affects of the administered world's many "Sub-Subs"—Melville's appellation for the minor employee, or "mere painstaking burrower and grub-worm," who dutifully assembles the cetological "Extracts" that open *Moby-Dick*[16]—rather than those of more iconic figures such as Ahab, Othello, or Lear, my focus will be on irritation *instead of* anger, envy *rather than* jealousy, and "stuplimity" *as opposed to* the transcendent feeling of the sublime. It is interesting to note here that while the texts chosen for the way they highlight these feelings are drawn from both high and mass culture, all are canonically minor. Something about the cultural canon itself seems to prefer higher passions and emotions—as if minor or ugly feelings were not only incapable of producing "major" works, but somehow disabled the works they do drive from acquiring canonical distinction.

Still, while partly a response to one philosopher's call for a study of feeling with a more idiosyncratic focus than those that "concentrate on analyzing the features of a handful of classic emotions,"[17] the "negativity" of the feelings in this book obtains at several levels that the classic emotions share. Like rage and fear, ugly feelings such as envy can be described as dysphoric or experientially negative, in the sense that they evoke pain or displeasure. They can also be described as "semantically" negative, in the sense that they are saturated with socially stigmatizing meanings and values (such as the "pettiness" one traditionally associates with envy); and as "syntactically" negative, in the sense that they are organized by trajectories of repulsion rather than attraction, by phobic strivings "away from" rather than philic strivings "toward." In the case of these explicitly agonistic emotions, informed by what one psychoanalyst calls the global affect of "against," the negativity at stake is algorithmic or operational, rather than value- or meaning-based, involving processes of aversion, exclusion, and of course negation.[18] It is these multiple levels of negativity that make the ugly feelings in this study so useful for *conjoining* predicaments from multiple registers—showing how sociohistorical and ideological dilemmas, in particular, produce formal or representational ones. The affect I call animatedness, for instance, will allow us to take the disturbingly enduring representation of the African-American as at once an excessively "lively" subject and a pliant body unusually susceptible to external control and link this representation to the rhetorical figure of apostrophe (in which a speaker animates or "gives life" to nonhuman objects by addressing them as subjects capable of response), and, further, to connect these to a symptomatic controversy surrounding the televisual aesthetics of dimensional animation, a technique in which clay or foam puppets are similarly brought to "life" as racialized characters by being physically manipulated and ventriloquized.

In this manner, even as the exaggerated expressiveness and hyperactivity associated with animatedness marks an important exception to the Bartlebyan aesthetic fostered by the other feelings in this book, it similarly draws our attention to the politically charged predicament of suspended agency from which all of these ugly feelings ensue. As the translation, into affect, of a state of being "puppeteered" that points to a specific history of systemic political and economic disenfranchisement, racialized animatedness actually calls attention to this predicament in a particularly emphatic way. It is the situation of passivity itself, and the allegorical significance it transmits to the ugly feelings that both originate from and reflect back upon it, to which I now want to turn in closer detail, by examining several moments of narrative inaction from two other American stories of the corporate workplace: the crime melodrama *Double Indemnity* (Paramount, 1944; directed by Billy Wilder, based on the novel by James M. Cain) and the conspiracy film *The Conversation* (Paramount, 1974; directed by Francis Ford Coppola). Like Melville's "Story of Wall Street," both films depict a worker's in-

creasingly alienated relationship to the corporation that employs
him, as well as to the institutions of the state. Both are also examples of film noir, a postwar genre commonly understood (even to
the point of cliché) as being aesthetically and ideologically driven
by an entire spectrum of dysphoric feelings: paranoia, alienation,
greed, jealousy, and so forth.

The inertial moments from the two films I want to examine
could not be more different from the films' more highly memorable moments of intense emotion, which (unsurprisingly) correlate
with significant actions propelling the plot forward: such as, in the
case of *Double Indemnity,* the kiss that seals the protagonist's decision to help his lover kill her husband, the murder itself, his final
confrontation with the femme fatale, and so forth. In contrast to
the "mere recital" of events, which Aristotle finds superior to visual
spectacle for the maximization of catharsis ("mere recital" entailing
a summary in which the duration of events narrated greatly exceeds that of their actual narration, such that "even without seeing
the things take place, he who simply hears the account of them
shall be filled with horror and pity"), the moments from the noir
films that concern us involve a narrative expansion or stretch, in
which "discourse time" becomes considerably longer than "story
time."[19] While it has been noted that cinema in general "has trouble
with summary," often resorting to devices ranging from montage
sequences to "cruder solutions . . . like peeling calendars," the preference for the narrative stretch over a compression that "forces us
to take in the entire story almost instantaneously" might also be
said to reflect the difference between the paranoia that suffuses the
postwar film noir and the fear that drives classical tragedy; as a
feeling without a clearly defined object, paranoia would logically
promote a more ambient aesthetic, one founded on a temporality
very different from the "suddenness" central to Aristotle's aesthetics of fear.[20] The anticathartic device of dilating the time in which
any particular incident takes place thus accentuates the manner in
which these uneventful moments mirror the general situation of

obstructed agency that gives rise to all the ugly feelings I examine, allowing them to function as political allegories in Arendt's sense above. But despite their obvious difference from scenes of high drama keyed to emotional tonalities which we are intended to recognize instantly, and even as their own affective quality remains comparatively undefined, these moments of conspicuous inactivity remain affectively charged. What seems indeterminate here, however, is actually highly determined. In fact, I would suggest that what each moment produces is the inherently ambiguous affect of affective disorientation in general—what we might think of as a state of feeling vaguely "unsettled" or "confused," or, more precisely, a meta-feeling in which one feels confused about *what* one is feeling. This is "confusion" in the affective sense of bewilderment, rather than the epistemological sense of indeterminacy. Despite its marginality to the philosophical canon of emotions, isn't this feeling of confusion *about* what one is feeling an affective state in its own right? And in fact a rather familiar feeling that often heralds the basic affect of "interest" underwriting all acts of intellectual inquiry? Turning to our two films, we may find it useful to refer to this very *specific* state of affective indeterminacy as the negative feeling of "disconcertedness"—the feeling of not being "focused" or "gathered." Such an ugly feeling is intimately tied (as we shall see) to the "loss of control" explicitly thematized in each moment of stalled or suspended action. Most important, in both films the dysphoric affect of affective disorientation—of being lost on one's own "cognitive map" of available affects—is concretely rendered through a *spatial* confusion made possible by a notoriously unstable narrative technique that film scholars have credited the genre of film noir with most fully instrumentalizing: subjective or first-person camera.

My first example involves a tracking shot from *Double Indemnity* that eventually captures the wounded protagonist, Pacific All-Risk Insurance agent Walter Neff (Fred McMurray), as he speaks into a dictaphone and concludes his narration of the events that have led up to his present condition (Figures 1a–c). Throughout the film, Neff's self-recorded narration, which eventually discloses his participation in two murders, is directly addressed to his avuncular boss and mentor at the insurance company, Barton Keyes (Edward G. Robinson), who has also been a major character in the story which Neff has been recounting and which the film presents to us through a series of voiceover-flashbacks. The shot that returns us to the scene of narration for the last time seems, initially, unambiguously objective—as would be thematically appropriate, given the symbolic import of the "impartial" recording instrument into which Neff speaks his story, and the fact that the depiction of a narrator in the actual act of telling or narrating (in this case, a technologically mediated, quasi-documentary act) will always have a stronger claim to objectivity than his subjectively filtered tale. As the camera comes to rest on the actor's profile, however, in a view so uncomfortably close that we can see the beads of sweat on his averted face, Neff slowly turns his head from the dictaphone toward the camera, as if to signal a realism-breaking awareness of its presence, or, more simply, a growing consciousness of being watched (Figures 1d–g). Our sense of the emotional tension that comes to inflect the shot is subsequently confirmed as Neff says, "Hello Keyes."

The cut to the compositionally contrasting shot that follows (Figure 1h), a long view revealing Keyes standing in the opened office door, unsettlingly reveals that the point of view of the preceding shot has in fact *been* that of Keyes, and that Keyes—in keeping with his general role as Neff's intellectual superior as well as the film's one representative of law and order—has been watching and listening to Neff's confession, unbeknownst to both Neff and the film's audience, for an indefinite time, if not all along. "How long have you been standing there?" asks Neff. "Long enough," is Keyes's response. The implications of the objective shot's curiously stealthy and *belated* subjectivization are as serious as its affective intensity is strong. Just as Keyes "sneaks up" on Neff at the level of

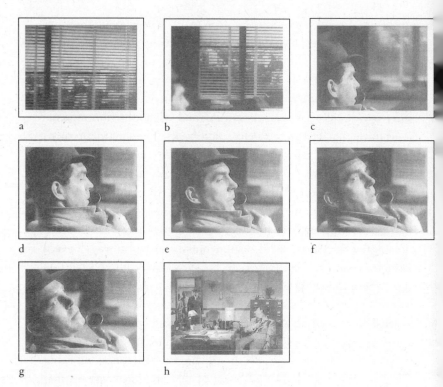

FIGURE I

discourse as well as at the level of story, and visually as well as narratively, as his point of view steals into and claims authorship over
a gaze initially owned by no subject in the diegesis, Neff is in a
double sense "caught," since it is understood that his capture in the
visual field surreptitiously overtaken by Keyes will entail his capture by the law. In fact, in the original, bleaker version of the film
which did not survive its studio censors, the arresting shot leads not
only to Neff's imprisonment, but to his execution by the state in a
gas chamber. In this manner, the moment when Keyes steps out of
the subjectively filtered world of the story told by Neff and enters
the more objective world in which Neff's act of telling takes place
is not only a moment designed to reaffirm his character's power

and authority (only Keyes, among all the other characters contained in the flashback sequences, is able to cross over from the past into the present), but one that produces an affective disorientation and qualitative change in the relationship between the two men.

Variations of this alternation between subjective and objective framing, and its use for the purpose of producing the highly specific feeling of feeling uncertain *about* what one is feeling—the "disconcertedness" which, in this case, heralds and morphs into the more articulated pathos of feeling "busted"—abound in film noir and its generic descendants. In Francis Ford Coppola's Watergate-era conspiracy film *The Conversation* (1974), we find the emotional effects of the technique maximized when it is used to produce the paranoia of a surveillance professional apprehended in the very gaze one would expect him to command. Like Cain's Pacific All-Risk Insurance agent and Melville's Wall Street scrivener, Harry Caul (Gene Hackman) is a white-collar worker who becomes increasingly alienated from and, eventually, overtly antagonistic toward the organization that employs him. Though we have already seen this opposition take the form of a work slowdown culminating in a full-blown stoppage (in "Bartleby"), as well as what Neff describes as an attempt to "crook the house," in *The Conversation* it appears as an effort to thwart a corporate conspiracy, revealed by a protagonist with much greater autonomy and libidinal investment in his work than his fictional predecessors had. Yet here the link between the moment of suspended action in the film's story and the frustrated agency of the film's male protagonist is much more structurally and thematically explicit as well as politically charged. For while Harry's stunted "faculty of action" appears in the guise of an individual problem, the film immediately reveals it as a synecdoche for a much larger social and in fact national ill, as exemplified by the collective apathy the eponymous conversationalists in the crucial opening scene discuss, as they observe sleeping homeless men (who may or may not be Vietnam war veterans) in a crowded public park—a setting that itself suggests a miniaturized representation of the social whole. Moreover, what we have else-where examined as a passivity with political resonance or implications is presented here as a passivity with respect to the domain of politics proper. For we learn that in an earlier phase of his surveillance career, while employed by a state prosecutor, Harry has refused, in the name of the "objectivity" conveniently idealized by his profession, to concern himself with the content of the surveillance cases assigned to him, regardless of the violent ends (including the murder of a local union official) which he suspects his government work may have furthered. Indexed here by the specific feelings of paranoia and guilt, rather than an affective absence or illegibility, Harry's political passivity, and correlative obsessions with maintaining his privacy and solitude, will become most evident in his inability to prevent a murder engineered by the private corporation for which (in a trajectory that neatly reverses Bartleby's move from the postal service's Dead Letter Office to a lawyer's firm on Wall Street) he has left the Attorney General's office to work—an inability he cannot overcome despite the technical expertise that has given him advance knowledge of the plot and thus his chance to redeem his past detachment. The allegorically charged moment of narrative stasis that concerns us occurs in the hotel room in which this murder (a sign as well as a direct consequence of Harry's political impotence) has taken place.

Dramatized, again, by a high ratio of discourse time to story time (and tellingly silent in the context of a film about conversations), the scene opens as Harry reenters this room after the traumatic experience of overhearing, from an adjacent room, the actual sounds of the crime. The take that concerns us begins with a view of Harry cautiously peering through the half-open door (Figure 2a). Moving in the direction of his gaze, the camera drops him from its visual field as it very slowly and methodically, much like a highly skilled surveillance professional, pans across the enigmatically unoccupied and immaculate room (Figures 2b–h). Because

Harry has abruptly disappeared from the visual field, as the pan continues we are made to understand that we are seeing what he sees. Without any break in its continuity or flow, the shot has thus already undergone a transition from objective to subjective. The relatively long duration of the pan seems intended, in fact, to secure the shot's surreptitious change in valence, to give the viewer time, as it were, to get used to its subjectivization. But as the camera completes its near 180-degree turn around the room, we are surprised by Harry's sudden *reappearance* at the far right edge of the visual field (Figure 2i). Here the shot undergoes its second transition, from subjective back to objective—for how else could Harry appear in a shot designed to represent his *own* gaze? In this case, the uncertainty over the authorship of the visual field highlights the pathos of the surveillance professional's increasing impotence and self-entanglement in the corporate conspiracy (a ghostly afterimage, if we follow Fredric Jameson's lead, of the social totality of late capitalism itself) in which he hopes to intervene.[21] In this otherwise uneventful and unemotional scene (one in which the enunciated content, or what we are shown, is that there is precisely "nothing to see"), Harry loses control of his own gaze—through a desubjectifying discourse that anticipates his own eventual transformation into an *object* of surveillance by the very corporation that has hired him, as the film's final scene depicting his failed effort to debug his own apartment ominously makes clear. In fact, the shot's cunning *re*-objectivization suggests just how uncertain this surveillance expert's grasp of the visual field has perhaps been all along.

Though *Double Indemnity* has already shown us how this alternation between subjective and objective enunciation can be used to produce irony as well as the uncanny affect of disconcertedness, the technique is used in *The Conversation* to produce another highly determinate feeling—paranoia—that not coincidentally replicates the subjective/objective oscillation in its basic structure: Is the enemy *out there* or *in me*? Confusion about feeling's objective or subjective status becomes *inherent* to the feeling. Our readings of the

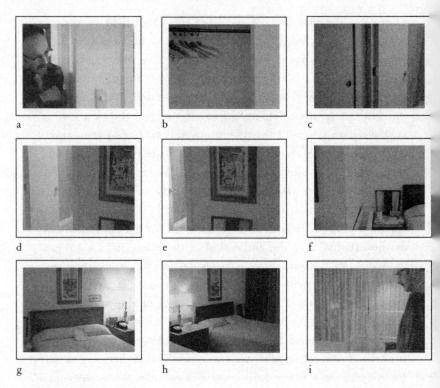

FIGURE 2

Bartlebyan moments of inaction highlighted above have thus pre-
pared us for a crucial reversal of the familiar idea that vehement
emotions—in particular, the strongly intentional or object-directed
emotions in the philosophical canon, such as jealousy, anger, and
fear—destabilize our sense of the boundary between the psyche
and the world, or between subjective and objective reality. In contrast, my argument is that a systematic problematization of the distinction between subjective and objective enunciation lies at the
heart of the Bartlebyan feelings in this book—minor affects that
are far less intentional or object-directed, and thus more likely to
produce political and aesthetic ambiguities, than the passions in the
philosophical canon. For just as the question of whether one's para-

noia is subjective or objective is internal to paranoia, the historically feminized and proletarianized emotion of envy has another version of this problematic at its core. While envy describes a subject's polemical response to a perceived inequality in the external world, it has been reduced to signifying a static subjective trait: the "lack" or "deficiency" of the person who envies. Hence, after a person's envy enters a public domain of signification, it will always seem unjustified and critically effete—regardless of whether the relation of inequality it points to (say, unequal ownership of a means of production) has a real and objective existence. In this manner, although envy begins with a clearly defined object—and it is the *only* negative emotion defined specifically by the fact that it addresses forms of inequality—it denies the very objectivity of this object. In doing so, it oddly bears a much closer resemblance to feelings lacking clearly defined objects, such as anxiety, than it does to an intentional emotion like jealousy. Envy is, in a sense, an intentional feeling that paradoxically undermines its own intentionality.

Marked by this conversion of a polemical engagement with the *objective* world into a reflection of a *subjective* characteristic, the confusion over a feeling's subjective or objective status that we have seen become internal to paranoia also seems internal to envy. Both are feelings that contain, as it were, models of the problem that defines them. Even an ostensibly degree-zero affect like animatedness has a version of this subjective/objective problematic at its core—namely, the question of whether "animation" designates high-spiritedness, or a puppet-like state analogous to the assembly-line mechanization of the human body famously dramatized by Charlie Chaplin in *Modern Times*. In the form of a dialectic of inside/outside, the subjective/objective problematic will likewise haunt Heidegger's and Hitchcock's strikingly similar conceptions of "anxiety," and will motivate the spatial fantasy of "thrownness" that sustains the affect's intellectual aura and prestige. In the form of a tension between psychological interiors and bodily exteriors, the subjective/objective problematic will become similarly integral to the affect of irritation—defined, as Nella Larsen will show us, by its very liminality as an affective concept (weak or mild anger), given its unusual proximity to a bodily or epidermal one (soreness, rawness, inflammation, or chafing).

The striking persistence with which the feelings in this book reflexively "theorize" or internalize the confusion between the subjective status and objective status of feeling in general can be taken as following from their relatively weak intentionality—their indistinctness if not absence of object. Indeed, while it is widely agreed that "emotions play roles in forms of action,"[22] the feelings in this study tend to be diagnostic rather than strategic, and to be diagnostically concerned with states of *inaction* in particular. Even the objects of envy and disgust, the most strongly intentional and dynamic feelings among my set of seven, and the only two that can be classified as emotions proper, are imbued with negativity. While envy, as we have seen, aggressively casts doubt on the objectivity of the very object that distinguishes it from other agonistic emotions (the social relation of inequality), disgust is constituted by the vehement rejection or *exclusion* of its object. Hence while disgust is always disgust *toward,* in the same way that envy is envy *of*— whereas it makes no sense to speak of stuplimity of or animatedness toward—its grammar brings it closer to the intransitive feelings in this study than to the other emotions with which it is traditionally classified. For while envy and disgust are clearly object-directed, their trajectories are directed toward the *negation* of these objects, either by denying them or by subjecting them to epistemological skepticism.

Not surprisingly, the boundary confusions built into the structure of these feelings, whether in the form of inside/outside, self/ world, or psyche/body, reappear in the aesthetic forms and genres they determine. They will therefore return in the series of representational predicaments I will mobilize these ugly feelings to read: ranging from controversies about the use of the "ugly" cinematic technique of claymation (dimensional screen animation) as a format for representing racial minorities on television, to the kind of bad or contagious mimesis—resulting in a symptomatic confusion between female self and female other, and even between phantasmatic identifications and observable acts of imitation—which crops up in accounts of female envy such as those found in *Group Psychology and the Analysis of the Ego* (Freud) and the lurid film *Single White Female*. While important to these specific aesthetic or representational controversies, the question of feeling's objective or subjective status has in fact been central to numerous philosophical investigations into the exact role and status of emotion in the aesthetic encounter. These investigations include debates over whether Aristotle uses *katharsin* to refer to something that takes place in the audience or that takes place in the tragic drama (that is, whether it refers to a response undergone by the viewing subject or to an event presented in the object viewed); John Dewey's effort to divorce expression from "the mere issuing forth or discharge of raw material" by describing "esthetic emotion" as "objectified" emotion; T. S. Eliot's closely related attempt to separate "personal emotion" from "art emotion," which he describes as a mixture or cocktail producing "feelings which are not in actual emotions at all"; the counterintuitive effort, on the part of Edmund Burke and other Enlightenment empiricists, to use emotional qualities to "objectify" or standardize judgments of taste (so as to avoid the problem of relativism it inevitably poses); and Gérard Genette's unapologetically subjectivist theory of aesthetic judgment as a mode of illusory projection, in which a quality or value reflecting the negative or positive feeling inspired by an object's appearance, in what amounts to a fundamentally subjective appraisal, is treated "as if" it were one of the object's own intrinsic properties.[23] For Genette, who claims to "out-Kant" Kant by fully acknowledging the relativism Kant's subjectivist theory of aesthetic judgment attempted to sidestep (by asserting the claim for universality in the judgment itself), aesthetic judgment *is* this illusory objectification. It is this process that produces what Genette calls "aesthetic predicates," affective-aesthetic values like "precious," "stilted," "monotonous," or "imperious," created from, or based upon, the feeling of pleasure or displeasure that accompanies our initial perception of the aesthetic object (*AR*, 90). Genette in fact describes these objectifying predicates, which bear a close resemblance to what I. A. Richards called "aesthetic or 'projectile' adjectives," as descriptive terms that "sneak in" evaluations of the object based on *feelings* about the object.[24] There is thus a sense in which the "aesthetic relation," which for Genette is more or less synonymous with "objectification," can be understood as an oblique effort to justify the presence of feeling in every aesthetic encounter.

The subjective-objective problematic, magnified by the relativism of aesthetic judgment and other classic problems in the discourse of aesthetics (including the contested notion of special "aesthetic feelings"), is central, as we have seen, to the ugly feelings in this book, as well as to the artistic forms and genres they generate. It will be a particular concern in my discussion of "tone" (Chapter 1), the affective-aesthetic concept that will implicitly inform all the analyses of the aesthetics of specific feelings that follow. Yet the subjective/objective problematic so central to the philosophy of aesthetics can also be traced back to the philosophy of *emotion* in general. It has become the über-question of recent theoretical writing on feeling in particular, as evinced in the analysis of emotion after "the death of the subject" (Rei Terada) or attempts to differentiate "emotion" and "affect" on the grounds that the former requires a subject while the latter does not (Lawrence Grossberg, Brian Massumi).[25] These questions reflect the extent to which the subjective dimension of feeling, in particular, in seeming to undercut its validity as an object of *materialist* inquiry, has posed a difficulty for contemporary theorists. The present spotlight on emotion in literary criticism can be understood partly as an attempt to redress its earlier exclusion on such "subjectivist" grounds, including its failure to be grasped by the more positivistic kinds of cultural-historical analysis and the more dryly technical kinds of semiotic analysis that dominated literary studies in the 1970s and 1980s, as well as by poststructuralist theories of literary language prevailing in the 1980s and early 1990s. In the former case, feeling's marginalization stemmed from its perceived incompatibility with "concrete" social experiences; in the latter (as Terada most fully examines), from its perceived incompatibility with poststructuralism's skeptical interrogation of the category of experience itself. Though emotion once posed an embarrassment to these very different critics for very different reasons, most critics today accept that far from being merely private or idiosyncratic phenomena, or reflecting a "romantically raw domain of primitive experiential richness" that materialist analysis will be unable to grasp (Massumi, *PV,* 29), feelings are as fundamentally "social" as the institutions and collective practices that have been the more traditional objects of historicist criticism (as Raymond Williams was perhaps the earliest to argue, in his analyses of "structures of feeling"), and as "material" as the linguistic signs and significations that have been the more traditional objects of literary formalism. Although feeling is not reducible to these institutions, collective practices, or discursive significations, it is nonetheless as socially real and "infrastructural" in its effects "as a factory" (Massumi, *PV,* 45).

The affect/emotion split originated in psychoanalysis for the practical purpose of distinguishing third-person from first-person representations of feeling, with "affect" designating feeling described from an observer's (analyst's) perspective, and "emotion" designating feeling that "belongs" to the speaker or analysand's "I." Yet Massumi and Grossberg have made claims for a stronger distinction, arguing not just that emotion requires a subject while affect does not, but that the former designates feeling given "function and meaning" while the latter remains "unformed and unstructured" (Massumi, *PV,* 260, note 3).[26] As Grossberg puts it, "Unlike emotions, affective states are neither structured narratively nor organized in response to our interpretations of situations."[27] Similarly, Massumi argues that while emotion is "a subjective content, the sociolinguistic fixing of the quality of an experience which is from that point onward defined as personal," affect is feeling or "intensity" disconnected from "meaningful sequencing, from narration" (*PV,* 28). The difficulty affective "intensity" poses for analysis is thus strikingly analogous to the analytical difficulty which Williams coined his term "structures of feeling" to address—that is, the kind posed by social experiences which "do not have to await definition, classification, or rationalization before they exert palpable pressures and set effective limits on experience and action."[28] In escaping qualification much like Williams' structures of feeling, which as "social experiences in solution" lie "at the very edge of semantic availability" (*ML,* 132), affective intensity clearly creates difficulties for more positivistic kinds of materialist analysis, even as it always remains highly *analyzable* in or as effect (Massumi, *PV,* 260, note 3).

While strong arguments have thus been made—primarily on the basis of a subjective/objective divide, but also in terms of oppositions like narrative/nonnarrative or semiotic/asignifying—for the idea that emotion and affect "follow different logics and pertain to different orders," some aspects of this taxonomic division will be more useful and important to this book than others (Massumi, *PV,* 27). Certainly less narratively structured, in the sense of being less object- or goal-directed, the intentionally weak and therefore often politically ambiguous feelings in this book are in fact much more like affects, in accordance with the definitions above, than emotions—which, for Martha Nussbaum, are "closely connected with action; few facts about them are more obvious."[29] Tied intimately, in contrast, with situations of what Dewey calls "being withheld from doing,"[30] the feelings in this book are obviously not as strategic as the emotions classically associated with political action; with their indeterminate or undifferentiated objects, in particular, they are less than ideally suited for setting and realizing clearly defined goals. Whereas Hobbes and Aristotle have shown how the principle of mutual fear actively binds men into the contracts that support the political commonwealth, and how anger advances the redressing of perceived injustices through retaliation, it is difficult to imagine how either of these actions might be advanced by an affective state like, say, irritation. While one can be irritated without realizing it, or knowing exactly what one is irritated about, there can be nothing ambiguous about one's rage or terror, or about what one is terrified of or enraged about. Yet the unsuitability of these weakly intentional feelings for forceful or unambiguous action is precisely what amplifies their power to diagnose situations, and situations marked by blocked or thwarted action in particular.

While the distinction between affect and emotion is thus helpful here in a number of ways, I will not be theoretically leaning on it to the extent that others have—as may be apparent from the way in which I use the two terms more or less interchangeably. In the chapters that follow, the difference between affect and emotion is taken as a modal difference of intensity or degree, rather than a formal difference of quality or kind. My assumption is that affects are *less* formed and structured than emotions, but not lacking form or structure altogether; *less* "sociolinguistically fixed," but by no means code-free or meaningless; *less* "organized in response to our interpretations of situations," but by no means entirely devoid of organization or diagnostic powers. As suggested above, ambient affects may in fact be better suited to interpreting ongoing states of affairs. What the switch from formal to modal difference enables is an analysis of the *transitions* from one pole to the other: the passages whereby affects acquire the semantic density and narrative complexity of emotions, and emotions conversely denature into affects. At the end of the day, the difference between emotion and affect is still intended to solve the same basic and fundamentally descriptive problem it was coined in psychoanalytic practice to solve: that of distinguishing first-person from third-person feeling, and, by extension, feeling that is contained by an identity from feeling that is not. Rather than also trying to dissolve this subjective/objective problematic by creating two distinct categories of feeling, this study aims to preserve it for its aesthetic productivity. We see this not just in the meaningful ironies or specific feelings generated by film noir's oscillations between first-person and third-person point of view, but also in the concept of cinematic or literary tone. For as anticipated by film noir's demonstration that certain kinds of ugly feeling (paranoia, disconcertedness) become maximized when we are most uncertain if the "field" of their emergence is subjective or objective, the tone of an artwork—which obviously cannot be reduced to representations of feeling within the artwork, or to the emotional responses the artwork solicits from its viewers—is a concept dependent upon and even constructed around the very problematic that the emotion/affect distinction was intended to dissolve.

By "tone" I mean a literary or cultural artifact's feeling tone: its global or organizing affect, its general disposition or orientation toward its audience and the world. Hence, while the concept I refer to includes the connotations of "attitude" brought to the term by I. A. Richards and other New Critics, I am not referring to the same "tone" they narrow down to "a known way of speaking" or a dramatic style of address. Instead, I mean the formal aspect of a literary work that makes it possible for critics to describe a text as, say, "euphoric" or "melancholic," and, what is much more important, the category that makes these affective values meaningful with regard to how one understands the text as a totality within an equally holistic matrix of social relations. It is worth noting here that literary criticism's increased attention to matters of emotion has predominantly centered on the emotional effects of texts on their readers, and, in the predominantly historicist field of nineteenth-century American studies, where the surge in the discussion of emotion has seemed particularly intense, on the expressivist aesthetics of sympathy and sentimentality in particular. But what gets left out in this prevailing emphasis on a reader's sympathetic identification with the feelings of characters in a text is the simple but powerful question of "objectified emotion," or unfelt but perceived feeling, that presents itself most forcefully in the aesthetic concept of tone. The absence of attention to this way of talking about feelings and literature not only is specific to recent literary scholarship on emotion (though it becomes particularly glaring in such a context), but points to a long-standing problem in philosophical aesthetics that we have already had a glimpse of above, in which an overemphasis on feelings in terms of purely subjective or personal experience turns artworks into "containers for the psychology of the spectator" (Adorno, *AT,* 275). Tone's original association with the New Critics, who not only de-emotionalized the concept but showed how easily it could be conscripted into a gentlemanly discourse of nuance and implication designed to produce and sharpen social distinctions (as the irony of T. S. Eliot demonstrates so well), may be partly responsible for the dearth of attention paid to tone in their wake, even in later literary structuralisms that provided reinvigorated analyses of other formal categories like plot, setting, and character. But while there has been a conspicuous absence of attention to tone itself, critics have continued to rely heavily on the notion of a text's global affect for the construction of substantive arguments about literature and ideology or society as a whole. The "euphoria" Jameson ascribes to a cluster of late twentieth-century artworks, for instance, is designed to do nothing less than advance his critique of postmodernism as the logic of late capitalism, in the same way that Walter Benjamin's isolation of "a curious variety of despair" in the Weimar poetry of Erich Kästner enabled him to diagnose a much broader "left-wing melancholy" that, as Wendy Brown notes, extends just as problematically into our contemporary political discourses.[31] Tone does a great deal of diagnostic and critical work for these writers and many others. Yet compared to other formal categories relied on for the analysis of literature in society, "tone" in my explicitly feeling-related sense, as a cultural object's affective bearing, orientation, or "set toward" the world, remains notoriously difficult to define.[32] In fact, because tone is never entirely reducible to a reader's emotional response to a text or reducible to the text's internal representations of feeling (though it can amplify and be amplified by both), the problem it poses for analysis is strikingly similar to the problem posed by uncertainties concerning a feeling's subjective or objective status. For we can speak of a literary text whose global or organizing affect is disgust, without this necessarily implying that the work represents or signifies disgust, or that it will disgust the reader (though in certain cases it may also do so). Exactly "where," then, is the disgust? Similarly, the "joyous intensity" Jameson ascribes to the work of Duane Hanson in his aforementioned essay on postmodernism does not imply that Hanson's hyperrealistic sculptures of tired, elderly museum guards and sagging, overweight tourists *represent* or *express* joy, or that they make the viewer *feel* joyous—as opposed to, say, mildly amused or unsettled.[33] Who is the subject, then, of the euphoria to which Jameson refers? Should this feeling belong to a subject? How is it even produced by the object from which it ostensibly emanates?

I ask these questions not to dispute the tone Jameson attributes to these postmodern artifacts—the exhilaration he is speaking of is clearly of the capitalist "special effect": flawless verisimilitude as a spectacular display of technological skill and power—but to underscore how central the subjective/objective problematic is to the concept of tone itself, such that to resolve or eliminate the problem would be to nullify the concept or render it useless for theoretical work.[34] Tone *is* the dialectic of objective and subjective feeling that our aesthetic encounters inevitably produce, much in the same way we have seen paranoia, the global affect of the noir films above, materially constituted by the systematic alternation of first- and third-person enunciations within a single shot. The fact that tone will always pose special difficulties as an *object* of analysis, particularly in the case of the frequently "atonal" texts foregrounded in this study of Bartlebyan feelings, does not imply that one must make its definition more positivistic: the concept's power resides precisely in its amorphousness. Accordingly, the goal of my first chapter is not to make the concept of tone less abstract or less "noisy" but to develop a more precise vocabulary for the "noise" that tone is. My primary guide in this venture will be Melville's last published novel, *The Confidence-Man* (1857), a notably "talky" text that offers a useful allegory of the very problem enabling tone to do its aesthetic work. It demonstrates how feeling slips in and out of subjective boundaries in a series of transactions involving the exchange of writing and money for affective goods.

This book thus begins with what might be called a pre-affective question, by addressing one of the most important though under-examined aesthetic functions of feeling in general. After that, we will examine one of the most "basic" ways in which affect becomes publicly visible in an age of mechanical reproducibility: as a kind of innervated "agitation" or "animatedness." On one hand, the state of being "animated" implies the most general of all affective conditions (that of being "moved" in one way or another), but also a feeling that implies being "moved" by a particular feeling, as when one is said to be animated by happiness or anger. Animatedness thus seems to have both an unintentional and intentional form. In a strange way, it seems at once a zero-degree feeling and a complex meta-feeling, which not only takes other feelings as its object, but takes only other *intentional* feelings as its object. For we can speak of someone's being "animated" by a passion like anger, but not by an objectless mood like nostalgia or depression, which tend to have a de-animating effect on those affected by them.

In its associations with movement and activity, animatedness bears a semantic proximity to "agitation," a term which is likewise used in the philosophical discourse of emotions to designate feeling prior to its articulation into a more complex passion, but that also underlies the contemporary meaning of the political agitator or activist. Yet while animatedness is bound up with questions of action—and even political action—in this general way, my primary focus will be on the social powerlessness foregrounded by its racialized version. It is precisely this racialization that turns the neutral and even potentially positive affect of animatedness "ugly," pointing to the more self-evidently problematic feelings in the chapters that follow. For as an exaggerated responsiveness to the language of others that turns the subject into a spasmodic puppet, in its racialized form animatedness loses its generally positive associations with human spiritedness or vitality and comes to resemble a kind of mechanization. At the same time, the minimal affect is turned into a form of emotional *excess,* and similarly stripped of its intentionality. Hence, in *Uncle Tom's Cabin* it no longer matters what emotion, negative or positive, moves or animates the African-American slave; rather, his or her animated state itself becomes the primary object of the narrator's quasi-ethnographic fascination. In this manner, the racialization of animatedness converts a way of moving *others* to political action ("agitation") into the passive state of *being* moved or vocalized by others for their amusement. The disturbing consequences of this conversion are most forcefully demonstrated in Ralph Ellison's *Invisible Man,* which draws on a "primal scene" of racial puppeteering to dramatize the death of a rising political leader, in a particularly violent account of the African-American "agitator" turned "animator" (or entertainer). Animatedness thus brings us back to the politically charged problem of obstructed agency that all the categories of feeling in this book will be used to interpret. It facilitates the transition from the general question of feeling in literature to the aesthetics of complex and highly particularized feelings such as envy, irritation, anxiety, stuplimity, paranoia, and disgust.

Given the predominant attention that critical work on emotion has devoted to the aesthetics of sympathy in recent years, we should note that it is precisely the obstruction of this "moral feeling" that "Bartleby" pointedly stages, as if Melville's intent were to create a character so emotionally illegible as to foreclose the possibility of sympathetic identification altogether (and also, in an interesting way I will elaborate later, charity and pity). As the following chapters pursue the Bartlebyan question of suspended agency beyond its nineteenth-century context through the twentieth century and into the present—where the figure of the Sub-Sub incarnated in the corporate employees in this introduction will morph, in a fashion that echoes the structure of *The Confidence-Man,* into an overly innervated factory worker, an envious temp, an irritated secretary, an anxious detective for hire, an exhausted would-be novelist, and a transcriber of responses to psychological questionnaires for a state-run psychiatric institute—they similarly highlight the limits of both expressiveness and identification, as my chapter on envy will draw out in particular. Here the work of emotion is taken up in another register of social difference—femininity—where it has seemed particularly overdetermined. Though both feminism and the patriarchal culture that is its constitutive outside have played roles in strengthening the association between emotion and women, the weight placed on this association also creates nervousness, with "women's feelings" imagined as always easily prone to turning ugly. Envy is one of the most conventionally imagined of these feelings, I argue, though in a manner that reveals the moral constraints imposed on female aggression within feminism as well as by its adversarial outside. Through readings of recent feminist debates as well as classic writings on envy and group psychology by Klein and Freud, I show how the agonistic feeling can be used to explore the fraught issue of antagonism's political value for feminism, and to disclose the limitations of sympathetic identification as our culture's dominant way of understanding the making of female homosociality and the formation of political groups.

Harnessed into the constellation of multiple negative affects that make up Friedrich Nietzsche's concept of *ressentiment* (as defined in *On the Genealogy of Morals*), envy is perhaps this book's most exemplary example of a politically equivocal feeling.[35] For *ressentiment* is Nietzsche's account of how a kind of moral authority, one that transforms social weakness from an undesirable situation one must struggle to overcome into a "blessedness" or virtue (*GM,* 34), "emerges from the powerless to avenge their incapacity for action, . . . enact[ing] their resentment of strengths that they cannot match or overthrow."[36] It is an account, in other words, of how a problematic valorization of powerlessness as "good" can easily emerge from the same situation of "withheld doing" that produces the ugly feelings foregrounded throughout this book. Here, then, is a rejection of the sentimental politics of Stowe that parallels the antisentimental aesthetic of "Bartleby," though made much more aggressively and from a very different place. There can be something useful, as Wendy Brown and other political theorists have stressed, about Nietzsche's assault on the idea that there is something morally beatific about being poor, weak, or disenfranchised,[37] even though Nietzsche is not interested in how one might actually eliminate the conditions that produce this "slave morality" from the viewpoint of the slave.[38] But despite its superficial resemblance to the "vengefulness of the impotent" that is Nietzsche's *ressentiment,* the ugly feeling of envy actually demonstrates that the two cannot be confused (*GM,* 37). For envy makes no claim whatsoever about the moral superiority of the envier, or about the "goodness" of his or her state of lacking something that the envied other is perceived to have. Envy is in many ways a naked will to have. In fact, it is through envy that a subject asserts the goodness and desirability of precisely that which he or she does not have, and explicitly at the cost of surrendering any claim to moral high-mindedness or superiority. Indeed, if envy and *ressentiment* have something in common, it is their shared status as targets of the very moral disapprobation (driven often by hate and fear) that Nietzsche summons the theory of *ressentiment* to attack. This correlates with what Jameson describes as *ressentiment*'s "unavoidable autoreferential structure," where the manager resents his employee, and what he resents most about him is the employee's *ressentiment.*[39] Hence, while the theory of *ressentiment* becomes productive for Brown's critique of contemporary feminism's "preference for moral reasoning over open political contest,"[40] it is ultimately on the side of Jameson's much blunter assessment of the nineteenth-century ideologeme that my own book comes down: "That this ostensible 'theory' is itself little more than an expression of annoyance at seemingly gratuitous lower-class agitation, at the apparently quite unnecessary rocking of the social boat." As an affective matrix devised as a "psychological explanation" for revolutionary or political impulses, which reduces social antagonisms to deficiencies of individual character or "private dissatisfactions," Jameson notes, "the theory of *ressentiment,* wherever it appears, will always itself be the expression and the production of *ressentiment.*"[41] Even if envy is not exactly the same feeling, then, as this moralizing pathos (though *ressentiment* is a matrix of a number of affects that can include envy), it is an antagonistic response to a perceived inequality easily discredited for similar reasons—especially, I argue, when the envious subject is a woman.

The political and aesthetic problems posed by the gendered and racialized feelings I examine in the chapters titled "Envy" and "Animatedness" converge in my discussion of Nella Larsen's *Quicksand.* The oft-noted psychological illegibility of the novel's biracial heroine has led to critical perplexities rivaling those generated by Bartleby. Though thinkers from Aristotle to Audre Lorde have highlighted anger's centrality to the pursuit of social justice, Larsen's novel prefers the "superficial" affect of irritation—a conspicuously weak or inadequate form of anger, as well an affect that bears an unusually close relationship to the body's surfaces or skin. Hyperbolized in Larsen's image of her protagonist as "an obscene sore," the novel's irritated aesthetic enables us to continue the exploration of the ideologically fraught relationship between emotion, race, and aesthetics as it comes to a head in the context of the Harlem Renaissance. The Bartlebyan predicament of suspended agency persists in the following chapters, as I explore how the intellectual prestige of "anxiety" is oddly secured by a male analyst's fantasy of himself as a "thrown projection," or passive body hurled into space, and as I also examine the paradoxical convergence of excessive excitation (shock) and the lack of excitation (boredom) in twentieth-century artforms ranging from Gertrude Stein's *Making of Americans* to the late modernism of Samuel Beckett's novels. While Kant's sublime involves a confrontation with the natural and infinite, the unusual synthesis of excitation and fatigue I call "stuplimity" is a response to encounters with vast but bounded artificial systems, resulting in repetitive and often mechanical acts of enumeration, permutation and combination, and taxonomic classification. Though both encounters give rise to negative affect, "stuplimity" involves comic exhaustion rather than terror. The affective dimensions of the small subject's encounter with a "total system" are further examined in the chapter titled "Paranoia," where Melville's scrivener reappears in the more contemporary guise of the poet-as-transcriber. He will return in person—but also as a figure for art itself, or rather the "harmlessness" that Adorno describes as the "shadow" of art's "autarchic radicalism" in a fully commodified society—in my afterword, which discusses the ugliest of all ugly feelings: disgust. As the allegorical personification not just of art but art's social inefficaciousness in a market society marked by the "pluralism of peacefully coexisting spheres"—the situation of limited agency from which all the ugly feelings and their attendant aesthetics ensue—Bartleby will preside over our final examination of the challenge that disgust's aesthetic of the intolerable poses to what Marcuse describes as the friendly or "repressive tolerance" that makes the scrivener seem "safely ignorable," for all his insistent negativity and ability to make his social invisibility as obtrusively visible as *Quicksand*'s "obscene sore." Art thus comes to interrogate the problematically limited agency of art foregrounded in the aesthetics generated by ugly feelings, and in a fashion, I will argue, unparalleled by other cultural practices. Whether in a direct or indirect manner, this Bartlebyan problem is one to which all of the following chapters will repeatedly return, even as animatedness, envy, irritation, anxiety, stuplimity, paranoia, and disgust are mobilized to investigate a multiplicity of other representational and theoretical dilemmas.

1 tone

How does one go about creating a "fake" feeling? And to what uses might an artfully created feeling be put? Melville's book *The Confidence-Man: His Masquerade* (1857) provides us with simple answers to both of these questions, in a miniature story passed on by one of the novel's noisy throng of "operators" and "transfer-agents" to a fellow passenger on the Mississippi steamer *Fidèle*.[1] After nonchalantly mentioning that "the president, who is also transfer-agent, of the Black Rapids Coal Company, happens to be on board here," the Company representative delivers the pitch to his mark:

> A month since, in a panic contrived by artful alarmists, some credulous stock-holders sold out; but, to frustrate the aim of the alarmists, the Company, previously advised of their scheme, so managed it as to get into its own hands those sacrificed shares, resolved that, since a spurious panic must be, the panic-makers should be no gainers by it. The Company, I hear, is now ready, but not anxious, to redispose of those shares, and

having obtained them at their depressed value, will now sell them at par, though, prior to the panic, they were held at a handsome figure above. (*CM,* 26–27)

The confidence-man knows that this story about a fictitious version of a feeling that, according to Hobbes, "happens to none but in a throng, or multitude of people," is both seductive and believable because of the ordinariness of what it describes: the stock market's sensitivity not only to economic factors but to affective ones, as well as the way in which a panic "contrived by artful alarmists" can generate repercussions identical to those of a genuine panic, producing a massive sell-off and "depressing" the value of stocks.[2] Such "spurious" emotions and their real effects become the primary focus of Melville's most formally innovative novel, last in a string of commercial and critical failures that began with *Moby-Dick* (1851) and continued with *Pierre* (1852). Indeed, the unpopularity of *The Confidence-Man,* the last novel Melville would publish in his lifetime, played a key role in his turn from the effort to make a living from writing fiction to his employment as a customs house inspector—a job that ironically required his swearing "to prevent and detect frauds in relation to the duties imposed by the Laws of the United States."[3]

It thus comes as no surprise that while continuing the savage parody of antebellum sentimentalism and the literary marketplace offered in *Pierre*'s account of a would-be serious novelist (who is, significantly, accused of being a "swindler" by his publishers for producing a "blasphemous rhapsody, filched from the vile Atheists, Lucian and Voltaire," under "the pretense of writing a popular novel for us"), *The Confidence-Man* broadens its area of attack to include any "positive" emotional attitude about virtually anything, ranging from Christian "benevolence" to cosmopolitan "conviviality," from a distinctively American "confidence" in the speculative antebellum economy (what one character calls "the Wall Street spirit") to a more general and romantic "faith" in humankind.[4] Unfolding in a series of transactions involving the exchange of money and writing for emotional goods, *The Confidence-Man* could be described as a interrogation of antebellum America's affective investment in "affective investments."[5] Published soon after Congress passed the 1854 Kansas-Nebraska Act, which allowed the Western Territories to become slave states, and in the same year as the financial panic known as the "Western Blizzard" (the name alludes to the swiftness with which the telegraph spread news of the embezzlement-related failure of a New York branch of the Ohio Life Insurance and Trust Company across the country), *The Confidence-Man* might be described as an exploration of the new emotional economy produced by the general migration of "trust" from personal relationships to abstract systems—a key theme in the twentieth-century sociology of modernity.[6] If "publicness, as the kind of Being that belongs to the Anyone, not only has in general its own way of having a mood, but needs moods and 'makes' them for itself," as Heidegger claims, it seems fitting that Melville's story about public exchanges facilitated by an anonymous agent becomes primarily preoccupied with how "confidence" and other feelings might be artfully created.[7]

What is important for our purposes is that every social and symbolic exchange in this story of public travel on the Mississippi, "the artery of trade and commerce . . . as well as the division between slave states and free," is an explicit demonstration of how feeling slips in and out of subjective boundaries, at times becoming transformed into psychic property, but at other times eluding containment.[8] In this it recalls the distinction between affect and emotion elaborated by Lawrence Grossberg and Brian Massumi, insofar as both approach emotion as contained by identity in a way that affect is not.[9] In calling attention to the process by which feelings are artfully contrived, and to the way in which these fake feelings may or may not be transposed into personally experienced emotions (like the real panic for investors that the alarmists have designed their illusory version to produce), *The Confidence-Man* provides a particularly compelling allegory for an investigation into the promiscuously used yet curiously underexamined concept of literary "tone." For there is a crucial similarity between the affective-aesthetic idea of tone, which is reducible neither to the emotional response a text solicits from its reader nor to representations of feelings within the world of its story, and the slippery zone between fake and real feelings, or free-floating and subjectively anchored feelings, foregrounded throughout *The Confidence-Man.*

Thus, while the tone I investigate here shares the connotations of "stance" that it has for critics like I. A. Richards and T. S. Eliot, I use it to mean something much more holistic and explicitly affective than the narrow concept employed by Richards in *Practical Criticism*—namely, a speaker's "attitude to his listener."[10] While the New Critics were the first to attempt a systematic definition and analysis of tone in terms of attitudes or dispositions (a project strikingly neglected in literary structuralism and semiotics), they also notably muted, and in some cases took pains to avoid, the affective dimensions of the problem. This de-emotionalizing tendency is already apparent in the way Richards separates "Tone" from "Feeling" in *Practical Criticism*'s list of the four kinds of poetic or literary meaning ("Sense, Feeling, Tone, and Intention"), even though the two categories are quite similar. For like "Tone," "Feeling" is defined as "an *attitude* . . . some special direction, bias, or accentuation of interest" (*PC,* 175). The primary difference is that those "attitudes" Richards classifies under "Feeling" apply specifically to "the state of affairs" created by the poem, whereas those classified under "Tone" apply to the relationship between the speaker and the implied listener—as if the latter relation could be neatly separated from the former, which is not often the case.[11] The tendency to *divorce* emotion from tone continues efforts by other formalists to expand and elaborate Richards' limited definition. These range from William Empson's concept of "Mood"—which widens Richards' notion of tone to include anything that relates "*any* supposed 'me'" suggested by the poem (and not just its speaker) to *any* supposed other or others (and not just the "listener" or "audience")—to Reuben Brower's likening of a poem's tone to its "dramatic situation," which Brower defines not just as "the implied social relationship of the speaker to his auditor" but also as "the manner he adopts in addressing his auditor."[12] Switching from poetics to narratology, we find a similar effort in Gérard Genette's concept of "voice," which designates the "situation" of a narrator with respect not only to the audience he is addressing, but to all events narrated and the manner in which these narrated events are presented.[13]

One cannot help noticing the inelegance, even clunkiness of these attempts to expand "tone" by simply adding extra relationships to the primary one between speaker and audience in Richards' original definition. This awkward quality might be attributed to a conspicuous avoidance of the dimension of feeling already deeply associated with "tone" and even "attitude" in everyday usage, as in the familiar "I don't like the [insert unstated but implied emotional quality] tone of your voice" or "That kind of [insert unstated but implied emotional quality] attitude will get you nowhere." One further suspects that the motivation for this avoidance comes from the perceived threat of a "soft" impressionism which has always haunted feeling's role in any analytic endeavor, and which theorists of aesthetic and critical judgment have repeatedly attempted to ward off in various ways: from Kant's appeal to the oxymoronic-sounding concept of "disinterested" pleasure, to its later echoes in Roger Fry's "disinterested intensity," to the explicit antipsychologism of William K. Wimsatt and Monroe C. Beardsley's "Affective Fallacy."[14] Yet the general strangeness of this evasion (particularly glaring in the case of Empson's deceptively named "Mood") comes to the fore when one considers how entirely appropriate emotive or affective qualities seem, as compressed assessments of complex "situations," for indicating the *total* web of relations sought after in each of these redefinitions. It is this holistic context we find emphasized, for instance, in Heidegger's theory of moods as "attunements" *(Stimmungen)* that arise from and shape or modulate the totality of Being-in-the-world, disclosing the "situ-atedness" *(Befindlichkeit)* that enables things to *matter* in determinate ways. As Charles Guignon notes, "From this standpoint our moods are not 'private' or 'personal,' but rather are essentially public, part of the 'world' instead of something *in* the 'self.'"[15]

It should be clear that by "tone" I mean less the dramatic "attitude" adumbrated by the New Critics than a global and hyper-relational concept of *feeling* that encompasses attitude: a literary text's affective bearing, orientation, or "set toward" its audience and world. In other words, I mean the formal aspect of a work that has made it possible for critics of all affiliations (Marxist, feminist, postcolonial, historicist) to describe a work or class of works as "paranoid" (Mary Ann Doane on the Hollywood "woman's film" of the 1940s), "euphoric" (Fredric Jameson on postmodern art and architecture), or "melancholic" (Anne Cheng on Asian-American literature); and, much more importantly, the formal aspect that enables these affective values to become significant with regard to how each critic understands the work as a totality within an equally holistic matrix of social relations. It is in this manner that Walter Benjamin isolates "a curious variety of despair" in the work of Weimar poet Erich Kästner, in order to launch a critique of the political mindset of the German left-wing intelligentsia to which Kästner belonged, and Cheng speaks of a "melancholia" suffusing texts by Asian-American writers that points back to long histories of systematic racism in U.S. culture and national policy.[16] To speak of tone is thus to generalize, totalize, and abstract the "world" of the literary object, in a way that seems particularly conducive to the analysis of ideology. There is a sense in which tone resembles the concept of collective mood frequently invoked by historians ("Cold War paranoia" and so forth), but poses the additional difficulty of aesthetic immanence, of being something that seems "attached" to an artwork. As the affective "comportment" of a literary text, the aesthetic notion of tone we will be working with bears less resemblance to any of its New Critical formulations than it does to

Susanne Langer's notion of a "significant form" whose import is "the feeling of the whole work," or Mikel Dufrenne's concept of the "affective quality" that constitutes the artwork's "expressed world," or even Roman Ingarden's notion of the "polyphonic harmony" that holds together all of the values and perspectives generated by a literary text's multiple "stratifications."[17] These attempts to account for the affective dimension of literature implied but ultimately avoided in New Critical definitions of "tone" provide much more salient models than any that are available in literary theory proper for the global concepts of feeling attributed to aesthetic objects by contemporary analysts of literature and ideology.

Langer is as impatient as any New Critic with the critical focus on a literary work's emotional effects on readers or with the emotions supposedly expressed by its author. Yet the question of feeling in art is nonetheless her primary concern in *Feeling and Form* (1953), and in fact is the problem her book's overarching theory of art as "significant form," a phrase she adopts from Clive Bell, is explicitly designed to solve.[18] As she notes, "The relation of art to feeling is evidently something subtler than sheer catharsis or incitement. In fact, the most expert critics tend to discount both these subjective elements, and treat the emotive aspect of a work of art as something integral to it, something as objective as the physical form, color, sound pattern of verbal text itself" (*FF,* 18). Searching for a precedent for her "more radical handling of feeling as something objective," Langer turns to Otto Baensch's "Kunst und Gefühl" (Art and Feeling; 1923), where the matter of what I am here calling tone is laid out as follows:

> The mood of a landscape appears to us as objectively given with it as one of its attributes, belonging to it just like any other attribute we perceive it to have. . . . We never think of regarding the landscape as a sentient being whose outward aspect "expresses" the mood that it contains subjectively. The landscape does not express the mood, but *has* it; the mood sur-

rounds, fills, and permeates it, . . . the mood belongs to our *to-tal impression* of the landscape and can only be distinguished as one of its components by a process of abstraction. (Quoted in Langer, *FF,* 19)

For Baensch, the "objective feeling" of a work of art is distinct from its sensory qualities precisely in this holistic character. Whereas sensory qualities "are combined and composed, so as to produce, *jointly,* the appearance of the object," the nonsensory quality called "feeling" is said to "surround and permeate this whole structure in fluid omnipresence" (*FF,* 21, italics added). The work's "feeling" thus "cannot be brought into an explicit correlation with its component elements," much as the "euphoria" Jameson attributes to Duane Hanson's latex sculptures of anxious-looking tourists is difficult to locate in any isolated formal feature.[19] At the same time, the feeling is not a free-floating phantom; rather, as Baensch notes, it is "always embedded and inherent in [an object] from which [it] cannot be actually separated, but only distinguished by abstraction: objective feelings are always dependent parts of objects" (quoted in *FF,* 20). While Langer uses this discussion to introduce her own comprehensive theory of art as a materially created abstraction, she dissolves Baensch's so-called paradox through what she herself describes as a simple and obvious move: by redescribing what he calls "feeling" as the artwork's "significant form" or "semblance" of feeling (in Schiller's sense of *Schein*). This form is best exemplified in the highly articulate but nondiscursive realm of music, which she examines in *Philosophy in a New Key.* As Langer notes, "The basic concept is the articulate but nondiscursive form having import without conventional reference, and therefore presenting itself not as a symbol in the ordinary sense, but as a 'significant form,' in which the factor of significance is not logically discriminated, but is felt as a quality rather than recognized as a function" (*FF,* 32).[20] But the same problem of a "significance" that is not reducible to signs or signification is important to literature, too, where "affect" seems a fugitive presence attached to or hovering in the vicinity of words. Indeed, Grossberg seems to have literature specifically in mind when he notes, "Affect is perhaps the most difficult plane of human life to define and describe, not merely because it is a-signifying (and contemporary theory is so heavily directed toward signifying practices), but also because there is no critical vocabulary to describe its forms and structures. But this does not mean that affect is some ineffable experience or a purely subjective feeling" (*OTP*, 80). It is clear, however, that tone often has an impact on these subjective responses, even if it cannot be reduced to them, and that it remains loosely fastened to signifying practices, even if it is not literally a sign itself. Adorno seems to be grappling with a version of this problem when he describes "mood in artworks" as "that in which the effect and the internal constitution of artworks form a murky amalgam that [go] beyond their individual elements," producing a "twilight" that Adorno seems to find irritating even as he acknowledges its centrality to any encounter with art (*AT*, 275).[21]

As this affective relay between subject and object, tone—though it presents all sorts of theoretical difficulties—is necessary for theoretical work. Indeed, since so much of ideological communication is tonal, it is in the arena of cultural politics that the concept matters most. Here, the ability to make forceful arguments about literature and society requires assessments of tone unthreatened by the potential objection that *because* what is being discussed is an affective quality, it is therefore hallucinatory or "make-believe." Indeed, as Grossberg argues, "Affect is the missing term in an adequate understanding of ideology, for it offers the possibility of a 'psychology of belief' which would explain how and why ideologies are sometimes, and only sometimes, effective, and always to varying degrees." He continues: "It is the affective investment in particular ideological sites (which may be libidinal or nonlibidinal) that explains the power of the articulation which bonds particular representations and realities. It is the affective investment which enables ideological relations to be internalized and, consequently, naturalized" (*OTP,* 83). While there is a sense in which analysts of art and ideology have been paying attention to tone all along, the difficulties the affective concept raises should not be shied away from but directly confronted—and doing so can only strengthen a critical practice that has always silently relied on it.

In fact, in its generality and abstractness, the concept of tone, which we might follow Langer in conceiving as an artfully created "semblance" of feeling, actually seems unpropitious for a purely formalist literary criticism—and this for the same reasons it seems so ideally suited for the analysis of ideology, which, as the materially embodied representation of an *imaginary relationship* to a holistic complex of real conditions, clearly shares tone's virtual, diffused, but also immanent character. This special adeptness or facility for the analysis of ideology is even more strongly suggested by the theory of "affective *a priori*" in the Husserlian aesthetics of Mikel Dufrenne—a theory which bears a close resemblance to Langer's equally antipsychologistic theory of "significant form" in its rejection of "make-believe" or the Sartrean "imagination" as explanations for "feeling in art." While Dufrenne's account also resembles Langer's in his emphasis on feeling's synthesizing, epideictic, and intellectual character, and its approach to the aesthetic object as essentially something perceived (and thus as requiring a theory of significance *specific* to apperception, as opposed to understanding or knowledge), it is also much more radical. For Dufrenne, all artworks have a singular "affective quality" or "atmosphere" that gives them their unity and that not only characterizes but constitutes the work's "expressed world." These affective qualities are revealed or "read" by our own feelings *(sentiments),* but are not identical to them. Holding all the sensuous and nonsensuous elements of the work together, as in the case of Baensch's "mood," the affective quality requires that the work be grasped as a whole, as a "total effect" that it encapsulates (*PAE,* 424). As Dufrenne writes, "The unity of an atmosphere is thus the unity of a *Weltanschauung;*

its coherence is the coherence of a characteristic or quality" (*PAE,* 177). Total and undifferentiated, the quality is also compared to "a supervening or impersonal [though always materially embodied] principle . . . somewhat like the collective consciousness which governs individual consciousness in times of agitation" (*PAE,* 168). As we have already seen in the case of the "joyous intensity" Jameson reads in Hanson's latex sculptures, this *Weltanschauung*-like quality cannot be decomposed: "We cannot reduce to their elements the melancholy grace of Ravel's *Pavana pour une enfante défunte,* the glory of Franck's chorales, or the tender sensitivity of Debussy's *La Fille aux cheveux de lin*" (*PAE,* 327).[22]

Already owing a great deal to Heidegger's theory of moods as manifestations of a "situatedness" that allows things to matter in specific ways,[23] Dufrenne's comparison of the artwork's organizing affective quality to "collective consciousness" or *Weltanschauung* needs only a slight push to return us to the possibility that the ideology of a literary text may be, in fact, revealed *more* in its tone—as for instance, in its "euphoria" or "paranoia"—than in any of its other formal features. This may offer another explanation for our observation that it is ideology-sensitive readers who seem to draw on tone most for their analyses of literature, and not (as one might expect from tone's historical and institutional associations) New Critical formalists or more technically oriented structuralists. In fact, in their common emphasis on the abstractness and synthesizing effects of a feeling already admixed with values or ideas, all the models for understanding tone introduced above—as "virtual emotion," as the semblance or "significant form" of feeling, or as an "affective *a priori*" that has "the unity of a *Weltanschauung*"—seem to suggest its distinctive resonance for the analysis of literature and ideology. Shifting emphasis slightly away from the question of what tone is, I will now attempt to offer a model for what tone *does* by taking this matter of "resonance" quite literally. My primary guide in this venture will be *The Confidence-Man,* a text that not only is filled with "spurious" and contrived emotions but obsessively reexamines the relationship between artfully fabricated feelings and subjectively experienced ones.

With questions of "resonance" in mind, we will tunnel into this famously noisy text through the writings of American psychologist Silvan Tomkins, a prolific writer in the field of clinical psychology since the 1940s, who published his major work, *Affect, Imagery, Consciousness,* in 1962–63 (Volumes 1 and 2) and posthumously in 1991–92 (Volumes 3 and 4).[24] Given the intense anti-psychologism of all the models of tone discussed above, this shift into the work of a clinical theorist of affect may seem somewhat odd. Yet Tomkins' theory of affect will provide the best model for understanding the complex way in which *The Confidence-Man* can be said to theorize tone's particular resonance for ideological analysis. In fact, Tomkins' theory of affect, directly aimed in later years at producing a "psychology of commitment" concerned with "the ebb and flow of affective investments in ideas and ideology," will act as a much-needed "tuning fork" that we can use to orient our assessment of the notoriously ambiguous tone in *The Confidence-Man.*[25]

Affective Amplification

At first glance, Melville's most emotionally unfriendly novel hardly seems a conducive site for any feeling-related inquiry, much less one into the complex aesthetic problem of literary tone. In addition to its unmerciful treatment of the particular feelings that compose what we might call the cheery side of antebellum capitalism (confidence, conviviality, charity, benevolence), the emotional ambiguity of the novel's discourse arguably makes *The Confidence-Man* more Bartlebyan than "Bartleby" itself. Much as the scrivener deflects the efforts of both the Lawyer and the reader to make him an object of sympathy (for it is made impossible for anyone to feel what Bartleby is feeling), *The Confidence-Man* seems to repel the reader's emotional engagement in some basic way. Its refusal of empathy partly explains the text's own relatively minor status in the American literary canon. It is a work that leaves even some Melville enthusiasts cold.

The novel's Bartlebyan refusal of empathy is intimately connected with its equally Bartlebyan problem of character—one that takes the form not just of a single psychologically inscrutable character, but of *too many* psychologically inscrutable characters. This superfluity, in turn, seems directly responsible for the novel's repetitive and even echolalic structure, as a narrative entirely made up of talk and of talk about talk. In many ways lacking a true protagonist, while buzzing with a multitude of barely differentiated "operators" and "operatees" who rotate in and out of the actantial positions that define what often seems like the same transaction, *The Confidence-Man* turns Bartleby into a narratological principle, diffusing the social minorness of the administered world's Sub-Sub into what Alex Woloch would call the "character system" of the novel itself.[26] This unusual proliferation of indistinct but insistently reappearing characters (all of whom seem more like representations of functions than like representations of persons) impacts as much on the novel's discursive noisiness as on its emotional opacity. Cecilia Tichi, for example, notes that by "depersonalizing dialogue, divorcing speeches from speakers, and restraining visual evocation"—acts directly facilitated by the removal of a clearly individuated protagonist demanding our attention and sympathy—the novel compels its reader to focus on the medium of language itself, dialing down imagery in order to dial up the reader's "aural sensitivity."[27] Tichi notes that in this restriction of visual detail, the goal of *The Confidence-Man* seems identical to that of its confidence "operator," as described while he listens to a story told by another barely visualized character: "To intensify the sense of hearing, he seemed to sink the sense of sight" (*CM*, 191). Like Bartleby, the confidence-man seems at once too present and not present enough. Recalling the way in which Melville underscores his copyist's social invisibility by describing him as "mildly disappear[ing]" after repeating his "formula," Tichi argues that while *The Confidence-*

Man's reader is also primarily intended "not to see, but to listen," she (or he) is "prevented from linking much of what [she] hears to its sources." For like the fake or "second-hand" panic described by the Black Rapids Coal Company agent, nearly all of the tales in the novel are "tales at second hand [which] make their narrators *conduits only,* dissociating them from any experiential action or moral weight the stories might bear," and thus making them into something like copyists or transcribers, vehicles for reproducing the language of others (Tichi, "MC," 642). The strategy of featuring a multiplicity of "narrative conduits" in lieu of a protagonist thus bears directly on the noisiness that leads Alexander Gelley to describe *The Confidence-Man* as a novel of "parasitic talk," a phrase that marries Heidegger's notion of "idle talk" with Michel Serres's concept of *parasites,* which in French "also means static, the noise or interference in an electronic transmission."[28]

In foregrounding a throng of functionally analogous characters who endlessly combine and recombine with one another, it is as if the novel systematizes Melville's earlier fondness for what Harrison Hayford calls "unnecessary duplicates." Talky, noisy, and characterized by this peculiar redundancy, *The Confidence-Man* is essentially atonal.[29] Though it is not hard to come up with affective adjectives to describe the novel—it is, for instance, an unfunny comedy whose politically charged, yet often flippantly treated themes include religious hypocrisy, the "metaphysics of Indian-hating," and of course the circulation of "fake" feeling—*The Confidence-Man*'s organizing affective quality remains so ambiguous that at times it even becomes difficult to tell if it tilts more to the negative or positive side of the feeling spectrum. While the novel is crammed with stories about ugly feelings (envy, greed, hate, distrust, misanthropy) and the generally unpleasant characters who feel them, we know that these internally represented feelings are not equivalent to its tone, which remains something like a "neutral," if strangely loud or insistent dial tone. One even hesitates to describe the novel as altogether "ironic," though it is tempting to appeal to irony as the distinctive feeling-tone of the genre of dark comedy. Indeed, we run into a kind of circularity if we make this move, insofar as irony is typically understood as "a judgmental stance . . . *inferred through a tone,*" usually "of mockery or ridicule or contempt."[30] One does repeatedly get the sense of ironic "targets" in the novel, but, as in the case of the vague objects of moods and other intentionally weak feelings, these targets often seem obscure. In fact, at times it seems as if *The Confidence-Man* has been aggressively constructed for the purpose of giving the reader the unpleasant feeling of ironies constantly missed or passing over her head— that is, the meta-ironic feeling of an irony intended for and available to everyone but oneself.[31]

Affect thus becomes a formal problem for the novel, even as it is more obviously one of its thematic concerns. In fact, I would argue that the formal problem of tone, which the novel itself allegorizes, is one that actually encompasses the more attended-to problem of character. For while *The Confidence-Man* is most evidently "Bartleby" writ large in its reliance on a multitude of barely distinguishable characters, rather than presenting its reader with the expected protagonist with whom she or he can identify, this device might be thought of as directly motivated by the fact that the text denies the reader sympathetic identification at all levels by foregrounding "objectified emotion." The novel's use of character is thus part and parcel of its larger preoccupation with affect, and it is precisely the complex nature of their interconnection that Tomkins helps us to understand.

Departing from Sigmund Freud, William James, and other contributors to his field by asserting affect's autonomy from drives, cognitions, and perceptions of physiological changes, Tomkins ultimately bases his theory of affect on a principle he calls "analog amplification." He describes affect as a mechanism that magnifies awareness and intensifies the effects of operations associated with other biological subsystems (drive, cognitive, motor, perceptual, homeostatic) by "co-assembling" with these other vital mechanisms:

"The affect amplifies by *increasing the urgency* of anything with which it is co-assembled. It is what I have called an analog amplifier" (*EA,* 53, italics added). Tomkins argues that affect fulfills this unique role "by virtue of three major conjoint characteristics—urgency, abstractness, and generality." As he notes, "In its urgency [affect] is insistent. It is insistent in a very abstract way—that [rates of internal bodily activity] are increasingly rapidly, or decreasing rapidly, or have increased too much. In its generality *it is capable of very great combinational flexibility with other mechanisms that it can conjointly imprint and be imprinted by,* thereby rendering its abstractness more particular and concrete" (*EA,* 52, italics added).

Paradoxically, the autonomy of affect ensues from its ability to "imprint and be imprinted by" nonaffective mechanisms. Indeed, it is affect's parasitical ability to "co-assemble" with drive, cognitive, motor, perceptual, and other functions that distinguishes it from these other functions (*EA,* 63), which do not perform the same work of combining and connecting others. In an equally counterintuitive fashion, affect's distinctive function of amplifying the awareness and effects of other functions is based on its ability to "simulate" them. Affect produces "urgent analogs" not only of the rate and duration of its "external activator" (the pistol shot, for instance, that activates surprise), but of the abstract profiles of "neural firing" generated by the external activator, profiles which Tomkins calls "innate activators." It is these "internal neural correlates" which determine the value or quality of an affect—positive affects being activated by rapid or gradual decreases in neural firing, negative affects by continuous, high levels of neural firing, and "neutral affects," like interest and surprise, by rapid or sudden increases in neural firing.

> Just as a pistol shot [and the internal neural firing that corresponds to it] is a stimulus which is very sudden in onset, very brief in duration, and equally sudden in decay, so its amplifying affective analog, the startle response, *mimics* the pistol

shot by being equally sudden in onset, brief in duration, and equally sudden in decay. . . . Affect, therefore, by being analogous in the quality of the feelings from its specific receptors, as well as in its profile of activation, maintenance, and decay, amplifies and extends the duration and impact of whatever triggers the affect. (Tomkins, *EA,* 88, italics added)

Without this production of amplifying analogs, Tomkins suggests, nothing in the world would assume the nature of a care or concern. Affect thus makes things matter much in the same way that Heideggerian moods make us attuned to our Being-in-the-world. As Tomkins puts it, "The affect mechanism is like the pain mechanism in this respect."

If we cut our hand, saw it bleeding, but had no innate pain receptors, we would know we had done something which needed repair, but there would be no urgency to it. . . . But the pain mechanism, like the affect mechanism, so amplifies our awareness of the injury which activates it that *we are forced to be concerned, and concerned immediately.* The biological utility of such analogic amplification is self-evident. The injury, in the absence of pain, simply does not hurt. The pain receptors have evolved to make us care about injury and disease. Pain is an analog of injury in its inherent similarity. Contrast pain with an orgasm, as a possible analog. If, instead of pain, we always had an orgasm to injury, we would be biologically destined to bleed to death. (*EA,* 88, italics added)

With this proliferation of analogs and analogies, we can see the "peculiarly high redundancy" Tomkins ascribes to "the affect system" emerge in his own prose style.[32] Not only using analogy as an argumentative strategy, but reusing the same analogies over a period of nearly thirty years (as Eve Sedgwick and Adam Frank note, "phrases, sentences, and sometimes whole paragraphs repeat" in a prose "whose rhythms remind one of Gertrude Stein's"), Tomkins writes in a way that might be said to mimetically amplify the basic principle behind his theory.[33] As he says, "Affect amplifies not only its own activator, but also the response to both that activator and *to itself*" (*EA,* 86, italics added). The high redundancy of the affect system, and the recursive reflexivity of its analog-amplifying principle, illustrate what Tomkins describes as "the luxuriant growth potential of analogs"—their capacity to multiply and proliferate seemingly without end (*EA,* 386). This echolalic effect becomes most intense, as we will soon see, when Tomkins develops his insight about affect's role in making things matter to us in general and extends it into an inquiry into its role in producing our investments in political ideologies.

Affect's "very great combinational flexibility" as a "co-assembler," however, is the principle on which Tomkins' theory of affective amplification most significantly relies. Tomkins stresses that the co-assemblages which affect fosters between itself and other mechanisms do not depend on exact matches or correspondences. Affect's combinatory function frequently hinges on an imperfect fit; in fact, "looseness" and "play" actually facilitate its role as co-assembler (*EA,* 52). While Tomkins acknowledges that the affect system still demands "sufficient limitation of mismatch" to carry out its functions, his desire to safeguard the principle of inexactness remains much stronger in the text, leading him to finally propose that "affect is a loosely matched mechanism evolved to play a number of parts in continually changing assemblies of mechanisms. It is in some respects like a letter of the alphabet in a language, changing in significance as it is assembled with varying other letters to form different words, sentences, paragraphs" (*EA,* 51). This linguistic analogy returns us to *The Confidence-Man,* whose eponymous agent not only demonstrates the "very great combinational flexibility" Tomkins associates with affect, but seems explicitly developed "to play a number of parts in continually changing assemblies of mechanisms," disappearing but always reappearing from chapter to chapter in a roughly analogous form. Tomkins' description of the affect system doubles beautifully, in fact, as an analogy not just for *The Confidence-Man*'s "character system" but for the novel as a whole—and in a manner that suggests the novel's propitiousness as a site in which to examine the implications of his amplification theory for a theory of tone.

If a literary work's organizing semblance of feeling cannot be identified entirely with a reader's response to it, or said to be a feeling represented or signified by the text, it evokes Massumi's description of affect as that which perpetually "escapes" the particular forms or perceptions in which it can be "captured," while also remaining "alongside" them. The phenomenon of "affective escape" by no means implies that the analysis of feeling is impossible, Massumi notes; it remains possible "as long as a vocabulary can be found for that which is imperceptible but whose escape from perception cannot but be perceived."[34] This challenge is explicitly met in Melville's novel through a vocabulary of affective "transfer" or transaction, subtended throughout by financial transactions in which values become disconnected from their tokens in the very act of exchange. Monetary value, after all, is precisely that which "escapes" the conspicuously unstable forms and embodiments in which it is captured in this novel (written vouchers, "golden eagles," shares in the Black Rapids Coal Company), and whose escape from perception is not only constantly perceived by the novel's characters but traced and registered by specific systems depicted within it. These include the stock market as well as the Black Rapids Coal Company representative's "transfer-book," toted from one encounter to the next like a proplike miniature of the novel itself, which is less a progression of causally connected events than a series of recorded exchanges. Set and written in a period marked by a highly unstable, unregulated, and excessively complicated currency system, which spawned heated debates over paper money and local forms of it in particular (the novel's publication preceded by nearly a decade the passage of the postbellum Legal Tender Act which instated the national "greenback," as well as the establishment of nationally chartered banks), *The Confidence-Man* explicitly links the question of how affect becomes transferred from one subject to another, and secured as a form of psychic property, to the question of monetary value's highly conspicuous flights from the forms designed to contain it, simply in the process by which these forms change hands. Such flights of value were prominent in the decade of financial anxiety in which Melville sets his novel, the aftermath of a panic sparked in part by Andrew Jackson's feuds with the National Bank. In Melville's novel, the exchanges of affect ("confidence") for written scrip or paper money (already an abstraction or representation of "confidence") also take place in the same year Congress passes the Fugitive Slave Act (1850), a detail that gives a politically charged inflection to the novel's more general preoccupation with "escape" and "capture." Indeed, the novel opens with a crowd reading a publicly posted text that offers "a reward for the capture of a mysterious imposter," followed immediately by a scene in which the same crowd surrounds an "unfortunate negro" bearing the numismatic name "Black Guinea," asking "had he any documentary proof, any *plain paper* about him, attesting that his case was not a spurious one" (*CM,* 14, italics added).

Fiduciary money, which underwrites all modern credit systems by "resting not on the value of the material composing it (paper, bronze, aluminum) but on *trust* in those who issue it,"[35] already signals a convergence of affect and money that Melville's novel will repeatedly reexamine. Such a monetary form not only points to the always potentially unstable relationship between value and the tokens used to capture it, but also shows how "the very materiality of the token can be dispensed with: a simple trace, a mark reduced to the very minimum will suffice. Is it not 'the greatest help and spur to commerce, that property can be so readily conveyed and so well secured by a *Compte en Banc,* that is, *by only writing one man's name for another's in the bank-book?*'"[36] It is precisely this conveyance and securing of fiduciary property, emotional as well as commercial, that Melville dramatizes by "writing one man's name for another's" throughout *The Confidence-Man,* using a spectrum of differently designated yet functionally identical agents.[37] As historian David Henkin argues, the link between language and money that the novel repeatedly scrutinizes was particularly heightened in a period in which the excessive proliferation of nonuniform paper currency transformed money into texts that actually had to be *read,* linking banknotes to leaflets, handbills, newspapers, and other forms of the "impersonal print authority" that "facilitated and dramatized the promiscuous circulation of strangers in an unfamiliar urban environment." In fact, as showcased at the end of *The Confidence-Man,* the overclose relationship between written text and currency spawned entirely new print genres, such as periodical counterfeit detectors and banknote reference guides, designed to teach people *how* to read what had become increasingly untrustworthy "money-texts."[38] As Chicago mayor John Wentworth reminisced in an 1876 lecture on the antebellum fiduciary system, "Nearly every man in Chicago doing business was issuing his individual scrip, and the city abounded with little tickets, such as 'Good at our store for ten cents,' 'Good for a loaf of bread,' 'Good for a shave,' 'Good for a drink,' etc., etc. . . . But after a while it was found out that men were over-issuing. The barber had outstanding too many shaves; the baker too many loaves of bread; the saloon-keeper too many drinks, etc., etc. Want of confidence became general. Each man became afraid to take the tickets of another."[39] The antebellum fiduciary system thus provided a site for an instrumental yet highly unstable convergence between money, written texts, and feelings, just as the *Fidèle* becomes the site for the convergence of confidence men and dupes.

One of the most prominent functions of the self-described "broker" of the fiduciary transactions taking place on the *Fidèle* is in fact a kind of "analog amplification." For all Melville's previous reliance on "unnecessary duplicates," none of his other characters has quite the "urgency, abstractness, and generality" of this parasitical transfer-agent, or quite the same "combinational flexibility."[40] In a sense, the set of interpretive problems posed by the kaleidoscopic nature of the confidence-man is not only strikingly homologous to the analytical challenge posed by "affect" in Silvan Tomkins' theory, but virtually identical to the problems posed by fiduciary money, and by antebellum money in particular in its excessively numerous forms. If "by 1850 so many types of bank notes circulated that only an expert with the aid of a catalog could set values on out-of-town notes," this situation could only intensify what Lendol Calder describes as the intimate link between "credit" and "character" in the antebellum economy, in which "character" (in the sense of temperament) was already functionalized "as a means of economic gain."[41] In *The Confidence-Man*'s catalog of out-of-town characters, however, the character who most prominently raises the financial issue of credit is also the one who most prominently raises the affective issue of what he calls "conviviality," "confidence," or "trust." Melville's novel itself takes the form of a series of analogous encounters between the confidence-man and a plethora of other subjects, gradually increasing in length and narrative complexity as the novel progresses. What ultimately links these episodes together is simply the reappearance of the parasitical transfer-agent, who in one incarnation as deputy of the Philosophical Intelligence Office ("the man with the brass plate") explicitly announces "analogy" as being the "quiet theory" or "strictly philosophical [principle] . . . upon which [his] office is founded" (*CM,* 160).

In his encounter with Pitch, the Missourian who initially denies having "slave sentiments" and boasts of being the citizen of a "free" state, this mimetic "doctrine of analogies" plays a key role in enabling the confidence-man to sell him a child laborer, using a steady accrual of images of unactualized potentiality, or, as Peggy Kamuf has underscored, images of credit, in which boys are compared to lily buds ("points at present invisible, with beauties at present dormant"), baby teeth ("so much the more reason to look for their speedy substitution by the . . . beautiful and permanent ones"), and caterpillars ("do they not bury themselves over and over again in the endless resurrection of better and better?").[42] Although the Missourian on whom the confidence-man tests this "quiet theory" initially challenges its effectiveness ("But is analogy argument? You are a punster"; *CM*, 165), he ends up reapplying the Philosophical Intelligence Office representative's "doctrine of analogies" in a retrospective analysis of their completed transaction:

> He resolves, but cannot comprehend, the operator, less the operation. Was the man a trickster, it must be more for the love than the lucre. Two or three dollars the motive to so many nice wiles? . . . Fain, in his disfavour, would he make out a logical case. The doctrine of analogies recurs. Fallacious enough doctrine when wielded against one's prejudices, but in corroboration of cherished suspicions not without likelihood. Analogically he couples the slanting cut of the equivocator's coat-tails with the sinister case in his eye; he weighs the slyboots' sleek speech in the light imparted by the oblique import of the smooth slope of his boot-heels; the insinuator's undulating flunkeyisms dovetail into those of the flunkey beast that windeth his way on his belly. (*CM*, 173–174)

At first glance, the return of the "doctrine of analogies" in Pitch's reevaluation of his purchase seems merely a tautological redoubling that yields nothing new, since the items he compares (slanting cut and sinister case; slyboots' sleek speech and smooth slope of boot-heels) are "loosely matched" images that corroborate an already established idea. Yet as the Missourian slides into a series of assonances and alliterations that might be said to culminate in a destabilization of "pitch," the sibilant excess of *ess* sounds here demonstrates how analogical "coupling" intensifies through the multiplication of analogies to a point at which it might be said to hiss or feed back, enabling Pitch to detect the presence of a separate, snaky element within the analogies the confidence-man has already produced. Most important, it demonstrates how the transaction between himself and the "analog amplifier" could not have been motivated by money alone.

For while Melville's transfer-agent overtly claims analogic coupling as the philosophical principle of his office, "[leading] me and my associates, in our small, quiet way, to a careful analytical study of man" (*CM,* 160), this office does not solely or even primarily involve brokering financial exchanges. Instead, the fiduciary agent's main function involves persuading the passengers on the *Fidèle*—in a time marked by insecurity over national cohesion, a malaise resulting from the slave system—that the range of negative affects or "sets toward" the world he encounters in them are not genuine dispositions in their own right, but rather effects of the *deprivation* of a positive feeling he calls "confidence" which he, uniquely, can provide. Part of the persuasion thus involves transforming this feeling into a commodity, but to do so involves convincing those with whom he "assembles" that the feeling he invokes is both fungible and possessable. In this sense, the operator's role involves a process that Brian Massumi and Lawrence Grossberg might describe as the subjective transpositioning of "affect" into "emotion," turning feeling uncontained by the subject into something his dupes experience as occasioned within them. This conversion of feeling into psychic property enables Melville's analog amplifier to switch the polarity of his dupes' worldviews from dysphoric to euphoric. While we find all the "positive" or friendly slavery-era feelings that *The Confidence-Man* indicts tellingly united in Melville's ultimate dupe, Captain Delano from "Benito Cereno" (1855), who is described as having a "singularly undistrustful good nature," a "benevolent heart," and "lightsome confidence"—such that even when briefly "operated upon" by "ugly misgivings" about Cereno's strange behavior on the slave ship *San Dominick,* Delano immediately discards them as uncharitable[43]—in Melville's last novel all of these affects are explicitly characterized by the fiduciary man himself as the ideological-affective underpinnings of antebellum capitalism and its traffic in human property in particular: "Confidence is the indispensable basis of all sorts of business transactions. Without it, commerce between man and man, as between country and country, would, like a watch, run down and stop" (*CM,* 171). In other words, confidence might be described as the "tone" of capitalism itself.[44]

It thus comes as no surprise that the confidence-man's conversions of feeling into psychic property are directly facilitated by transfers of ostensibly less ineffable commodities, such as shares of stock (though in a potentially nonexistent company) or vials of herbal medicine (which may only be colored water). The text repeatedly emphasizes the codependency of both transactions. In fact, the confidence-man's role as fiduciary seems to involve deliberately inducing confusion over whether his interactions with the passengers involve the exchange of affects *or* goods. For instance, when a sick man asks "How much?," referring to the medicine peddled by the confidence-man in his incarnation as "herb-doctor," the analog amplifier replies, "As much as you can evoke from your heart and soul." When the sick man asks in bewilderment, "how?—the price of this medicine?," the confidence-man's response ("I thought it was confidence you meant; how much confidence you should have. The medicine,—that is half a dollar a vial") deliberately calls the identity of the purchase into question, demonstrating the ease with which the affect and money are confused (*CM,* 107).

Yet the fact that the confidence-man's function as feeling-broker assumes *primacy* over his role in facilitating exchanges of money for (seemingly) less intangible goods, is illustrated by the fact that his interaction with Pitch, though ostensibly about the latter's purchase of the child laborer, culminates with Pitch more visibly eager and anxious about the possibility of acquiring feeling instead (raising the question of whether "even I, I myself, *really ha[ve]* this sort of . . . confidence"). Significantly, Pitch does not seek verification from this agent that the transfer of the nonaffective commodity has genuinely taken place (unlike other characters in the novel, he makes no demand for a bill of sale, voucher, or receipt), but does nervously appeal to the agent for reassurance about his potential to subjectively possess the feeling which has simultaneously been transacted ('Do you think now, candidly, that—I say candidly—candidly—could I have some small, limited,—some faint, conditional degree of confidence . . . ? Candidly now?"; *CM,* 170). The fact that the confidence-man is appealed to on this basis alone (his capacity to verify whether or not the feeling has in fact been transferred into Pitch's possession) suggests that the only thing "special" about the confidence-man, distinguishing him from any other antebellum salesman, is his ability to broker deals in feeling. His "office" thus involves ensuring that the possibility of the Missourian's "really having" the affect will end up *mattering more* to the Missourian than the possibility of possessing *or* not-possessing the boy, while also ensuring that the very fact of its assuming priority for him will directly facilitate and enable the sale of the boy *as* property.

Though the encounter with Pitch demonstrates that the exchange of money for goods ultimately becomes secondary in importance to the affective transaction it subtends, in other episodes monetary exchange is posited as the only way of guaranteeing that the affective transaction has actually taken place, providing the "receipt," "voucher," or "documentary proof" (forms of written verification demanded continually throughout the novel) for the affective transaction's felicity. We see this reflexive logic amplified in the encounter between the agent, described as a "ge'mman wid a big book," and the miser—an interaction that stands out among the many others analogous to it in the novel, since as a hoarder unwilling to place tokens of value into circulation, the miser assumes the role of an element which blocks exchange and whose symbolic function posits a serious threat to this transfer-based text as a whole. The encounter between these two figures unfolds as follows: (1) After performing a small service for the coughing miser, providing him with water on his request, the confidence-man suggests affect as a viable substitute for the money the miser claims to lack, capable of being tendered in lieu of dollars to neutralize the debt which the service performed has instated; (2) the miser agrees to this replacement and, when asked directly by the confidence-man to give him "confidence," does so verbally; (3) the confidence-man verbally acknowledges that this transfer has taken place, but then demands money in order to verify it. The affect thus acquires a monetary value by being initially offered as the money's replacement, while money acquires the function of a written "receipt" confirming the felicity of the miser's speech act, on which the success of the affective transfer depends:

> Revived at last [by the water], [the miser] inclined toward his ministrant, and, in a voice disastrous with a cough, said: "I am old and miserable, a poor beggar, not worth a shoestring—how can I repay you?"
>
> "By giving me your confidence."
>
> "Confidence!" he squeaked, with changed manner, while the pallet swung; "little left at my age, but take the stale remains, and welcome."
>
> "Such as it is, though, you give it. Very good. Now give me a hundred dollars."
>
> Upon this the miser was all panic. His hands groped toward his waist, then suddenly flew upward beneath the moleskin pillow, and there lay clutching something out of sight. Meanwhile, to himself he incoherently mumbled: "Confidence? Cant, gammon! Confidence? hum, bubble!—Confidence? fetch, gouge!—Hundred dollars?—hundred devils!"
>
> (*CM,* 95–96)

Significantly, a demand for the affective transaction's *verification* in nonaffective terms precipitates a disfiguration of both syntax and meaning in the miser's response. The words that compose his response not only reflexively refer to this semantic corrosion (the meaningless words of "cant"), but enact it in a quasi-onomatopoeia.

"Hum" and "bubble" are presented here as sounds or noise, much like the miser's cough ("ugh, ugh").

In this sense, one might say that there is a *redoubling* of the dissonance the confidence-man has introduced into the miser's language in the very words that indicate it. More significantly, in response to the demand that some monetary token be exchanged in order to confirm that the passing of affect from one individual to the other via language *has really taken place,* the miser's language turns anaphoric, a repetitive rather than substitutional schema which, in this case, resists syntactic closure in favor of sonorous patterning.[45]

> Confidence? Cant, gammon!
> Confidence? hum, bubble!
> Confidence? fetch, gouge!

It is at this moment, one marked by a failure to verify affect's successful conveyance and securing as psychic property, and a failure to bring closure to a circuit of social exchange, that anaphora begins to *drown out* analogy, however dominant the latter logic appears to have been in organizing the novel's set of fiduciary transactions by establishing similarity-based correspondences between the items exchanged (money and affect, language and money). In other words, a positional parallelism in which sound is foregrounded as an independent feature (Nathanson, *WP,* 140), comes to override an ideational parallelism at the exact moment the subjective proprietorship of a feeling, ostensibly secured by analogical equivalences between affect, money, and language, is rendered questionable and unstable simply by the *amplification* of these equivalences. Moreover, the disturbance of this proprietary relationship between subject and feeling is echoed in anaphora's capacity to disturb the relationship between a substance and its formally distinct attributes, simply by foregrounding the "intensive variations of which [these attributes] are capable."[46] Like the proprietorship of feeling ultimately destabilized by the confidence-man's attempt to push the analogical correspondences between affect and money to an extreme, showing how their exchange might be continued ad infinitum, subject-predicate linkages could be described as "loosened" in anaphora, insofar as its rhythmic pattern tends to emphasize the spectacular variation and proliferation of predications *over* the bond or logical connection between any individual predicate and its subject (Nathanson, *WP,* 140). Note, for example, how the miser's linguistic eruptions recall the pattern of the inscriptions theatrically displayed on the deaf-mute's slate, at the opening of the novel:

> "Charity thinketh no evil."
> "Charity suffereth long, and is kind."
> "Charity endureth all things."
> "Charity believeth all things."
> "Charity never faileth."

As Melville's narrator notes, "The word charity, as originally traced, remain[s] throughout uneffaced, not unlike the left-hand numeral of a printed date" (*CM,* 3). Significantly, this display of anaphora at the local and stylistic level (parallel repetition of beginning words or phrases in succeeding lines or sentences) mirrors the fact that *The Confidence-Man* is actually anaphoric in its narrative *structure,* insofar as its entire plot consists of a series of exchanges involving one term which remains constant while the elements co-assembled to it rotate and change:

> CM and crowd
> CM and merchant
> CM and young scholar
> CM and clergyman
> CM and miser
> CM and sick man
> CM and soldier of fortune
> CM and cripple
> CM and Missourian
> CM and barber

CM and the stranger
CM and the stranger's disciple
CM and old man, etc.

Yet the unity of even this repeated "substance," however contrasting with the intensive variation of its co-assembled elements, is deceptive. For the "CM" position is itself pluralized through another anaphoric structure, involving (among others):

The man with the brass plate
The man with the big book
The man with a traveling cap
The man with a weed
The man in the snuff-colored surtout
The man with the gold sleeve-buttons
The man in a gray coat and white tie
The man with the hook nose, etc.

In fact, as the novel progresses and the interactions between the analog amplifier and others accumulate in number, the principle of analogy becomes engulfed by anaphora *simply by being repeated*—a Sub-Subish strategy which will reappear in my other chapters on ugly feelings, and in which one disrupts a system not by breaking or challenging the rules from above but by adhering to a rule too well.[47] Here, the overwhelming of analogy by anaphora could be described as a shift from *logos* to *pherein,* from ratiocination to "bearing," which produces an increase in resonance in *The Confidence-Man* as a whole—a novel-wide "vibration" whose disruption of signifying communications at the local level is marked by the presence of "hum" or "bubble" in speech. In this manner, the "quiet theory" of analogy, when simply amplified by the transfer-agent during his successive operations, dissolves into anaphoric noise.[48]

Thus, while the transactions in feeling supervised by the novel's "analog amplifier" depend on his ability to intensify the correspondences between affect, money, and language that render each potentially substitutable for the others, the anaphorization of speech marks the moment in which these correspondences dissolve in a schema foregrounding repetition *over* substitution and sonority *over* semantics, culminating in a "hum" reconfiguring feeling in excess of the terms in which it has initially been transacted. The subjective ownership of the feeling that supports the fiduciary system cannot be verified, and it is in the doomed effort *to* verify its subjective ownability that feeling "escapes" in a series of noisy linguistic bursts. In the case of the miser, it could be said that the positive affect of "confidence" is set at odds with itself simply by being amplified to the point at which it begins to feed back, distorting his language in a manner that points to the paradoxical breakdown of larger correspondences between affect, money, and language once the analogous relationship between these value systems is reflexively appealed to as a basis for verifying that a transfer of feeling has actually taken place. What is more important, the new dissonance introduced into the language of the miser suggests that the negative situation of the confidence's unfeltness is itself perceived, and in a manner that generates a secondary feeling that is indeed actually experienced: "Upon this the miser was all panic."

The systematic disruptions of communicative language throughout the novel are thus far from incidental to its preoccupation with affective transactions, which remain central to the text precisely in their (extremely noisy) elision from epistemological verification. Generated by a subject's failure to authenticate the subjective ownership of feeling by appealing to values produced by analogous systems of circulation and exchange, these dissonant patterns call attention to feeling's paradoxical ability to introduce interference in the very circuits of commerce and communication we have seen it enable. Thus, while *The Confidence-Man* illustrates feeling's role in lubricating acts of antebellum circulation and exchange, it also illustrates its potential to suspend the closure of these exchanges once its unfelt status as a *semblance* of feeling is disclosed, making it impossible to identify the feeling entirely with the discursive or symbolic economies it traverses and in which it intervenes. For while the text shows the potential of affect to generate effects across linguistic and economic domains, magnifying awareness and increasing the urgency of the effects it produces, its anaphoric "feedback" points to the impossibility of sustaining any analogy-based substitutability between language, money, and affect. None of the "deals" involving or supported by feeling can be properly closed, in other words, without producing a stutter or echo ("Confidence! . . . Confidence! . . . Confidence!") registering its "escape."

It is here that *The Confidence-Man* offers its most compelling allegory for the problem posed by tone, as well as for tone's unusual resonance for the analysis of literature and ideology: in these audible demonstrations that whether the feeling is vested in abstract systems or in personal relationships, the world of the novel's story *runs on a feeling that no one actually feels*. More specifically, the world is run by a feeling (confidence, trust) that no one in the novel can verify or publicly prove he possesses, *even* with aid of tokens (money, vouchers, receipts) that are essentially abstractions of that unfelt "confidence," and whose values presuppose and depend on it. Against this general atmosphere of "affective jingoism," here a possible motivation for the novel's own affective or tonal ambiguity emerges (Massumi, *PV,* 42). We can also understand why the inability to affirm the subjective ownership of "confidence" causes the characters in the novel so much consternation or panic, much the way the proximity between real and virtual feeling in the concept of tone can produce anxiety for the literary theorist. Though the unfeltness of confidence is *itself* perceived (and in a manner that subsequently generates a second and actually experienced feeling that, in the case of many of the dupes, seems much like the affective confusion or "disconcertedness" where one feels confused about *what* one is feeling), to admit that one cannot verify having or feeling confidence in the world of Melville's novel, even as one may possess tokens that "capture" the feeling and affirm its presence *in every act of exchange,* is to imply that the feeling underwriting the system of fiduciary money on which the modern antebellum economy depends is somehow "ontologically obscure," as fake as the "panic contrived by artful alarmists" we encountered at the beginning of this chapter. If, indeed, "confidence is the indispensable basis of all sorts of business transactions" and "without it, commerce between man and man, as between country and country, would, like a watch, run down and stop" (*CM,* 171), a public admission of not really "having" the feeling, of being unable to isolate or locate it, either in oneself or in the fiduciary transactions that would seem to affirm its existence above all (since trust is what enables them to take place), raises the specter of a potential threat to the system itself. Such admissions of lacking confidence would have seemed particularly ominous to readers who witnessed the dramatic collapse of banking institutions during the Panic of 1836. Yet while the epistemological difficulty posed by this fictitious feeling may make the "market individualists" depicted in the novel feel disconcerted or panicky, its unfelt or virtual status, as a mere "idea" or "semblance" of feeling, is precisely what holds together the system of fiduciary exchange and the public sphere conflated with it.[49] Hence, while "the confidence man exposes the absent core of marketplace reality" (as Michael Rogin argues), or, more precisely, discloses the "spurious" feeling at this reality's center, such exposure hardly threatens the marketplace's ability to function—much as the fakeness of the panic in the Black Rapids transfer-agent's narrative poses no limit to its potential effects.[50] The unfelt feeling enables *all* economic transactions in the novel's fiduciary system to take place, including the commodification and transfer of the feeling itself— stopping short only at facilitating the verification of its own subjective capture. And as the encounter with Pitch demonstrates in particular, this unfelt feeling (which has no problem promiscuously circulating even if it cannot be entirely isolated from the tokens whose fungibility depend on it) can be put to powerful ends. For in this case, what Cecilia Tichi calls "the posting of private psychic property" facilitated by the confidence-man's analogies between having confidence and owning supposedly less virtual goods (phony stock, fake medicine, and so forth) culminates not only with the transfer of property for money, but with the sale of a young person as property ("MC," 651).

Dominated by the "Wall Street spirit" and "slavery sentiments" masked by "benevolence," the public sphere of *The Confidence-Man* runs on a feeling that everyone recognizes for its personal utility but that nobody "has," just as the "world" of the aesthetic object in Dufrenne's phenomenology is constituted by an "affective quality" that is perceived rather than experienced. In both cases, the difficulty lies not in the ontological difference between real emotion and virtual emotion, but rather in their proximity. For as Langer notes in a comment recalling the very situation the "artful alarmists" in Melville's novel have intended their fake feeling to create, "It takes precision of thought not to confuse an imagined feeling, or a precisely conceived emotion that is formulated in a perceptible symbol, with a feeling or emotion actually experienced in response to real events. Indeed, the very notion of feelings and emotions not really felt, but only imagined, is strange to most people" (*FF,* 181). Yet the point of the Black Rapids agent's story is precisely that an illusory panic can easily *generate* a "double" that is actually experienced in response to real events, reminding us of how tone influences our subjective responses to a literary work even if it cannot be assimilated to them. We can thus see that *The Confidence-Man* is not only a novel crowded with doubles, but a novel about the feedback that this kind of affective redoubling produces—one that discloses the ease with which confidence, the seemingly neutral "tone" of capitalism itself, can short-circuit in panic, disconcertedness, and other ugly feelings when its semblance character is made apparent, revealing the virtual as well as ideological character of the feeling on which the world of Melville's novel runs.

If the noise that reveals the virtual/ideological character of this feeling is the outcome of a certain kind of reflexivity, similar to the feedback produced by an overproximity between the transmitter and receiver of an electronic signal, it comes as no surprise that a similar "noise" comes to haunt Silvan Tomkins' affect theory when he explicitly turns its principle of "analog amplification," initially deployed to show how affect makes things matter, to an analysis of our affective investments in ideas and ideology. Starting in the 1960s, we find Tomkins redirecting his laboratory studies of the affect system toward the development of a "psychology of commitment" concerned with "the dynamics of seduction by ideas, of disenchantment with ideas, of addiction to ideas, of commitment to ideas and the integration of both individuals and societies through commitment"—a project that would include specific attention to "the role of violence and suffering in either discouraging or encouraging commitment to ideology, as for example in the deepening and strengthening of both the anti-democratic and democratic ideology by the threat of fascism and again by the challenge of the Negro for integration in American society" (*EA,* 110). While newly engaged in this analysis of affect's role in structuring social and collective behavior, Tomkins (a former playwright) starts using the word "script" to describe the set of rules governing the relationships between various affective "scenes," with "scene" defined as the basic unit of analysis for understanding "persons," understood as biological entities "embedded in a historical, sociocultural, and civilizational matrix"—as distinct from "human beings," who are simply the biological entities.[51] This new focus on interpellated or social subjects also leads Tomkins into differentiating "magnification" from "amplification":

A single affect is scripted innately to amplify its own activator [and co-assemble with it and the responses it triggers] in a single momentary scene. But when amplified scenes are *co-assembled,* as repeated, the resulting responses to such a set represent magnification, or amplification, of the already separately amplified scenes. Now it is the *set* of such co-assembled scenes

that is then amplified by fresh affect, and which I am defining
as magnification, in contrast to the simpler script involved in
any innate amplification of the single scene. . . . What is essential for magnification is the ordering of sets of scenes by rules
for their interpretation, or evaluation, or production, or pre-
diction . . . so that these scenes *and* their rules are themselves
amplified by affect. (*EA*, 315, italics in the original)

Note how the basic principles of Tomkins' systems theory, "co-
assembly" and "amplification," are taken to increasing levels of
reflexive complexity here. Affect not only co-assembles and amplifies its activator and responses "in a single momentary scene," but
these single scenes are themselves co-assembled in a way which
triggers fresh responses and affect that then amplify the already
amplified scenes. (Though I am merely paraphrasing Tomkins' argument, my sentence is likely to induce vertigo.) These newly
"magnified" scenes form a set ordered by "rules for predicting, interpreting, responding to, and controlling [them]," and these rules,
along with the magnified scenes they govern, are further amplified
by affect. Given that many amplifications of amplifications are involved in this theoretical scenario, Tomkins' use of the word "magnification" reflects an effort to control the echolalia that his core
concept of "analog amplification" threatens to produce when extended beyond the analysis of the affect mechanism itself (where
the "single momentary scene" is all that really matters) to its implications for the person "embedded in a historical, sociocultural, and
civilizational matrix." To draw on one of Tomkins' own explana-
tory analogies, this echolalia might be described as the dissonance
produced when an amplification system redoubles or feeds back
upon itself. As Tomkins writes in 1978,

[My original] theory of affect as amplification was flawed by
[one] serious ambiguity. I had unwittingly assumed that in
both electronic amplification and affective amplification there
was an increase in gain of the *signal*. If that were the case, *what*

> *would be amplified would remain essentially the same except that*
> *it would be louder.* But affects are separate mechanisms, involv-
> ing . . . responses quite distinct from the . . . responses they are
> presumed to amplify. (*EA,* 87, italics added)

The passage implies that affective amplification produces "an increase in gain" of something *other* than "signal," and, moreover, an
increase that introduces *difference* into the system; otherwise, "what
would be amplified would remain essentially the same." Affective
amplification does not simply turn up the volume on what is already there, but points to the presence of something "separate."
Tomkins places a particular emphasis on this difference-through-
amplification when discussing magnification. As he notes, "Scenes
are magnified not by repetition, but by repetition with a *difference.*
. . . Sheer repetition of experience characteristically evokes adaptation, which attenuates, rather than magnifies, the connected scenes"
(*EA,* 325). Returning to Tomkins' own analogy between electronic
and affective amplification, the "increase in gain" of the unnamed
element, defined here only as that which is not signal, reveals difference in the form of an unexpected excess: something akin to the
noisy interference the parasitical confidence-man introduces into
his fiduciary transactions in order to disclose the illusory character
of the feeling that has made them possible.

Tomkins gives us an additional twist on tone's special conducive-
ness, as precisely this kind of "resonance," for the analysis of "the
ebb and flow of affect investment in ideas and ideology"—using a
model that strikingly recalls his original description of the relationship of affect (as a "loosely matched mechanism") to the psychic
and bodily mechanisms it amplifies.

> Now let me introduce the concepts of ideo-affective postures,
> ideological postures and ideo-affective resonance. (1) By ideo-
> affective postures I mean any *loosely organized* set of feelings
> and *ideas about feelings.* (2) By ideological postures I refer to

any *highly organized* and articulate set of *ideas about anything.*
. . . (3) By ideo-affective resonance we mean the engagement of
the loosely organized beliefs and feelings (of the ideo-affective
postures) by ideology (as we have defined it), where the ideo-
affective postures are sufficiently similar to the ideological pos-
ture, so that they reinforce and strengthen each other. Ideo-affective resonance to ideology is a love affair of a loosely organized set of feelings and ideas about feelings with a highly
organized and articulate set of ideas about anything. As in the
case of a love affair the fit need not at the outset be perfect, so
long as there is sufficient similarity . . . to set the vibrations between the two entities into sympathetic coordination with each
other. . . . It is possible, and indeed common for different individuals to resonate in different manners to the same ideology.
(*EA*, 111–112)

We might echo Melville in saying that here, with a significant increase in reverberation, the doctrine of analog amplification returns—though once again "magnified" to a higher order of social
meaningfulness and complexity. Just as affect mimetically amplifies
the other psychic and bodily mechanisms with which it co-assembles, "ideo-affective resonance" results when sets of feelings and
ideas about feelings are loosely matched ("the fit need not at the
outset be perfect") with "sufficiently similar" ideas about other
things (as for instance, in *The Confidence-Man,* ideas about character, property, slavery, and the fiduciary system itself), so that they
"reinforce and strengthen" each other. And not just with an increase in gain or loudness, but with the addition of "something separate," registered in a dissonance akin to the feedback generated by
the operator's transactions. Hence, in addition to *parasite,* transfer-
agent, and analog amplifier, the confidence-man's "function" might
be described as that of ideo-affective resonator, both for the characters he co-assembles on the *Fidèle,* and for the reader of the novel.

Like the "confidence" that runs the world of Melville's novel, holds or co-assembles all of its elements together, and makes all of its internal exchanges possible, tone is a feeling which is perceived rather than felt and whose very *nonfeltness* is perceived. There is a sense, then, in which its status as feeling is fundamentally negative, regardless of what the particular quality of affect is. In *The Confidence-Man,* we find this subjective perception of unfelt feeling repeatedly registered in the language of the operator's operatees, in the form of an excessive "vibration" that the confidence-man produces simply by underscoring the redundancy of trying to buy the "feeling" that underlies all acts of buying in a fiduciary system—a vibration that, for a single brief moment, disrupts the reflexive relay. For even as noise can produce order, as Jacques Attali notes, "order by noise is not born without crisis," however minor a form that crisis may take.[52] In our case, the noise discloses nothing less than the logic of what Jean-Christophe Agnew calls the "placeless market," a market which is dependent on a virtual feeling that cannot be felt and whose power to lubricate nonaffective exchanges rests precisely on its resistance to being psychically captured as one's own. Hence, it is less true that confidence lies at the basis of all transactions in the social world of the novel (as the confidence-man attests) than that a semblance of the feeling does. When the "confidence" enabling these exchanges of objects becomes an object of exchange itself, the fiduciary transactions automatically feed back, producing a noise that indicates not so much a glitch in the system as the way in which that system requires each transaction to "place the [real feeling] farther out of reach."[53] Accordingly, the noisy interferences Melville's parasite introduces into the exchanges he supervises do not so much disrupt the feeling-based economy of the novel as demonstrate how it works, "deploying the ambiguities and contradictions of market exchange to deconstruct Common Sense, the conventional novel, and in the end, Melville's own relation to his reader."[54] Indeed, as a system of exchange based on a highly codified feeling that is continually reproduced and circulated even as it cannot be subjectively felt, Melville's novel harnesses the logic of this market for an inquiry into the role of virtual emotion in literature in particular.[55] It seems fitting, then, that Melville's most anti-psychological novel, one explicitly preoccupied with the politically ambiguous uses of semblances of feeling, takes care to ensure that readers remain uncertain about what its own organizing semblance of feeling might be.

Coda

Like the *Fidèle,* which accumulates passengers as it travels the Mississippi in a series of stops, this chapter has brought us from one theoretical landing to another. We have moved from Langer's inquiry into how a semblance of feeling enables an artwork to have an import or "factor of significance" relatively autonomous from what it signifies, to Tomkins' investigation into the general structure of our caring—how not just art but the world itself comes to matter—by theorizing what feeling actually is and does. We saw how this attention to affect's role in generating "concern" naturally deepened, with an increasing noisiness as well as complexity, into an analysis of its role in generating our investments in ideas and ideologies, which Melville's novel broadens to include ideologies about affect itself. Further still, we noted how this arrival at the convergence of affect and ideology seemed to be accompanied by noise—in particular, a noise produced by a certain kind of recursive reflexivity. In this last section, I will steer this nexus of issues back to a specifically aesthetic context, returning us to the question of how the model of tone that *The Confidence-Man* offers bears on the novel's own curious resistance to affective engagement as a whole.

Let us begin by noting the "noise" Tomkins says he unexpectedly encountered in the early 1960s in his effort to analyze photographs of the human face as an "affective transmitter"—photographs which were actually images of "fake" feeling, or emotional expressions carefully simulated by actors:[56]

> At [one] time I spent a few years and several thousand dollars of government money in ultra-speed photography of the face. I assumed that at speeds of 10,000 frames a second, micro-analyses of the face would yield "secrets" of affect and human nature analogous to those the microscope had revealed about biological structures. Although microexpressions of the face do reveal some important information, they also create *a great noise*. At 10,000 frames a second the smile becomes an interminable bore, forfeiting much vital information which can be seen easily by the naked eye or by conventional slow motion photography (*EA*, 41, italics added)

This anecdote about a dubious "micro-analysis" of a series of still photographs may call to mind a famous scene from Michelangelo Antonioni's *Blow-Up* (1966; story by Julio Cortázar). During a stroll in a London park, Thomas (David Hemmings), a professional photographer, randomly snaps pictures of a man and woman. He later enlarges them at increasing levels of magnification, to a point at which the individual grains of the silver emulsion become visible and produce a kind of snow or static in the images.[57] When Thomas studies the magnified prints pinned to his studio walls, he comes to believe, despite (but more likely because of) the grainy interference that increasingly enters them, that the black-and-white photos reveal a second man hiding in the bushes with a pistol, and tell the noirish story of a duplicitous woman leading her lover to his death. Hence, while Tomkins and Thomas both encounter an asignifying excess in the act of interpreting a series of photographs, for Tomkins the "noise" ends up resisting, rather than appearing to promote, the disclosure of a "secret."

Indeed, while best known for its preoccupation with photography, *Blow-Up* eventually shifts its attention to the amplification

of sound. In fact, the scene of visual magnification is explicitly paralleled by a scene of acoustic amplification that unfolds when
Thomas wanders into a Yardbirds rock show, one of the film's
foregrounded scenes of an encounter with art. During the musical
performance, which is attended by an impassive crowd that seems
strangely detached from this context, a hiss and crackle starts to
emanate from the guitarist's electronic amplifier. Resulting from
output unintentionally reentered into the system as input (such that
the amplifier begins amplifying its own amplification of the signal,
in addition to the signal itself), the feedback eventually drowns out
the melody and words of the ballad being played. While this unintended crackle, generated by an overproximity between transmitter
and receiver, explicitly recalls the static that appears in Thomas'
photographic enlargements (both result from relatively routine
techniques of amplification, though one is achieved via a darkroom
enlarger and the other via electronic equipment), like the "great
noise" encountered by Tomkins, it ends up disrupting rather than
facilitating narrative sequencing and order. Just as there are conservative as well as disruptive models of feedback—one in which the
controlled return of output as input allows the system to "learn"
and readjust itself, the other in which an overdetermined relay between output and input generates an unintended surplus that cannot be reabsorbed—we could say that the guitarist's feedback involves "a redundancy of resonation that plays up . . . (feeds back
disconnection, enabling a different connectivity)" versus "a redundancy of signification that plays out or linearizes" (Massumi, *PV,*
26). As it plays "up," the feedback seems to indicate something
about the state of the "channel" through which the signal is transmitted, even as it begins to interfere with the signal itself.[58] It is
thus something like Gelley's *parasites,* as well as the "dial tone"
in one psychoanalyst's account of the crucial distinction between in-
dicators and signals in affective communication: "When the telephone rings, an intentional signal addressed to us is being produced, informing us that a communication is to be expected

through our telephone at this moment. But when we are near our telephone, as we happen to hear *a low buzzing sound,* then we realize that the receiver is off the hook. What we are hearing is the dial tone which we use as an indicator informing us of the state of the telephone; but it is not an intentional communication directed at us."[59]

In the example of the telephone, "noise" and "signal" function as noninterfering parts of a communicative system, but in *Blow-Up*'s scene of musical performance the conflict between these two elements is explicitly staged as a battle between guitar and amplifier. In an unsuccessful effort to control the excessive resonance, the guitarist begins to hit his instrument against the amplifier from which it emanates, which eventually breaks off the neck of the guitar. It is this allegorical "victory" of the amplifier feedback *over* the intended signal that animates the previously motionless crowd, which is suddenly drawn back into the scene and begins behaving as one expects the audience of a rock show to behave. Bringing movement and feeling back into the ironically frozen world of "Swinging London" (though the excitement that finally breaks loose at the rock show seems not directed toward anything in particular, but rather a burst of undifferentiated arousal), this intrusion of noise into signal, or of asignifying "indications" into intentional communications, seems to make affective engagement possible in some basic or zero-degree way. It is as if the staged conflict between noise and signal enables the diegetic audience (and perhaps the film audience as well) to become reattuned to the performance, recovering a "situatedness" that enables what they are encountering to matter, if not exactly to mean.

As a form of surplus resonance or feedback *that intensifies engagement with an aesthetic object,* the amplifier crackle in *Blow-Up* provides yet another useful analogy for tone's critical function. Like the noisy hisses in Melville's novel, which register the "escape" of feeling from the very circuit of exchange it enables once its unfeltness is perceived, the film's dramatization of amplifier feedback points to the way in which tone can be thought of as a form of "orderly disorder": a materially created semblance of feeling that nonetheless dissolves into static when one attempts to perform a "micro-analysis," or to break it down into isolated parts.[60] There is a crucial difference, however, between the allegorical imports of the amplifier feedback in *Blow-Up* and the versions of feedback we encounter in Melville's novel. For in the way *The Confidence-Man* turns from how feelings become "mattering mechanisms" (in the positive sense presented above) to the ways in which affective engagements become sites for interpellation and manipulation, it becomes clear that its emphasis slants in a more negative direction. Indeed, as a novel which is *not* easily engaged with emotionally, and whose tonal noisiness might even be said to actively resist the reader's conscious efforts at an affective connection, *The Confidence-Man* is in many ways the counterexample of the phenomenon that both it and *Blow-Up* allegorize, namely the way in which feeling—even an unfelt but perceived semblance of feeling—makes the world, and art in particular, matter. Melville's last novel might even be said to obtrude itself as a text that readers will have *trouble caring about*—a phrase whose strangeness we will return to shortly. Hence, while the figure of a "noise" produced by a recursively reflexive structure comes to assume a central role in *Blow-Up*, in Tomkins' theory of affective amplification, and in *The Confidence-Man*, Melville's novel has a very different stake in deploying it. This stake is in fact twofold. For in its depiction of an overdetermined relay between subject and object, or between a signal's transmitter and receiver, that not only produces noise but is momentarily broken by the very noise that it produces, *The Confidence-Man*'s theory of literary tone seems aimed at contesting two kinds of reflexivity in art and aesthetics that both take the form of affective mirroring.

The first of these is the literary strategy of sympathy that prevails in the novels of Melville's contemporaries, a perfectly symmetrical circuit of affective "communication" in which the reader feels what a character feels. The second, more complicated version is the concept of "projection," which we might think of as tone's greatest adversary in the domain of philosophical aesthetics. The strength of this adversary is what appears to be its post-Kantian common-sensicality: what a critic calls "tone" is simply a subject's emotion-based appraisal of an artwork, treated *as if* it were an intrinsic property of the work itself. From this perspective, the "feeling" of the object is merely a mirror reflection of the subject's affective response to it, each confirming the other in an imaginary loop. Here what we call tone seems just another word for the category that Genette calls "aesthetic predicates": qualities reflecting the negative or positive feelings which a work inspires in the viewer and which the viewer then phantasmatically appends to the work, as in the case of Santayana's definition of "beauty" as "pleasure objectified," or, to draw from Genette's own examples, "graceful, elegant, dull, vulgar, powerful, heavy, light, pretty, deep, superficial, noble, stilted, charming, classical, academic, subtle, crude, moving, sentimental, uniform, monotonous, sublime, grotesque, etc."[61] If, in the aesthetics of sympathy perfected by the nineteenth-century realist novel, I feel what a character in the work feels, in the aesthetic theory of projection, or what Theodor Lipps called "empathy," the work's "feeling" is a duplicate of what *I* feel.[62] One model reverses the direction of the other, though in both cases the reflexive circuit between subject and object, or "transmitter" and "receiver," is seamlessly closed. There is, admittedly, an attractive neatness to both the literary strategy of sympathy and the theory of aesthetic empathy or projection, by no means implausible or unuseful models of how feeling can make a work of art become an object of our concern *by the production of immediacy.*

Yet there are clearly other ways in which feeling facilitates aesthetic engagement. Indeed, it is precisely the kind of affective reflexivity embodied in the dynamics of sympathy and empathy that Melville's novel wants to disrupt, simply by demonstrating how its imaginary symmetry cannot in fact be sustained. As we have seen, the confidence-man's strategy is to introduce a break in the relay, however fleeting or momentary, not by challenging its principle of reflexivity but by amplifying it. The novel's emphasis on the ensuing dissonance should not be taken as a celebration of chaos, but rather as an effort to put forward a different model of affect's role in our aesthetic encounters, and, indeed, one which it explicitly pits against the imaginary circuit of sympathy. It is this model that reveals the full extent of the confidence-man's "operation" within the novel and the full force of tone's dialectical character. For the subjective nature of the *secondary* feeling—panic, consternation, disconcertedness—produced once the confidence-man has forced his dupes to perceive the semblance character of the feeling which runs their world, suggests that the dupes have been made to *care* about *the very fact of its unfeltness,* that somehow the affect's "escape" from subjective containment itself matters. Care or engagement, while produced by an "affective amplification" similar to the versions in *Blow-Up* and Tomkins' psychology of commitment, thus comes to have a negative structure in Melville's novel, since what has become an object of concern to the dupes is precisely the phenomenon of a *separation* between subject and feeling. This negative model of aesthetic engagement, as paradoxically fostered through affect's surprising ability to produce distance rather than immediacy, sheds new light on our previous characterization of Melville's novel—based precisely on a reading of its tone—as one that reflexively conscripts the very atonality it theorizes to become a novel which readers will have "trouble caring about." The expression has an oxymoronic quality: things that we are unconcerned with should not make us troubled. Yet a closer inspection reveals that what at first seems oxymoronic about the idea of "having *trouble* caring" about something is in fact its meta-affectivity, paralleling the way in which the perception of an unfelt feeling produces a secondary, dysphoric emotion in Melville's novel. There are obviously things we do not care about—end of story. But then there are things we do not care about in which the very absence of care subsequently becomes disturbing. Put simply, the novel conscripts its own affective ambiguity to ensure that which we cannot *not* care about it *without feeling,* well, *bad.* It is important to note the aggressiveness of this maneuver, as well as where it seems directed. Indeed, the novel's largest stake in offering this negative model of affective/aesthetic engagement might be said to be that of problematizing literature's own status as an object of general unconcern in a world organized and driven by the "Wall Street spirit." But note that Melville's strategy is to do so not by making his novel plead more loudly for emotional attention, but rather by using its affective atonality to *intensify* its status as an object of *unconcern,* such that the response the novel produces (if not the novel itself, directly) becomes, in spite of its negative status as an affective deficit or lack, something that generates an ugly feeling and can no longer be ignored. *The Confidence-Man* could thus be said to redirect our attention, albeit in a highly negative and indirect way, to the broader question of our very engagement with art in a world dominated by practical and instrumental concerns, by allegorizing the problematic status of affect *"in"* art concentrated in the concept of tone. Indeed, there is a sense in which tone provocatively reveals an "aesthetic attitude" at the heart of the *critical* mindset that makes ideological analysis possible, and even at the center of the ideological analysis of aesthetic ideologies themselves.

The Confidence-Man's theory of tone as a noisy feedback loop or form of "affective amplification" is thus nothing less than a theory of aesthetic engagement that goes straight to the heart of literature's Bartlebyan status in the administered world—that is, the limited social agency that renders it *not much of a concern* in the first place. Here, affect discloses the dialectic of distance and immediacy at the center of aesthetic engagement, and in a way that offers a response to one of the most difficult questions in philosophical aesthetics—the *motivation* for the mechanism of projection—which we find Langer posing in the following way:

Santayana regarded beauty as "pleasure objectified"—the
spectator's pleasure "projected" into the object that caused it.
Just why and how such projection occurs is not clear; it is not
imputation, for we do not . . . think Dürer's crucified Christ,
the Disciple and the swooning Mother below the cross, and the
cross itself, is "having" our alleged pleasure in the picture.
What the picture "has" is beauty, which *is* our projected, i.e.
objectified pleasure. But *why* is subjective pleasure not good
enough? Why do we objectify it and project it into [the form
of] "beauty," while we are content to feel it directly, as delight,
in candy and perfumes and cushioned seats? (*FF,* 18–19, italics
added)

Here, with its demonstration of the momentary disconnection produced by an overdetermined relay between "transmitter" and "receiver," Melville's novel matter-of-factly responds: We project the
feeling that the object inspires to create a *distance* between ourselves
and that feeling. But why are we compelled to separate ourselves
from the feeling that the object elicits? Precisely *because* our feeling
has made the object into an object of concern. In other words, the
desire for detachment is a direct consequence of the kind of interest
our feeling about the object has fostered, and it is precisely this
combination of steps—an affective engagement *that itself prompts
distancing*—that constitutes the object as an *aesthetic* object: to introduce such a distance into our affective relationships to candy
and perfume would be to make them aesthetic objects as well.
The creation of distance in turn produces fresh affect and ensures
that aesthetic engagement will be maintained—in a feedback loop
made possible by *a momentary disconnection in the circuit.* Perhaps,
then, empathetic projection is not as powerful an antagonist to the
notion of tone as it would initially seem. Indeed, in demonstrating
how affect "feeds back *disconnection,*" though in a manner that
"enabl[es] a *different* connectivity," *The Confidence-Man*'s model of

tone actually further elucidates the concept of projection by fore-grounding the gap at its center. One might say that in a crucial re-doubling, it uses affect to force aesthetic engagement—always al-ready facilitated by affect—out of its mirror stage.

The idea of an aesthetic engagement fostered by distanciation rather than immediacy is hardly unfamiliar. Indeed, it returns us to Kant's enduring notion of "disinterestedness" as the defining fea-ture of aesthetic experience, and to its reinforcement by the explic-itly emotional notion of detachment in Edward Bullough's "'Psy-chical Distance' as a Factor in Art and an Aesthetic Principle" (1912). What is new and surprising is the idea of "detachment" be-ing produced *by affect*—the idea of a distance attained not *from* feeling, but *by* feeling. Indeed, the concept of tone which we have arrived at through Melville's model of the dissonance produced by "affective amplification" reveals that the affective distance which the aesthetic relation requires can *only* be produced affectively. In other words, it is not only that in aesthetic engagement we become disconnected from feelings associated with practical aims (such as the highly interested affect of "confidence" which the confidence-man disconnects from his dupes), but that it is *a feeling itself* that does the work of this distancing (as when the noisy tone of the novel ensures that its reader will have "trouble caring about it"). Given that the world Melville depicts, one in which the public sphere and the market have become virtually co-extensive, is also one in which *every* feeling seems functionalized or yoked into some form of personal or social utility, his novel might be described as highlighting the problem of tone to revitalize a form of "disinter-estedness"—though with full awareness of how dangerously close this disinterestedness always comes to sliding into *noninterest* in a society where art's narrowly delimited agency allows it to be safely ignored. *The Confidence-Man*'s tone enables it to highlight the thin line between these positive and negative understandings of aes-thetic disinterest, even at the cost of making itself resistant to sym-pathetic connection.

As an affective relay between subject and object in which feeling paradoxically produces a "beyondness" rather than nearness or immediacy, tone is in some sense a more specific, value-inflected version of aura, which Benjamin described as "the unique phenomenon of a distance, however close [the object] may be."[63] In the fragments posthumously gathered as the "Paralipomena" to *Aesthetic Theory*, Adorno interprets Benjamin's notion of aura in a way that links it back to the Kantian notion of aesthetic disinterestedness, by describing this "phenomenon of a distance" more specifically as a "distancing . . . from practical aims" modeled on "nature when it is not seen as an object of action." In doing so, Adorno tellingly likens aura (with a swift and very grudging acknowledgment of its family resemblance to Heidegger's "mood") to "the *atmosphere* of an artwork, that whereby the nexus of the artwork's elements points beyond this nexus and allows each individual element to point beyond itself" (*AT*, 274, italics added). In a salient echo not just of Baensch, but of Langer's point that an artwork's semblance of feeling is always something formed from materials and through the use of techniques, Adorno continues: "Precisely this constituent of art, for which the existential-ontological term 'being-attuned' provides only a distorted equivalent, is what in the artwork escapes its factual reality, what, fleeting and elusive . . . can nonetheless be objectivated in the form of artistic technique" (*AT*, 274). Even as Adorno himself opens the door to emotion by this ambivalent reference to "mood," his theorization of aura or "atmosphere" as "an objective determination of the artwork" is marked by the same hesitation about appealing to feeling that we saw in the New Critical accounts of tone. But note how the idea of a distance attained not *from* feeling, but *by* feeling, sheds light on a curiously circular moment that emerges in Adorno's following sentence— one that reinforces the analogy between nature and aura which he has already introduced: "An artwork opens its eyes under the gaze of the spectator when it emphatically articulates something objective, and this possibility of an objectivity that is not simply projected by the spectator *is modeled on the expression of melancholy or serenity,* that can be found in nature when it is not seen as an object of action" (*AT,* 275). With this striking invocation of individuated feelings *as an index of objectivity as such,* affect returns through the back door to Adorno's theory of aura, as the product of an over-determined relay in his argument. For here, Adorno's previous analogy between an artwork's "objective phenomenon of a distance," and nature when distanced from practical aims, might be said to feed back "melancholy" and "serenity" as semblances of feeling—and in a manner which suggests, in a reversal of our earlier description of tone as a specific version of aura, that what critics call "aura" is actually an unspecified kind of tone. For as Tomkins notes about affect, tone's generality and abstractness should not distract us from the fact that it is always "about" something. Ironically, nothing demonstrates this better than Melville's affectively ambiguous novel, whose atonal tone we have seen to be ultimately "about" the simultaneously orderly and noisy character of tone itself.

2 animatedness

In *Moving Pictures: How They Are Made and Worked* (1912), part of a series of volumes with the overall title "Conquests of Science," Frederick A. Talbot announced that "Americans have brought the 'one turn one picture' movement to a high state of perfection, and have produced some astonishing pictures as a result of its application." A technical explanation of "one turn one picture," Talbot's term for stop-motion animation, is offered by the example of the "popular film" *Animated Putty:* "A lump of this material was shown upon a table. Suddenly it was observed to become agitated, and to resolve itself gradually into statues and busts of well-known people, so cleverly wrought as to be instantly identified."[1]

Anticipating the animation technique that would be trade-marked decades later in the United States as Claymation, Talbot's film featuring a lump of earthy matter seems a particularly fitting means for explaining stop-motion cinematography, given how primitive this "trick" was perceived to be. Despite the novelty and sophistication associated with special effects in general, the stop-motion technique "brought . . . to a high state of perfection" by

Americans is not only "one of the simplest of trick effects," but "one of the most tedious to perform":

> The lump of material lies on the table. . . . The camera is set up. The modeler advances to the table whilst the shutter is closed and moves the clay slightly towards the desired result. He then steps out of the picture, and the camera handle is turned sufficiently to expose one picture and to cover the lens again. The modeler comes forward once again and advances a little further with his work; after which he retires from the scene, and the second stage is recorded upon the next picture. [. . .] This alternate process of shaping the putty a little at a time, and photographing every separate movement, is continued until the bust is completed.
>
> It is essential that the progress should be very gradual, or else the material would look as if it took shape by spasmodic jumps and the illusion would be destroyed. (*MP*, 236)

Harking back to the familiar medium of still photography, film animation was thus seen as a kind of technological atavism. As Talbot writes, "It will be observed . . . that this magical effect is not produced in accordance with the generally accepted principles governing cinematography. It is merely a series of snap-shots taken at certain intervals, and could be produced just as well by a hand-camera if one had sufficient plates or film" (*MP*, 236). The simultaneously basic yet exceptional character of this special effect is underscored by the ideological fantasy which *Animated Putty* seems to suggest: that of an "agitation" that is quickly stilled, and even seems conveniently to "resolve itself" as the film's lumpen protagonist is transformed into "cleverly-wrought" images of humans of unmistakable social distinction: "a bust of the King, of the American President, or some other illustrious personage" (*MP*, 236).

The fact that such preclassical "trick films" tended to feature scenes of production in the absence of human agents—for instance, a film in which "a stocking [is] knitted before the audience by unseen hands," or a "magical carpenter's shop" picture in which "tools are manipulated without hands and where the wood . . . is planed, sawn, chiseled, and fashions itself into a box . . . by an apparently mysterious and invisible force"[2]—suggests a further irony: that films based on a technically "backward" and labor-intensive principle were precisely those that most spectacularly imagined the utopian possibilities of a technology so advanced as to put an end to human labor altogether (*MP,* 238, 237).[3] In contrast to the "vigor and spirit" of the saws and knitting needles "moved to action," humans appear strikingly inert in most of the dimensional animation films cited by Talbot, as in the case of a short depicting a shoeshine man "going to sleep at his task, and the footwear cleaning itself while he dreams, brushes running to and fro to remove the dust, apply the blacking, and to give a vigorous polishing off" (*MP,* 235). From this ambiguous interplay between agitated things and deactivated persons, one could argue that what early animation technology foregrounds most is the increasingly ambiguous status of human agency in a Fordist era. These questions of agency will figure importantly in this chapter as we focus on one of the most basic ways in which affect becomes socially recognizable in the age of mechanical reproducibility: as a kind of "innervation," "agitation," or (the term I prefer) "animatedness." Indeed, the rudimentary aspect of stop-motion technology parallels the way in which the affective state of being "animated" seems to imply the most basic or minimal of all affective conditions: that of being, in one way or another, "moved."

But as we press harder on the affective meanings of animatedness, we shall see how the seemingly neutral state of "being moved" becomes twisted into the image of the overemotional racialized subject, abetting his or her construction as unusually receptive to external control. This surprising interplay between the passionate and the mechanical will be our focus as we move through readings of texts by William Lloyd Garrison, Frederick Douglass, Harriet Beecher Stowe, Ralph Ellison, and the short-lived but aesthetically and politically controversial Claymation television show *The PJs* (1998–2001), tracing the affect's transformation into a racializing technology in American cultural contexts ranging from nineteenth-century abolitionist writing to the contemporary cartoon. In order to unpack the ideologeme of racialized animatedness, we will keep returning to the questions of human agency associated with the much more general concept of "animation" that underlies it—with "animation" designating not only a "magical" screen practice, but also a rhetorical figure and the general process of activating or giving life to inert matter. It seems fitting, then, to begin by examining another scenario in which a "lump" plays a key role in dramatizing the process by which an object becomes imbued with life, though this time in a manner that explicitly foregrounds the problematic connections between emotion and race.

"A foul lump started making promises in my voice," notes the speaker in John Yau's poem cycle "Genghis Chan: Private Eye" (1989–1996), giving new "life," "vigor," or "zest" to a cliché or overfamiliar metaphor for one's inability to speak due to undischarged emotion: "a lump in my throat."⁴ In fact, the exhausted metaphor could be described as doubly "revitalized," insofar as the inhuman entity obstructing human speech in the original adage is itself brought to "life" in Yau's poem, perversely ventriloquizing the Asian-American speaker. If *Animated Putty* demonstrates the quieting of an agitated lump as it "resolves itself" into the facsimile of a person, in "Genghis Chan" an increasingly vocal lump appears to take *possession* of the person, as if it were the first lump's evil twin. We thus move from a human character who is "all choked up," rendered inarticulate by some undischarged feeling, to a situation in which the "lump" responsible for this rhetorical disempowerment suddenly individuates into an agent capable of speaking *for* the human character—and, more dangerously, in a manner contractually binding him to others without his volition.

For Nietzsche, it is precisely the act of promising that humanizes the subhuman: "To breed an animal *with the right to make prom-*

ises—is this not the paradoxical task that nature has set itself in the case of man?"[5] In a striking echo of this question, the disturbing power of the inhuman entity in "Genghis Chan" to silence *and* contractually obligate the racialized speaker similarly echoes Nietzsche's observation that "something of the terror that formerly attended all promises, pledges, and vows on earth is *still effective*" (*GM,* 61). As Nietzsche notes, "Man himself must first of all have become *calculable, regular, necessary,* even in his own image of himself, if he is able to stand in security for *his own future,* which is what one who promises does!" (*GM,* 58, original italics). We could argue, however, that Yau's lump promises not so much to make a claim for its own humanity, as to force the human whose voice it has appropriated into the social role of this promising—and therefore regular and accountable—subject. If for Nietzsche "the long story of how *responsibility* originated" is that of how "one first *makes* men to a certain degree . . . uniform, like among like . . . , and consequently calculable" (*GM,* 58), the story of the lump who turns Genghis Chan into a pledging individual might be read as an allegory of how the Asian-American becomes forced into the position of model minority—that is, the person "made" uniform, accountable, and therefore safely "disattendable," at the cost of having his or her speech acts controlled by another.[6]

"Genghis Chan: Private Eye" thus offers a genealogy of an American racial stereotype—that of the Asian as silent, inexpressive, and, like Bartleby, emotionally inscrutable—which stands in noticeable contrast to what we might call the exaggeratedly emotional, hyperexpressive, and even "overscrutable" image of most racially or ethnically marked subjects in American culture: from Harriet Beecher Stowe's ebullient Topsy (1852) to Warner Brothers' hyperactive Speedy Gonzales (1950),[7] to the hand-wringing Jews, gesticulating Italians, and hot-tempered Greeks in films ranging from *The Jazz Singer* to *My Big Fat Greek Wedding.* Versions of these excessively "lively" or "agitated" ethnic subjects abound in American literature as well—for example, in Melville's novel *The Confidence-Man* (1857), where "Irish enthusiasm" is described as "flam[ing] out" and irritating gentleman "of sense and respectability,"[8] and in Anzia Yezierska's *Bread Givers* (1925), where Sara Smolinksky's struggle with what she perceives to be her problematic overemotionality becomes a key part of her trajectory toward cultural assimilation and where nearly every page contains an ejaculative "Ach!" or "God!" Whether marked as Irish, Jewish, Italian, Mexican, or (most prominently in American literature and visual culture) African-American, the kind of exaggerated emotional expressiveness I call animatedness seems to function as a marker of racial or ethnic otherness in general. As Melville's narrator notes about his "Irish" enthusiasts, "To be full of warm, earnest words, and heart-felt protestations, is to create a scene; and well-bred people dislike few things more than that."[9]

And though this exaggerated expressiveness is absent from the racial stereotype whose origins are allegorized in "Genghis Chan," the image of the disturbingly "lively" lump suggests how *much* "animation" still seems required for its production. Insofar as we often regard the cliché as a "dead image"—what Robert Stonum calls a "fossilized" metaphor whose "expired figurative life" is rarely capable of being "restored or reinvented"—the poem's transformation of "a lump in the throat" into one that makes promises might be said to dramatize "giving life" in more ways than one.[10] Moreover, in presenting the transformation of the inanimate "lump" into a living, speaking agent within a series of poems whose title marries the violent Mongol Genghis Khan with the impassive Charlie Chan (the American cinema icon from the 1940s turned into a television cartoon in the 1970s through Hanna-Barbera's *The Amazing Chan and the Chan Clan*), Yau amazingly uses all the definitions of "animate" and "animated" provided by *Webster's Collegiate Dictionary.* With both terms, we move from references to biological existence ("endowed with life or the qualities of life: ALIVE"), to socially positive emotional qualities ("lively," "full of vigor and spirit," "zest"), and finally to a historically specific mode of screen representation ("made in the form of an animated cartoon").[11] While all these meanings become spectacularly condensed in Yau's "lump," the already counterintuitive connections in the standard dictionary definition of "animated"—between the organic-vitalistic and the technological-mechanical, and between the technological-mechanical and the emotional—are further complicated by the way in which the orientalized and cartoonish Genghis Chan introduces race into the equation.

With such a surplus of "animations" at work in "Genghis Chan," it is as if Yau's poetic series is suggesting that to be "animated" in American culture is to be racialized in *some* way, even if animation's affective connotations of vivacity or zealousness do not cover every racial or ethnic stereotype. Indeed, "Genghis Chan" shows the extent to which animation remains central to the production of the racially marked subject, *even* when his or her difference is signaled by the pathos of emotional suppression rather than by emotional excess. Yet it is the cultural representation of the African-American that most visibly harnesses the affective qualities of liveliness, effusiveness, spontaneity, and zeal to a disturbing racial epistemology, and makes these variants of "animatedness" function as bodily (hence self-evident) signs of the raced subject's naturalness or authenticity. Here, as epitomized in Stowe's character Topsy, the affective ideologeme of animatedness foregrounds the degree to which emotional qualities seem especially prone to sliding into *corporeal* qualities where the African-American subject is concerned, reinforcing the notion of race as a truth located, quite naturally, in the always obvious, highly visible body.

In abolitionist William Lloyd Garrison's preface to the *Narrative of the Life of Frederick Douglass* (1845), we find this connection between the physical and emotional aspects of "being animated" put to work in his testament to the slave narrative's authenticity, one of the genre's standard features. Garrison directs us to the singular authorship and verisimilitude of Douglass' narrative, but also to the text's power to "move" the reader: "He who can peruse [this narrative] without a tearful eye, a heaving breast, an afflicted spirit,—without *being . . . animated* with a determination to seek the immediate overthrow of that execrable system . . .—must have a flinty heart and be qualified to act the part of the trafficker 'in slaves and the souls of men.'"[12] The syntactic parallelism of the list-like construction ("without W, X, Y,—without Z") invites us to read "being animated" as synonymous with the terms that precede it, which indicate an impassioned state betrayed by involuntary movements of the body ("tearful eye," "heaving breast"), but also as the endpoint of an action implicit in the form of the list itself, which, through its presentation of discrete elements separated by commas, might be said to enact a segmentation of the human body into a series of working parts (the eye, whose function is to shed tears; the breast, whose function is to heave). Hence, the anticipated animation of Douglass' reader seems not only to involve an unusual immediacy between emotional experience and bodily movement, but to be the "outcome" of a process by which bodily movement is broken down into phases. At the same time, however, Garrison's "animation" designates the process by which these involuntary corporeal expressions of feeling come to exert a politicizing force, activating the reader's desire to "seek the immediate overthrow" of an entire system. There is an intimate link here, in other words, between "animation" and the "agitation" that subtends our concept of the political agitator. Facilitating the transition from the image of a body whose parts are automatically moved, to the oppositional consciousness required for the making of political movements, what Garrison calls "being animated" also hinges on a particularly immediate relationship to Douglass' language, which is depicted as having a spontaneous and direct impact on both the body and mind of the reader.

Figured as this intensified attunement or hyperreceptiveness to the language of others, the animation of Douglass' reader that Garrison anticipates is strikingly similar to the kind of animatedness Harriet Beecher Stowe assigns to racialized subjects in *Uncle Tom's*

Cabin (1852): "The negro mind, impassioned and imaginative, always attaches itself to hymns and expressions of a vivid and pictorial nature; and as [the hymns were being sung], some laughed and some cried, and some clapped hands, or shook hands rejoicingly with each other."[13] In this passage, animation turns the exaggeratedly expressive body into a spectacle for an ethnographic gaze—a spectacle featuring an African-American subject made to move physically in response to lyrical, poetic, or imagistic language. A similar excessive responsiveness to poetic discourse, but with different effects, is implied in Stowe's description of Uncle Tom himself:

> Nothing could exceed . . . [the] earnestness of his prayer, enriched with the language of Scripture, which seemed so entirely to have wrought itself into his being, as to have become a part of himself, and to drop from his lips unconsciously. . . . And so much did his prayer always work on the devotional feelings of his audiences, that there seemed often a danger that it would be lost altogether in the abundance of the responses which broke out everywhere around him. (*UTC*, 79)

In this case, the animatedness ascribed to Tom, which seems to threaten to animate his audience in turn, takes the form not of bodily movement but of a kind of ventriloquism: language from an outside source that "drop[s] from his lips" without conscious volition. Hence, the animation of the racialized body in this instance involves likening it to an instrument, porous and pliable, for the vocalization of others.

In this function, animation seems closely related also to apostrophe—lyric poetry's signature and, according to Jonathan Culler, most "embarrassing" rhetorical convention, in which absent, dead, or inanimate entities are made present, vital, and human-like in being addressed by a first-person speaker.[14] As Barbara Johnson notes, apostrophe can thus be described as a form of ventriloquism, in which a speaker "throws voice . . . into the addressee, turning its silence into a mute responsiveness."[15] Here one recalls the scene of Tom's enthrallment (and ventriloquization) by Scripture. This link between apostrophe, animation, and enthrallment can also be found in Garrison's preface:

> This Narrative contains many affecting incidents . . . but I think the most thrilling one of them all is the description DOUGLASS gives of his feelings . . . on the banks of the Chesapeake Bay—viewing the receding vessels as they flew with their white wings before the breeze, *and apostrophizing them as animated by the living spirit of freedom.* Who can read that passage, and be insensible to its pathos and sublimity? ("P," 249, emphasis added)

Just as Tom's prayer "work[s] on the devotional feelings" of his audience, here animation becomes a thrill that seems highly contagious—easily transferred through the animated body to its spectators. This transferability is reinforced by Garrison's use of the oblique conjunction "as," which makes it difficult to distinguish the subject performing the animation from the object being animated. One wonders if Garrison finds this scene "thrilling" because it provides the spectacle of Douglass animating the ships—investing these inanimate objects with the "living spirit of freedom"—or if the thrill comes from witnessing the animation of Douglass himself, either by the same "living spirit of freedom" or through his own expressive act of apostrophizing.

Regardless of where we locate the thrill Garrison describes, it is important to note that both Stowe and Garrison find it necessary to dramatize the animation of racialized bodies for political purposes: in Stowe's case, to demonstrate the intensity of the slave's devotional feeling in order to support a Christian indictment of slavery as a sin; in Garrison's, to signify Douglass' power as a writer and mobilize his readers to the antislavery cause. In both cases, the connection between animation and affectivity is surprisingly fostered through acts resembling the practice of puppeteering, involving either the body's ventriloquism or a physical manipulation of its parts. Yet the "thinging" of the body in order to construct it, counter-intuitively, as impassioned is deployed by both abolitionists as a strategy of shifting the status of this body from thing to human, as if the racialized, hence already objectified body's reobjectification, in being animated, were paradoxically necessary to emphasize its personhood or subjectivity.

Rey Chow, in her essay "Postmodern Automatons," argues that becoming animated in this objectifying sense—having one's body and voice controlled by an invisible other—is synonymous with becoming automatized, "subjected to [a manipulation] whose origins are beyond one's individual grasp."[16] In a reading of Charlie Chaplin's hyperactive physical movements in *Modern Times* (1936), Chow suggests that film and television, as technologies of mass production, uniquely disclose the fact that "the 'human body' as such is already *a working body automatized,* in the sense that it becomes in the new age an automaton on which social injustice as well as processes of mechanization 'take on a life of their own,' so to speak" ("PA," 62, italics in original). For Chow this automatization of the body, as an effect of subjection to power, coincides with the moment the body is made into the object of a gaze; being animated thus entails "becoming a spectacle whose 'aesthetic' power increases with one's increasing awkwardness and helplessness" ("PA," 61). While Chow describes this simultaneous visualization and technologization as a condition of the modern body in general, she also observes that certain bodies are technologized in more pronounced ways than others. Hence, "the automatized other . . . takes the form either of the ridiculous, the lower class, or of woman" ("PA," 63). From a feminist perspective, this point enables Chow to argue that the main question facing third-world subjects constantly invoked, apostrophized, or ventriloquized by first-world theorists is the question of how to turn automatization into autonomy and independence: "The task that faces 'third world' feminists is thus not simply that of 'animating' the oppressed women of their cultures but of making the automatized and animated condition of their own voices the conscious point of departure in their interventions" ("PA," 66, 68).

Automatization, in the Fordist or Taylorist sense dramatized by Chaplin (and Chow), becomes a useful, if slightly anachronistic, synonym for the kind of animation already at work in the antebellum writings of Garrison and Stowe; in both situations, the human body is "subjected to [a manipulation] whose origins are beyond one's individual grasp" and becomes "a spectacle whose 'aesthetic' power increases with one's increasing awkwardness and helplessness." What makes the affect of animatedness distinctive, however, is the way in which it oddly synthesizes two kinds of automatism whose meanings run in opposite directions, encompassing the extremely codified, hyperrationalized routines epitomized by the factory worker's repetitive wrenching movements in *Modern Times* but also, as Rosalind Krauss notes, "the kind of liberating release of spontaneity that we associate with . . . the Surrealists' invocation of the word 'automatism' (as in psychic automatism)."[17] As this "peculiar blend" of the spontaneous with the formulaic, the unpremeditated with the predetermined, and the "liberating release" of psychic impulses with "the set of learned, more or less rote conventions *(automatisms)* contained within [a system or traditional medium],"[18] the concept of animatedness not only returns us to the connection between the emotive and the mechanistic but also commingles antithetical notions of physical agency. On one hand, animatedness points to restrictions placed on spontaneous movement and activity; in *Modern Times,* for example, it emerges from the exclusion of all bodily motion apart from the one assigned to the assembly-line worker. On the other hand, the affect can also be read as highlighting the elasticity of the body being animated, as evinced in Sergei Eisenstein's praise of "plasmaticness" in his analysis of Disney cartoons. Just as animatedness integrates the two contrasting meanings of automatism, then, the affect manages to fuse signs of the body's subjection to power with signs of its ostensive freedom—by encompassing not only bodily activity confined to fixed

forms and rigid, specialized routines (Fordist or Taylorist animation), but also a dynamic principle of physical metamorphosis by
which the body, according to Eisenstein, seems to "*triumph* over the
fetters of form" (what we might call "animistic" animation).[19] It is
clear that for the filmmaker, the excessive energy and metamor-
phic potential of the animated body make it a potentially subversive or powerful body, whereas for Chow, the very qualities that
Eisenstein praises as liberatory—"plasmaticness," elasticity, and pliancy—are readable as signs of the body's utter subjection to power,
confirming its vulnerability to external manipulation and control. Although in the last instance Chow's pessimistic reading of the
animated-technologized body as a Taylorized body seems more
persuasive than Eisenstein's optimistic one, the two perspectives
point to a crucial ambivalence embedded in the concept of animation—ambivalence that takes on special weight in the case of racialized subjects, for whom objectification, exaggerated corporeal-
ity or physical pliancy, and the body-made-spectacle remain doubly
freighted issues.

The category of racial difference has thus come to complicate the
meanings of animation on television: a visual medium Jane Feuer
has described as increasingly governed by an ideology of liveness—
that is, "the promise of presence and immediacy made available by
video technology's capacity to record and transmit images simultaneously."[20] Recalling the similarly direct and immediate impact of
language on the racialized subjects in Stowe's *Uncle Tom's Cabin,*
liveness's "promise of presence and immediacy" has thus been particularly crucial to what Sasha Torres calls "the definitionally televisual events" of the 1990s which "have involved, if not centered
on, persons of color."[21] As Torres notes, historically significant
broadcasting events such as the Clarence Thomas confirmation
hearings, the trial of O. J. Simpson, the videotaped beating of
Rodney King, and, more recently, *Court TV*'s coverage of the trial
of the New York City police officers indicted for the murder of
Amadou Diallo have made it impossible to ignore "the *centrality*

of racial representation to television's representational practices," while also indicating the primacy of "liveness" in informing what race "*look[s]*" like on television."[22]

What bearing, then, does the *liveliness* associated with "animation," in all of its various meanings, have on what race "looks like" to viewers in a medium where liveness signifies live action and a simultaneity between event and transmission—principles fundamentally opposed to the stop-motion technology on which contemporary screen animation often depends? While it is the live broadcasting event that has made race central to television, as Torres argues in "King TV," it could be said that animation on television foregrounds the centrality of liveness to the representation of racial difference in a particularly intense way, even though at a certain level the genre runs counter to medium-specific meanings of "liveness," which, as Feuer notes, is less an ontological reality than an ideological one: "As television in fact becomes less and less a 'live' medium, in the sense of an equivalence between time of event and time of transmission, the medium in its practices insists more and more on the live, the immediate, the direct, the spontaneous, the real."[23] Although we have already seen—via the writings of Stowe and Garrison—how a similar ideology informs the relation between animation and racial identity in earlier modes of cultural production, the epistemological inflection linking these attributes to the racialized feeling concepts above (what are vivaciousness, liveliness, and zeal if not affective correlates to "the immediate, the direct, the spontaneous, [and] real"?) makes television an ideal site for examining animation both as screen genre and as a technology for the representation of racial difference.

At the end of the twentieth century, questions related to animation and the politics of racial representation rose to the fore in debates surrounding Fox Television's dimensional animation comedy series, *The PJs* (1998–2000). *The PJs* was the first prime-time program in American television history to feature a completely non-white, non-middle-class, and non-live-action cast, as well as the first to depict its characters in foamation, a three-dimensional, stop-motion animation technique trademarked by Will Vinton Studios (once producer of the infamous California Raisin commercials, which featured anthropomorphized black grapes singing and dancing to a classic Motown hit).[24] Introduced to the network's lineup in the fall of 1998 and featuring multicultural but primarily African-American characters living in an urban housing project, *The PJs* generated controversy several months prior to more widely publicized debates over the "whitewashing" of network television, described by Kweisi Mfume as "the most segregated industry in America" during his July 1999 keynote address to the 90th annual NAACP convention.[25] Starring Eddie Murphy (who was also one of the producers) as Thurgood Stubbs, the superintendent of the fictional Hilton-Jacobs projects, the program was soon the target of criticisms from a number of grassroots organizations, who accused it of carrying an antiblack message. These criticisms came from a variety of directions, including the Black Muslim group Project Islamic Hope, as well as the Coalition against Media Exploitation, headed by African-American writer and activist Earl Ofari Hutchinson. In an interview on the Cable News Network (CNN) in February 1999, Hutchinson voiced his objection to the show: "It does not present an accurate or honest depiction of the African-American community. It does present racially demeaning and offensive stereotypes."[26] A similar criticism came from the director Spike Lee, who described the cartoon as "really hateful, I think, to black people."[27] In spite of his polemicism, the "I think" in Lee's statement reveals a crucial ambivalence over the political and aesthetic aims of *The PJs,* and over the use of animation for the representation of racial minorities in general—an ambivalence I would like to explore by focusing on some of this technology's intended and unintended effects.

The shocking quality that Lee, Hutchinson, and others attribute to *The PJs* points to how the program fundamentally disrupted the "look" of race on mainstream network television, since the traditional way in which racial minorities have had a presence in this arena has been through live-action representations of upwardly mobile nuclear families—not through animated cartoons featuring the urban poor. In particular, Hutchinson's criticism of the show for failing to present "an accurate and honest depiction of the African-American community" reflects the insistent demand for mimetic realism in the representation of blacks on television—a demand which is both reflected and resisted in the equally insistent call for what Philip Brian Harper terms "simulacral" realism. Based on the premise that representations actively shape, define, and even occasionally usurp social realities, simulacral realism involves the conviction that "an improvement in [the] social status [of African-Americans] can result from their mere depiction in mainstream television programming."[28] In contrast, mimetic realism insists that television faithfully mirror a set of social conditions viewed as constituting "a singular and unitary phenomenon known as '*the* black experience.'"[29] It is this latter demand that Hutchinson sees *The PJs* as betraying, though similar criticism was directed earlier at *The Cosby Show*—a black-produced program that could not be more opposed to *The PJs* in form, content, and tone. This contradiction reinforces Harper's observation that while the tension between mimetic and simulacral realism continues to structure critical discourse on black television, their opposing demands often run "smack up against [each other]."[30] Yet in its three-dimensional animation format, *The PJs* changed the terms of the existing debate. The conflict between simulacral and mimetic realism became a moot issue, since neither demand—that television faithfully mirror "the black experience" or that it aim at bettering the social status of actual African-American subjects—could be properly applied to a show that so insistently foregrounded its own artifice. Calling attention not just to the exaggerated physicality but also to the material composition of its characters—that is, to their existence as dolls with outsized plastic heads and foam latex bodies—*The PJs* pushed the issue of racial representation outside the "two realisms" binary. Though in doing so it risked the appearance of merely resuscitating a much older style of racial caricature which realism was once summoned by African-American artists to combat, the show actually introduced a new possibility for racial representation in the medium of television: one that ambitiously sought to reclaim the grotesque and/or ugly, as a powerful aesthetic of exaggeration, crudeness, and distortion, which late twentieth-century African-American artists seemed to have become barred from using even for the explicit purpose of antiracist critique.

As the only prime-time comedy to feature residents of subsidized housing since Norman Lear's *Good Times* (1974–1979), and the only animated program featuring nonwhite inner-city dwellers since *Fat Albert* in the early 1970s (the decade of "socially relevant" programming), *The PJs* also produced a shift in the content of network television.[31] As Armond White has noted, every joke on the show "implies a correlated social circumstance,"[32] enabling the program in its first season to address topics such as access to food, health care, public education, and safe and livable housing. Since the show dealt with racism in a larger socioeconomic context rather than as a problem of prejudice between individuals, its targets were frequently government institutions: the welfare system, hospitals, the police, and the federal Department of Housing and Urban Development (HUD). The humor becomes most acerbic when Thurgood visits the local HUD office, which he does in nearly every episode. The sign greeting him displays a variety of sardonic messages, ranging from "HUD: Putting a Band-Aid over Poverty for 30 Years!" to "HUD: Keeping You in the Projects since 1965."

The PJs also replaced the traditional sitcom's main social unit, the nuclear family, with the community formed by the project's inhabitants. In one episode, the tenants try to raise money for one elderly resident, Mrs. Avery, when it is discovered she has been secretly subsisting on dog food. Since Mrs. Avery is too proud to "take charity," the only way Thurgood can convince her to accept the food and health care supplies donated by tenants is by disguising them as gift baskets from the state welfare system and Medicaid. The joke here is the illusion that these beleaguered institutions are still efficient—even benevolent—in their intended functions, and that the bitter task of perpetuating the illusion of efficiency, rather than exposing it, becomes the only way of ensuring that services are actually performed.

In another episode, after suffering a near-fatal heart attack, Thurgood is informed that he requires medication he cannot afford. The only solution is for him to participate in an experimental drug program. The problem is that Thurgood's cholesterol level and blood pressure aren't high enough to officially qualify him for the program, so the episode turns on his efforts to jack them up in order to receive the medication he needs to live. Once again, the show's humor finds its basis in the contradictions of an unjust system, targeting the institutional ineptness that translates into actual harm or injury to the bodies of the urban poor. In this manner, *The PJs* insists that racism involves more than the mobilization of stereotypes, that in fact it extends far beyond matters of visual representation. While this is a relatively simple point, it nonetheless invites us to push beyond the prevailing methods in media studies, where a focus on analyzing stereotypes dominates the conversation about race to the extent that racism often becomes inadvertently reduced to bad representation, and antiracist politics are often depicted merely as a struggle over the content of specific images. Yet the struggles depicted on *The PJs* are rarely about imagery; indeed, in a culture where it is impossible to separate racism from class politics, the struggles remain lived and felt primarily in relations of power not visible at all. In this sense, what the show ultimately offers is a Foucauldian rather than a liberal humanist critique of racism; as Armond White notes: "When government workers appear or Thurgood and his wife visit social agencies, conversations take place in a void. Voices of authority are always faceless. . . . Thurgood's trek though a blizzard to retrieve his wife's journal left at a hospital emergency room is interrupted by cops who stay in their vehicle while announcing their shakedown through a bullhorn: 'Frisk yourself!' This humor puts *The PJs* in league with some of the most daring and derisive agit-pop such as Public Enemy's '911 Is a Joke' and its colorful, comic music video" ("*TPJS*," 10).

This is not to say, however, that *The PJs* simply bypasses the issue of representing blackness on television in order to foreground other aspects of social inequity. The show also contains the internal references to African-American history and culture that Kristal Brent Zook finds integral to the antiracist identity politics of the first black-produced sitcoms in the early 1990s, which, unlike previous white-produced shows *about* African-Americans, attempted to foreground struggles over the representation of blackness within the black community as a whole.[33] But in contrast to the paintings by Varnette Honeywood featured on the walls of the *Cosby* living room, or the framed photograph of Malcolm X prominently featured on the set of *Roc* (key examples cited in Zook's study), the references to black history and culture in *The PJs* are primarily references to black television culture—pointing to the fraught legacy of African-Americans on television not only in the form of tribute but also in playful, irreverent, and ambivalent ways. For instance, the Hilton-Jacobs housing project is named after Lawrence Hilton-Jacobs, the actor who portrayed Freddie "Boom-Boom" Washington in *Welcome Back Kotter*. The mere reference to the older situation comedy suggests a relationship between tokenism and ghettoization, as well as the failures of liberal cultural progressivism (as reflected in the demands for issue-oriented programs like *Kotter* in the 1970s and early 1980s) to create public policy capable of producing serious changes in the infrastructure of U.S. cities ("*TPJS*," 10). Also invoking Sherman Helmsley's "apartment in the sky" in the theme song's description of the Hilton-Jacobs as a "low-rent highrise," and using Janet DuBois, singer and composer of the memorable theme song for *The Jeffersons,* as the voice of Mrs. Avery, *The PJs* constantly "confronts the legacy of the 70s black sitcom—rather than simply joining in" ("*TPJS*," 10). The show also offered a running commentary on the cultural legacy of black television in the 1980s and early 1990s. The most genteel character in *The PJs,* for example, is a parole officer named Walter, whose signature trait is an affable chuckle closely resembling the laugh of the expensively clad family doctor on *The Simpsons,* who in turn seems to be a gentle parody of Bill Cosby's Dr. Huxtable.

Yet as a situation comedy based entirely on caricature, *The PJs* is forced to confront the problem of stereotypes directly. Questions concerning caricature and typecasting, moreover, necessarily come to the fore in genres informed by the mode of comedy, which has traditionally relied on the production of what Stanley Cavell calls individualities rather than individuals, or on the presentation of social types: opera's villains and buffos, Shakespeare's clowns and melancholics, Jane Austen's snobs and bores, and the television sitcom's nosy neighbors and meddling mothers-in-law. Although there remains an irreducible difference between types and stereotypes, or between social roles and "individualities that [project] particular *ways* of inhabiting a social role," this difference becomes especially uneasy when it involves certain social roles that have been drastically limited in ways that others have not.[34] Thus, while the overwhelming emphasis on stereotype analysis in liberal media criticism often limits critical intervention to the analysis of the content of specific images or to assessments of the extent to which contemporary images conform to or deviate from previous ones, it remains important to acknowledge the reasons for this emphasis, which clearly underlie the specific criticisms by Hutchinson and Lee. The stakes of traditional stereotype analysis will continue to be high, not only because depictions of raced subjects in the mass media have been so severely limited but also because raced subjects continue to exert less control over how existing images are actually deployed—quite often with symbolically violent effects. Moreover, in conjunction with the continued haunting of black, live-action television comedy by blackface minstrelsy—a legacy that critics such as J. Fred MacDonald, Herman Gray, Robin Means Coleman, and Kristal Brent Zook have extensively explored—the tradition of viciously racist cartoons in American screen culture ensures that the intersection of comedy with animation in the visual representation of racialized bodies becomes a particularly loaded issue.[35] Thus, while arguments have been made for cel animation's ideologically disruptive properties in its incipience as an early film genre,[36] in products ranging from MGM's *Bosko* series in the 1920s to numerous cartoon features in the following two decades (including Disney's *Alice Hunting in Africa,* Warner Brothers' *Tokio Jokio,* and Walter Lantz's *Jungle Jitters* and *Scrub Me Mama with a Boogie Beat*), two-dimensional animation became one of the most culturally prominent technologies for the revitalization of extant racial stereotypes, giving new "life" to caricatures that might otherwise have stood a greater chance of becoming defunct or inactive.[37]

Since the animated subjects in *The PJs* are three-dimensional dolls made of spongy latex fitted over metal armatures, hand-drawn cel animation is not the technology responsible for (what many critics viewed as) the aesthetically disturbing "look" of the television program's characters, or for the disturbing way in which their bodies were made to move. Yet this two-dimensional ancestor, patented in the United States by Earl Hurd and John Bray in 1915, nevertheless haunts the controversial sitcom through the pictorial separation process on which the older technology depends. For as I will discuss in more detail shortly, the stop-motion process used to animate the characters on *The PJs* inadvertently introduced a fragmentation of the body that recalls cel animation's method of "separating portions of a drawing onto different layers to eliminate the necessity for re-drawing the entire composition for each movement phase" (Thompson, "ICAT," 107). As Kristin Thompson notes, the "slash system" developed by Raoul Barré in the mid-1910s provided an easily standardized and therefore industrially amenable method for this breakdown of figures into discrete parts, such that "a drawing of an entire character could be cut apart and traced onto different cels." Oddly anticipated, perhaps, by the activation of isolated body parts ("tearful eye," "heaving breast") in Garrison's account of the reader "animated" by Douglass' *Narrative,* the slash system's separation of the body, at each stage of its movement, into discrete portions and poses was particularly suited to the kind of animation specific to modern Fordist production—that is, to animation as automatization:

> Using the slash system, the background might be on paper at the lowest level, the characters' trunks on one sheet of clear celluloid, and the moving mouths, arms, and other parts on a top cel. For speech and gestures, only the top cel need be redrawn, while the background and lower cel are simply re-photographed.
>
> This technique not only saves labour time for a single artist, but it also allows specialisation of labour. That is, one person may do the background, while another does certain main poses of the character, and yet another fills in the phases between these major poses. In fact, the animation industry has followed this pattern, with key animators (doing the major poses), "in-betweeners," and "opaquers" (filling in the figures with opaque paint) in addition to those performing the specialised tasks of scripting and planning. The specialisation process and the establishment of the first production companies for animated films took place about 1915–1917—at the same time as the establishment of the Hollywood motion picture system in general (also characterised by greater and greater specialisation of tasks—the "factory" system). (Thompson, "ICAT," 107–108)

If Fordist or Taylorist automatization constitutes a specialized type of animation, as Chow suggests, the celluloid slash system could be described as an animation technology that animated its workers in turn—a functional doubling that not only recalls the anticipated animation of Douglass' readers by the scene of his own animation or by his act of animating, by apostrophizing, the ships, but also evokes the capacity of Uncle Tom's exaggerated responsiveness to biblical language to animate or enthrall the spectators of his own animation—such that "that there seemed often a danger it would be lost altogether in the abundance of the responses which broke out everywhere around him."

Thus, it is not just the material basis of two-dimensional cel animation or its explicitly racial-comic legacy that comes to haunt *The PJs'* mode of production (which involves the same automatization of labor as its technological predecessor), but the antebellum meanings, both racial and emotional, that already haunt the former. Before launching a more detailed analysis of how the three-dimensional animation technology in *The PJs* operates, in a manner enabling the older racial, emotional, and technological connotations of animation to remain active within it, I'd like to recall a key scene from Ralph Ellison's *Invisible Man* in which similar questions converge.

Walking through midtown Manhattan, Ellison's narrator suddenly finds himself part of a larger audience watching a black doll puppeteered by Tod Clifton, a Harlem community leader and activist he has admired:

> I moved into the crowd and pressed to the front where at my feet I saw a square piece of cardboard upon which something was moving with furious action. It was some kind of toy and I glanced at the crowd's fascinated eyes and down again, seeing it clearly this time. . . . A grinning doll of orange-and-black tissue paper with thin flat cardboard disks forming its head and feet and which some mysterious mechanism was causing to move up and down in a loose-jointed, shoulder-shaking, infuriatingly sensuous motion, a dance that was completely detached from the black, mask-like face. It's no jumping-jack, but *what,* I thought, seeing the doll throwing itself about with the fierce defiance of someone performing a degrading act in public, dancing as though it received a perverse pleasure from

its motions. And beneath the chuckles of the crowd I could hear the swishing of its ruffled paper, while the same out-of-the-corner-of-the-mouth voice continued to spiel:

Shake it up! Shake it up!
He's Sambo, the dancing doll, ladies and gentlemen.
Shake him, stretch him by the neck and set him down,
—He'll do the rest. Yes!. . . .

    I knew I should get back to the district but I was held by the inanimate, boneless bouncing of the grinning doll and struggled between the desire to join in the laughter and to leap upon it with both feet, when it suddenly collapsed and I saw the tip of the spieler's toe press upon the circular cardboard that formed the feet and a broad black hand come down, its fingers deftly lifting the doll's head and stretching it upward, twice its length, then releasing it to dance again. *And suddenly the voice didn't go with the hand.*[38]

I would like to foreground several aspects of this literary account of the racial body made into comic spectacle, which eventually will prepare us for a closer investigation of how visual format in *The PJs* affects the ideologically complex questions of animatedness as an affective quality, the agency of mechanized or technologized bodies, and the comic representation of racially marked subjects.

    We can begin by noting that the narrator is simultaneously attracted and repelled by the sight of the doll being animated. His effort to negotiate responses at odds with one another—a desire to join in the audience's laughter and a desire to destroy the object provoking it—suggests an ambivalence closely related to the contradictory qualities of the object itself: the doll is "grinning" while it dances, as if in empathetic attunement with the enthusiastic, lively response of its spectators, yet it is also described as "fierce" and "defiant"—words suggesting antipathy toward the audience at which it grins. These affective contradictions call attention to the disjunctive logic informing the total scene, from the way the doll's spasmodic body movements are described as "completely detached" from its immobile, mask-like face, to the image of the animator's voice suddenly "not going with" the animator's hand. Despite the insistent processes of mechanization at work, nothing seems in sync in this scene—though it is precisely the mechanization which makes the disjunctiveness visible. In fact, it is the very moment when Tod Clifton's body is disclosed as the "mysterious mechanism" making the doll move (his toe against the doll's feet, his hand pulling the doll's neck) that this fragmentation and disruption of the synchronized movement takes place. The human agent anthropomorphizes the puppet, as we would expect, but the puppet also mechanizes the human, breaking his organic unity into so many functional parts: pressing toe, stretching hand, commanding voice.[39] Like the slash system's separation of the drawn figure's moving body parts from its immobile ones (and the automatization of human labor this technology fostered), or the animated breast and eye that induce the animation of Douglass' reader, Clifton's manual manipulation of the doll produces an animatedness that boomerangs back onto its human agent, separating his own body into isolated components and movements. The nonliving entity that is animated (or, as Chow would say, automatized) comes to automatize its animator.

The unexpected mechanization of the human animator by the inhuman object he animates, a situation we have already witnessed in the case of Yau's "foul lump" (a repulsive piece of matter invested with "vigor" and "zest" to the extent that it becomes capable of overtaking and commanding the racialized speaker's voice), seems to represent the ultimate form of human subjection. Here the human agent is not only automatized or mechanized but ironically made so through the process by which he mechanizes an inhuman entity; his passive, corporeally fragmented condition is thus engendered by his own animating activity. Yet Ellison's scene of boomeranged animation might also be read as an allegory for how the "postmodern automaton," Chow's metaphor for the subjected subject in general, might acquire agency within his or her own automatized condition, enabling the mechanized human to politically comment on—if not exert some form of direct resistance to—the forces manipulating him or her. Here we might take a closer look at the sentence with which the passage concludes: "And suddenly the voice didn't go with the hand." If the hand is clearly Clifton's hand and thus belongs to the animating agent's body but the voice no longer corresponds to this body, Ellison's sentence provokes us to ask whose voice is coming out of Clifton's mouth. Regardless of whether the source can be identified, we can pinpoint one of the intended receivers. On one hand, the voice who says, "Shake it up! Shake it up! He's Sambo, the dancing doll, ladies and gentlemen!" is obviously directed at the collective audience enthusiastically witnessing the doll's animation—the "ladies and gentlemen" who are named and addressed. But on the other hand, the voice that in the same breath utters "Shake him, stretch him by the neck and set him down" seems to direct itself at *Clifton,* issuing specific commands about how to move the doll, to which Clifton immediately responds. (We hear the imperatives "stretch him by the neck and set him down," then see Clifton do precisely that). In this sense, the voice emanating from the doll's ventriloquist, or animator, and directed primarily at those witnessing the spectacle of its animation, is directed at the animator as well. But the fact that Clifton is being addressed or hailed by this voice, which is, moreover, a voice that does not correspond with his body, doubly emphasizes that it is a voice not his own. It is as if Clifton is ventriloquizing the doll in order to foreground his own ventriloquization, or animation, by an unidentified external agent.[40] It could even be said that Clifton animates the doll not only to comment polemically on his own animated condition (since what he does to the doll and what the doll does to him indicate something being done to both man and doll simultaneously) but also to contest his own seemingly unequivocal status as the doll's true animator. Yet in putting forth the statement,

"Perhaps *I* am not the true animator in this scene of racial animation," Clifton paradoxically exercises a critical, albeit highly negative, form of agency within the context of his dramatized subjection.

The excessively "lively," racialized doll in *Invisible Man* brings us back to the three-dimensional animation technology at work in *The PJs.* This racial comedy in which all humans are represented as dolls made of metal and latex playfully inverts Henri Bergson's notion that the comic results from our perception of something rigid or mechanical "encrusted on the surface" of the supple or living; in *The PJs,* we have rigid structures "encrusted" with a layer of supple, skin-like material.[41] The animation of these three-dimensional figures takes place at two distinct levels: the body and speech. Like Ellison's representation of Clifton as animated by both "the hand" and "the voice," *The PJs'* dolls are "endowed with the qualities of life" not only by being physically manipulated but also by being ventriloquized by the voices of human actors. So there are actually two animating agents or agencies here: the animator is the technician who moves the dolls' limbs into discrete poses to be photographed, yet the process would be incomplete without the actors' vocalizations.

To create the illusion that the spongy dolls we see are unified and autonomous beings, *The PJs'* stop-motion imaging technology requires that every movement by a character, including the mouth movements (which are choreographed to correspond to the words spoken by the actor assigned to the character), be broken down into discrete positions, adjusted in small increments, and shot one frame at a time, with each shot previewed on a digital video assist before being recaptured on film. But because the movements of the mouth in speaking are much faster, more dynamic, and more complicated than the movements of arms or legs, the animators end up using a set of about forty "replacement mouths" for each character, rather than changing the configuration of a single mouth permanently fixed on the body.[42] We can thus see how the separation principle of early twentieth-century cel animation is reapplied in the three-dimensional method. Although the body parts are sculpted rather than hand-drawn on layers of celluloid, the concept of detaching mobile from immobile elements remains essentially the same.

Each *PJs* character is thus given his or her own set of independently molded plastic mouths, corresponding to the pronunciation of discrete consonants and vowels. Yet the technique of constantly attaching and reattaching differently shaped mouths poses the difficulty of ensuring that the forms are fitted in the exact location each time; as one of the show's directors informed me, "Sometimes they move a little to the side of the face and we get what is known as 'slippery mouth' syndrome, which is quite painful to watch."[43] What results is an unintended, excess animatedness on top of the intended, functional one, recalling the "spasmodic jumps" Talbot describes as being a threat to the illusion of "liveliness" in *Animated Putty* (*MP,* 236). With every word spoken by the character, the mouth slides a bit from its initial position; the longer a character speaks, the more his mouth gives the impression, when viewed on our television screens, of threatening to fly off the body completely. The mouths of *The PJs'* characters could thus be described as just a little *too* animated, particularly if we view the mouth as "subjected to [a manipulation] whose origins are beyond one's individual grasp" at two distinct levels already (Chow, "PA," 61): through vocalization by an actor and through bodily arrangement by the animator. And the characters are perhaps even "subjected to external manipulation" on a third front, given the fact that the mouth functions as a symbolically overdetermined feature in racist constructions of blackness, in the same way that eyes become overdetermined, synecdochic sites of racial specificity in representations of Asianness.

Like the corner-of-the-mouth voice emanating from Clifton, the unintended slippery-mouth effect in *The PJs* produces a disjunctiveness that in turn facilitates animation's uncanny redoubling: the mouths create surplus movement apart from those originally scripted for them, assuming a liveliness that is distinct from the "life" given to them by the animators and that exceeds their design and control. In this sense, the very sign of the racialized body's automatization functions as the source of an unsuspected autonomy. It might be said that the excess liveliness produced by this particular body part suggests something like the racialized, animated subject's "revenge," produced not by transcending the principles of mechanization from above but, as in the case of Chaplin's factory worker, by obeying them too well.[44]

In the consistency of their bodies, then, the characters in *The PJs* call attention to the uncomfortable proximity between social types and stereotypes in a material yet highly metaphoric fashion: by embodying the contradiction between the rigidity we typically associate with social roles and the elasticity or "plasmaticness" hyperbolized by screen animation, which produces the visual effect of characters constantly threatening their own bodily limits.[45] In this manner, *The PJs* reminds us that there can be ways of inhabiting a social role that actually distort its boundaries, changing the status of "role" from that which purely confines or constricts to the site at which new possibilities for human agency might be explored. Recalling the distinction between rigidity and elasticity central to Bergson's theory of laughter, animatedness in *The PJs* depends on something literally elastic "encrusted on the surface" of the mechanical. This elasticity is the sign of the body's automatization (since the pliancy of an object suggests its heightened vulnerability to external manipulation), but functions also as the source of an unaccounted-for autonomy. As the slippery-mouth effect demonstrates, the animation of the raced body seems capable of producing an excess that undermines the technology's power to constitute that body *as* raced.

While the scene of Clifton's doll provided my first example of how the racialized body might produce this surplus animatedness, or a "lifelike movement" exceeding the control and intention of its would-be manipulators, the redoubling of animation in this scene is explicitly figured as violent. Emanating from Clifton's mouth and addressed to the mob around him, the invitation to "stretch" the doll's neck, with its allusion to lynching, invokes a fantasy of inflicting harm or injury to animated objects in which the narrator himself becomes implicated, though his initial desire to "leap upon it with both feet" is replaced by the slightly less violent act of spitting on it instead: "I looked at the doll and felt my throat constrict. There was a flash of whiteness and a splatter like heavy rain striking a newspaper and I saw the doll go over backwards, wilting into a dripping rage of frilled tissue, the hateful head upturned on its outstretched neck still grinning toward the sky" (Ellison, *IM*, 423). A fantasy of aggression against the doll invoked by its very own animator ("stretch him by his neck") thus leads to an act of real aggression that strips it of its human qualities and agency, turning the dancing figure into a pile of wet paper. More horrifically, the violence inflicted on this animated body culminates in violence toward the human who animates it, since the aftermath of Ellison's dancing-doll episode is Clifton's murder by the police. This murder is described as if in slow motion: the narrator sees Clifton's body "suddenly crumpling" with "a huge wetness growing on his shirt," such that his death explicitly mirrors the doll "wilted" by the narrator's wet spit (*IM*, 426). The link between animation and violence cannot be dismissed here, and it is a link that reinforces the disturbing likeness between human animator and animated object: Clifton's "crumpled body" and the wilted body of the doll.

Here the act of animation begins to look inherently and irredeemably violent. If this is in fact the case, the idea of an animated object "animating its animator in turn" can only have negative implications. Yet when the narrator later raises the possibility that his aggressive behavior toward the puppet may have been indirectly responsible for the murder of its puppeteer, Ellison's text suggests that the violence at stake here lies less in the doll's animation than in its deanimation. What results in both cases is the cessation of movement. Seeing Clifton's body crumple, the narrator describes himself as unable to "set [his] foot down" in the process of climbing a curb, just as crumpling the doll with his spit replaced his act of lifting his foot to crush it (*IM,* 426). The image of the narrator arrested in action, with his foot in the air each time, suggests that the deanimation of the doll (its fantasized and real disfiguration and reconversion into dead matter) leads not only to the death of its human operator but also to the deanimation of its human witness, freezing him in his attempt to destroy the object as if to foreground his complicity. Violence here takes the symbolic form of the body's arrested motion, as opposed to its mobilization; moreover, it is aggression toward the animated object that results directly in bodily harm and injury, and not, however symbolically disturbing it may have been, the object's animation itself. Once the narrator confronts the possibility that this aggression might have been misplaced, the deanimated doll, as an ambiguous symbol of both life and death, oppression and survival, becomes a burden he feels compelled to protect and safeguard, carried in his briefcase along with a chainlink given to him by former slave Brother Tarp.

Without losing sight of the seriousness of this scene from Ellison's novel, I would like to conclude by interrogating the possibility of foreclosing comic animation altogether as a strategy for representing nonwhite characters. One *Village Voice* critic argues for such a possibility in his *PJs* review: "While I don't believe that any technique should be rejected out of hand, I might make an exception for claymation . . . whose golliwog aspects come unpleasantly front and center when used to depict nonwhites, as here."[46] This argument for rejecting animation entirely in the depiction of racially marked characters hinges on a reference to the technique's propensity for the grotesque, an aesthetic based on crudeness and distortion. Yet in the last *PJs* episode aired by Fox prior to the show's cancellation and its subsequent move to the currently "more black" Warner Brothers network, the show's writers seemed to offer a direct response to this critical position, in a moment I think of as the episode's "lump" scene. In this episode (a "Christmas Special" broadcast on December 17, 1999), two of the Hilton-Jacobs residents, Thurgood's Latino chess partner Sanchez and his Korean brother-in-law Jimmy, rummage in the basement to find makeshift supplies for the project's annual Christmas pageant. Since they lack a baby-Jesus doll for the nativity scene, Sanchez hunts for a substitute and pulls a lumpy, crudely anthropomorphized object out of a box. The object resembles a Mr. Potato Head toy but on closer inspection seems to be an actual potato, or, rather, a Claymation or foamation replica of an actual potato, with eyes, nose, and lips loosely arranged on its surface to resemble a face. Sanchez suggests using the potato to represent the baby Jesus. Jimmy skeptically responds, "I don't know—this thing is pretty freaky. It might scare children!" At the same time, we see Thurgood's head appear in the right background, symmetrically juxtaposed with the potato in the left foreground. The parallel between the show's star and the clay blob is reinforced by the manner in which the camera lingers on this shot. The shot further contrasts its ensemble of "bad" or crudely animated characters (Jimmy + Thurgood + potato) with the statue of the black Wise Man propped up in the opposite corner—a "good" realist representation of a human that is, ironically, the only truly inanimate figure in a scene where dolls debate the aesthetic properties of dolls. Or, more specifically, a scene in which dolls representing humans engage in a debate about whether a lump looks human enough to *qualify* as a doll.

Recalling the invisible man's repeated description of Clifton's puppet as "obscene" (*IM,* 428), the description of the clay-like, crudely humanized object as "pretty freaky" seems pointedly aimed at the show's detractors, implicitly equating charges of the program's antiblack characterization with a fearful overreaction to crudely anthropomorphized objects in general, regardless of the social identity assigned to them. This comment is reinforced by a later moment in the same episode—one as crudely deconstructive as the lump seems crudely animated—which highlights the same principles of disjunction and detachability at work in the scene of animation from *Invisible Man.* In a moment of distress which com-

FIGURE 3

pels Thurgood to pray to the Hilton-Jacobs' baby-Jesus substitute
(the potato), he anticlimactically discovers that he has to reattach
and rearrange its facial features first, since all of these parts have
slid off the lumpy object onto the floor. Slippery-mouth syndrome,
once again. Thus, the last Fox *PJs* episode offered its audience a little *mise en abyme* of its own mode of production, in which the
crudeness and distortion attributed to its foamation characters became hyperbolized in a very poorly animated potato.

We have returned full circle to the "foul lump" in "Genghis
Chan: Private Eye." Yau's relatively unusual format—a series of
twenty-eight numbered poems each bearing the same title, published over a span of eight years and across three collections of
his writing—demands that each poem's relationship to the name
"Genghis Chan" be reconsidered as the sequence unfolds, like a
succession of identically captioned but visually different pictures or
cartoon panels. The aesthetic of mechanical reproduction suggested
by this serial format reinforces the link between Yau's poems and
modern screen practices, as already implied by the title's reference
to the animated cartoon and live-action versions of Charlie Chan.
At first, the name in the titles clearly seems to designate the poem's
first-person speaker, an "I" whose overtly stylized, hard-boiled language suggests a subjectivity that is always already character or
type—perhaps even a cartoonish type produced not just by a particular filmic or televisual genre but by a filmic or televisual medium: "I am just another particle cloud gliding on the screen / . . . /
I am the owner of one pockmarked tongue / I park it on the hedge
between sure bets and bad business" (Yau, *RS,* 194). Like a projected mass of photons, the "I" described as "just another particle
cloud gliding on the screen" inhabits a landscape marked by Yau's
typically surreal imagery, which persistently disrupts and transforms the topoi of 1930s and 1940s crime fiction: "I was floating
through a cross section / with my dusty wine glass when she entered."

> It was late
> and we were getting jammed in deep.
> I was on the other side, staring at
> the snow covered moon pasted above the park.
> A foul lump started making promises in my voice. (*RS,* 189)

The very first poem in the "Genghis Chan" series thus ends by per-petuating a confusion between human subjects and inhuman ob-jects: Is the last line foregrounding the lumpishness of the speaker, or the speakerliness of lumps? In contrast to the Romantic lyric tra-dition, in which animation conventionally takes the form of apos-trophe, animation here depends on an inversion of the Romantic rhetorical device: instead of a subject throwing voice into an inhu-man entity in order to anthropomorphize it, or turn this object into another subject who can be addressed ("O Rose!"), we have a nonhuman object that becomes animated by usurping the human speaker's voice from a position inside the human's body. Yet the re-sult of this ambiguous moment of animation is another slippery-mouth effect. For in appropriating the "I"'s voice and agency, the lump immediately questions the connection between the proper name "Genghis Chan" and the poem's first-person speaker: Per-haps it is not Genghis who is speaking in all the poems that follow but, instead, the foul entity residing in his throat? It is key that this theft of the "I"'s voice takes place in the first poem. As the series progresses, moreover, the ambiguity surrounding the identity of the speaker becomes increasingly pronounced. In the last poem that appears in *Radiant Silhouette,* the "I" vanishes completely and is re-placed by the second-person "You" in a series of commands: "You will grasp someone's tongue with your teeth and pull / You will prefer the one that bleeds on the carpet / to the one that drools on your sleeve" (Yau, *RS,* 195). By the conclusion of the series, we can no longer be certain who is speaking in the poem or what is being referred to by its title. (Who is "Genghis Chan"? Is Genghis Chan a who or a what?) We can be sure, however, of the gap that opens between the human speaker and his own voice and body. Hence, if the proper name in the series title stands for neither person nor thing but for a specific relationship—the discontinuity introduced between the speaker and his voice, between a body and its tongue, between a poem and its title—"Genghis Chan" could be described as a term that designates animation's ability to undermine its own traditional status as a technology producing unified racialized subjects. And since this relation of discontinuity intensifies as Yau's sequence progresses, what it seems to offer in its totality is less a portrait of someone named Genghis Chan than a flickerbook-like demonstration of the technique of Genghis Channing.

Like the unintended surplus animation in *The PJs,* which resulted when a racialized body part became increasingly detached from its fixed position the more it was made to speak, the "Genghis Chan: Private Eye" series in *Radiant Silhouette* culminates in two disembodied sites of vocalization: a tongue parked on a hedge, another bleeding on the carpet or (less preferably) drooling on a sleeve. While undeniably grotesque, Yau's reanimation of the always already animated, racialized body ultimately pits a kind of material elasticity against the conceptual rigidity of racial stereotypes, recalling the "sponge," a blob-like object similar to the tongue and particle cloud to which the speaker earlier likens himself. Given this combination of elasticity and self-discontinuity, "Genghis Channing" might be described as a practice of threatening one's own limits (or the roles in which one is captured and defined) not by transcending these limits from above but by inventing new ways of inhabiting them.

Like the scene from *Invisible Man* and *The PJs,* Yau's series suggests that racial stereotypes and clichés, cultural images that are perversely both dead and alive, can be critically countered not just by making the images *more* "dead" (say, by attempting to stop their circulation), but also, though in a more equivocal fashion, by *reanimating* them. Thus, while animatedness and its affective cousins (liveliness, vigor, zest) remain ugly categories of feeling reinforcing the historically tenacious construction of racialized subjects as excessively emotional, bodily subjects, they might also be thought of as categories of feeling that highlight animation's status as a nexus of contradictions with the capacity to generate unanticipated social meanings and effects—as when the routine manipulation of raced bodies on screen results in an unsuspected liveliness undermining animation's traditional role in constituting bodies *as* raced. Thus, as an affective spectacle that Garrison finds "thrilling," Stowe "impassioning," and Ellison's narrator "obscene," animation calls for new ways of understanding the technologization of the racialized body as well as the uneasy differential between types and stereotypes—if only through a slippery-mouth method riskily situated, like Genghis Chan's parked tongue, in the uncertain territory between "sure bets and bad business."

3. envy

Though once at the center of feminist debates, the notion of "penis envy" now seems just an old saw, more deserving of obsolescence than sustained analysis or critique. Yet this theoretical concept, formulated by Freud in 1914 as a structuring principle of gender differentiation and quickly diffused into popular culture, remains something of a shibboleth to be reckoned with in the domain of feminist psychoanalytic theory. The standard objection to penis envy in this discourse has been that the idea entails a "characterization of feminine sexuality as deficiency."[1] While it usefully identifies a persistent stereotype of femininity subtending the concept of penis envy, such a critique relies on an equally commonplace approach to "envy" itself—one which treats it as a term describing a *subject* who lacks, rather than the subject's affective *response* to a perceived inequality. In other words, the traditional feminist critique of penis envy regards envy as saying something about the subject's internal state of affairs ("deficiency") as opposed to a statement by or from the subject concerning a relation in the external world.

Rey Chow's comment on Gayatri Spivak's invocation of the affect provides a useful example of this traditional approach. Responding to Spivak's own criticism of Julia Kristeva's "ethnocentric sense of 'alienation' at the sight of some Chinese women in Huxian Square" (a moment Kristeva describes in *About Chinese Women*), Chow writes:

> Spivak charges Kristeva with being primarily interested in her own identity rather than these other women's. While I agree with this observation, I find Spivak's formulation of these other women's identity in terms of "envy" troubling: "Who is speaking here? An effort to answer that question might have revealed more about the mute women of Huxian Square, *looking with qualified envy* at the 'incursion of the West.'" Doesn't the word "envy" here remind us of that condition ascribed to women by Freud, against which feminists revolt—namely "penis envy"? "Envy" is the other side of the "violence" of which Fanon speaks as the fundamental part of the native's formation. But both affects—the one of wanting to *have* what the other has; the other, of destroying the other so that one can *be* in his place—are affects produced by a patriarchal ideology that assumes that the other at the low side of the hierarchy of self/other is "lacking" (in the pejorative, undesirable sense). . . . The fate of the native is then like that of Freud's woman: Even though she will never have a penis, she will for the rest of her life be trapped within the longing for it and its substitutes.[2]

Chow's discomfort with the presence of "envy" in this feminist exchange—an exchange about differences between women—seems based on an assumption that Spivak is invoking the term in the same way it is usually invoked in psychoanalysis as well as a culture which has enthusiastically assimilated it: as a static sign of deficiency rather than a motivated affective stance. Yet the parenthetical qualification of this deficiency, as lack "in the pejorative, undesirable sense," reveals Chow's awareness that there are indeed ways of lacking signaled by envy that are not necessarily pejorative or morally coded, but in fact the consequences of economic inequality.

By perhaps overhastily aligning the envy Spivak attributes to the peasant women with penis envy, a particular situation of "not having" produced by a complex network of social relations, inclusive of but not limited to patriarchal ideology, becomes reduced to an illusion wholly contained within a highly specialized Western discourse of sexual difference.[3] Moreover, by describing envy as the "other side" of the hostility or violence evinced by Fanon's colonized subject, thus replacing an aggressive stance toward owners of property with a more passive longing *for* property, Chow seems to pass over what Spivak finds most significant in the Huxian peasants' gaze at the European intellectual on tour—namely, antagonism.

Given what Helmut Schoeck describes as envy's potential "to draw unenvious people into class conflict" and other forms of social struggle—"Who does not envy with us is against us!"[4]—why is a subject's enviousness automatically assumed to be unwarranted or petty? Or dismissed as an overreaction, as delusional or even hysterical—a reflection of the ego's inner workings rather than a polemical mode of engagement with the world? Unlike anger, another affective support of oppositional consciousness with the capacity to become "a legitimate weapon in social reform" (Schoeck, *E,* 172), envy lacks cultural recognition as a valid mode of publicly recognizing or responding to social disparities, even though it remains the *only* agonistic emotion defined as having a perceived inequality as its object. This invalidation is most powerfully exemplified by envy's integration into the nineteenth-century ideologeme of *ressentiment:* the "diseased passion" which, as Fredric Jameson notes, enabled the discrediting of genuine political impulses by ascribing them to "private dissatisfactions" or psychological flaws.[5] Hence, once it enters a public domain of signification, a person's envy will always seem unjustified, frustrated, and effete—regardless of whether the relation it points to is imaginary or not.

If emotions are fundamentally strategic and "play roles in forms of *action,*" as Rom Harré suggests, the fact that we tend to perceive envy as designating a passive condition of the subject rather than the means by which the subject recognizes and responds to an objective relation suggests that the dominant cultural attitude toward this affect converts its fundamentally other-regarding orientation into an egocentric one, stripping it of its polemicism and rendering it merely a reflection of deficient and possibly histrionic selfhood.[6] Moralized and uglified to such an extent that it becomes shameful to the subject who experiences it, envy also becomes stripped of its potential critical agency—as an ability to recognize, and antagonistically respond to, potentially real and institutionalized forms of inequality.

It is impossible to divorce the pervasive ignobility of this feeling from its class associations or from its feminization, which might explain why the envious subject is so frequently suspected of being hysterical. As historian Peter Stearns has argued, whereas envy and jealousy were "dramatically transformed" into female characteristics in the nineteenth century, in the twentieth century this feminization was accompanied by intensified social prohibition against their expression.[7] These emotions thus doubly "dispositioned" female subjects, since they confronted women with paradoxical injunctions with respect to a gender ideal: femininity entails being naturally or inevitably prone to envy or jealousy, but also never prone to envy or jealousy. If by the twentieth century women were viewed as "more susceptible" to envy and jealousy than men, according to American psychologist George Stanley Hall (1904), the same passions were increasingly viewed as, "on several counts, more *inexcusable* in a woman than a man," according to E. B. Duffy's 1873 bestseller *What Every Woman Should Know.*[8] In this sense, the feminine subject, when speaking *of herself,* would be forced to speak, as Søren Kierkegaard suggests in *The Sickness unto Death* (1849), a "different language." As Kierkegaard notes, "Envy is concealed admiration. An admirer who senses that devotion cannot make him happy will choose to become envious of that which he admires. He will speak a different language, and in this language he will now declare that that which he really admires is a thing of no consequence, something foolish, illusory, perverse and high-flown. Admiration is happy self-abandon; envy, unhappy self-assertion."[9] Focusing on the emotion that places female subjects in such a disjunctive position, this chapter examines how envy's modes of negative or "unhappy self-assertion," including a negative relationship to property we might call "unhappy possessiveness," contribute to—but also enable a critical interrogation of—existing gender norms.

The fact that the feminization and moralization of envy have operated in collusion to suppress its potential as a means of recognizing and polemically responding to social inequalities, casting suspicion on the possible validity of such a response and converting it into a reflection of petty or "diseased" selfhood, should alert us to the fact that forms of negative affect are more likely to be stripped of their critical implications when the impassioned subject is female. Envy's concomitant feminization and moral devaluation thus points to a larger cultural anxiety over antagonistic responses to inequality that are made specifically by women. As we shall see in the next section, this anxiety about female antagonism in general comes to a particular head in academic feminism, especially when it involves representations of antagonistic relations *between* women.

"Who Killed Feminist Criticism?"

It may seem like poor taste and timing to use a reading of a lurid thriller like *Single White Female* (Barbet Schroeder, 1992) as a way of addressing conflicts in academic feminism today—not only because it involves hanging a large coat on a small peg (however one might prefer this to hanging small coats on large pegs), but because the film has already been the object of a vogue in critical attention that has long since passed. In its blunt contrasting of an idealized femininity (white, middle-class, cosmopolitan, and heterosexual) marked "benevolent," with a bad or threatening femininity (working-class, provincial, and putatively lesbian) marked "envious," embodied respectively in the figures of Allison Jones (Bridget Fonda) and Hedra Carlson (Jennifer Jason Leigh), *Single White Female* inspired numerous feminist critiques almost immediately after its release, all of which "justly attack the film for its potent misogyny and homophobia," and several for its attitudes toward class and race.[10] More recently, Karen Hollinger contextualizes Schroeder's film, which is based on John Lutz's novel *SWF Seeks Same* (1990), as part of a "major backlash" in response to the political conservatism of the 1980s and 1990s, a conservatism she finds particularly visible in the popular reemergence of the "manipulative female friendship film."[11] Grouping *Single White Female* with other, contemporaneous Hollywood thrillers about the violent aggression unleashed by envious working-class women, films such as *The Hand That Rocks the Cradle* (Curtis Hanson, 1992) and *Poison Ivy* (Kat Shea Ruben, 1992), Hollinger argues:

> These films often rejuvenate antiquated stereotypical representations of female relationships from woman's films of the 1930s and 1940s. They represent women's friendships as plagued by jealousy, envy, and competition for men, and they teach women to beware of and fear one another. By focusing so strongly on conflicts between women, they obscure other issues related to women's position in society, relieve men of any responsibility for women's problems, and suggest, instead, that women should grant men primary importance in their lives because they are the only ones upon whom women can rely. ("B," 207)

Given that *Single White Female* features an initially happy domestic alliance between Allie and Hedy and chronicles the way in which it becomes increasingly "conflicted"—to the point that Hedy ends up bludgeoning Allie's best friend and neighbor and leaving him for dead, stabbing Allie's boyfriend through the eye with the heel of a

FIGURE 4

stiletto pump, murderously chasing Allie with a grappling hook, and finally being killed by Allie with a screwdriver in the back—it is hard not to agree with the assessment above.

But should we *not* focus strongly on "conflicts between women," as Hollinger's statement also seems to imply?[12] Even if attention is shifted to vexed, antagonistic, or unhappy female relationships at the exclusion of other issues (as any act of "focusing" will entail), the emphasis in itself does not seem to be an obvious sign of an antifeminist agenda. In the wariness it reflects, however, Hollinger's statement points to the fact that the representation of female conflicts remains a particularly loaded issue for feminists, particularly when these antagonistic relationships often gain greatest cultural visibility through hyperbolic, violent narratives fitting the paradigm above. There is legitimate cause for the fear that female conflicts may be subject to representational manipulation by feminism's external enemies—a fear reflected in Susan Gubar's reference to "a culture all too willing to exploit disagreements among women in a backlash against all or some of us."[13]

But how are polemical "conflicts between women" within feminism figured by feminists themselves? For an example, we can turn to a controversial debate between Gubar and Robyn Wiegman in *Critical Inquiry* (1998–1999) concerning the very topic of polemical antagonism's role in academic feminism.[14] In this exchange, murder is invoked not just once but twice, and both times at the very beginning of each critic's essay. In both cases, the reference to violence is both immediate and strategic, as if to provocatively induce the same "thrill" associated with the thriller genre. Originally called "Who Killed Feminist Criticism?" Gubar's "What Ails Feminist Criticism?" starts with an explanation of why she decided not to use the more graphic and accusatory title; Wiegman begins her critical response to Gubar by invoking Amanda Cross's *Murder Without a Text,* a mystery novel featuring "a seasoned feminist scholar bludgeoning a student to death." Since both essays characterize the nature of the feminist disputes they discuss as fundamentally generational, it is difficult not to read Wiegman's invocation of the Cross story (older feminist kills younger feminist) as a canny way of reversing the roles of murderer and victim assigned in Gubar's essay (younger feminists kill older feminism), as well as a way of foregrounding the murderous scene of "feminist betrayal" that Gubar calls forth but then quickly disavows by substituting the metaphor of illness ("What Ails?") for the original image of killing ("SO," 363). The culturally familiar narrative of generational injury and rivalry between women invoked by both Gubar and Wiegman (though in a much more ironic and self-conscious way by the latter) also bears a striking resemblance to the narrative of *Single White Female*'s 1950 predecessor, *All about Eve* (directed by Joseph Mankiewicz). For in using thriller imagery to dramatize generational disputes or "betrayals," and in being framed by subsequent commentators as a conflict between an older feminist and a younger feminist previously the student of the former, the Gubar-Wiegman debate not only recalls the Amanda Cross story cited by Wiegman, but the Mankiewicz film's depiction of the antagonistic rivalry that develops between an older theater star (Bette Davis) and the younger woman (Anne Baxter) who begins as her admirer and pupil. If the themes of envy and ingratitude in this film may remind readers of Melanie Klein's eponymous 1957 essay, the Kleinian implications of the Gubar-Wiegman exchange are reinforced in a letter by "Amanda Cross" herself (a.k.a. Carolyn Heilbrun), describing the debate as a mother-daughter dispute— "another battle in the war of generations" ultimately explicable in terms of infantile aggression.[15] As Cross/Heilbrun writes:

> My initial astonishment at finding my story quoted in *Critical Inquiry* soon dwindled to dismay as I understood the rudeness offered to my character, Beatrice Sterling [the seasoned feminist scholar], was not far from the tone Professor Wiegman chose as appropriate for addressing Professor Gubar, who had fought early feminist academic battles when Professor Wiegman was at her mother's knee. . . . Why Professor Wiegman agreed to answer Professor Gubar in such a mode is explicable . . . chiefly upon maternal principles. ("L," 397–398)

In the Gubar and Wiegman essays, then, we have an accusation of symbolic murder by a seasoned feminist scholar and an allegory in which a seasoned feminist scholar murders her accuser. In Heilbrun's response, these violent motifs are compounded by the introduction of two related themes: infantile rage and aggression toward a maternal figure, and envy and ingratitude. It thus becomes as difficult to avoid seeing parallels between the Gubar-Wiegman debate and a film like *All about Eve* as it is to avoid finding this association distasteful. For such a comparison seems to do exactly what Hollinger says *Single White Female* does: "rejuve-

nate antiquated stereotypical representations of female relationships from woman's films of the 1930s and 1940s" ("B," 207). The
fact that a contemporary intellectual debate about the role of antagonism in feminism *could* be so readily aligned with a mid-cen-
tury Hollywood narrative about female aggression does seem quite
troubling.

But aside from the fact that both key players in this feminist debate use violence themselves as a way of framing their arguments,
is there something inherently untenable about women's use of metaphorical violence, even "murderous desire," as a way of critically
discussing conflicts between women? While images of "murderous
desire" can obviously be used to distort and exploit disagreements
between feminists from feminism's outside, does the Gubar-Wiegman debate not also demonstrate that such images can be imagina-
tively and provocatively used to address such disagreements from
within? Yet while Gubar suggestively invokes the image of murderous aggression to frame and advance her argument, in addition
to mobilizing the polemical discourse of accusation and blame, she
pinpoints this aggressivity in other feminists as the cause of feminism's demise. Thus, she finds bell hooks's *"curiously condemnatory*
vocabulary," "[Hazel] Carby's *hostility,"* and "the *aggression* . . .
surfac[ing] in Spivak's competing for perceptual supremacy over
First World feminist critics" equally culpable.[16] Ironically, this criticism of "condemnatory vocabulary" would seem to confirm its centrality to the enterprise of feminist scholarship, insofar as Gubar's
own critical intervention clearly relies on it. Instead of simply re-
formulating Gubar's question to address the undeniably important
issue of how collective enterprises are constituted and sustained—
"Who or what is responsible for conflicts within feminism?"—we
might consider posing another question addressing the same issue
in a different way: "To what extent do homosocial group formations like feminism *rely* on antagonism and its associated images,
metaphors, and paradigms of aggression?" *Single White Female,*
surprisingly, has much to offer in this regard, since the hyperbolic

violence that characterizes female conflicts in this film becomes most concentrated in its main narrative event: the production of a de-singled femaleness. In fact, the transition from single to compound female identity is not only motivated and facilitated by aggression, but the ultimate goal of the female-female struggle on which the film's story depends.

Though it is precisely the transition from singular to compound subjects that initiates group formation and therefore politics, it is the rhetorical enactment of this transition that Gubar finds politically suspect (in a metaphorical fashion) in the prose style of Judith Butler. Described as leading to "mistakes in agreement," Butler's grammatical error is, according to Gubar, symptomatic of a fundamental incompatibility between feminism and poststructuralism— a discourse Gubar finds complicit with race theory in "sidelining" the "first three stages" of feminist criticism and "marginalizing" the aesthetic. Here the problem is not with the feminist subject's emotional mindset, as is the case in Gubar's critique of Spivak's "aggression" and Carby's "hostility," but with the linguistic subject's *discursive* status as compounded. Gubar writes:

> One especially revealing feature of Butler's style is the preponderance of subject-verb disagreements. I want to speculate that this penchant, by reflecting the difficulty of sustaining a Foucauldian critique of the singular self and the biological body, reveals the tensions continually at play in efforts to combine poststructuralism with feminism. Since my argument depends on a pattern of mistakes in agreement, I will cite . . . examples here from *Gender Trouble* . . . :
>
> "The *totality* and *closure* of language is both presumed and contested within structuralism."
>
> "The division and exchange between this 'being' and 'having' the Phallus is established by the Symbolic, the paternal law." . . .

> Note how prone Butler's prose is to a compound subject with a singular form of verbs that eschew action and instead denote a condition or stipulate a mode of existence. Her dual subjects often involve not persons but abstractions, which are treated as if they have combined in her mind into a single force that therefore requires the singular verb.[17]

Interestingly, while the critique aimed at feminists of color is *psychological,* the critique aimed at the feminist poststructuralist is *grammatical:* the problem here is not with emotional qualities like hostility or aggression but with a situation in which dual or compound subjects are combined "into a single force that therefore requires the singular verb." According to Gubar, this misuse of compound subjects "bespeaks a quandary, for it demonstrates how often the most vigilantly antitotalizing theorist of poststructuralism relies on stubborn patterns of totalization (two treated as one)" ("WAFC," 898).

In a reversal of her critique of Spivak, Carby, and hooks, which pits universality against particularization, Gubar here plays the particular against what she construes as a false universal. But aside from the fact that the statement above drastically elides the substantial difference between "totalization" and the treatment of two abstract qualities as one (as seems appropriate when the qualities engender effects or are acted upon in tandem), isn't the combining of dual or multiple subjects into a single force or agency precisely the way in which group alliances (even fraught or uneasy ones such as feminism) are formed? If such a transition "bespeaks a quandary," Gubar's discomfort with Butler's grammatical enactment of it might be said to bespeak uneasiness about the "compound subject" in general. Since Gubar's argument links poststructuralism and race studies or ethnic studies as complicit in causing the demise of feminist criticism, thus "creating a confederacy among knowledge formations that are not often seen as collaborative culprits" (Wiegman, "SO," 368), one might also ask how the *discursive* threat of the paradoxically doubled-yet-single subject associated with poststructuralist feminists relates to the *psychological* threat of aggression associated with feminists of color. In other words, what is the relationship between female aggression and the grammar of de-singled subjects? Or between the subject of emotion and the subject of language? Oddly enough, these questions are ones that *Single White Female* directly addresses. But to see how requires some working-through of the terms in which the female relationships in this film have been traditionally conceived.

Emulation and Antagonism

Single White Female is perhaps best summarized as a story about the violent production, if ultimately also the destruction, of non-singular female subjectivity, in both cases by means of antagonism between women. In other words, the film narrativizes the making of a compound female subject while depicting the process as both dangerous and unstable. Because this central aspect of the movie turns on Hedy's emulation of Allie in manner and appearance, as well as on Hedy's intensely emotional attachment to her (with the two attitudes closely linked and similarly pathologized) readings of the film have continued a line of psychoanalytically informed inquiry into the complex relationship between identification and desire. This identification/desire dialectic, and its role in the construction of gendered and sexual spectatorship, was feminist film theory's main object of focus in its almost exclusively psychoanalytic phase in the 1970s and 1980s, from Laura Mulvey's "Visual Pleasure and Narrative Cinema" to Mary Ann Doane's equally classic response to it in "Film and the Masquerade." Thus, like popular "woman's films" that foreground extremely close but troubled female attachments—films ranging from *Rebecca* (Alfred Hitchcock, 1940) to *The Prime of Miss Jean Brodie* (Ronald Neame, 1968)—*Single White Female* has made its way into longstanding but still ongoing debates concerning the relationship between "wanting to be" and "wanting to have" as primary in constituting sexual and gender norms. Although tracing the history of these detailed arguments about desire and identification lies beyond the agenda of this chapter, I want to highlight two issues raised particularly in commentaries on cinematic representations of close but uneasy female relationships: first, the danger of conflating the two dynamics, as Teresa de Lauretis warns in her reading of *All about Eve* and *Desperately Seeking Susan* (directed by Susan Seidelman, 1985), since the conflation leads to mistaking "homosocial, i.e. woman-identified bonding" for lesbian sexuality; and, second, the danger of too-rigidly separating them, as Jackie Stacey argues in a reading of this same pair of films.[18] Thus, Scott Paulin suggests:

> Perhaps identification and desire are "not to be confused" in that they cannot occupy the same moment in time, but surely an oscillation between the terms is possible, just as a film spectator can be encouraged to oscillate between identification and desire for a character, regardless of gender. At the very least, whether this situation has a counterpart in "reality," films like *All about Eve* and *Single White Female* fantasize a space in which such oscillation can and does occur.[19]

In what follows, my intention is not to ignore questions related to the desire/identification dialectic (indeed, Freud's essay on identification will play a key role in the analysis), but rather to suggest that its dominance in the critical discourse surrounding "films like *All about Eve* and *Single White Female*"—that is, films that foreground the subject of unhappy or negative bonds between women—often limits the other feminist *and* psychoanalytic ways in which they might be read. For an almost exclusive focus on these poles tends to produce a reading that overlooks or underestimates the importance of antagonism in these alliances.[20] As a dynamic that is reducible to neither desire nor identification (though desire and identification often inform it), aggressive conflict is emphasized as the relation of primary narrative significance between women in these films. Though psychoanalytic theory facilitates our understanding of how one might simultaneously desire and bear aggression toward an other, identify with one's aggressor, or form an antagonistic relation with someone with whom one identifies (this being the easiest of all to imagine from a classic Oedipal perspective), in the last analysis the terms are not conflatable: antagonism is not identification, nor is it a subspecies or variant of desire. Freud himself would come to insist on these separations in *Beyond the Pleasure Principle* (1920), where aggressivity is clearly established as the manifestation of an independent drive, parallel rather than secondary to sexual instincts.[21] In Freud's postwar writings, in fact, the dynamic is viewed as being on equal standing with the sexual in the process of subject formation, thus preparing the way for Klein's insistently negative theories of constitutional aggression and infantile envy.[22] Moreover, his crucial reformulation of aggression as a separate phenomenon irreducible to sexuality enables Freud to introduce one of his few accounts of subject formation in which the subject is neither necessarily marked by nor entirely produced in gender difference. Wariness, then, of a critical tendency to reduce antagonism to a mere side effect of desire or identification (as already anticipated by the shift in the later works of Freud), is one of my motivations for shifting the analysis of the vexed female relationships foregrounded in films like *All about Eve* and *Single White Female* away from these conceptual poles. Instead of focusing on desire and identification as the primary psychic functions informing the uneasy attachments between women featured in this subgenre of the "woman's film," I will examine how these processes work when they are inscribed within the logics of *envy* and *emulation*. Though it is neither useful nor possible to understand envy and emulation apart from questions of identification and desire, I will focus on the latter feelings primarily insofar as they relate to the former.

My second motivation for making some form of break from the

identification/desire paradigm relates to another tendency common to readings focused solely on these two poles: the conflation of emulation with identification. For example, what Ellen Brinks accurately describes as Hedy's "mimetic performance"—in which Hedy imitates Allie's appearance and manner to such a degree that the viewer has difficulty telling the two women apart—is referred to as "mimetic *identification*" in the title of Brinks's essay. As Brinks writes: "For Hedy, 'to look like' is a way 'to become.' . . . Instead of the purely acquisitive desire *to have* the clothing or the man that Allie possess or enjoys (something which would assume an already constituted *subject* who desires some *thing* or *object*), Hedy 'does the double' in order to create a subjective identity for herself. She desires *to be, to be like,* or *to become* Allie" ("MI," 4; original italics). Here the attempt to copy or double *Y* is explicitly equated with the wish to be *Y,* with the agency of these attempts attributed to some unfinished or not "already constituted" subject *X.* Similarly, Scott Paulin uses the fact of Hedy's actively copying Allie's "look" as a basis for claiming, "It is clear that Hedy identifies with Allie as an ideal, that she envies her and 'wants to be her.'"[23]

As a mode of admiration that takes the form of striving toward an ideal or idealized object, emulation in *Single White Female* is depicted as this striving gone horribly awry, displaced or rerouted, as it were, from object to subject. Female emulation in particular—one woman's emulation of another woman—is represented in the film as an unstable mode of admiration that easily slides into aggression, or, more specifically, as a mimetic behavior that initiates a trajectory: from the reverence of an ideal to full-blown antagonism toward the subject embodying that ideal. We can thus see the logic underlying the popular psychological view which takes emulation to be a process that naturally subtends envy, a cultural idiom *Single White Female* uses in order to feminize and pathologize both behaviors. Hence, the film's greatest ideological contradiction involves positioning Allie as the embodiment of a feminine ideal whose admiration by Hedy or other women is to be expected, even mandated, while depicting any act of striving toward that ideal as troubling or problematic. Hedy's attempts to emulate Allie are thus perceived by Allie as a threat, and presented as a kind of warning sign of the beginnings of a trajectory from reverent fascination to aggression. In *All about Eve,* such a trajectory is ironically foreshadowed in the two sides of Margot's response to Eve's emulation. When Margot's maid, Birdie (Thelma Ritter), points out, "She's studying you—like you was a book, or a play, or a set of blueprints—how you walk, talk, eat, think, sleep," Margot replies, "I'm sure that's very *flattering,* Birdie [i.e., deferential, an act of homage] and I'm sure there's *nothing wrong with it* [i.e., hostile, aggressive]." Since in *Single White Female* emulation is explicitly posited as the act that inaugurates this transition from admiration to enmity, Allie's disturbance by Hedy begins when she discovers the signs of Hedy's imitative behavior, all of which involve acts of appropriation or progressively forceful claims to property: Hedy's unasked borrowing of her clothes, the discovery of duplicates of these clothes in Hedy's closet, Hedy's change of hair color and style to match her own, her own letters hoarded in Hedy's shoebox of personal mementos.

According to the film's narrative logic, then, Hedy's emulation of Allie *is* an accurate indication that she envies her. But is it synonymous, as Brinks and Paulin claim, with a form of identification? For it seems obvious that emulating someone does not necessarily entail wishing to *be* that someone, or even that one desires to take over the social or symbolic position he or she occupies in order to enjoy its privileges. In fact, we can easily imagine antagonistic situations in which emulation is motivated by reasons antithetical to a wish or fantasy to be the other, situations in which one emulates in order to overtake or eclipse the other, even "dispossess" her by claiming exclusive recognition for the attributes that define her. Instead of being a means of altering one's self in *deference* to another, emulation can be a form of aggressive *self-assertion:* performed with the purpose of causing the other anxiety or distress, or, to use a

Kleinian expression, with the intent of "spoiling" her by rendering her own identity unstable. In Hitchcock's *Vertigo* (1958), Judy's second, extremely reluctant and even painful assumption of the role of "Madeleine" under pressure from Scottie (James Stewart) provides an example of how emulation can also be performed without unconscious or conscious desire to transform one's own identity after the fashion of the other. Thus, emulation in more aggressive forms of parody, including political satire and cultural mimicry, often works as a sort of prophylactic against or antidote to identification: it makes manifest an incongruity or disjunction, enables one to forcefully assert one's difference from the other whom one emulates. Similarly, by foregrounding the antagonism between Hedy and Allie (which hyperbolically escalates into murderous violence), *Single White Female* calls attention to the fact that Hedy's acts of emulation actually work against "phantasmatic efforts of alignment, loyalty, [and] cohabitation," as Judith Butler describes identifications.[24] Moreover, these acts of copying give rise to the very distinction between emulation and identification, since they transform Hedy's attitude from philic "striving-toward" to a phobic "striving-against." Surely the film insists on uncoupling emulation from identification. Why, then, the critical tendency to equate them? Or to treat the former as evidence of the latter?

"Group Psychology" and Freud's Exemplary Females

If the Gubar-Wiegman exchange and *Single White Female* both highlight, in very different ways, the question of how aggression relates to the production of "compound subjects" necessary for group formation, *Group Psychology and the Analysis of the Ego* (1921), Freud's attempt to "contribute toward the explanation of the libidinal structure of groups" and theorize the emergence of what he calls "group feeling," becomes a crucial text in addressing the same issue.[25] And as Diana Fuss notes, "Identification," the seventh chapter of *Group Psychology,* is where Freud "first begins to systematize the complicated dialectical relation between identification and object-choice in the formation of the sexed subject," formalizing the concepts on which major debates in feminist film theory have been based.[26] The tendency in psychoanalytically informed film criticism to conflate copying and identification makes sense to a degree if one takes a closer look at the slipperiness in Freud's original account of identification in *Group Psychology*—a slipperiness that in fact *encourages* the confusion of these two dynamics when they pertain to female subjects.

If one's identification with an other is, as Freud initially argues based on his example of a boy's pre-Oedipal relation to his father, *a fantasy or wish* to be like him, or replace him in his role with respect to another, emulation would seem to be the means by which identifications are pursued rather than established—since identification, as Butler reminds us, is a phantasmatic trajectory, not an actual *event* said to taken place.[27] Copying or imitating is not equivalent to wishing. The first is a form of behavior through which a fantasy might be enacted; the second refers to the psychic act of fantasizing. But a slipperiness between the two dynamics enters Freud's account of identification once he turns from the example of the relationship between a boy and his father, and attempts to develop his initial thesis by analyzing identification "as it occurs in the structure of a neurotic symptom" in girls and women. We can locate the moment of transition in the last sentence of the following, frequently cited paragraph:

> It is easy to state in a formula the distinction between an identification with the father and the choice of the father as an object. In the first case one's father is what one would like to *be,* and in the second he is what one would like to *have*. The distinction, that is, depends upon whether the tie attaches to the subject or to the object of the ego. The former kind of tie is therefore already possible before any sexual object-choice can be made. It is much more difficult to give a clear metapsycho-

logical representation of the distinction. We can only see that identification endeavors *to mold a person's own ego after the fashion of the one that has been taken as a model.* (*GP,* 47; last italics added)

Molding one's own ego "after the fashion" of another person taken as a model, which might be described as an act of transforming the self by example, sounds very much like an act of emulation. Here it becomes easy to understand why critics tend to conflate the purely imaginary act of "wishing to be"—which, as Butler reminds us, "does not belong to the world of events"[28]—with the realizable event of self-transformation through imitation. In the sentence above, Freud seems to conflate the two himself. Yet even in this expanded concept of identification as having "ego-molding" as its aim or goal, imitative behavior is still not reducible to the original fantasy of being the idealized other, though it now comes extremely close, construed as both the fantasy's objective (what it directly seeks or "endeavors") and the means by which it might be achieved.

The slippage between mimetic self-transformation (event) and identification (fantasy) that Freud's sentence introduces has much to do with the fact that it works less as a logical extension of the remarks preceding it, and more as a proleptic introduction to the topic of the paragraph that follows. Whereas the first paragraph discusses identification in the purely phantasmatic terms of a boy *wishing* to be his father (no mention of actual mimetic behavior yet), the second introduces the case of a girl imitating her mother's cough, visibly behaving "after the fashion" of her mother as model. Thus, the proposition in Freud's last sentence, insofar as it implies an actual inducement to imitation by example, "belongs" more to the second paragraph than the first, which it concludes. Here is the previously quoted passage in its larger context:

It is easy to state in a formula the distinction between an identification with the father and the choice of the father as an object. In the first case the father is what one would like to *be,* and in the second he is what one would like to *have.* The distinction, that is, depends upon whether the tie attaches to the subject or to the object of the ego. The former kind of tie is therefore already possible before any sexual object-choice can be made. It is much more difficult to give a clear metapsychological representation of the distinction. *We can only see that identification endeavors to mold a person's own ego after the fashion of the one that has been taken as a model.*

Let us now disentangle identification as it occurs in the structure of a neurotic symptom from its rather complicated connections. Supposing that a little girl (and we will keep to her for the present) develops the same painful symptom as her mother—for instance, the same tormenting cough. (*GP,* 47–48, italics added)

Rather than directly addressing the questions raised in the first paragraph (concerning the distinction between object-choice and identification), the rhetorical function of "We can only see . . ." is to prepare us for the subsequent paragraph, which deliberately diverts focus from *fantasies* of being and having that are generated in a male psyche to the observable, empirical *behavior* of female subjects. The sentence also marks the termination of the male homosocial relation as a paradigmatic basis for Freud's theory of identification; from this point on, all of his "theoretical sources" consist of relations involving women—including not just the hypothetical little girl's replication of her mother's cough, but (in order of appearance) Dora's mimicry of her father's cough, a contagious outbreak of jealousy at an all-girls boarding school, and a "genesis of male homosexuality" based on maternal fixation. In this manner, what is most significant about Freud's first mention of mimetic behavior in his discussion of identification is its location within his series of examples, or its relationship to the way his examples are ordered. The pivotal sentence—"*We can only see that identification endeavors to mold a person's own ego after the fashion of the one that has been taken as a model"*—marks a crucial transition in Freud's argumentative strategy, a transition in which he relocates the basis of his definition from a generalized account of normative human development (the production of male heterosexual subjectivity) to particular instances of neurosis in girls, women, and homosexual men (the production of hysterical "feminine" subjectivity). The shift from *imaginary fantasies of being* to *observable acts of copying* in Freud's example-driven theory of identification thus coincides with a shift from boys and fathers to girls and mothers, normative to neurotic, general to particular, definition to example, and "typically masculine" to "feminizing" relations (*GP*, 46)—an alignment of terms suggesting that there is a markedly hierarchical logic at work in the essay.[29]

Once Freud resituates his theory in a specifically feminine register, identification and emulation immediately become interchangeable. Starting with the example of the little girl's imitation of her mother's cough, Freud uses one as a synonym for the other throughout *Group Psychology*. When he speaks of "the identification" in the case of the little girl who copies her mother's cough, the phenomenon he refers to is precisely that of the replicated symptom—*not*, as one might expect from his previous discussion of the boy's identification with his father, her ontologically distinct act of fantasizing. Fantasy and behavior are further collapsed in Freud's third female "source" (*GP*, 49) which comes from his failed analysis of Dora. In an infamous account of how sexual object-choice "regresses" to identification based on Dora's imitation of her father's cough, Freud uses her mimetic behavior as evidence of this regression: "Where there is repression and where the mechanisms of the unconscious are dominant, object-choice is turned back into identification—*the ego assumes the characteristics of the object*" (*GP*, 48, italics added).

As identification becomes increasingly theorized within a world of feminine subjects and feminizing relationships, it becomes increasingly depicted as a fantasy that not only strives toward but assumes the characteristics of a nonphantasmatic event—one that *can* be said to happen. And as Freud moves through his examples—(1) the boy and his father; (2) the hypothetical girl imitating her mother's cough; (3) Dora imitating her father's cough; (4) the jealousy outbreak at the all-girls boarding school; (5) the young man with the maternal fixation—the ontological distinction between wishing and acting which seemed fairly obvious in the case of the boy-father relationship is ever more reduced. In other words, the further Freud locates his theory away from the original paradigm of male heterosexuality, the easier it becomes to equate identification with emulation. Thus, by the time we reach Freud's fifth example (concerning "the genesis of male homosexuality"), things have become "transformed" indeed. "Things take a sudden turn: the young man does not abandon his mother [at the onset of adult sexuality], but identifies with her; *he transforms himself into her,* and now looks about for objects which can replace his ego for him, and on which he can bestow such love and care as he has experienced from his mother" (*GP,* 50, italics added). Initially a phantasmatic trajectory directed toward the other, identification is now redefined as a trajectory whose destination is the actual transformation of the *self:* "identification . . . *remolds the ego*" (*GP,* 51).

Thus, the increased proximity between identification and mimetic acts of self-transformation that coincides with a shift in the gender of Freud's examples *also* strategically coincides with an increase in the "exemplarity" of these examples—if we understand the example not just in the logical sense of a particular instance of a general principle, but in the social sense of an inducement to imitation (Fuss, *IP,* 41). Once Freud shifts to examples involving female subjects to illustrate his theory of identification, the proximity between identification and mimesis increases because the "examples" *within* these examples—the models providing the fashion after which subjects "remold" themselves—increase in their capacity to encourage or induce emulation. *The more feminine the example, the more exemplary the example.* As if femininity itself were a hyperbolic mode of exemplarity? Or, to turn a famous phrase of Lacan's, structured "like" an example?

The logic underlying Freud's use of examples thus suggests not only that identification is bound up with emulation more closely in social relationships involving women than in male-male configurations, but that female subjects have a closer relationship to exemplarity in general. An extension of this logic implies that to be feminine is to be an *unusually exemplary* example—an entity inducing imitation in others while at the same time appearing "after the fashion" of a previously established model. Thus, the virtuous Clarissa (from Samuel Richardson's novel of the same name; 1747–1748), a character repeatedly compelled to serve as "an example to her sex," became most of all an example *of* exemplarity, when thousands of eighteenth-century parents named their daughters after her. It could be said that in "Identification," Freud's exemplification of femininity—which emerges in this essay as precisely the kind of subjectivity produced by identifications where phantasmatic alignments with the other become indistinguishable from events of mimetic self-transformation—induces *the feminization of exemplarity*.

This correlation between femininity and exemplarity is reinforced through a shared principle of transmissibility, which Freud figures as "infection." The metaphor is introduced in the fourth of his progressively or increasingly female-centered examples of identification—which significantly turns on a hypothetical anecdote about jealousy. Concerning the contagious outbreak of this emotion among "girls in a boarding school," Freud's example invokes the image of infection in order to reinforce the already implicit linkage of femininity with imitation and iterability.[30]

> There is [another] particularly frequent and important case of symptom formation, in which the identification leaves entirely out of account any object-relation to the person who is being copied. Supposing, for instance, that one of the girls in a

boarding school has had a letter from someone with whom she is secretly in love which arouses her jealousy, and that she reacts to it with a fit of hysterics; then some of her friends who know about it will catch the fit, as we say, by mental infection. The mechanism is that of identification based on the possibility or desire of putting oneself in the same situation. The other girls would like to have a secret love affair too, and under the influence of a sense of guilt they also accept the suffering involved in it. It would be wrong to suppose that they take on the symptom out of sympathy. On the contrary, the symptom only arises out of the *identification,* and this is proved by the fact that *infection or imitation* of this kind takes place in circumstances where even less pre-existing sympathy is to be assumed than usually exists between friends in a girls' school. One ego has perceived a significant analogy with another upon one point—in our example *upon openness to a similar emotion;* an identification is thereupon constructed on this point, and, under the influence of the pathogenic situation, is displaced on to the symptom which the one ego has produced. The identification by means of the symptom has thus become the mark of a point of coincidence between the two egos which has to be kept repressed. (*GP,* 48–49, italics added)

Here, as Freud moves from individual acts of feminine identification to feminine identifications en masse, note how identification's equivalence with imitation slides into a further equivalence with infection. Since the logic of exemplarity in Freud's essay has already suggested that feminine identifications, unlike their masculine counterparts, cannot easily be detached from acts of imitation, or from the example's social function of *compelling* imitation, it comes as no surprise that feminine identifications are viewed here as contagious, since, as Freud notes in his earlier work *Totem and Taboo* (1912), "*examples* are contagious" (Fuss, *IP,* 42, italics added). Whereas identification and emulation remained ontologically distinct phenomena in the case of the boy-father relation, we have seen how difficult it becomes to separate them in examples involving women. Not all identifications, then, but feminine identifications in particular—that is, phantasmatic alignments with *women* —become coeval with mimetic acts of self-transformation "after the fashion" of another as model. Leading to the production of female selfhood, feminine identifications are more "contagious" than masculine ones since they *work* like examples. Hence, while all genders may be performative or mimetic in structure, involving "the stylized repetition of acts in time," *Group Psychology* suggests that some genders are more mimetic than others, and that its own rhetoric of exemplarity is anything but neutral to the logic of gender difference.[31]

If femininity is structured like an inducement to imitation or example, and envy or jealousy intensify this relation, how might Hedy's envious attitude toward Allie in *Single White Female* constitute a way—a strategic and perhaps even feminist way—of negotiating her relationship to gender itself?

Bad Examples

Reinforcing Stearns's historical observations, the implicit equation of femininity and exemplarity in "Identification" runs parallel with, and is in fact strengthened by, Freud's feminization of envy. For unlike his other "theoretical sources," the boarding school anecdote enables Freud not only to posit that identifications can "leave entirely out of account any object-relation to the person who is being copied," but also to demonstrate that infectious identifications can be partial rather than whole—"borrow[ing] a *single* trait from the person who is its object," hence becoming even easier to establish and transmit (Freud, *GP,* 48). It is important to note that the shared trait in this example is the female subject's unquestioned predilection for envy and jealousy: "One ego has perceived a significant analogy with another upon one point—in our example upon *openness to a similar emotion:* an identification is thereupon constructed on this point, and, under the influence of the patho-genic situation, is displaced on to the symptom which the one ego has produced" (*GP,* 49, italics added).

According to Freud's account, identification leads to or implies imitation particularly where feminine subjects are concerned, and even more so where jealous females are concerned; in fact, we have seen how in this emotional arena, under the aegis of an "infection" metaphor, the two processes become virtually synonymous. Given that a fictitious envying scenario provides an ideal setting for this linkage of terms to become visible as such, the gendered logic at work in "Identification" seems to support Paulin's assertion con-cerning what is most obvious about the central relationship in *Sin-gle White Female:* "It is clear that Hedy identifies with Allie as an ideal, that she envies her and 'wants to be her'" ("SSG," 51). Here again, a fictional account of envy between women seems to provide a way of demonstrating emulation's coextensiveness with iden-tification. As noted earlier, *Single White Female* does make obvi-ous Hedy's attempt to appropriate for her own use—literally bor-rowing, as in the case of "partial," nonsexual identifications—the markers of Allie's identity. Hedy wears Allie's clothes with, and then without, her permission, and eventually she buys duplicates of the clothes themselves. She pays to have her hair cut in the same style and dyed the same color as Allie's, which brings their resem-blance close enough to the point that when dressed in clothes like Allie's, she effectively passes for Allie to others who know her.

Yet insofar as emulation turns the thing emulated (whether this be a single characteristic or a whole person) into a thing that can be copied, and in doing so transforms that thing into something slightly other than what it was, it is possible to interpret Hedy's mimeticism not as the enactment of a wish to be Allie, or an effort to transform herself into Allie and occupy her place, but rather as an attempt to transform *Allie.* As the film's plot reveals, it is the emulated subject's life and not the emulator's that most radically changes as result of the latter's actions.[32] Defined throughout by an ability to shapeshift, Hedy maintains a comparatively consistent identity. In contrast, by being "copied," the single Allie is transformed by Hedy's mimetic behavior into something she previously was not: a duplicate. If Freudian identification is a process where the subject makes himself *one* with the other person, Hedy's emulation of Allie could be described not as an endeavor to achieve oneness, but as a process of making twoness.[33] In their semiotic study of rivalry, which presents envy and emulation as indissociably linked, Greimas and Fontanille describe emulation as implying "an unfinished process, S1's process, in relation to another subject, S2, whose process is treated as finished."[34] But paradoxically, in *Single White Female* the "unfinished" subjectivization is less that of the emulating person than that of the person she emulates, since it is Allie's sense of selfhood and her relationships with others which are ultimately altered. In one of their final encounters, Allie herself acknowledges this outcome. As she says to Hedy, "I'm like *you* now."

Thus, in spite of the overcloseness between the two dynamics that emerges in *Group Psychology,* Hedy's mimetic behavior seems to have surprisingly little to do with Freud's notion of identification, in the sense of either a fantasy about her own transformation (the desire to be or be like Allie) or a fantasy of replacing Allie in her relationships with other people. The film makes the latter particularly clear: though Hedy deceptively seduces Allie's boyfriend Sam, she does so to force him to vanish from both Allie's life and her own, using the seduction as blackmail. Nor does Hedy express any interest in Allie's other few relationships: her platonic friendship with gay upstairs neighbor Graham, or her disastrous business alliance with the unattractive and rapacious Mitch. Far from attempting to usurp Allie's place within these relationships with men, Hedy's aggressive acts of emulation actually aim at *dissolving* them. Moreover, Allie's bitter comment, "I'm like *you* now," makes it clear that Hedy's mimetic behavior has not been aimed at molding herself, qua "unfinished" ego, after the fashion of the "finished" model supplied by Allie. In fact, insofar as the comment suggests that what Hedy's mimeticism has striven toward is the alteration of Allie (implying a trajectory whose destination is the other, rather than the self), its underlying fantasy bears more of a resemblance to what Jean Laplanche and J.-B. Pontalis call "centrifugal" identification, in which the subject identifies the other with herself, than to Freud's centripetal model, in which the subject identifies herself with the other (Laplanche and Pontalis, *LP,* 206).

Yet insofar as centrifugal identification simply reverses the direction of Freudian identification, Hedy's emulation of Allie evades this categorization as well. While her mimetic behavior does appear aimed toward Allie's transformation, the transformation does not take place after the fashion of Hedy's own self, as a positive entity that can be taken as model. Hedy's emulation of Allie "molds" Allie, in other words, but not based on the model of who Hedy is or could be said to be. For in a crucial and innovative departure from John Lutz's novel, the film dramatically reveals who and what Hedy really is: an identical twin who lost her sister when she drowned at the age of eleven, and hence a person deprived of not just her "double" but her sense of *herself* as a nonsingular or compound female subject.[35] Significantly, Hedy retells the story to Allie to make the loss of nonsingular identity more "original" and even constitutive, situating the moment at birth rather than at the actual childhood accident: "I was *supposed to be* a twin but she was stillborn. I grew up feeling a part of me was missing." In conjunction with its many visual motifs of female doubleness—ranging from an opening shot featuring twin girls applying makeup to each other, to the numerous two-shots depicting Hedy and Allie staring at their own mirrored reflections—the film extravagantly foregrounds this disclosure to suggest that what Hedy ultimately desires is the recovery of this *no longer existent identity.* Hedy's efforts to mold or transform Allie are thus paradoxically based on the model of what Hedy defines herself as lacking. Allie is refashioned

FIGURE 5

not after the example of who Hedy is but who Hedy is *not:* a female twoness, a nonsingular or compound female subject.

In this sense, Hedy's attitude toward Allie does not conform to Freud's notion of identification, involving the transformation of self after the model of the other; yet neither does it conform to Laplanche and Pontalis' notion of centrifugal identification, involving the transformation of the other after the model of the self. For in this case, *neither subject provides the model* for what the emulation produces. Female twoness or nonsingularity, the idealized trait or attribute whereby a partial identification might be established, is indeed the "point of coincidence" between Hedy and Allie, but is a trait that is conspicuously missing. It emerges, paradoxically, only through the process of imitation itself. Prior to Hedy's transformation of Allie by assuming her characteristics, twoness is precisely what both single white females self-consciously lack. This seems particularly true for Hedy, whose identity the film takes pains to define as the negation of twoness.

Where is the exemplary attribute located, then? If mimetic transformation, as it occurs in partial modes of identification, requires the "borrowing" of an attribute from one subject by the other, how can this attribute be "lent" when initially possessed by neither party? Hedy's emulation of Allie does in fact successfully mold *Allie* after the model of female twoness, yet unlike the "openness to a similar emotion" in Freud's scenario, twoness is not a quality that Hedy possesses, and thus does not provide the "significant analogy" by which a partial identification might be established. Rather, the "property" of female twoness becomes a product of the emulation, rather than an existent preceding and informing it. Thus, while Hedy's imitation of Allie depends wholly on literal acts of borrowing (involving jewelry, perfume, skirts, stiletto-heeled pumps, and other explicitly gendered commodities), the transformation of Allie toward which her mimetic behavior aims is paradoxically facilitated through the transfer of a property neither subject owns. If there is a "borrowing" at stake in Hedy's behavior toward Allie, then, it is not the kind of borrowing that for Freud makes partial identifications possible. When he uses the term "borrowing," Freud means "taking," the appropriation of an element belonging to the other for the self's own use. Yet borrowing can also be thought of as a form of receiving, "with the implied or expressed intention of *returning the same or an equivalent*."[36] This secondary definition, which involves the dual actions of receiving and returning rather than the single act of appropriating, suggests that in the case of Hedy and Allie's relationship, the attribute borrowed (twoness) has no existence prior to being returned. To be more specific, the attribute borrowed has no existence prior to being returned as identical to something that the self has already received from the other. If, as suggested earlier, envy involves forms of "unhappy self-assertion" subtended by a negative relationship to property, Hedy's aggressive emulation of Allie ensures that for both

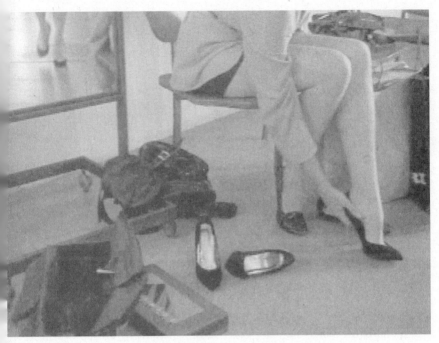

FIGURE 6

subjects, property will be redefined as something constantly transferred and circulated rather than something actually possessed, in
the sense of being traceable back to an original owner.

Given the strange and paradoxical relationship between self-
definition and property that Hedy's emulation produces, it makes
sense that the exchange of material possessions between the two
women becomes a significant source of discomfort for Allie. This
uneasiness about borrowed property is inextricably linked to Allie's
intellectual uncertainty about her status as feminine oneness or
twoness: Am I a single white female, or a nonsingular one? Is my
nonsingular femaleness a property I can actually own? Or is it
something I only receive back from the other as an entity previously lent? Different attitudes toward borrowing become a crucial

site of difference between the film's central characters.[37] In the Freudianism-overloaded scene depicting the purchase of the fetishistic stiletto pumps Hedy will eventually use to pose as Allie, trick Sam into sex, and stab him through the eye afterward, we hear the voices of Hedy and Allie over a close-up of their legs, both wearing identical shoes.

> *Hedy:* Hey, what do you think?
> *Allie:* I think YOU should get them.
> *Hedy:* Oh god, do YOU like them?
> *Allie:* Well, I think they go with that dress.
> *Hedy:* You take them.
> *Allie:* Well . . .
> *Hedy:* I'll just borrow them when I want to.[38]

The initial conflict over who will end up owning the shoes is dispelled by Hedy's encouragement that Allie should take them, while confidently asserting her own right to receiving and returning them. This claim is met with no objection. In the very next scene, however, when Allie is awkwardly caught rifling through Hedy's possessions in Hedy's room and Hedy attempts to ease the tension by saying, "Anything of mine you want is yours, go ahead: share and share alike," Allie's response is notably hesitant.[39] She explains or attempts to legitimate this hesitation by reasserting her status as a female oneness: "But I don't really know about that. I'm an only child." It is at this point that Hedy reveals her own undesired female oneness—but by defining it solely in terms of the *loss* of a female twoness, she implicitly links her propensity for borrowing and lending property to the very attribute or property she defines herself as lacking. Compound femaleness is a property Hedy does not herself possess and thus cannot lend, but that she nonetheless endeavors to "return" to Allie—retroactively constituting Allie as the owner or original possessor of a property that subsequently *can* be "lent." A radically negative relationship to property thus subtends the forms of negative yet forceful self-assertion enabled through Hedy's mimetic behavior.

Thus, if a fantasy is being expressed through Hedy's mimeticism, it cannot be described as Hedy's identification with Allie, as Brinks and Paulin suggest: "She desires *to be, to be like,* or *to become* Allie"; "It is clear that Hedy identifies with Allie as an ideal, that she . . . 'wants to be her.'" Nor, according to Freud's criteria, can it even be described as a partial or limited identification, since this depends on a notion of "borrowed attributes" presupposing prior ownership of the property transferred. In fact, if identification is a fantasy that constitutes who one is, Hedy's mimetic and envious behavior seems motivated by the *undoing* of identification, since the event her emulation strives toward, imagines, or phantasmatically stages is the *other's* transformation after the fashion of what the self is *not*.[40] In its goal of escaping or undoing female singularity, Hedy's fantasy might be described as a fantasy of female compoundedness. As such, it bespeaks a desire to redefine "femaleness" as what Freud calls "group feeling." Throughout *Group Psychology,* Freud says group feeling derives from a social organization that begins with and can be limited to two members, a point enabling him to use twosomes throughout his book as allegorical representations of group formations as a whole.

Though Freud's essay and Schroeder's film both create fictional accounts of female homosociality that emphasize its negative emotional dimensions, they use the affective configurations they establish to offer very different arguments about the relationship between identification and emulation, as well as about how this relationship consolidates gender roles and produces "group feeling." In Freud's schoolgirls scenario, envy or jealousy-motivated imitation is depicted as highly conducive to the *formation* of feminine identifications. In *Single White Female,* however, envious imitation results in the reversal of these identifications—that is, in fantasies about a female other that take that other, or an attribute she possesses, as a model or example to be imitated—insofar as the imitation is shown to *paradoxically undo that other's exemplarity*. Hedy's copying of Allie ensures that Allie will become replicable, much like the mass-produced clothes she wears and the fashion software programs she designs. Yet unlike these items, what Allie becomes cannot be described as a copy *of* or *after* some previously established or positively existing model. We could say that Hedy's envious emulation of Allie transforms Allie into an imitation without an original, but it is perhaps more interesting to formulate this another way: in envying and imitating Allie, Hedy is able to transform Allie into an example—something that appears "after the fashion" of a category already defined—*voided of its exemplarity*. Allie becomes an example that does not exemplify—a particular instance or manifestation of X (female twoness or compoundedness) that does not refer "back" to X as a value already in place. In other words, in being emulated, Allie comes to embody and exemplify a standard that cannot be positively defined or located—that has no ontological coherence or consistency—prior to its exemplification. Hedy's behavior turns Allie into a compound subject precisely by making her into a *bad example*.

Yet the compound subjectivity Allie comes to embody by means of Hedy's emulation is revealed to be unstable, and (the ending of the movie proves) impermanent. As Paulin notes, "What the film's title reflects is an endpoint, and the fundamental work of the film is to produce the 'single white female' we are promised" ("SSG," 33). The conclusion thus reinstates the situation with which the film begins. Hedy, self-defined as a subject painfully lacking or missing compound subjectivity, dies through her paradoxical efforts to "borrow" it. And Allie, also initially and painfully singular, but temporarily transformed into an example of female twoness or compoundedness through Hedy's mimetic behavior, ultimately kills the borrower who has been "returning" the attribute to her. In doing so, Allie ends the cycle of receiving and returning that has paradoxically *generated* the attribute, and reverts back to her original singularity.

Yet despite this endpoint, in which female singleness regains precedence over compoundedness by means of an emulator's violent elimination ("screwed" and "stabbed in the back" with a screwdriver, as it were), *Single White Female*'s story about female homosociality and ugly feelings raises important questions about aggression, gender, and group formation that fully pertain to the conflicts—and the conflicts about the political value of conflict—in feminism today. At the very least, the film's violence demonstrates what seems like an almost obvious point: while identifications and female identifications in particular may be mimetic, imitation does not require or presuppose identification; in fact, it can actively strive to reverse and undo identifications, ensuring their failure or even preempting their formation. By insisting on the difference between identification and emulation in the context of a complex female-female relationship, *Single White Female* enables us to see how not identifying might be the enabling condition for female homosociality, rather than an obstruction to it.[41] If aggressive acts of not identifying can play as active a role as identification in facilitating the transition from single to group femaleness, this usefully highlights the primary and (as Chantal Mouffe and Ernesto Laclau and others have argued) even constitutive importance of antagonism to collective political formations such as that of feminism.

Since the film depicts envy in terms of a transition from admiration to antagonism, we could also argue that envy enables a strategic way of *not* identifying which, in facilitating and ensuring this very transition, preserves a critical agency whose loss is threatened by full-blown idealization of the attribute admired. In this sense, it could be said that a subject might envy and emulate not just as a safeguard against fully identifying herself with the quality emulated—say, "femininity"—but precisely in order to convert her admiration into polemicism, qua critical force or agency. Envy's critical potential thus resides in its ability to highlight a refusal to idealize quality *X,* even an ability to attack its potential for idealization by transforming *X* into something nonsingular and replicable, while at the same time enabling acknowledgment of its culturally imposed desirability.

In Melanie Klein's "Envy and Gratitude" (1957), it is precisely the idealized object that gives rise to envy and is attacked and spoiled. Klein also describes primal envy as a form of deproprietorization or theft, in which the envier robs the object of what it possesses: "In both male and female, envy plays a part in the desire to take away the attributes of the other sex, as well as to . . . spoil those of the parent of the same sex" ("EG," 201). Significantly, envy is further viewed as underlying all forms of "destructive criticism," including in particular any distrust, skepticism, or contestation of the analyst's interpretations on the part of the analysand ("EG," 184). In this theory of envious aggression as critical aggression, or as a refusal to assimilate without contesting an authority figure's interpretations ("EG," 184), the ideal or good object envied and phantasmatically attacked is attacked precisely because it *is* idealized and good—as if the real source of antagonism is less the object than idealization itself.[42] It is important to note here that in envying the good object, the Kleinian infant ultimately seeks to transform it by phantasmatically disfiguring or spoiling it, hence rendering it something no longer desirable, as well as something that can no longer be possessed.[43] Significantly, Klein also suggests that such envious attacks are both accompanied and intensified by the subject's belief that the idealized object is a source of persecution; hence, the envied breast becomes a "devouring" breast. But if envy thus enables the subject to formulate the assertion, *"This idealized object persecutes me,"* might we not interpret Hedy's aggression toward the idealized, singular white femininity Allie initially embodies, or her envious effort to transform it into some form of compoundedness, as an attempt to forcefully put forth a similar proposition? That is, an attempt to identify that particular feminine ideal, one functioning as property whose possession can be claimed, as a persecutory, devouring, or brutally assimilating one?

This approach to envy—which Freud suggests, toward the end

of *Group Psychology,* is an *inevitable* factor in group formation—
bears some interesting applications with respect to aspects of being
feminist that are "actively lived and felt" and thus run the risk of
"not [being] recognized as social, but taken to be private, idiosyncratic, and even isolating."[44] Let's say there is a certain model of
femininity that I recognize as culturally desirable and invested with
a certain degree of power. If from a feminist standpoint what I
struggle with most is my having been acculturated into admiring
and desiring that femininity, envy would seem to enable me to critically negotiate rather than simply disavow or repudiate this desire,
which would entail positing myself as immune to acculturation.
Moreover, envy would facilitate a transition from desire to antagonism that might enable me to articulate what I have been trained to
admire as something possibly threatening or harmful to me. As
Klein notes, it is only once the ideal object is envied that it becomes
viewed as persecutory—a view that in turn mobilizes the subject's
efforts to criticize and transform it, and transform its value or status as property in particular, spoiling it and "rob[bing] it of what it
possesses" ("EG," 188).[45]

While Freud's dramatization of jealousy in "Identification" reinforces the suggestion that femaleness—the concept that is feminism's inaugurative yet most contentious point of reference—may
be structured like an example, in *Single White Female* envying becomes a way of stripping this "example" of its exemplarity, demonstrating that one's status as a particular embodiment of a general
principle can take place without the principle's being determined in
advance. This obstinate paradox, I would argue, offers a viable and
compelling way of approaching feminist "group feeling." For if the
concept enabling our sense of ourselves as a collective is actively
produced by its various bad and good embodiments, rather than
preestablished as a quality for us to passively mold ourselves after
or secondarily reflect, the concept becomes more plastic and viable
for transformation—though indeed more unstable, as Schroeder's
film demonstrates. Yet what the film fails to demonstrate is that

this instability can actually constitute the concept's political agency and force. For while it guarantees that the unifying principle *X,* or membership condition of group *X,* will always be in flux, this flux is more likely to be determined by the members themselves—produced by group *X's* bad or unexemplary examples, rather than fostered or imposed by its outside. Hence, if (as Wiegman argues) there is to be a productive "transition from the critique of patriarchal masculinism to internal struggle within feminism," a transition in which we shift from a mode of critique "embroiled, indeed embattled, in a heterosexual paradigm in which women's relationships to men are centrally interrogated" to one that is "fundamentally a homosocial circuit in which feminism signifies from the conflicted terrain of relations among women" ("SO," 363), the affective dimension of feminism, including all its ugly feelings, needs be to taken far more seriously than it has been so far.

It is crucial to note that near the conclusion of *Group Psychology,* in "The Herd Instinct" (chapter 11), Freud says envy in fact *precedes* the establishment of identifications that enable group formation, suggesting that ultimately "social feeling is based upon *the reversal of what was first a hostile feeling* into a positively-toned tie" (*GP,* 67, italics added). If Hedy's aggressive emulation of Allie suggests that envy produces compound or nonsingular subjects by reversing or undoing identifications, Freud's thesis here is that the identifications on which group formations depend are only secondarily established through a reversal of envy. Thus, envy oddly emerges as primary in the production of "group feeling," which results only after the subject, in the face of cultural disapproval, comes to recognize "the impossibility of his maintaining his hostile attitude without damaging himself" and is subsequently *forced* (the verb is Freud's) "into identifying himself with [others]." The subject's identification-based sense of collective belonging emerges only after he is forced to give up his ugly feeling: "What appears later on in society in the shape of *Gemeingeist, esprit de corps,* 'group spirit,' etc., does not belie *its derivation from what was originally envy*" (*GP,* 67; italics added). The example Freud chooses to support this argument once again involves a group of women and girls—this time in terms of their too close, too mimetic, and hence too "feminine" relation to popular culture:

> This transformation—the replacing of jealousy by a group feeling in the nursery and classroom—might be considered improbable, if the same process could not later on be observed again in other circumstances. We only have to think of the troop of women and girls, all of them in love in an enthusiastically sentimental way, who crowd around a singer or pianist after his performance. It would certainly be easy for each of them to be jealous of the rest; but, in the face of their numbers and the consequent impossibility of their reaching the aim of their love, they renounce it, and, instead of pulling out one another's hair, they act as a united group, do homage to the hero of the occasion with their common actions, and would probably be glad to have a share of *his* flowing locks. Originally rivals, they have succeeded in identifying themselves with one another by means of a similar love for the same object. (*GP,* 66)

The language of the passage suggests that Freud's initial, gender-neutral examples of primal envy—sibling rivalry and dynamics in "the nursery and classroom"—may have struck him as lending inadequate support to his theory. It is as if in order to make the thesis of envy's primary role in the production of "social feeling" *truly convincing,* Freud needs to introduce the image of a female throng or multitude, the quasi-militaristic "troop of women and girls." The best or most effective example again seems to be a feminine example—which brings us back to how Hedy's envious emulation of Allie provides a way of critically negotiating her relation to femininity *as* exemplarity.

If a bad example is an example that destabilizes the argument it is supposed to bolster, or constitutes the idea it is merely supposed to reflect, it could be argued that *all* examples are potentially bad examples, "harbor[ing] terrible powers of deviation and digression."[46] In Richardson's novel, we can see a certain logic behind the fact that the myriad descriptions of Clarissa as an "example to her sex" are equaled in number only by references to her as a "perverse girl," as if to suggest that what is most perverse about Clarissa is her exemplarity itself. As Hillis Miller writes, "The choice of examples . . . and their ordering, is never innocent. Does not my choice of examples load the dice, predetermine the conclusions I can reach and, like all examples, in fact form the essence of the argument it is apparently only meant to exemplify?"[47] Similarly, Andrzej Warminski shows how G. W. F. Hegel's attempt to explain the difference between an idea and its example—as the difference between a primary and active, and a secondary and passive mode of representation—actually rests on the *use* of a example, reversing the roles he initially assigns them.[48] Hedy's aggressive emulation of Allie produces a similar reversal, turning Allie into an example of a general principle or property (female nonsingularity or compoundedness) that has no existence *prior* to its exemplification, and thus cannot be said to be reflected secondarily. In this sense, Hedy's mimetic behavior suggests that when the production of nonsingular or compound identity is at stake, the best kind of examples are always the bad ones. This in turn suggests that bad examples of *X* might be good for group *X,* since they compel its members to constantly question, reevaluate, and even redefine what it is that they supposedly exemplify.

While we have seen Miller's observation that a theorist's choice of examples "is never innocent" borne out in Freud's "Identification," exemplarity may not always be a choice. Once a group has fought for and attained a certain degree of political recognition, the demand that its members be "good examples" can easily turn repressive, especially when the demand emanates from outside rather than from within. This imperative often takes the following form: "You, having declared yourself an example of *X*—perhaps in the initial struggle to secure social recognition and visibility for *X*—

must now *exemplify* X as a fixed concept which you merely refer back to or reflect." A corollary of this logic would be the following: "In your failure to adequately exemplify *X*, you threaten the validity and legitimacy of *X*, as well as any group formation or collective identity based on *X*." To use Gubar's metaphor, the implication is that a group becomes "sick" when its members become examples that do not properly exemplify. This assumption that collective strength depends on good exemplarity bears a close resemblance to the concept of the ego ideal that Freud develops in *Group Psychology,* as well as the common assumption that one must identify with whatever one emulates or strives toward. All suppose that collectives are formed on the basis of models established *in advance* for the purpose of being imitated, and that it is a shared relation to an established model that secures the identification of individuals with one another—which in turn leads to the formation of groups. Yet while having to exemplify can be a demand imposed, even violently imposed, on members of a group from those seeking to define and control its parameters from without, being an example can be a site of change from within. One acknowledges or declares oneself an example of *X,* a "real particular case" among numerous other cases, precisely in order to make and shape what *X* is.

As a political as well as theoretical discourse, feminism necessarily implies a compound subject, or at the very least a nonsingular one. Indeed, as Wendy Brown suggests, there is an etymological sense in which the making of compound subjects *is* politics, insofar as the ancient Greek term *politeia* designates "the singularly human practice of constituting a particular mode of collective life."[49] The political act of feminist group formation thus entails producing "group feeling," though not necessarily the antagonism-free, identification-based "group feeling" nostalgically mourned in "What Ails Feminist Criticism?" It would be ludicrous to suggest, of course, that feminist collectivity should be literally modeled on the affective relations depicted in *Single White Female,* or any other film depicting "women's friendships as plagued by jealousy [and] envy."[50] *Single White Female* is clearly a bad example of female homosociality, since its final reaffirmation of oneness depicts the desingularized female subject as threatening, destructive, and ultimately untenable. But however and in whatever way bad, the film's unusual account of how compound subjects *might* be formed provides an interesting alternative to Freud's more popular model of social and political organization in *Group Psychology,* where group formation ultimately depends on identifications of individuals with one another based on a mutually shared model already established and in place. In contrast, the film mobilizes envy to demonstrate the capacity of female subjects to form coalitions based on something other than "similar love for the same object," to emulate attributes without identifying with them, and to function as examples that do not properly exemplify, actively defining and redefining the category they would seem only to passively reflect (Freud, *GP,* 66). What is most surprising and interesting about *Single White Female* with respect to how we approach conflict within feminism today is how it depicts female compoundedness as actively strengthened through these disidentificatory and antiproprietory practices, if not directly by the ugly feeling that inspires them.

Indeed, since here the compound subject is produced not by making two into one (as in the case of what Gubar takes to be Butler's symptomatically bad grammar), but rather by making one into two, *Single White Female* could be said to allegorize the state of contemporary feminism as internally divided or split, yet *held together* by this very split. We have seen how the transformation of one into two, exacerbating the confusion between identification and mimesis already perpetuated by Freud's "feminine" examples, is presented by the film in terms of the paradox of exemplarity itself. In an essay that examines the work of exemplarity in the concept of genre, Derrida describes this paradox as follows: "The trait which marks membership inevitably divides, the boundary of the set comes to form, *by invagination,* an internal pocket larger than the whole; and the outcome of this division and of this abounding

FIGURE 7

remains as singular as it is limitless."[51] With this strikingly anatomical word choice on the part of a philosopher scrupulously attentive
to language, the logic of exemplarity that subtends the "law of
genre" once again seems strangely susceptible to feminization. But
in a much more surprising fashion, *Single White Female* seems not
only to understand the division and doubling that produces compound subjects in terms of "bad exemplarity," but also to present it
in terms of the racial divide we have seen Gubar discuss, with respect to contemporary feminism, at the beginning of this chapter.

Here we are finally confronted with one of the most puzzling
aspects of *Single White Female*. Why is the detail of whiteness
foregrounded in the film's title, when the issue of race seems so
conspicuously *not* taken up by the film as whole?[52] Indeed, why

does Allie oddly describe herself as white—"SWF seeks female to share apartment in west 70s"—in an advertisement not for a sexual or romantic partner (where the specification of race has become a convention), but for a roommate?[53] Allie's specification of her own race seems all the more gratuitous, given that in a yet another telling departure from Lutz's *SWF Seeks Same, Single White Female* is careful to present Allie as "color-blind," indifferent to the race (if not the gender) of the roommate she seeks. The reference to race thus comes across as irritating, an unessential element inexplicably highlighted, but then just as inexplicably dropped from the story once Allie chooses Hedy over the other candidates she interviews (one of whom is in fact a woman of color) and the film becomes exclusively focused on the relationship between the two women played by white actresses.[54] This is, of course, a homosocial relationship most visibly marked by class difference—as is the case in Patricia Highsmith's more widely known novel about male envy and emulation, *The Talented Mr. Ripley.*[55] Yet in striking contrast to the *vast* class difference between the envious male protagonist and the man he aggressively emulates in *The Talented Mr. Ripley,* a text to which Lutz's suspense novel explicitly invites comparison by invoking the "Highsmith tradition" on its jacket, the social distance here is the relatively minor one between a middle-class computer programmer and a lower middle-class clerk employed at an bookstore—both of whom live in the same apartment, pay the same amount of rent, and can more or less afford the same shoes.[56] In both the novel and the film, these relatively minor class differences are presented as disturbingly easy to mask simply by the acquisition of the right female commodities, which exemplify undifferentiation itself: "Everyone's basic black dress was like someone else's" (Lutz, *SWF,* 158). The self-solicited comparison to *Mr. Ripley*—the male version of *Single White Female*'s story of female envy and emulation—is especially revealing here, since it suggests that among women, even slight and supposedly easy-to-disguise differences in socioeconomic status lead almost immediately to hyperbolic conflict and violence, whereas they need to be enormous to culminate in violence between men. The difference between the scale of the class differences that set off the aggressive mimetic behavior in *Single White Female* and *Mr. Ripley,* not only exaggerates the pettiness of female envy in contrast to male envy (reinforcing the feminization of the emotion in general), but contributes to the stereotype of women as unusually prone to envious hatred of other women in particular. This is precisely the stereotype which Gubar rightly worries that feminism's hostile outside might exploit, and which her critique of internal feminist conflict drawn along racial lines is pitted against.

Though female conflict is obviously *Single White Female*'s central preoccupation, we have seen how its reference to race irritatingly persists, like the whine of a mosquito, even as the film draws attention to the supposed ease with which class differences between white women can be socially masked simply by the acquisition of the right commodities: a better haircut, better shoes. But what if we take Hedy, the female character of unspecified race sought by a woman who oddly calls attention to her own whiteness, as performing a kind of "darkface" in reverse? That is, if we see Hedy as a woman of color in whiteface, an "other" appearing to Allie under the cover of the "same"? This reading not only accounts for the disconcerting way in which racial difference seems simultaneously extraneous and central to *Single White Female,* but reveals another motivation for the film's insistence that Hedy's mimetic behavior cannot be confused with an identification or desire for adequation with the woman she emulates (in this case, a woman who describes herself as white). Instead, as we have noted, Hedy's emulation of Allie is presented as a form of aggressive *self*-assertion. It is thus interesting to speculate how *Single White Female* might or might not have been a very different movie if the actress playing Hedy had been a woman of color—say, the contemporary performance artist

FIGURE 8

Nikki Lee, whose work on the aesthetics of "imperfect doubles" has focused precisely on the question of how race complicates the politics of group affiliation.

But let me suggest, in a final turn of the screw (or, in the spirit of the film, the screwdriver), that "race" in *Single White Female,* already visible only by means of its conspicuous nonpresence in the story, is itself a signifier for a struggle based on a distinction in social class—and what is more, a signifier for a class envy or antagonism that cannot be entirely dissipated through economic mobility, or that remains resistant to being reconciled through the mere acquisition of property. Here *Single White Female* simply follows the lead of American popular culture, in its longstanding preference and well-demonstrated facility for imagining this kind of class antagonism—that is, *irreconcilable* class antagonism—in terms of race *rather* than class. If "class" is the term in the series of struggles defined by categories of social difference (race, class, gender, sexuality) that is "simultaneously one of the terms in the series and a structuring principle of the entire series,"[57] "race" names the struggle in which it is most taken for granted that no degree of acquiring what the envied other has—money, education, phallus, or, in the case of *Single White Female*'s story of female-female struggle, the right hairstyle and shoes—will *ever* culminate in the other and one becoming indistinguishable. The peculiar irritation which race might be said to produce in this film about ugly feelings is the explicit focus of the next chapter.

4. irritation

Nella Larsen's 1928 novel *Quicksand,* now well established as a classic of the Harlem Renaissance due to the recovery work of feminist scholars, seems infused with a strange "irritation"—a minor, low-intensity negative affect—at virtually all of its levels. If every literary work has an organizing quality of feeling akin to an "atmosphere," as we have seen critics argue in Chapter 1, *Quicksand*'s famously enigmatic protagonist appears to have a microclimate of her own. While Helga Crane is presented as unusually prone to being irritated by nearly anything around her, we are informed (by *Quicksand*'s mostly covert omniscient narrator), that "[Helga] herself was unconscious of that faint hint of offishness which hung about her and repelled advances . . . that stirred in people *a peculiar irritation.*"[1] The nimbus of "offishness" that both distances Helga *from,* and makes her irritating *to* other characters in the novel, aptly doubles as a description of *Quicksand*'s own affective "atmosphere," as well as of the novel's emotional effects on its audience. As Barbara Johnson notes, "Helga repeatedly reaches states of relative contentment—in Harlem, in Denmark, in Alabama—only to fall into depression again for no obvious reason. Chapter breaks often occur where psychological causation is missing. . . . And it is the difficulty of defining the causes of Helga's suffering that leads to irritation in many readers."[2] Paradoxically conjoining an image of distance or emotional detachment with an image of physical contact or friction, the novel seems to summon the idiom of irritation both to "put us off" and to "rub us the wrong way."

Concentrated in the protagonist's signature aloofness as well as in the withholding of psychological explanations for her actions, "irritation" becomes the index of a more general affective opacity at work throughout *Quicksand,* operating at the level of discourse as well as story, and at the level of reception as well as internal structure and form. As we shall see, the "peculiar irritation" that permeates this novel at so many levels is itself further distinguished by a peculiar "offishness"—though here in the more abstract sense of an incongruity or disproportionality. The "offish" (in the sense of "off-key" or "off the mark") quality that comes to inflect the novel's organizing affect is very much in keeping with the way Aristotle characterizes irritation in the *Nicomachean Ethics:* "Those people we call irritable are those who are irritated *by the wrong things, more severely and for longer than is right.*"[3] In exploring *Quicksand*'s particular investment in this minor and, one might say, inherently "disproportional" feeling, this chapter shifts my book's inquiry into race and affect from the aesthetics of emotional excess or "overscrutability" associated with "animatedness" (Chapter 2), back to the Bartlebyan aesthetics of affective illegibility. And more specifically to what we might call the problem of incorrect or "inadequate" anger.

Indeed, the minor negative affect associated with Helga Crane can be linked to what we might call the "Bartlebyization" of her character in the novel, which "demotes" her from would-be artist or intellectual to a clerical worker with discriminating tastes.[4] After her short stint as a teacher in a Southern vocational college, and prior to working as a secretary for an insurance company in Harlem, Helga is hired by a traveling female lecturer for a job that involves "correcting and condensing" her employer's clichéd speeches on the "race problem." Helga is "galled" by the secretarial position, but accepts with the recognition that "she couldn't afford anger" (*Q,* 35). Her main task involves reorganizing Mrs. Hayes-Rore's irritating "patchworks" (37), which consist of "ideas, phrases, and even whole sentences and paragraphs . . . lifted bodily from . . . Wendell Phillips, Frederick Douglass, Booker T. Washington, and other doctors of the race's ills" (38). This work not only places Helga in the position of Melville's Sub-Sub Librarian (another compiler of "Extracts") but also, as she dutifully "corrects" Mrs. Hayes-Rore's patchy corpus of textual grafts, into that of an accomplice—an act that uncannily anticipates Larsen's own act of assuming "the abject position of plagiarist that ended her career as a writer."[5] Helga Crane's "peculiar irritation" can thus be thought of as the signature affect of the modern Sub-Sub: the "word-worker" or mere "processor" of the language of others who is in many cases also a socially thwarted or obstructed author. Helga Crane has been described as a thwarted artist by most critics of the novel. But while the predominant focus has been on how Helga's artistry is deflected into exercises of aesthetic judgment in interior decorating and fashion, or, in a kind of reverse sublimation which proves much less successful, rechanneled into sexual relationships with men, we might instead read it as more simply being displaced to the social and economic margins of literary culture itself.[6]

Larsen herself worked full-time as a "General Assistant" in the New York Public Library system, both before (1922–1926) and after (1929) the completion of *Quicksand* and *Passing* (1929). During this time she enrolled in the city's Library School, where she took classes in classification, cataloging, reference work, and bibliography. Possibly blocked by racial policies from pursuing a diploma (which would have been necessary for professional advancement to

the positions of curator or administrator), Larsen left the school after receiving a junior certificate, which did allow her to be promoted from "grade 1" to "grade 2" in the library's tiered personnel
system, with a raise from $82.66 to $109.75 a month.[7] Larsen's wage
labor as a librarian actually marks an intermediate phase between
her remarkably short-lived career as a novelist and an earlier career
in nursing, which Larsen would resume permanently in the wake
of the plagiarism scandal that put an end to her career as a writer
only months after she was awarded a Guggenheim Fellowship in
1930. There is thus a sense in which Larsen's time at the library enabled her to make a "transition" of sorts—from working with ill
bodies, to working with words on "race's ills."[8] In what follows, we
will see these two images—diseased body and racially dis-eased
corpus—twist together in *Quicksand*'s organizing concept of irritation.

The idiom of "irritation" that dominates *Quicksand* actually enables
the novel to address two significant impasses in the criticism which
surrounds it. The first emerges from the tension between two
aesthetic positions at the heart of literary modernism: the claim to a
racially *distinctive* aesthetic, as advanced by many of the Harlem
Renaissance's most prominent artists and critics under the political
rubric of "uplift"; and the aestheticization of racial difference itself, as promoted not only by European artists attracted to the aesthetics of primitivism but by African American artists as well.
Indeed, as Michael North argues, the aestheticization of "blackness" in particular became a way for artists of all races in the early
decades of the twentieth century to secure their credentials as
modernists.[9] Institutionally, Larsen's novel can be seen as framed
by these clashing but also occasionally intersecting attitudes about
race and aesthetics. The novel's publication by Albert A. Knopf
came about partly through the patronage of Carl Van Vechten, a
close friend of Larsen's to whom she would dedicate her second

novel, *Passing* (1929), but most widely known for his exotic portrayal of Harlem residents in the 1926 bestseller *Nigger Heaven*. At the same time, *Quicksand*'s critical success was informed by W. E. B. Du Bois's praise of the novel (in a *Crisis* review comparing Larsen's "delicately woven plot" to the "glaring colors" of Claude McKay's 1928 *Home to Harlem*) for strengthening the category of a literature distinctive to and exemplary of "Negro America," while refusing to "cater [to] that prurient demand on the part of white folk" for an equivocally beatified or aestheticized blackness.[10]

Given that *Quicksand* was caught in a battle between aesthetic claims advanced by a white modernist (Van Vechten) who described himself as "violently interested in Negroes" and a black modernist (Du Bois) who described the white's interest as "a blow in the face," the first problem that the novel's idiom of irritation will allow us to address is one related to the book's historical reception.[11] The second problem, however, relates to the contemporary critical discourse surrounding Larsen's novel, which since the 1980s has turned *Quicksand* into one of those texts for which there seems to be a single, if not unpersuasive, reading. While expressive gaps or discontinuities are often cited to bolster the aesthetic credentials of other modernist novels (say, by Hemingway and Faulkner), these same gaps in *Quicksand*—famous, as we have seen, for its refusal to provide explanations for Helga's mood swings or their dramatic consequences for the novel's jagged plot—have tended to be treated less under the aesthetic rubric of formal innovation than under the psychological rubric of "repression." Most critics of the novel have not used the term in a Freudian sense, but have relied instead on a popularized version, in which "repression" more simply refers to an absence or deficit of expression, and "expression" is implicitly identified with liberation. Hence, the reading of *Quicksand* which has come to inform nearly all analyses of the novel, regardless of the individual critic's stance or methodology, takes the novel's emotional blank spots as a sign of Helga's "unacknowledged sexuality." This repression is perceived to ensue directly from her entrapment between two equally disabling models of selfhood: the construction of the black woman as hypersexualized primitive (an image promulgated by certain kinds of modernism) and middle-class ideals of chaste "ladyhood" (promulgated by the genteel, nineteenth-century American tradition of sentimental "mulatta" fiction from which *Quicksand* consciously departs).[12] In strenuously attempting to avoid both of these dubious identifications, which clearly correspond to the primitivism-versus-uplift "binarism in which the African-American novel of the time found itself trapped," Helga tragically sinks.[13] Yet there are aspects of Larsen's language which suggest that *Quicksand* cannot be reduced to a story about an African-American woman's sexual or emotional hangups. To say this is not to argue against a reading of the novel as a demonstration of "the psychological costs of racism and sexism,"[14] but rather to extend the meaning of what such costs entail, and to explore their implications beyond a critical framework in which an ideal of "total intelligibility" is posited as the antidote to repression (and, as such, a guaranteed pathway to psychic and social freedom).[15]

In fact, the lack of precipitating causes for Helga's restlessness seems in keeping more with the logic of irritation than with that of repression. For irritation is a mood, distinct from emotion in that it lacks an explicit occasion or object. As Annette Baier notes, "Emotions . . . are about *something,* not everything, while moods, if they are about anything, seem to be about nearly everything."[16] For this reason, "we can ask what makes a person depressed, solemn, irritable . . . and sometimes get an answer, but the answer need not tell us what they are depressed about, what occasion they are solemnizing, [or] what irritates them. . . . Moods are either objectless, or have near all-inclusive and undifferentiated objects. They sometimes involve emotions searching for appropriate objects."[17] The formal or structural problem of inexplicit psychological causation is thus strikingly similar to the state of irritation itself. In fact, Baier's definition of mood as an emotion searching for an "appropriate object" doubles beautifully as a description of *Quicksand*'s plot. Structured by Helga's abrupt but unexplained relocations from one subculture or community to another, the novel's sharp turns seem driven entirely by the quest to assign an "about something" to its protagonist's psychic life.

What is most noticeable about irritation in *Quicksand* is not only its insistent presence in a novel where psychological motivations for the heroine's actions are generally withheld (leading to what one *Opportunity* reviewer in 1928 described as the "incompleteness" of Helga's characterization) but the variety of contexts in which it appears—contexts ranging from the very inconsequential to the very serious.[18] We find Helga repeatedly "irritated," "galled," "exasperated," or "annoyed" by things like "the smell of stale food and ancient tobacco" on a train, and "the thick cups and the queer dark silver" in the dining room of a Chicago YWCA, which irritate Helga so much that she ends up eating at a restaurant despite having no money to spare (*Q*, 25, 48, 31). Here, in suggesting an overdetermined responsiveness to her environment or hyperactive judgment of taste, Helga's irritation seems closely related to the "nervousness" that late nineteenth-century physicians associated with the heightened sensitivities of the dandy, the intellectual, and the "overly civilized" person in general.[19]

Unattractive teacups seem relatively appropriate as the object of a weak feeling like irritation. Yet we find Helga responding identically to situations that seem more weighty. These include an incident Helga remembers as the "annoying . . . affair," in which a white preacher who has been invited to speak at Naxos (the black vocational college in which we first encounter Helga, employed as a teacher) urges the black audience "to stay in their places." "He spoke of his great admiration for the Negro race, no other race in so short a time had made so much progress, but he had urgently besought them to know where and when to stop" (*Q*, 3). Though it is clear that Helga perceives the racism of the speech and is sensitive to her institution's complicity with its message (and she does later recall the moment with much stronger emotions), her initial response to the relived incident is rendered in language identical to the language describing her dissatisfaction with the teacups: "The day had been more than usually crowded with distasteful encounters and stupid perversities. . . . And annoying beyond all other happenings had been that affair of the noon period, now again thrusting on her already irritated mind" (2).

In another weighted moment that would seem to incite a much stronger response than Helga's signature irritation, she recognizes the real motives underlying the generosity of one of her closest family members: "In his contemptuous way [Uncle Peter] was fond of her. . . . Even so, Helga Crane knew he would be more likely to help her because her need would strengthen his oft-repeated conviction that because of her Negro blood she would never amount to anything, than from motives of affection or loving memory. This knowledge, in its present aspect of truth, irritated her to an astonishing degree" (*Q*, 6). It is ironically the superficiality of irritation, in this and many other racially charged moments in the novel, that makes it conspicuous; indeed, what seems most "astonishing" is less the "degree" of Helga's irritation than the response itself. In fact, irritation and its close relations—bother, annoyance, vexation, aggravation, pique—might be described as negative affect in its weakest, mildest, and most politically effete form. One is tempted to vote it the dysphoric affect least likely to play a significant role in any oppositional praxis or ideological struggle—including the "sub-cutaneous propaganda" Alain Locke praised as circulating under the aesthetic veneer of Van Vechten's controversial *Nigger Heaven,* or the "propaganda" Du Bois famously embraced as a site and stake of struggle for African-American artists to whom art's entitlement to polemicism was denied.[20]

Drawing from Aristotle's analyses of anger in *Rhetoric* and the

Nicomachean Ethics, Philip Fisher notes that "anger in its legitimate form has its source in the . . . perception of injustice."[21] The observation that justice conversely requires anger, and cannot be imposed solely by reason, underscores the passion's centrality to political struggles throughout history—a point also made provocatively by Audre Lorde.[22] Yet while numerous thinkers have valued anger for its connections to justice, its *justifiability* seems always in question. It is therefore not just any person, but "the person who is angry at the right things and towards the right people, and also in the right way, at the right time and for the right length of time," whom Aristotle praises.[23] The emphasis on proportionality and correctness clearly raises the specter of the person angry in the wrong ways and at the wrong times, a topic that Aristotle goes on to address. As Fisher notes, "The capacity for correct anger is, like each of Aristotle's virtues, positioned between two equally negative extremes, one an excess, the other a defect. The excess of anger is obviously the bad-tempered or irascible man. . . . But it is the defective extreme of anger, for which we have no word, that excites Aristotle's close attention. The in-irascible man *does not feel anger when he should*" (*VP,* 173, italics added). Irritated as much by tarnished silver and badly designed teacups as by the racism of her closest family member, Helga Crane seems a perfect example of this in-irascible person. Yet Aristotle, in the *Nicomachean Ethics,* classifies irritability not as one of anger's deficiencies but as one of its excesses—"The people we call irritable are those who are irritated by the wrong things, *more severely and for longer* than is right" (*NE,* 106, emphasis added). What this seeming contradiction makes clear is that Helga's irritation is *both* an excess and a deficiency of anger: in response to the memory of the white preacher's racism, she does not seem sufficiently angry; in response to clunky china and bad smells, she seems far too angry. As an insistently *inadequate* reaction, one occurring only in conspicuous surplus or deficit in proportion to its occasion, Helga's irritation marks the very opposite of "having the *correct* capacity for anger" (*VP,* 175, italics added).

Though Aristotle's term for the in-irascible person is "slave" or "fool," persons who do not become angry in situations where we expect them to are, in our day, more likely to be described as "repressed." There is thus a sense in which the predominance of irritation actually seems in keeping with the popularized concept of repression most critics appeal to in order to explain or account for *Quicksand*'s formal gaps and elisions. These range from the surprising lack of a psychological elaboration that would help us understand "the self-defeating or self-exhausting nature of Helga's choices" (as Barbara Johnson notes) to what Linda Dittmar describes as the text's general "reluctance to utter" at the level of individual sentences (*WWA*, 145).[24] Dittmar explicitly mobilizes the concept of repression to account for this expressive deficiency: "Combining factual reporting and stylistic repression, [Larsen's] writing signals a struggle to inhibit emotion" (145). Dittmar locates this inhibition in Larsen's own "historically constituted 'positionality' as a black woman . . . writing about racism from a position of personal ambivalence and within a social context that inhibits protest" (145). Hence, the inhibition of emotion in Larsen's writing mirrors Helga's psychological illegibility, as well as the emotional inhibition characterizing the middle-class black culture to which Larsen belonged. Novel, protagonist, and author are thus all characterized, in one way or another, as repressed.

It's tempting to read *Quicksand*'s irritated style and thematics as supplying further evidence for this interpretation, since the superficial affect often seems invoked to mask or strategically distance Helga from deeper emotions she seems unwilling to express.[25] But if one of the things that makes Helga's irritation striking is its off-putting superficiality, it is worth noting that the minor and inconsequential status of this affect is in fact integral to its colloquial definition. Before offering synonyms for the term "irritation," for instance, a typical thesaurus asks the user to make a choice between "mild anger" (versus "anger") and "soreness."[26] This semantic fork sheds further light on irritation's conspicuous insufficiency—and, one is tempted to say, inappropriateness—as an emotional response to most of what Helga experiences in *Quicksand*. For the split between the bodily sensation that is "soreness" and the emotional quality that is "mild anger" foregrounds irritation's liminality or instability *as* an emotional response. Whether "irritation" is defined as an emotional or physical experience, synonyms for it tend to apply equally to psychic life *and* life at the level of the body—and particularly to its surfaces or skin. In addition to "inflammation," "rawness," and "chafing," for example, "irritation" qua "soreness" also signifies "hypersensitivity," "susceptibility," and "tenderness," words with explicitly affective dimensions easily turned, as we have seen, into signifiers of social distinction in the late nineteenth-century discourse of "nerves." Conversely, one of the synonyms for "irritation" qua "mild anger"—namely, "aggravation"—carries the implication of worsening or worrying a wound or sore, with "sore" itself signifying both a condition of the skin or body (an ulcer, abrasion, or inflammation) and, in twentieth-century slang, a state of indignation or resentment. Irritation's marginal status thus seems related to the ease with which it always threatens to slip out of the realm of emotional experience altogether, into the realm of physical or epidermal sensations. In doing so, it calls up Frantz Fanon's self-conscious use of a cutaneous metaphor to *replace* "internalization" in his analysis of racism's psychological effects: "If there is an inferiority complex in [the black subject], it is the outcome of a double process: primarily, economic; subsequently, the internalization—or, better, the epidermalization—of this inferiority."[27]

Yet the blur between psychic and corporeal (or internal and external) experience that "irritation" produces comes most to the fore in descriptions of the emotional life of *Quicksand*'s protagonist—for example, "The smell of stale food and tobacco irritated Helga like a physical pain" (*Q*, 25). Here "irritation" is first presented as an emotional response to a bodily sensation ("smell"), but then becomes elaborated, *as* an emotional response, by a simile comparing it to the sensation of bodily pain. The closeness of the two meanings of "irritation" becomes similarly evident in references to Helga's "*lacerated* pride," during a conversation in which the principal of Naxos mistakenly assumes her to be a member of the black middle class; to her "*pricked* . . . self-assurance," when she suspects that her Danish suitor's hesitation in proposing marriage is a result of her blackness; and to her "*stinging* hurt," when she is turned away at the door by her white step-aunt in Chicago. It surfaces most of all in Helga's description of herself as "an obscene *sore*" in the lives of her white relations, one "at all costs to be hidden."[28] All of these allusions to a bodily surface that is lacerated, pricked, stinging, or sore are used to describe Helga's emotional responses to situations in which racial and class differences are explicitly at stake. But while Helga's status as an "obscene sore" is specifically depicted as a problem for her white family, it poses an equal problem for the black bourgeoisie: "Negro society, she had learned, was as complicated and as rigid in its ramifications as the highest strata of white society. . . . You could be queer, or even attractive, or bad, or brilliant, . . . if you were a Rankin, or a Leslie, or a Scoville. . . . But if you were plain Helga Crane, of whom nobody had ever heard, it was presumptuous of you to be anything but *inconspicuous and comfortable*" (*Q,* 8). It is hard to imagine a more perfect antithesis for the "inconspicuous and comfortable" than the highly noticeable site of physical discomfort posed by an "obscene sore." As a strangely cutaneous feeling located on the border between emotional and bodily experience, and thus "superficial" in more ways than one, Helga's irritation often (and unsurprisingly) comes off as an inadequate response to situations which, in a novel that makes questions of race and class central, would seem apt to provoke something "deeper."

To pursue this issue further, we can return to the context in which Helga's irritation is first compared to a "physical pain," when Helga travels to Chicago from Naxos in the black car of a segregated train:

Across the aisle, a bronze baby . . . began a fretful whining, which its young mother essayed to silence by a low droning croon. In the seat just beyond a black and tan young pair were absorbed in the eating of a cold fried chicken, audibly crunching the ends of the crisp, browned bones. A little distance away a tired laborer slept noisily. Near him two children dropped the peelings of oranges and bananas on the already soiled floor. *The smell of stale food and ancient tobacco irritated Helga like a physical pain.* A man, a white man, strode through the packed car and spat twice, once in the exact centre of the dingy door panel, and once into the receptacle which held the drinking-water. *Instantly Helga became aware of stinging thirst.* Her eyes sought the small watch at her wrist. Ten hours to Chicago. (*Q,* 25, italics added)

Note how carefully the sentence describing Helga's "irritation" is placed in this passage, neatly and evenly dividing the description of the car's other African-American occupants (whose relatively innocuous presence Helga responds to with her characteristic emotion, which is decidedly inflected with class here) from the account of the white man's aggressive act of soiling the car and its drinking water. The arrangement makes particularly conspicuous the fact that Helga's emotional response to the latter is *not* described. Instead, the reaction the act provokes is a bodily one: "*stinging* thirst." While underscoring the unusually close relationship between the emotional and bodily connotations of "irritation," the chiasmic structure of the passage simultaneously highlights the difference between the two. Although there is nothing scandalous about a somatic reaction to an act that directly affects and even endangers one's physical well-being (having no drinking water for ten hours is a serious matter),[29] the carefully structured contrast between the causes of this "stinging thirst" and the preceding irritation "like a physical pain" places both reactions in a defamiliarizing light: we see Helga responding emotionally to a *physical* sensation (the smells of food and smoke) and reacting bodily to an *emotional* expression (of racial hatred or contempt). The formally crisscrossed nature of Helga's response to the incident on the train—a response that seems simultaneously excessive and deficient—is reinforced by the sentence with which the paragraph concludes: "Ten hours to Chicago. Would she be lucky enough to prevail upon the conductor to let her occupy a berth, or would she have to remain here all night, without sleep, without food, without drink, and with that disgusting door panel to which her purposely averted eyes were constantly, involuntarily straying?" (*Q*, 25).

Here, the object of Helga's "superficial" reaction to the racially charged incident has become a literal surface (the door panel covered with spit), rather than the action itself or the emotion it expresses. Though in the context of a long journey in close quarters it is not hard to imagine that one might be bothered more by the presence of a revolting substance than by the details of its origin,[30] Larsen's text also seems to be hinting at the political effeteness of Helga's signature affect. Indeed, far from "demarcat[ing] a world of justice" (Fisher, *VP*, 177) in a novel where matters of racial injustice are clearly central, Helga's irritation at this moment would seem to confirm the dominant reading of *Quicksand* as a "repressed" text. What is more, her irritation is likely to irritate the reader. It is as if the novel wants us to ask: Why does Helga's response to the racist incident seem so "off"? If the function of emotional utterances is to solicit a response "in kind" from the other (as Stanley Cavell argues), why does Helga seem to choose the wrong *object* to respond in kind to here?[31]

Though these are serious questions, I pose them primarily to call attention to a sanctimoniousness that unavoidably permeates the way we are *prompted* to respond to Helga's *lack* of emotional responsiveness to an expression of racial hatred. Indeed, the novel seems to call up our moral judgment of this affective deficit precisely in order to problematize it. For by responding to the change in her environment which the white man's act *produces,* and not to the feeling which his act *expresses,* Helga ultimately undercuts the racist's power to make his own feeling the determining standard by which the adequacy of her own response might be gauged. Which raises a number of additional questions. Is there an "adequate" or "sufficient" response to racist expressions? What would such a response be? Does our irritation at Helga's inadequate one imply that the appropriateness or legitimacy of emotional responses to racist sentiments should be evaluated on the basis of adequacy? Or that propriety, as well as proportionateness, is at stake in the way one formulates responses to these expressions? I should clarify that my effort here is not to morally salvage Helga's irritation by suggesting that the affect may not be as banal or superficial as it seems. For the affect's intransigent superficiality is precisely what allows Larsen to problematize the assumption that the subject to whom racist violence is directed has a duty to respond, and to respond in a manner that is *neither in excess nor lack of the violence inflicted.* In other words, it is irritation's radical *in*adequacy—its stubborn "offishness" or incommensurateness with respect to objects throughout the novel—that calls attention to a symbolic violence in the principle of commensurability itself, when there is an underlying assumption that an appropriate emotional response to racist violence exists, and that the burden lies on the racialized subject to produce that appropriate response legibly, unambiguously, and immediately.[32]

In *The Vehement Passions,* Philip Fisher argues that there are two main ways in which literary texts solicit emotion from their readers: sympathy, in which "I feel what the other is feeling," and the less familiar case of what he calls volunteered passion, "where we feel something exactly because the other does not" (*VP,* 142). In the former case the text solicits "feeling alongside another's explicit emotional state," whereas in the latter the text produces "a blank spot where the reader . . . [steps] in to supply the missing fear, grief, shame or anger" (*VP,* 144). Hence, while sympathy—a dynamic central to the genre of sentimental "mulatta" fiction from which

Larsen's novel self-consciously departs—involves the mimetic reproduction of an emotional state, volunteered passion obliges readers to "fill in the state ourselves without a represented model for us to copy" (*VP,* 145). Yet irritation's striking inadequacy in *Quicksand*—in addition to allowing the novel to critique the demand for an "appropriate" response to racist vehemence—ultimately deflects readers from responding in either of these two ways. One of its aesthetic outcomes is thus a relationship between text and reader that is as vexed or "offish" as Helga's irritation itself—in which *both* our sympathy with the protagonist *and* the emotion we might volunteer on her behalf are aggressively refused.

Thinking back to the incident on the train can help us understand this maneuver more concretely. Here, we as readers are diverted from feeling the anger we may think Helga "ought" to have felt, because the "offishness" of her alternative response immediately shifts attention from the displacement of the stronger emotion to the actual response.[33] Hence, the minor and inadequate affect of irritation manages not only to usurp and upstage anger, but even to upstage the fact of anger's absence. Yet the outcome suggests a double standard that further problematizes the dissatisfied response the text initially solicits from us—suggesting that Larsen has laid an affective and ideological trap for its readers. For since we are first and foremost irritated by Helga's irritation, instead of immediately becoming angry at the racist's actions (as we expected Helga herself to be), the conspicuous inadequacy of Helga's response not only changes the *value* of the response solicited from the reader (from anger to irritation) but changes its *object* (from the racist to Helga). This shift, which clearly mirrors Helga's own "wrong" object choice, explains why the affect that drives Larsen's novel, in addition to blocking the reader's ability to volunteer passion, equally forecloses the dynamic of sympathy. Though the parallel between the reader's irritation and Helga's does seem to suggest "feeling alongside another's explicit emotional state" (*VP,* 144), we do not feel what the other is feeling *in response to the same occasion.* What may initially look like sympathy is actually the reverse. We are less irritated *alongside* Helga than *at* Helga; we feel what she feels, but not in response to the original source of her own distinctively corporeal and noticeably "insufficient" response.

It is time to take a more direct look at the questions which have accumulated here. First, why does Larsen's novel induce us to react to Helga's physical discomfort in a way that eventually discomforts *us?* Why is a novel with a title like *Quicksand*—with all its connotations of depth—so driven by an affect associated with surfaces? Or, to return to Fanon's image, why does *Quicksand* choose to "epidermalize" the internal, as opposed to Locke's move of locating a literary text's politics below its aesthetic skin? Second, given that both *Quicksand*'s irritating absence of psychological causation and Helga's stubbornly inadequate irritation produce "blank spots" that seem ideally suited for eliciting volunteered emotion, why does Larsen's novel deliberately incite but then block our attempts to fill in its gaps? Why, in a similarly unfriendly fashion, does it encourage us to feel in parallel with its protagonist without allowing us to sympathize with her? The two parts of my second question can be combined to pose a slightly different one: What is at stake for this Harlem Renaissance novel, aesthetically and ideologically, when it uses the affective idiom of irritation—a strangely aggressive kind of weakness—to produce a racialized protagonist with whom we can neither fully identify nor fully disidentify? And what does any of this have to with the competing positions on race and aesthetics that I have said *Quicksand*'s irritation allows the novel to interrogate?

Though the minimalism of irritation would seem to position it as the antithesis of a concept defined by emotional excess, there is a sense in which Helga's irritation plays a role similar to that of animatedness. Both affects suggest a kind of hyperresponsiveness to the subject's external surroundings, as reflected in Helga's "acute sensitiveness" (*Q,* 34). Yet it is the image of the racialized body as an unusually responsive and expressive body that Helga's irritation often seems mobilized to negate. Throughout *Quicksand,* we see Helga repeatedly locating this excessive responsiveness in other African-American subjects—including, ironically, the woman who most shares her aversion to it. The attribution of racialized zeal to Anne Grey, who "while proclaiming loudly the undiluted good of all things Negro, . . . disliked the songs, the dances, and the softly blurred speech of the race" (*Q,* 48), takes place in the context of Helga's sudden, psychologically unexplained irritation at Harlem itself:

> Not only did the crowds of nameless folk on the street annoy her, she began also to dislike her friends. Even the gentle Anne distressed her.
>
> Perhaps because Anne was obsessed by the race problem and fed her obsession. She frequented all the meetings of protest, subscribed to all the complaining magazines, and read all the lurid newspapers spewed by the Negro yellow press. She talked, wept, and ground her teeth dramatically about the wrongs and shames of her race. And, though she wouldn't, even to herself, have admitted it, she reveled in this orgy of protest. (*Q,* 48)

It is precisely the fervency of Anne's dedication to racial politics—a politics encompassing a "deep and burning hatred" of white people—which becomes the object of Helga's minor irritation, as if her irritation were a prophylactic against emotional vehemence in general (*Q,* 48):

> Helga had been entertained by this racial ardor in one so little affected by racial prejudice as Anne, and by her inconsistencies. But suddenly these things *irked her with a great irksomeness* and she wanted to be free of this constant prattling of the incongruities, the injustices, the stupidities, the viciousness of white people. It stirred memories, *probed hidden wounds, whose*

poignant ache bred in her surprising oppression and corroded the
fabric of her quietism. (Q, 49, italics added)

There is something chafing about the rhetorically clumsy phrase,
"irked her with a great irksomeness," as if the narrative discourse
were becoming stylistically irritated by the irritation of its focal-
izer.[34] Note also that Helga's irritation at Anne's "racial ardor" is
described as the aggravation of an epidermal abrasion (Anne's
fervency probes hidden wounds), as well as the eating-away of a
surface (it corrodes the fabric of Helga's quietism). Yet Helga's irritation is provoked as much by Anne's seemingly inconsistent preference for the work of white artists over black artists as it is by her
"racial ardor" or "orgy of protest." As the narrator notes, Anne
"preferred Pavlova to Florence Mills, John McCormack to Taylor
Gordon, Walter Hapden to Paul Robeson" (Q, 49). While Anne
stands up "for the immediate advancement of all things Negroid,"
she is also described as "turn[ing] up her finely carved nose at their
lusty churches, their picturesque parades, their naïve clowning on
the streets" (Q, 49, 48). Yet what Helga perceives as the disjunction
between Anne's race pride and activism, and Anne's aesthetic pref-
erences, seems no more contradictory than Helga's own mixed
reactions to the very dubiously racialized qualities that provoke
Anne's disdain.

This contradiction becomes most evident in a scene where "racial ardor" becomes "entertainment" in a much more literal context. Though her irritation with Anne's fervency partly compels
Helga to leave Harlem for Denmark, Helga encounters another
version of it during a minstrel performance in a Copenhagen
vaudeville house, in the "gesticulating black figures" that she un-
willingly finds herself watching. Described as "silent, motionless"
throughout the performance, while the Danish audience around
her "applauded with delight" (Q, 82), Helga responds in a markedly unresponsive way that pointedly contrasts with the animated-

ness of the black entertainers, as well as with the equally animated
response of the white spectators:

> They were reaching for their wraps when out upon the stage
> pranced two black men, American Negroes undoubtedly, for
> as they danced and cavorted, they sang in the English of
> America an old ragtime song that Helga remembered hearing
> as a child, "Everybody Gives Me Good Advice." At its conclu-
> sion the audience applauded with delight. *Only Helga Crane
> was silent, motionless.*
>
> . . . How the singers danced, pounded their thighs, slapping
> their hands together, twisting their legs, waving their abnor-
> mally long arms, throwing their bodies about with a loose
> ease! And how the enchanted spectators clapped and howled
> and shouted for more!
>
> Helga Crane was not amused. Instead *she was filled* with
> a fierce hatred for the cavorting Negroes on the stage. She
> felt shamed, betrayed, as if these pale pink and white people
> among whom she lived had suddenly been invited to look
> upon *something in her* which she had hidden away and wanted
> to forget. And she was shocked at the avidity at which [Axel]
> Olsen beside her *drank it in.* (*Q*, 82–83, italics added)

In contrast to the "loose ease" with which the performers are
"throwing their bodies about" and the "howling" of the white audience, Helga's silent immobility initially suggests emotional distance from both the spectacle of racial animatedness and its equally
animated consumption by the white audience. Her distance takes
the form of the proposition: *That is not me.* The moment of emotional disengagement is amplified by the narrator's own withdrawal from Helga's consciousness at the exact moment Helga's
unresponsiveness is being recounted. The sentence, "Only Helga
Crane was silent, motionless," constitutes one of the noticeably few
moments when the novel disrupts the fixed internal focalization

that prevails in the text as a whole; the reader is suddenly confronted with a gap between the perspective of the narrator and that of the character, and this gap, as one might expect, appears in a description of what the character does *not* feel or perceive. Yet as soon as the focalization resumes—with the distinctively Helga-ish expression, "Helga Crane was not amused"—the text appears to suggest that Helga's lack of responsiveness to the performance is in fact an outward display that hides strong emotions: the hatred and shame with which she is "filled." This particular "filling" of a "blank spot," a void created by an initial absence of responsiveness or expressiveness on the part of the character, assumes a troubling meaning that helps us further understand the novel's motivations for impeding our own ability to volunteer Helga's unfelt emotions—since the primary thing Helga is "filled with" is racial hatred. It is at the very moment that Helga's "blank spot" is replenished, moreover, that the disidentification initially implied by her unresponsiveness to the performance turns, surprisingly, into the sign of an equally unsettling identification: "She felt shamed, betrayed, as if these pale pink and white people among whom she lived had suddenly been invited to look upon something *in her* which she had hidden away and wanted to forget."

In other words, with the narrator's act of refilling the blank spot created by what Helga does *not* feel, through the resumed use of internal focalization and the simultaneous revelation that Helga's unresponsiveness may in fact have been the external cover for an internal shame, Helga's *That is not me* suddenly turns into a *That is me*—and what's more, a *That is me* which hinges on the phantasmatic perception of others perceiving something *inside* the "me" that the "I" herself cannot. Helga's unexpected identification with the animated black performers thus coincides with the introduction of a depth-model account of racialized subjectivity—a disturbing notion of the self as a receptacle or container not only for the emotions that "fill" it, but for an extra unidentified "something" as well. This construction is reinforced by the image of voracious ingestion in the description of Axel Olsen: he "drank it in." Significantly, it is unclear whether the "it" which Olsen is drinking in (with an "avidity" which mirrors that of both the black entertainers and the white audience) refers to the performance itself or to the unspecified yet implicitly racial "something" in Helga of which her hatred and shame have made her conscious. We are thus given the impression that Olsen is vampirically draining "blackness" from the filled container which Helga has figuratively become, as an effect of both the show and the white audience's response to it.[35]

Though Helga later perceives that the performance mirrors a truth about the aestheticization of her own blackness for the consumption of the Danes, the "disquiet" provoked by the spectacle and her relationship to it ultimately leads her to the strangely contradictory conclusion that race is in fact a "something" which is innate or internal. More disturbingly, Helga's newfound understanding of racial specificity—a depth-model account in which race is perceived to derive from a mysterious substance located inside the subject—is presented as an understanding she receives from white Europeans: "All along they had divined its presence, had known that *in her was something, some characteristic,* different from any that they themselves possessed" (*Q,* 83, italics added). In other words, it is a construction of racial difference *as* deeply internal that Helga comes to internalize. And in spite of the depth and interiority the Danes ascribe to her racial specificity, Helga nevertheless comes to perceive "it" as a "characteristic" or "thing" more perceptible to the whites around her than to herself—part of a knowledge not only implicitly superior to Helga's own, but from which she has been excluded.

We can thus see how Larsen might summon the superficial affect of irritation to explicitly counteract the problematic notion of the racialized self as a container "filled" by emotions (a notion produced by the Copenhagen minstrel show), as well as to counteract the rhetoric of "deepness" Helga appeals to thereafter in efforts to assert her racial specificity. Her acceptance of the Copenhagen community's perception of race as an "it," "something," or substance hidden inside the subject is revealed, for example, in her ensuing rejection of Axel Olsen's marriage proposal: "You see, I couldn't marry a white man. I simply couldn't. It isn't just you, not just personal, you understand. It's deeper, broader than that. It's racial" (*Q*, 88). While read by critics as a moment in which Helga instrumentally summons a display of racial identification and solidarity as "an offensive move to conceal her sexual discomfort," or as a decoy "to conceal her ambivalent feelings about sex," Helga's equation of the "racial" with the "deeper" in her rejection of Olsen recurs in a later attempt to explain her motivations to her Danish uncle, where the avoidance of sex no longer seems an issue: "It's just something—something deep down inside of me" (*Q*, 91).[36] The depth-model construction of racial specificity Helga receives and accepts from the Danes appears again later, after Helga's return to Harlem, in a reflection on the nature of racial solidarity: "How absurd she had been to think that another country, other people could liberate her from the ties which bound her forever to these mysterious, those terrible, these fascinating, these lovable dark hordes. . . . Ties not only superficially entangled with mere outline of features or color of skin. *Deeper. Much deeper than either of these*" (95, italics added). Across various moments in the text, then, we find racial specificity figuratively located in the depths of the subject, and racial affinity described in terms of ties "much deeper" than superficial ones based on skin color.

Yet there is an intense critical irony at work in these varying associations of race with depth, since Helga mobilizes a rhetoric of deepness not only to claim but also to *reject* blackness. In fact, Helga's conception of blackness both as a submerged "something" (in the aftermath of the Copenhagen minstrel show) and as something "deeper" (in her assertion of racial solidarity in response to Olsen's marriage proposal) relies on a language virtually identical to the language describing the racial *disidentification* which precipitated Helga's move from Harlem to Denmark in the first place:

"She *didn't,* in spite of her racial markings, belong to these dark segregated people. She was different. She felt it. It wasn't merely a matter of color. *It was something broader, deeper,* that made folk kin" (*Q,* 55, italics added). Now here is Helga asserting an equally strong racial *solidarity* with other African-Americans: "Ties not only superficially entangled with mere outline of features or color of skin. Deeper. Much deeper than either of these" (*Q,* 95). Let's break the two passages into half and align the halves together:

Ties not only superficially entangled with mere . . . color of skin.
She felt it wasn't merely a matter of color.

Deeper. Much deeper than either of these.
It was something broader, deeper . . .

Though the reference to a depth beyond the mere superficialities of color is used, in one pair of sentences, to *assert and celebrate* blackness, and in the other, to *repudiate or disavow* blackness, the two pairs are virtually interchangeable. Like an obscene sore, the contradiction in Helga's identical appeals to "deepness" to justify diametrically opposed psychological investments and political stances —racial affinity and racial disconnection—is both conspicuous and discomforting. And this conspicuous, discomforting contradiction is reinforced by similar contradictions surrounding Helga's responses to other racialized artforms, as well as by contradictions in her own directly professed views on race and aesthetics.

In addition to the ragtime music performed by the black vaudevillians in Copenhagen, the cultural forms either positively or ambivalently marked "black" in Larsen's novel include a jazz performance Helga attends in a Harlem cabaret, and a religious song sung by African-American choir members in a Harlem church. Significantly, all of these productions by African-American artists induce uncharacteristically strong emotional responses in the normally merely irritated Helga. We have already seen how the ragtime singers facilitate Helga's identification (albeit indirectly and negatively) with a distinctively white and European construction of blackness as a "something" hidden deep inside the self—a dubious identification that coincides, moreover, with the equally dubious "filling" of Helga's blank spot with hatred and shame. The jazz and church-choir performances, however, appear to erase the self altogether—at least at first. Both aesthetic productions immediately induce violent and almost identical experiences of self-loss:

> She was drugged, lifted, sustained, by the extraordinary music, *blown out, ripped out, beaten out,* by the joyous, wild, murky orchestra. The essence of life seemed bodily motion. And when suddenly the music died, she dragged herself back to the present with a conscious effort; and a shameful certainty that not only had she been in the jungle, but that she had enjoyed it, began to taunt her. She hardened her determination to get away. She wasn't, she told herself, a jungle creature. (*Q,* 59, emphasis added)

The jazz is described as invading and destroying Helga's self—blowing, ripping, and beating it out—in an exciting, arousing way. The temporary loss of self the music induces, however, is counter-intuitively followed by Helga's disidentification with a construction of racial selfhood she perceives the music to have fostered. It is this disidentification ("She wasn't, she told herself, a jungle creature") that leads to Helga's decision to break her attachments to the Harlem art scene and leave it altogether.

Helga's response to the religious song performed by the Baptist choir—an aesthetic production that could not be more different from the jazz played at the cabaret—is equally complex. Again, Helga's initial response to the music is one of self-loss. In fact, this erasure of selfhood is thematized in the lyrics of the song performed, through a refrain that gradually changes from "All of self and none of Thee," to "Some of self and some of Thee," to "Less of self and more of Thee," and finally to "None of self and all of

Thee." The last line, as Barbara Johnson notes (*FD,* 48), is "acted out" by Helga rather than stated directly in the text:

> And as Helga watched and listened, gradually a curious influ-
> ence penetrated her; she felt an echo of the weird orgy resound
> in her own breast; she felt herself possessed by the same mad-
> ness; she too felt a brutal desire to shout and to sling herself
> about. . . . Maddened, she grasped at the railing, and with no
> previous intention began to yell like one insane, drowning ev-
> ery other clamor, while torrents of tears streamed down her
> face. She was unconscious of the words she uttered, or their
> meaning: "Oh God mercy, mercy. Have mercy on me!" but
> she repeated them over and over. (*Q,* 113)

Like the jazz performed at the Harlem club, the hymn sung by the African-American singers at the Harlem church induces an "ec-static disappearance" of self (Johnson, *FD,* 49). But in this case, the initial experience of self-loss leads to an identification with a sub-ject position ("pore los' sinner") that eventually *strengthens* Helga's ties to a black community, rather than severing them.[37] Thus, al-though both aesthetic experiences initially involve a radical nega-tion of selfhood, one culminates in a feeling of racial disconnection whereas the other instantiates a sense of belonging—so strong that it leads Helga to convert to the Baptist faith, marry Reverend Pleasant Green, and move with him to his parish in the rural South. More precisely, though Helga encounters two African-American artforms that create subjective "blank spots," one blank is immediately filled with an identification that in turn secures Helga's allegiance to a new black community, whereas the other is filled with a racial *disidentification* ("She wasn't . . . a jungle crea-ture") that leads her to break ties with another black community.

Yet by emphasizing the subjective gaps or erasures initially in-duced by both artforms, the text suggests that black-authored art-forms do not necessarily have to promote, confirm, or buttress identifications with either positive or negative constructions of blackness, even if they have the potential to do so. In fact, *Quicksand* seems to suggest that it is the ability to both facilitate *and* not facilitate identifications with constructions of blackness that gives the black-authored artforms in the novel their power—much the way Glenn Gould's power as an artist resides, as Giorgio Agamben has argued, in his exercising his potential to *not*-play as much as his potential to play.[38] To put this slightly differently, it is as if *Quicksand* were polemically asserting the right of black artforms to create and *preserve* "blank spots," shedding new light on the novel's motivation for preventing its own emotional or expressive gaps from being "filled." But since an artform's potential to not-facilitate racial identification should not be confused with its potential to facilitate racial disidentification (the first involves the absence of psychic affiliation or alignment, whereas the second involves negating an alignment that has been previously established), we can see how Larsen takes this stance one step further. She suggests that black-authored artforms do not necessarily promote disidentifications with positive or negative constructions of blackness, even if they may have the capacity to do so.

Yet, as if Larsen were trying to call attention to the ideological deadlock between primitivist and uplift aesthetics, the fact remains that her irritated protagonist is compelled to either identify or disidentify with constructions of racial identity in *all* of her encounters with artforms created by African-Americans. Helga is forced to fill every blank spot that every aesthetic experience induces—forced to say either *That is me* or *That is not me* in response. Since she is constrained to formulate at least one of these two propositions, Helga is confronted with a forced choice in which the psychic effects of racial oppression (and not repression) are highlighted. For Larsen is careful to show that the models of black identity and community that Helga must *either* identify *or* disidentify with, in *all* of her aesthetic experiences, are equally loaded with negative and positive meanings. Both identification and disidentification, moreover, have ambivalent consequences. Neither the new ties to a black community that the choir performance establishes (precipitating Helga's move to the rural American South), nor the racial disidentification that the nightclub performance brings forth (precipitating Helga's move from Harlem to Denmark), results in happiness for the character; in fact, the former implicitly leads to her death. Since no act of filling subjective blank spots seems capable of remaining unproblematic in *Quicksand,* in conjunction with the vigilance with which the novel protects its own affective gaps (as we have seen in its ability to block our efforts to volunteer emotion), it could be argued that this seemingly "repressed" text makes an explicit and even manifesto-like statement on the rights and entitlements of African-American art—and on its right to *not* express, and to *preserve* its expressive vacancies in particular.

We have seen how irritation's location in the uneasy zone between psychic and bodily experience produces an oscillation between insides and outsides: "external" sensations (pain, inflammation, stinging) are used to elaborate "internal" or psychological states. This oscillation is stylistically reinforced by the novel's dependence on free indirect narration, which, in merging aspects of Helga's "silent but implied speech" with the narrator's "factual reporting," produces a blur between subjective and objective enunciation that parallels the novel's irritating play between interiors and exteriors.[39] Free indirect narration is so consistent throughout the novel that the few moments of its disruption—where a blank spot suddenly appears in the focalization, or where the narrator's perspective is clearly separated from the character's—seem almost like lacerations or "obscene sores" in *Quicksand*'s narrative fabric. Though we have already seen one of these discontinuities emerge in the minstrel-show episode, the most conspicuous and discomforting involve moments that have something to do with *skin.*

Helga's much-discussed love of colors and surfaces is most apparent when linked to a racially specific aestheticism. In the following passage, she polemically espouses this attitude:

> Something intuitive, some unanalyzed driving spirit of loy-
> alty to the inherent racial need for gorgeousness told her that

bright colors *were* fitting and that dark-complexioned people *should* wear yellow, green, and red. . . . One of the loveliest sights Helga had ever seen had been a sooty black girl decked out in a flaming orange dress. . . .

These people [at Naxos] yapped loudly of race, of race consciousness, or race pride, and yet suppressed its most delightful manifestations, love of color, joy of rhythmic motion, naïve, spontaneous laughter. (*Q,* 18, italics in the original)

Conspicuous here is the ease with which Helga's claim to a racially distinctive aestheticism—the "inherent racial *need* for gorgeousness"—slides into an *aestheticization* of racialized bodies, suggesting a discomforting proximity between positions frequently polarized in debates at the heart of the Harlem Renaissance. In fact, the "sooty black girl decked out in a flaming orange dress" anticipates Helga's voyeuristic fascination with the minor character of Audrey Denney, whose appearance is flagged by a paler variation of the same colors, black and orange, associated with the first object of Helga's aestheticizing gaze. "Across dozens of tables . . . through slits in the swaying mob, Helga Crane studied her. Her pitch-black eyes, a little aslant, were . . . surmounted by broad brows, which seemed like black smears. The extreme *décolleté* of her simple apricot dress showed a skin of unusual color, a delicate, creamy hue, with golden tones. 'Almost like an alabaster,' thought Helga" (*Q,* 60).

Here is the first disruption of free indirect style I want to focus on, where the text not only *directly* attributes a thought to Helga, but brackets it off with quotation marks. It is significant that the moment in which Helga's thoughts are suddenly set apart from the narrator's coincides with the comparison of Audrey Denny to a sculpture, as if to suggest that the narrator wants no part of Helga's aestheticization of Audrey. Yet the language of Helga's aesthetic evaluation of Audrey is a near-replica of the passage in the novel's opening chapter where Helga herself is described *by the narrator.*

Just as Helga evaluates Audrey in painterly and sculptural terms, as "an alabaster" of "creamy hue" marked by "black smears," so Helga is first presented as a sculpture that has "delicately chiseled" features and "well-turned" limbs and that is "well-fitted" to its setting's "framing of light and shade." Ironically, then, the narrator distances herself from Helga at the exact moment when Helga's aesthetic appraisal of another black woman comes into phase with the narrator's own aestheticization of Helga. It is precisely when the two aesthetic stances seem most to converge that the discourse insists on their separation, as if to stylistically foreground the incommensurateness on which the concept of "irritation" depends.

These contradictions are exacerbated when Helga's early meditation on color and "joy of rhythmic motion" as a reflection of racial solidarity and *pride* is followed by a nearly identical mediation on color and motion as a reflection of racial disidentification and *contempt*. Note, for example, how Helga comes to regard the colors and "bodily motion" displayed at the jazz performance in the cabaret:

> For the hundredth time she marveled at the gradations within this oppressed race of hers. A dozen shades slid by. There was sooty black, shiny black, taupe, mahogany, bronze, copper, gold, orange, yellow, peach, ivory, pinky white, pastry white. . . . She saw black eyes in white faces, brown eyes in yellow faces, gray eyes in brown faces, blue eyes in tan faces. Africa, Europe, perhaps with a pinch of Asia, in a fantastic motley of ugliness and beauty, semi-barbaric, sophisticated, exotic, were here. *But she was blind to its charm,* purposely aloof and a little contemptuous, and soon her interest in the moving mosaic waned. (*Q,* 59–60, italics added)

The revelation of Helga's surprising contempt for the same display of color we have previously seen her celebrate coincides with yet another moment in which the narrator's language suddenly severs itself from the consciousness of the character with which it is normally merged. The free indirect style of the passage suggests that the narrator and Helga share a tendency to "marvel" at color variations, yet the passage culminates in the phrase "But *she was blind* . . . ," which pointedly distances the narrator from the character. Yet whereas the rupture of free indirect style triggered by Helga's comparison of Audrey to "an alabaster" suggested the narrator's unwillingness to participate in Helga's act of aestheticizing a black woman, in this case the dissociation of their perspectives suggests that the narrator finds some "charm" in the aestheticization of racialized bodies that Helga does not. Just as we have seen virtually identical references to "deepness" strengthen Helga's racial ties in one context and dissolve them in another, here antithetical positions on the question of racial aestheticization are produced through an identical stylistic maneuver. In one case, the discontinuation suggests the narrator's refusal to subject a black female body to Helga's aestheticizing gaze; in the other, it suggests a refusal by *Helga* to perceive black bodies from the aestheticizing gaze of the *narrator.*

The formalist way in which *Quicksand*'s narrator and protagonist come to exchange stances regarding the aestheticization of black bodies—that is, through another chiasmus—emphasizes the impossibility of describing the novel's position on this issue as an ideologically unified or consistent one. For while critics have read Helga's "love of color" as an unequivocally positive way of expressing and celebrating her racial and gender identity—a means of enabling her "to create . . . a palette that will unify her life rather than leave it divided" and "to construct a female identity, to use her attractiveness as power"[40]—the ironic splitting of the narrator's perspective from Helga's suggests a more skeptical view about color's role in facilitating "race consciousness, race pride." In fact, the contradictions highlighted by these stylistic discontinuities could even be read as a subtle parody of the thematization of color in Harlem Renaissance fiction. Note, for example, how closely the aforementioned reflection on color echoes similar litanies in Van Vechten's *Nigger Heaven:*

On all sides of the swaying couple, bodies in picturesque cos-
tumes rocked, black bodies, brown bodies, high yellows, a
kaleidoscope of color transfigured by the amber searchlight.
Scarves of bottle green, cerise, amethyst, vermilion, lemon.

Couples were dancing in such close proximity that their bodies
melted together as they swayed and rocked to the tormented
howling of the brass, the barbaric beating of the drum. . . .
Blues, smokes, dinges, charcoals, chocolate browns, shines, and
jigs.[41]

In the latter passage, the names of colors blur disturbingly into
denigrating names for African-Americans. All of these color catalogs, moreover, appear in the same setting as Larsen's "moving mosaic"—that of a Harlem nightclub, dance hall, or cabaret. This is
likewise the case in Claude McKay's *Home to Harlem*:

Dandies and pansies, chocolate, chestnut, coffee, ebony, cream,
yellow, everybody was teased up to the high point of excitement.

Civilization had brought strikingly exotic types into Susy's
race. And like many, many Negroes, she was a victim to that.
. . . Ancient black life rooted upon its bases with all its fascinating new layers of brown, low-brown, high-brown, nut brown,
lemon, maroon, olive, mauve, gold. Yellow balancing between
black and white. Black reaching out beyond yellow. Almost-
white on the brink of a change. Sucked back down into the
current of black by the terribly sweet rhythm of black
blood . . .[42]

Larsen was well aware that paeans to skin color had become a familiar convention of Harlem Renaissance fiction, deployed in the
aestheticization of black bodies by white and black artists alike. In
Quicksand, however, "skin" functions much more ambivalently as
an ideologeme by which racial identifications are both negated and
asserted through aesthetic position-takings; it produces contempt

and disaffiliation in one instance, and self-esteem and solidarity in the other. At moments where contradictions explicitly concerning the coupling of race with aesthetics come most to the fore, we find them exacerbated by gaps or discontinuities in *Quicksand*'s own narrative fabric. In fact, it is precisely at moments where a position on race and aesthetics seems most clearly articulated that these contradictions become most conspicuous. Instead of remaining an unbroken surface for pleasurable aesthetic contemplation and the racial affinities this would seem to foster, "skin," as a trope, might be described as a discomforting scab which Larsen obsessively picks at and which the novel never allows to heal—insofar as *Quicksand*'s skin-color rhapsodies systematically disrupt its otherwise fluid integration of Helga's consciousness with third-person narration.

In fact, Helga Crane's strange irritation suggests a version of "the erupting symptomatic body display[ing] monstrous and unreadable forms to a horrified society" that critic and artist Laura Kipnis, in her work "Marx: The Video," associates with Marx's chronic affliction with carbuncles.[43] Dramatized by the way in which Kipnis superimposes filmed images of riots and political protests on top of her actor's epidermal lesions, Marx's painful, self-described "proletarian disease" not only turns his epidermis into a "battleground" during the writing of the first volume of *Capital* (a historical fact documented in Marx's correspondence with Engels, as Kipnis notes), but suggests the process of "a body [becoming] sarcastic, . . . [not] a body you could take in the drawing room. This was an ill-mannered body."[44] In a similar though considerably less revolutionary vein, *Quicksand*'s irritation not only epidermalizes states we normally understand as internal, but equates the psychological costs of racism and sexism with obscene sores on a body otherwise quite at home in the drawing rooms of the bourgeoisie. Interfering with Helga's tendency to blend into these genteel environments (in the novel's opening paragraph, we see her "skin like yellow satin" blend into the "oriental silk," "dark tapestry," and other luxurious fabrics surrounding her), these sores constitute sites of conspicuous discomfort not only to characters within the novel, but to its readers as well. In fact, the predominance of irritation in the novel, at the level of form and structure as well as that of content, comes to provocatively suggest the image of a literary text in a minor but continuous state of inflammation or discomfort—and one whose "sores" resist the dubious beautification to which black skins and female bodies are repeatedly subjected in the novel.

Though Larsen turns the black-authored literary text into a "stinging," "pricked," and "lacerated" surface, *Quicksand*'s irritation should not be confused with an attempted "strengthening of the corporeal as the bearer of race's meaning."[45] On the contrary, *Quicksand*'s cutaneous affect explicitly questions this "visible epistemology of black skin" by pushing its logic to an extreme. There could not be a more telling contrast, for instance, than the one between the epidermal rawness of the feeling and perceiving African-American *subject* in the novel, and the unbroken smoothness of the skin that is *objectified* in the novel—as if only *looked-at* black skin can be free of inflammation or soreness. Indeed, Helga's own epidermal discomfort—her "peculiar irritation"—seems to signify a price paid for the pleasure she and others (including the narrator and even the novel itself) derive from aestheticizing the black skin of others. The image *Quicksand* projects of sores on a *textual* corpus, or of itself as an *irritated narrative,* raises the ante, enabling the novel to further dramatize the violence Robyn Wiegman ascribes to the idea of race as "a constituted 'fact' of the body" and its epidermis in particular.[46] Thus, if there are narrative lesions or ruptures in *Quicksand* that discomfort the reader, they are ruptures which function as "felt" outbreaks of contradiction, telling symptoms of race's *overdetermined* equation with the black body in American culture. Troubling the reader's ability to identify or completely disidentify with its protagonist or narrator, whose discordant positions on race and aesthetics both attract and repel us, these sores foreground *Quicksand*'s larger effort to distance itself from the sentimental tradition of mulatta fiction and its politics of compulsory sympathy, while also enabling the text to resist the imperative that productions by African-American artists *fill in their blanks,* facilitating *either* identification *or* disidentification with existing constructions of black identity. Moreover, the sores enable the text to resist the closely related demand that artforms by racialized subjects be expressive at any cost. *Quicksand*'s use of irritation to challenge the assumption that, in order to politically or aesthetically matter, feelings must be located below the surface or "under the skin" plays a key role in furthering this polemical assertion. In addition to countering the conflation of "deficient" or "inadequate" expression with *re*pression, which it does by vigilantly protecting *Quicksand*'s own expressive and emotional blank spots, Helga Crane's strange irritation undermines a longstanding tradition of confining feeling to internal spaces, as well as the moralized opposition between depth and surface used to distinguish feelings viewed as politically efficacious and adequate to their occasions, from those which are not.

5. anxiety

*[Since] more general psychological problems are involved in
the question of the nature of projection, let us make up our
minds to postpone the investigation of it . . . until some
other occasion.*
> — Sigmund Freud, "On the Mechanism of
> Paranoia"

*I am also postponing, for a short time, the exposition of my
analysis of anxiety.*
> — Louis Althusser[1]

In the two epigraphs above, the issues of anxiety and projection
paradoxically intersect by virtue of the fact that both are averted,
deferred for analysis to a future which never arrives. This post-
ponement ironically underscores anxiety's own special temporality:
the future-orientedness that makes it belong to Ernst Bloch's category of "expectation emotions." While "filled emotions" (such as
envy, greed, and admiration) are "those whose drive-object lies

ready, if not in respective individual attainability, then in the already available world,"[2] "expectant emotions" like anxiety, fear, and hope "aim less at some specific object as the fetish of their desire than at the configuration of the world in general, or (what amounts to the same thing) at the future disposition of the self."[3] For Bloch, "expectant" feelings are thus distinguished from "filled" ones by their "incomparably greater anticipatory character," which in turn puts them into a closer relationship to time in general: "All emotions refer to the horizon of time . . . but expectant emotions open out entirely into this horizon."[4]

Yet while intimately aligned with the concept of futurity, and the temporal dynamics of deferral and anticipation in particular, anxiety has a spatial dimension as well. In psychological discourse, for example, anxiety is invoked not only as an affective response to an anticipated or projected event, but also as something "projected" onto others in the sense of an outward propulsion or displacement—that is, as a quality or feeling the subject refuses to recognize in himself and attempts to locate in another person or thing (usually as a form of naïve or unconscious defense).[5] Althusser refers to this kind of projection in a description of his own psychiatric evaluation:

> In my own case, it is striking that the most well-intentioned doctor in the world . . . projected onto me his own anxiety . . . [and] as a consequence of this projection and confusion, was partly mistaken about what was really happening inside my head. [My] doctor's attention was fixed on a specific anxiety which he passed *to* me rather than observed *in* me, thus shifting it from its "object," or rather from the absence or loss of any "object," to the representation of *his* anxiety projected on to me.[6]

Yet this account of projection as the externalizing trajectory by which anxiety becomes displaced seems paradoxically internal to Freud's definition of anxiety itself. In his attempt to redefine neurotic anxiety, for example—from its initial formulation as "fermented" libido, or sexual energy transformed from being accumulated without discharge, to the experience of unpleasurable endogenous excitations treated *as if they were coming from without*—Freud shifts from viewing anxiety as an "inside" matter to viewing it as a matter of the very distinction *between* inside and outside. This shift becomes most noticeable in Freud's eventual appeal to the experience of birth, the archetypal emergence/expulsion, as "the first experience of anxiety, and thus the source and prototype of the affect of anxiety."[7]

The notion of anxiety as already involving some form of outward trajectory, *prior* to its being projected or displaced onto others, is suggested not only by its "prototypicalization" in birth, but also by a much earlier definition mobilized by Freud to distinguish realistic anxiety from its neurotic form. Whereas realistic anxiety emerges in the context of an external threat, neurotic anxiety seems to involve an extra step: "In neuroses [the psyche] is overtaken by anxiety if it notices that it is incapable of allaying a sexual excitation that has arisen from within. Thus it behaves *as though it were projecting this excitation to the outside*."[8] This comment suggests that the externalizing mechanism of "projection" may in fact constitute *part* of the phenomenon of anxiety, as opposed to a psychic operation subsequently performed *on* one's anxiety—an implication reinforced by Freud's tendency in his later work to equate projection with phobic avoidance in general,[9] and by his proto-Kleinian view of projection as a form of *expulsion,* as a trajectory retroactively constituting the very distinction between the ego's inner reality and outside world.[10] Yet the exact nature of the relationship between anxiety and projection in Freud's work remains ambiguous, for several reasons. For one thing, the question of whether anxiety preexists or becomes determined by its outward displacement (a question which Freud never asks directly) seems not only paradoxical but irresolvably circular. For another, Freud never ends up fully elaborating or providing a formal theory of projection, though he

consistently refers to the mechanism in his efforts to theorize phobia and paranoia.[11] In his case study of Daniel Schreber,[12] he isolates
it as a prospective object of analysis, only to immediately postpone
discussing the topic; indeed, Laplanche and Pontalis note that "for
the most part, when Freud mentions projection he avoids dealing
with the matter as a whole" (*LP,* 352). Moreover, at times the concept of projection is conspicuously absent from Freud's theory of
anxiety where one expects it most, such as when the "castration
anxiety" that afflicts all boys is perceived as the carrying out of a
paternal threat. There is an opportunity here to claim that the boy
displaces his fear of castration onto the father, resituating his experience of dread in an external source, yet no mention of projection
informs this famous account of anxiety as a gender-specific and
gender-determining phenomenon.

Thus, the question of timing that one normally associates with
anxiety's affective grammar (When?) can also become a question
of location (Where?). By examining spatialized representations of
anxiety in works by Herman Melville, Alfred Hitchcock, and Martin Heidegger, all involving fantasies of the intellectual subject as a
thrown or airborne entity, I hope to show that the externalizing aspect of "projection" which the image of thrownness hyperbolizes
can be perceived not just as a strategy for displacing anxiety, but as
the means by which the affect assumes its particular form. These
accounts of anxious subjectivity, in which actual and phantasmatic
acts of throwing reinforce the boundary between center and periphery, and thus the distinction between "here" and "yonder" on
which the experience of threat depends, depict anxiety less as an inner reality which can be subsequently externalized than as a structural effect of spatialization in general.[13] Moreover, in all three accounts the image of thrownness secures a strategic sort of distance
for the knowledge-seeking subject, enabling him to differentiate
"here" from "yonder" even in the absence of the fixed positions
from which nearnesses and farnesses are ordinarily established or
gauged.[14]

In Western intellectual history, the concept of anxiety seems to have acquired a certain epistemological cachet, having given rise to an all-purpose term stretching across knowledge formations and disciplinary vocabularies. Pointing to the general prominence of phobia as a signifying economy in modern culture, expressions such as "anxiety of influence," "middle-class anxiety," and "millennial anxiety" use the negative affect they invoke as a handy way of immediately establishing a skeptical or critical stance toward the phenomena described.[15] Yet while the concept of anxiety is useful as a critical framing device, it also has a history of being gendered in Western culture, particularly in the discursive arenas where it has played the largest role. Psychoanalysis is the strongest example, since its primary model of gender differentiation, the castration complex, relies partly on affective categories to fully distinguish "masculine" and "feminine" attitudes toward a perceived loss. In response to this imagined privation, only male subjects are capable of experiencing genuine anxiety or dread, whereas female subjects are allotted the less traumatic and therefore less profound (certainly more ignoble) affects of nostalgia and envy. Freud notes with reference to little girls: "We can hardly speak with propriety of castration *anxiety* where castration has already occurred."[16] The castration complex as originally formulated by Freud in his case study of Little Hans could thus be read (albeit somewhat perversely) as barring female subjects from anxiety as a subject-determining orientation, whereas the ambient phobia not only plays a privileged role in the process of gendered ego formation for male subjects, but comes to precipitate the formation of the paternal superego.

Similarly, in the Continental tradition of existentialist philosophy, the privileging of anxiety as a key for interpreting the human condition is accompanied by its being secured as the distinctive—if not exclusive—emotional province of male intellectuals. The obsessive young men and agitated scholars in Søren Kierkegaard's pseudonymous writings, for example, seem fused together in Don Giovanni, the hypermasculine and flamboyantly heterosexual hero of Mozart's opera, who is described as anxiety itself: "There is an anxiety in him, but this anxiety is his energy. In him, it is not a sub-jectively reflected anxiety; it is *substantial* anxiety. In the overture there is not what is commonly called—without knowing what one is saying—despair. Don Giovanni's life is not despair; it is, how-ever, the full force of the sensuous, which is born in anxiety; and *Don Giovanni himself is this anxiety,* but this anxiety is precisely the demonic zest for life."[17] While Kierkegaard is careful to distinguish this anxiety from melancholia (the life of Don Giovanni, a vitalist to the core, "is not despair"), the agitated male subject seems to be a modern variant of the male melancholic, a figure with a much older cultural history. It could in fact be argued that the state of un-ease or agitation eventually codified as "anxiety" gradually replaced melancholia as the intellectual's signature sensibility (as earlier claimed by Richard Burton in *The Anatomy of Melancholy*).[18] Even prior to the coupling of "nerve sensitiveness" with intellectual supe-riority in the nineteenth-century concept of "neurasthenia" (which physician George M. Beard, in his 1881 study *American Nervous-ness,* celebrated as a disease of modernity's "overly civilized" indi-viduals),[19] by the end of the eighteenth century and in the wake of Romanticism in particular, Stephen Rachman argues, "cerebral ac-tivity and worry" had become a generally recognized token of gen-teel literary culture and its "bookish lads."[20] The connection be-tween literariness and anxious agitation was so pervasive that by the early 1800s an American clinician could observe, "All men who possess genius . . . are endued by nature with more than usual sen-sibility of nervous system."[21] The heightened nervous sensibility as-cribed by clinicians to "men of letters" in the eighteenth century and to "brain-workers" in the nineteenth century could thus be viewed as paving the way for anxiety's privileged status in the liter-ature and philosophy of the twentieth, from what Tom Lutz de-scribes as the general fascination with "neurasthenic protagonists" on the part of American writers and intellectuals in the early 1900s,[22] to the prominent place Martin Heidegger gives this affect in his phenomenology of moods.

Displaying such centrality across periods and knowledge formations (literature, literary culture, philosophy, psychoanalysis), how
does anxiety come to acquire its special status in Western culture as
the distinctive "feeling-tone" of intellectual inquiry itself? To approach this question, this chapter considers dramatic accounts of
symbolic displacement in three texts preoccupied with the "moody
organization" of knowledge-seeking subjects: Melville's *Pierre,*
Hitchcock's *Vertigo,* and Heidegger's analysis of anxiety in *Being
and Time.* In each case, the projective configuration anxiety assumes becomes inextricably bound up with the trajectory of a male
analyst's quest for understanding or interpretation. Thus, while
remaining firmly tied to questions of futurity in psychoanalysis
(where, in the case of boys, castration is "projected" as an anticipated event) and to the matter of time itself in Heidegger's analysis
of Dasein's self-interpretive agency, anxiety nevertheless emerges in
these texts as a general effect of spatialization involving thrown,
hurled, or forcibly displaced objects.

In wishing to highlight the spatial discourse returning to haunt
anxiety's temporal definition, as well as the way in which this disposition seems to have acquired its intellectual cachet across periods
and disciplines, I have deliberately chosen to examine this phenomenon through a synchronic constellation of texts. All of these texts
forefront, though in very different ways (filmic, novelistic, and
philosophical), how the representation of anxiety, as an anticipatory
structure explicitly linked to a male subject's quest for interpretive
agency, oddly becomes dependent on a spatial grammar and vocabulary—from the way *fleeing, turning, falling,* and *sinking* come to
inform Heidegger's analysis of anxious Dasein in terms of futural
possibility, to the manner in which the anticipation of a castrating
event in *Pierre* culminates in a fantasy of the male intellectual as a
stone hurled through space. The topologies of dispositioning produced here, marked by physiological motifs of dizziness or vertigo,
suggest that the logic of "anxiety" and that of "projection," as a
form of spatial displacement, converge in the production of a distinct kind of knowledge-seeking subject.

The Detective

In keeping with the film noir convention of using the private investigator as a democratic figure for the male intellectual, *Vertigo* (1958) presents its protagonist, Scottie (James Stewart), not just as a retired detective but as a "hard-headed scholar," in the words of the wealthy industrialist who hires him. The most memorable spatialized representations of Scottie's psychic life are, unsurprisingly, connected to the theme of his acrophobia. Shot on location in Northern California, and featuring many of the area's tallest landmarks (Coit Tower, the National Forest sequoias, the San Juan Bautista Mission church tower), *Vertigo* offers an "objective correlative" for Scottie's emotional mindset that seems tailored to the verticality of its setting. The most famous cinematic gesture in the film, a track-out/forward zoom from an initially static shot representing the protagonist's point of view from a site of elevation (looking down from a rooftop, as in the film's opening chase sequence, or from a staircase), dramatizes the acrophobe's "vertigo" by suddenly elongating the vertical distance depicted, creating the illusion that the ground is sinking beneath his gaze.

Yet Scottie's psychic life is not reducible to his officially diagnosed—and visually verticalized—"fear of heights." For his notably anxious mindset could be described equally well in terms of a horizontal oscillation between two sites of feminine self-discontinuity, embodied in the figures of "Madeleine" and Judy (both played by Kim Novak). Insistently nonidentical to themselves, the women are symbolically negative presences, defined more by who they are not than by who they are. Thus, the film's romantic pathos resides in Scottie's inability or refusal to perceive Judy as Judy, seeing her rather as not Madeleine. Yet the figure Scottie first encounters as Madeleine is *also* not Madeleine, because she is Judy playing the part of the wife of Gavin Elster (a corporate shipbuilder) and because this "Madeleine," as part of the fictitious persona Judy is asked to assume, is *also* at times not "Madeleine," insofar as she is supposedly subject to self-estranging possession by a dead woman named Carlotta Valdez. Ironically, while Carlotta Valdez and Madeleine Elster provide the models that "Madeleine" and Judy copy, it is these authentic originals who are figured as "projections" of the latter. For while Carlotta and Madeleine are women who do not impersonate other women, they are also absent or occulted figures; one is dead to begin with, and the other is murdered in the middle of the film. The film thus confronts us with a paradox: it is the self-identical, nondissimulating women who seem ghostly or supernatural (especially since they are barely if ever represented on screen), while the split, doubled, dissimulating women played by the movie star Kim Novak are the ones both we and Scottie find most actual or real. In this sense, Scottie's horizontal oscillation cannot be interpreted as an oscillation between fixed or unchanging poles, since Judy and "Madeleine" are not only self-discontinuous figures, but presented as "screens" on which other female figures (Madeleine and Carlotta) are projected.

There is another form of "projection," however, that is established relatively early in *Vertigo* as strangely bound up with Scottie's masculinity. Immediately after the film's opening "primal scene" marking the onset of Scottie's acrophobia, we meet Scottie wearing what he calls a "corset" and restlessly playing with a cane, while his friend Midge (Barbara Bel Geddes) works at her job as a designer of ladies' undergarments. At one point, the viewer hears Scottie in a voiceover while onscreen is a close-up of one of Midge's drawings, which features a female torso in a brassiere. The joke linking Scottie's corsetedness to a deficit of masculinity runs through most of the scene:

> *Scottie:* [Stretching to retrieve dropped cane.] Ouch.
> *Midge:* I thought you said no more aches and pains.
> *Scottie:* Yeah, it's this darn corset. It binds me.
> *Midge:* No three-way stretch? How very un-chic.
> *Scottie:* Those police department doctors have no sense of style.
>   Well, anyway, tomorrow will be the day.
> *Midge:* Why, what's tomorrow?

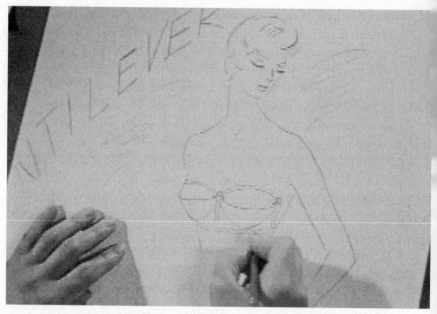

FIGURE 9

> *Scottie:* Tomorrow? The corset comes *off* tomorrow! I'll be able to
>   scratch myself like anybody else tomorrow, and I'll throw this
>   miserable thing out the window and be a free—*a free man.*

Becoming "a free man" is clearly at issue or stake for Scottie at the
beginning of the film, a desired outcome rather than an established
fact. This anticipated remasculinization, according to Scottie's own
description, rests on the act of throwing a "miserable thing" out a
window. Yet Scottie's fascination with corsets and other feminine
things seems based on a preoccupation with a more abstract phenomenon: the mechanics of projection in general. Midge accordingly appeals to physics rather than erotics (as might be expected)
to account for Scottie's highly particular interest in a brassiere he
finds in her apartment. Responding to Scottie's quasi-scientific curiosity ("I've never run across one like *that* before"), she matter-of-

factly explains: "Revolutionary uplift. No shoulder straps, no back straps, but it does everything a brassiere should do. It works on the principle of the cantilever bridge. An aircraft engineer down on the Peninsula designed it. Worked it out in his spare time."[23] Scottie's enthusiastic response, "Kind of a hobby—a do-it-yourself kind of thing," signals that this apparatus designed for bodily projection will come to serve as inspiration and model for his own entrepreneurial, "do-it-yourself" effort to overcome his acrophobia, bringing the externalizing design of the brassiere and his affective relation to space into a rather unusual alignment. The conflation of topologies becomes increasingly pronounced as *Vertigo* foregrounds Scottie's growing anxiety in conjunction with his developing quest for knowledge about "Madeleine." Thus, while the trajectory of retired Scottie's own "spare time" investigation seems strangely anticipated by the motif of a thrown corset, and even more strangely motivated by the projective design of a mechanically innovative, male-engineered brassiere, his pursuit of understanding eventually comes to involve a succession of encounters with other thrown objects—culminating in a fantasy of *himself* as a projectile.

Initially posed to the "hard-headed scholar" as the task of disclosing the truth behind one woman's mysterious possession by another, this red herring quest leads not only to Scottie's anxious oscillation between "Madeleine" and Judy, female figures that render each other self-discontinuous, but to an oscillation between the dead or occulted "originals," Carlotta Valdez and Madeleine Elster —the real women who in absentia paradoxically function as imaginary extensions of "Madeleine" and Judy, who are in turn depicted as extensions of each other. In this sense, each of the film's women —real or fictional, contemporary or historic, alive or dead—assumes the status of a "projection," in the sense of something extending outward from and beyond something else. This projectedness is grimly reinforced by the fact that all four women, in one way or another, eventually become projectile objects, violently hurled or thrown. Thus, the imaginary act of ejecting a feminine

FIGURE 10

object out the window in order to become "a free man," as anticipated in Scottie's quip about his corset, inaugurates a chain of
events in which Scottie becomes a helpless or coerced witness to the
throwing of *actual* women. When Scottie consults a local history
buff about the origins of Carlotta Valdez, for example, the man explains she was the mistress of a wealthy manufacturer who cast her
off after she bore his illegitimate child: "I don't know how much
time passed, or how much happiness there was, but then—*he threw
her away.* He had no other children; his wife had no children. So he
kept the child and threw her away. Men could do that in those
days; they had the power, and the freedom." The characterization
of Carlotta as thrown away by her industrialist lover explicitly
mirrors the act of shipbuilder Gavin Elster, who kills his wife
by throwing her from the top of the mission church tower. The
throwing of Madeleine Elster is preceded by yet another mirror-

reflection act: the imitation Madeleine throws herself into San Francisco Bay, in a staged suicide attempt intended to replicate Carlotta's death. These dizzyingly interlinked cases of "being thrown" come full circle at the film's conclusion, as Scottie help-lessly witnesses Judy's accidental fall from the same church tower where he has previously witnessed the faked death of "Madeleine" and, unbeknownst to him at the time, Madeleine's actual one.

In this sense, all four of the women Scottie encounters—already presented as projections or imaginary extensions of one another—are also *thrown projections*. The film accentuates the redoubling of this concept (a thrown projection is, after all, a construct that enacts the same principle twice over, describing the projection of a proj-ection, or the thrownness of something already thrown) in a grisly way by presenting the image of the real Madeleine flattened against the surface of the roof on which her body lands after being pushed by her husband from the church tower. It is as if the film were de-liberately evoking cinema's dependency on images projected onto a screen—or, as Laura Mulvey and others have argued in the case of classical narrative cinema, on the images of *women* projected onto a screen.[24] In each case the projection's spectacular redoubling is de-liberately performed as an event to be witnessed by Scottie. The throwing of the real Madeleine from the church tower, for exam-ple, and the act designed to foreshadow it (when Judy, in the role of "Madeleine" spiritually possessed by Carlotta, hurls herself into the bay), are both willfully orchestrated by Gavin Elster for the gaze of his hired investigator. Accordingly, Scottie becomes increasingly in-scribed within this spatial logic as he grows affectively entangled in what at first seemed a straightforward hermeneutic quest.

"Projection" in *Vertigo* thus does not designate a subjective oper-ation whereby preexisting feelings of the subject are displaced onto others, but rather designates the objective mechanism by which the feeling emerges. As Scottie's anxious mindset and the trajectories defined by the thrown objects he witnesses eventually become con-substantial, it becomes clear that he does not project or externalize his anxiety as a preexisting inner condition; rather, his anxiety seems inextricably bound up with this dislocating and externalizing function. Like the Freudian concept of catharsis qua emotional discharge, as theorized by Jonathan Lear, Scotty's anxiety "comes packaged" with its own logical (spatialized) explanation—it is an affect containing its own "theory" or formative principle.[25] Lear's observation that "the conceptualization of an [affect] is a development within the [affect] itself" suggests that "projection" is not something that *happens* to Scotty's feeling but is something like "a justification of its own occurrence," enabling the feeling to manifest itself as such (*LPN*, 68, 50). *Vertigo*'s implication, like that of Lear's theory, is that feelings may be formed and even "shaped" by the means used to project, "discharge," or "expel" them.[26]

Hence, the film's convergence of trajectories—that of Scottie's already intertwined quests for knowledge and masculine agency, the spatialization of his anxiety, and the pathway of objects hurled into space—becomes most pronounced in Scottie's dream, in which he phantasmatically becomes a thrown object as well. Introduced by an exterior shot of Scottie's apartment—a shot featuring Coit Tower, whose blinking light seems to initiate the succession of images which follows—Scottie's dream reveals a partial identification with the fictitious Madeleine that hinges precisely on her status as a projectile object. It shows him walking in a cemetery and peering into an empty grave by an unmarked stone—an exact reenactment of the phony dream "Madeleine" describes to him as part of the possession hoax: "It's an open grave and I stand by the gravestone looking down into it." In the dream, Scottie's gaze into this site of nothingness—a patch of black that strangely gives the impression of surface rather than depth—propels him into a fantasy of *himself* as a projected projection, a point the film underscores by depicting Scottie's body as a black silhouette hurled toward the same surface on which Scottie later witnesses the real Madeleine flattened. The dream instigates another redoubling of projection, depicting the thrown entity as a quasi-filmic image.

FIGURE II

The dream sequence explicitly links the projective logic of Scottie's anxiety to an aversive encounter with nothingness. This is emphasized by the fact that the place from which his trajectory as thrown or falling object begins, the open grave, is more accurately described as a "nonplace." Having established Scottie's initial look at this emptiness, the film abruptly cuts to a defamiliarized close-up of Scottie's horrified face that makes him seem like both the witness *and* the object of his subsequent fall. In this manner, the film substitutes the subject himself, and his thrownness in particular, for the hole or emptiness that is the original locus of his gaze. If we recall Kierkegaard's famous description of anxiety as having no object—or rather having "nothing" as its object—it seems as if Scottie's encounter with this objectlessness compels him to volunteer *himself* as the "object," reemphasizing the spatial configuration of his state of mind.

In redefining the male subject as thrown projection, Scottie's anxiety discloses his role as part of the elaborate system of projections designed and overseen by the film's predominantly invisible or offscreen males: the wealthy patriarch from "Old San Francisco" (who throws away Carlotta Valdez), the corporate shipbuilder running the new San Francisco (who throws away Madeleine Elster), and even the military engineer and bra designer from what we now call Silicon Valley. As successful capitalists who symbolize the "do-it-yourself" mentality Scottie admires, these male entrepreneurs are among the few fixed or *inertial* subjects in the film, unaffected by the mechanical forces which they set into play and to which other characters in the film are subjected. Though Scottie is clearly one of these thrown or projected characters, he ultimately differs from the other figures (all women), since in his case the redoubling of projection enables him to regain his equilibrium by the film's conclusion. The closing shot depicts Scottie obviously cured of his phobia: we see him standing on the edge of the church tower gazing directly down at the surface where Judy's hurled body has implicitly landed. In this sense, *Vertigo* could be described as a story of the process of restoring a "sick" male spectator to "healthy" masculine viewership of (mostly female) images flattened against a screen, a process that works perversely by *replicating* the spatial logic of his original phobia, or anxiety. Though previously unable to gaze at thrown projections, Scottie regains the capacity to do so by—paradoxically—identifying with the thrownness of a feminine figure engineered by Gavin Elster. Yet the identification with "Madeleine" as hurled image perversely inspires Scottie to *continue* the tradition of male engineering that Elster represents, attempting to remake Judy into "Madeleine" by using the former as a template

FIGURE 12

on which to cast the image of the latter. Only in replicating Elster's original operation does Scottie become fully aware that "Madeleine" was "projected" even prior to being thrown—an awareness that returns Scottie to the stability shared by the film's other men. While the logic of *Vertigo* thus renders Scottie's moody organization consubstantial with a projective dispositioning, the *act* of projecting is concomitantly claimed as a distinctly masculine prerogative. The safeguarding of this practice becomes clear in a scene early in the movie, when Scottie's friend Midge, excluded from his intellectual quest despite her efforts at involvement, attempts an analogous act of "projection" by painting her own face onto an otherwise exact copy of Carlotta's portrait. While this maneuver is somewhat similar to Scottie's own use of Judy as a template for "Madeleine" (though Midge reverses the trajectory by superimposing a living woman onto the mythic one), Scottie reacts with a revulsion so intense that Midge finally drops out as a potential co-investigator. Thus, while persons of both genders become equally subject to the mechanical forces of projection, the film demonstrates that this operation can be *performed* only by subjects who are male—a privilege limited to aircraft engineers, corporate shipbuilders, and "hard-headed scholars."[27]

The Phenomenologist

The doubly projective nature of anxiety in *Vertigo*—an anxiety instigated by an encounter with negativity from which the male analyst, in what begins as a hermeneutic quest for knowledge about a woman, withdraws and veers away as thrown—comes very close to the nature of the anxiety linked to the demonstrative pronoun "there" [*Da*] in Heidegger's *Being and Time* (1927), where anxiety's consubstantiality with a projective displacement elevates it to "a distinctive way in which Dasein [Being-there] is disclosed." More specifically, this disclosure is that of Dasein's "*'thrownness'* . . . into its 'there'; indeed, it is thrown in such a way that . . . it is the 'there.' The expression 'thrownness' is meant to suggest *the facticity of its being delivered over*" (*BT,* 174). For Heidegger, *all* moods or states-of-mind—anxiety in particular—"*disclose Dasein in its thrownness,*" but do so primarily "*in the manner of an evasive turning away*" (*BT,* 175). The projective nature of Scottie's anxiety thus bears a striking resemblance to the aversive trajectory Heidegger attributes to a mood (*Stimmung*) in general—as a mode of discovery based on self-distanciation: "In a state-of-mind Dasein is always brought before itself, and has always found itself, not in the sense of coming across itself by perceiving itself, but in the sense of finding itself in the mood that it has . . . in a way of finding which arises not so much from a direct seeking, as rather from a fleeing. The way in which the mood discloses is not one in which we look at thrownness, but one in which we [predominantly] turn away" (*BT,* 174).

For Heidegger, thrownness not only "has the character of throwing and of movement" (*BT*, 223) but entails *a form of surrender* to the holistic complex of "the world," revealing its nature as a totality of contexts or involvements to which Dasein finds itself always already consigned, and hence "something by which [it] can be threatened." "A state-of-mind not only discloses Dasein in its thrownness and its submission to that world which is disclosed with its own Being; it is itself the existential kind of Being in which Dasein constantly surrenders itself to the 'world,' and lets the 'world' 'matter' to it in such a way that somehow Dasein evades its very self" (*BT*, 178). We can thus find the affective organization of Scottie's intellectual quest paralleled in what Pierre Bourdieu calls the "philosophically stylized pathos" of Heidegger's analytic (*PO*, 10),[28] insofar as both trajectories insist on and proceed from the externalizing structure of moods. As Charles Guignon observes, "for Heidegger moods are not 'subjective" or 'psychic' in any sense"; neither are they "fleeting experiences which 'color' one's whole 'mental attitude.'"[29] As such, moods cannot be grasped by turning "inward": "Having a mood is not related to the psychical in the first instance, and *is not itself an inner condition* which then reaches forth in an enigmatical way and puts its mark on Things and persons."[30] Contrary to the widespread understanding of feeling, in which states of mind are in fact inner phenomena disclosed *by* their extension outward into the world, for Heidegger "Being-in-the-world," a function of consignment to "thrownness" or externalization, is precisely what states of mind like anxiety disclose. Thus, in divulging Dasein as always already thrown, much as Scottie's anxiety facilitates awareness of his own status as surrendered to "projection" in *Vertigo*'s elaborate system of projections, Heideggerian mood also imparts (as Giorgio Agamben puts it) "the fact that Dasein is not brought into its *Da* of its own accord." Agamben says further: "The originary discovery of the world is, thus, always already the unveiling of . . . a thrownness" to which Dasein has already surrendered.[31] "Discovering" the world is thus a matter not of *knowing* the world, but of consignment to one's "being delivered over" to it as something that "matters."

For the moody analyst in *Vertigo,* as we have seen, this consignment to "projectedness" is both disclosed through and fundamental to his quest for knowledge, as if his anxiety and his investigative practice were coeval trajectories. Similarly, Heidegger begins his discussion of a uniquely phenomenological method of interpretation—the famous "hermeneutic circle"—by immediately establishing moods as ontologically coextensive or "equiprimordial" with understanding, the phenomenon which in turn grounds the existential structures of interpretation and discourse. Drawing on Kierkegaard's argument in *The Concept of Anxiety* about the indissociable relation between affect and concept, in which every cognitive structure is said to "presuppose a mood"—so much so, that "an error in the modulation" becomes "just as disturbing as an error in the development of thought"—Heidegger says that "state-of-mind always has its understanding and understanding always has its mood."[32] Mood and understanding are not only equiprimordial, but organized by intimately related projectile logics. Whereas mood discloses Dasein's "thrownness" as its "Being-in-the-world," or mode of submission or surrender to the world, understanding actively throws or "projects" itself upon possibilities. Heidegger explains this as follows:

> Understanding has in itself the existential structure which we call *"projection."* With equal primordiality the understanding projects Dasein's Being both upon its "for-the-sake-of-which" and upon significance, as the worldhood of its current world. . . . Projecting has nothing to do with comporting oneself towards a plan that has been thought out, and in accordance with which Dasein arranges its Being. On the contrary, any Dasein has, as Dasein, already projected itself; and as long as it is, it is projecting. As long as it is, Dasein . . . always will

understand itself in terms of possibilities. . . . Projection, in throwing, throws before itself the possibility *as* possibility, and lets it *be* as such. As projecting, understanding is the kind of Being of Dasein in which it *is* its possibilities as possibilities. (*BT,* 184–185)

Understanding, then, is the enactment of the same "mechanical" principle to which Dasein has already been consigned (thrown), and to which it is made aware of being consigned through a state of mind. Having established the equiprimordiality and interpenetrability of mood (the disclosure of throwness) and understanding (a form of projecting), Heidegger examines interpretation as a phenomenon grounded in understanding, and analyzes discourse, in turn, as a derivative mode or byproduct of interpretation, one based on the "leveling down" of the primordial possibilities inherent in the latter.[33] Continuing this process of "leveling down," Heidegger characterizes language as being grounded in, or an offshoot of, discourse. Finally, "only after this discussion of language has been concluded, is the everyday being of the 'there' presented in terms of the existential structure of falling"[34]—the last of the four existentials which Heidegger uses to disclose "care" as the unifying structure of Dasein's being.

For Heidegger, falling (into the world) is an existential mode of everyday Dasein revealed in the "interconnection" between idle talk, curiosity, and ambiguity—which are the paler, everyday versions of discourse, understanding, and interpretation. Despite the moral and theological connotations of the word "fall," Heidegger insists that "the term does not express any negative evaluation." It must not be taken "as a 'fall' from a purer and higher 'primal status,'" or as a "bad or deplorable ontical property of which, perhaps, more advanced stages of human culture might be able to rid themselves" (*BT,* 220). Rather, it is a term "used to signify that Dasein is proximally and for the most part *absorbed in* 'the world' of its concern." Falling is thus "a kind of motion" that constitutes an essential part of Dasein's topology (*BT*, 224). This "downward plunge [*Absturz*]" is a movement opposite to the dynamic of projection (223). Whereas projection "presses forward" (184), falling "tears away": "Dasein plunges out of itself into itself, into the groundlessness and nullity of inauthentic everydayness. . . . This downward plunge . . . has a kind of motion which constantly tears the understanding away from the projecting of authentic possibilities. . . . Since the understanding is thus constantly torn away . . . the movement of falling is characterized by *turbulence*" (223).

Sounding not unlike an "aircraft engineer," Heidegger uses this property of falling to clarify an aspect of thrownness hitherto unstated: "Falling is not only existentially determinative for Being-in-the-world. At the same time turbulence makes manifest that the thrownness which can obtrude upon Dasein in its state-of-mind has the character of throwing and of movement. Thrownness is neither a 'fact that is finished' nor a Fact that is settled. Dasein's facticity is such that as long as it is what it is, Dasein *remains in the throw*, and is sucked into the turbulence [of public everydayness]" (223, italics added). Like the offscreen male technocrats in *Vertigo*, Heidegger functions like a projectionist in more ways than one, creating an abstract system in which beings are not only thrown but suspended *in* "the throw," recalling cinema's term for the crucial distance between projector and screen on which the legibility of filmed images depends. The topology defined by Heideggerian moods thus strikingly resembles a filmic one, turning on the relation between Dasein's status as thrown projection and the possibilities on which it projects. Reinforcing this visual metaphor, Heidegger describes understanding's "projective character" as that which "goes to make up existentially what we call Dasein's *"sight"* (*BT*, 186). The implicit "distance" between Dasein's site of projection and the possibilities where thrown projections land becomes the focus of Heidegger's interpretation of anxiety, which culminates in his positing the affect as a distinctive method of gauging this distance or throw.

This analysis of anxiety begins only after Heidegger has concluded his discussion of falling and has established the holistic complex of Being-in-the-world as consisting of four aspects: "falling and disclosed, thrown and projecting." Significantly, he introduces this particular state of mind in the context of searching for an analytic strategy that will make Dasein "accessible as *simplified* in a certain manner," enabling the "structural totality of . . . Being" to "come to light in an elemental way" (*BT,* 226). Heidegger lays out the problem as a methodological one, that of finding a way of "grasping the structural whole of Dasein's everydayness in its totality" or of bringing out Dasein's Being "in such a unitary manner that in terms of it the essential equiprimordiality of the structures we have pointed out, as well as their existential possibilities of modification, will become intelligible." Heidegger immediately turns to anxiety as a potential solution, describing it as "an understanding state-of-mind in which Dasein has been disclosed to itself in some *distinctive* way" (*BT,* 226, italics added) and thus as "one of the most far reaching and most primordial possibilities of disclosure . . . [lying] in Dasein itself." "In working out this basic state-of-mind and characterizing ontologically what is disclosed in it as such, we shall take the phenomenon of falling as our departure point, and distinguish anxiety from the kindred phenomenon of fear. . . . As one of Dasein's possibilities of Being, anxiety—together with Dasein itself as disclosed in it—provides the phenomenal basis for explicitly grasping Dasein's primordial totality of Being. Dasein's Being reveals itself as *care*" (*BT,* 227). Not just a mood but a "phenomenon which functions methodologically" (230), anxiety is—paradoxically—distinctive because it is "basic," as if it were a generic template for all other kinds of mood.

As he promised, Heidegger begins the analysis of anxiety as this distinctive yet basic state of mind by returning to his analysis of falling, previously defined as the existential structure of Dasein's absorption in the world of discourse and the public interpretations of the "they." Just as moods disclose thrownness in an evasive way, falling as absorption in this inauthentic realm "make[s] manifest something like a *fleeing* of Dasein in face of itself [as authentic potentiality]." Yet "to bring itself face to face with itself is precisely what Dasein does *not* do when it thus flees"; rather, "it turns *away from* itself" (*BT,* 229). It is in this very act of turning away that Dasein "is disclosed 'there,'" revealing the disclosive, "interpretive" character of the evasive maneuver itself.

Having established "turning away" in falling as a mechanism of disclosure or interpretation, Heidegger suggests that anxiety performs a similar function, and proceeds to demonstrate this by distinguishing it from fear. In fear, one does not really "flee"; rather, one "shrinks back" (a weaker version of fleeing) in the face of something threatening, defined as "a detrimental entity within-the-world which comes from some definite region but is close by and is bringing itself close, yet might stay away." But since Dasein turns away from *itself* in falling, "that in the face of which it thus shrinks back must, in any case, be an entity with the character of threatening; yet this entity has the same kind of Being as the one that shrinks back: it is Dasein itself. That in the face of which it thus shrinks back cannot be taken as something 'fearsome,' for anything 'fearsome' is always encountered as an entity within-the-world. . . . *The turning-away of falling is grounded rather in anxiety, which in turn is what first makes fear possible*" (*BT,* 230). Whereas in fear one shrinks back from a definite entity within the world, in anxiety one flees from something "completely indefinite" and "incapable of having an involvement." As Heidegger elaborates, "Nothing which is ready-at-hand or present-at-hand within the world functions as that in the face of which anxiety is anxious" (*BT,* 231).[35] In Heidegger's affective topology, however, the "no*thing*" one encounters in anxiety is also a "no*where,*" lacking a definite position or location in the world. In other words, "that which threatens cannot bring itself close from [a particular] direction," since "anxiety does not 'see' any definite 'here' or 'yonder' from which [the threatening] comes" (*BT,* 231). The combination of "nothing and nowhere" causes the world itself, Dasein's total network of involvements, to assume the character "of completely lacking significance" (*BT,* 231): "The threatening does not come from what is ready-to-hand or present-at-hand, but rather from the fact that neither of these 'says' anything any longer" (393). Yet this "nothing and nowhere" paradoxically makes the world manifest as such, *in* its lack of signifying value: "The utter [asignifyingness] which makes itself known in the 'nothing and nowhere,' does not signify that the world is *absent,* but tells us that entities within-the-world are of so little importance in themselves that on the basis of this insignificance of what is within-the-world, *the world in its worldhood is all that still obtrudes itself*" (231, italics added). This maneuver enables Heidegger to posit not only that "that which anxiety is anxious about is Being-in-the-world itself" (232), since it brings Dasein "face to face with its world *as* world" (233, italics added), but also that the "nothing and nowhere" about which it is anxious is its own "being possible."[36]

It is at this point that anxiety, already privileged as a distinctive mode of disclosure which is fit "to take over a methodological function *in principle* for the existential analytic" as a whole, becomes elevated into an "individualizing" and redemptive mode of affective self-discovery. Anxiety rescues or "brings Dasein back from its falling," countering this movement by retrieving it "from its absorption in 'the world'":

> In anxiety what is environmentally ready-at-hand sinks away, and so, in general, do entities within-the-world. The "world" can offer nothing more, and neither can the Dasein-with of Others. Anxiety thus takes away from Dasein the possibility of understanding itself, as it falls, in terms of the "world" and the way things have been publicly interpreted. Anxiety throws Dasein back upon that which it is anxious about—its authentic potentiality-for-Being-in-the-world. Anxiety individualizes Dasein for its ownmost Being-in-the-world, which, as something that understands, projects itself essentially upon possibil-

> ities. Therefore . . . anxiety discloses Dasein as *Being-possible,* and indeed as the only kind of thing which it can be of its own accord as something individualized in individualization.
> (*BT,* 232)

Anxiety not only saves Dasein from falling, but restores its individuality and *capacity for projection* (i.e., its capacity for understanding and interpretation), which is precisely the outcome of the anxious detective's trajectory in *Vertigo.* Anxiety's distinctive "throw" in Heidegger is in fact a mirror image of Scottie's pathway to recovering his status as "free man."

While grounded in the existentials of throwing, projecting, and falling, Heidegger's interpretation of anxiety as interpretive methodology implicitly rests on a fourth kind of "movement": the sinking of the "environmentally ready-at-hand" which counters Dasein's absorption in the world and its entities as meaningful or "saying something." As we have seen, Heidegger's thesis that anxiety distinctively and uniquely discloses Dasein as "*Being towards* its ownmost potentiality-for-Being" (*BT,* 232) rests on the idea that anxiety brings Dasein "face to face with the world *as* world," or as something asignifying. But the disclosure of this asignificance occurs through the "motion" of recession or withdrawal: the world appears asignificant in anxiety only because "in anxiety what is environmentally ready-at-hand *sinks away*" (*BT,* 232, italics added). While Dasein's thrownness, projection, and falling are carefully developed as existentials, however, this "sinking" of the environmentally ready-at-hand is not. Given Heidegger's attention to figures of recession and their importance to his work as a whole, the absence of phenomenological elaboration here is striking, particularly when contrasted with the detailed ontological analyses Heidegger provides of the other "kind[s] of motion" concomitantly used to establish anxiety's unique interpretive function (*BT,* 223). If the world's spatial abatement or "sinking" in anxiety is what manifests its asignificance and thus what "brings Dasein back from its falling" (235), one wonders if the term's conspicuous occlusion from existential analysis might not have something to do with the fact that the image of a sinking that counters the movement of falling introduces a problem of relativity that recalls *Vertigo*'s famous track-out/zoom. Is Dasein's falling or fleeing toward entities-in-the-world *really* a "downward plunge," or is this plunge an illusion fostered by the downward dropping of the world itself? In any case, the "movement" of sinking in Heidegger's account of anxiety foregrounds how this "basic state-of-mind" enables Dasein to achieve a certain kind of distance even in the absence of the *fixed* positions by which distances are ordinarily determined, since the region from which anxiety "throws" Dasein back from falling, thus ensuring its *separation* from that region, is not only a site lacking real coordinates but one already subject to spatial displacement.

Given the proclamation of anxiety's "fitness to take over a methodological function in principle for the existential analytic" as a whole, and the fact that Heidegger's text is the very performance and demonstration of this existential analysis, the philosopher's interpretation of anxiety amounts somewhat to a comment on the moodiness of his own hermeneutic practice. In effect, he is saying: As everyday Dasein's existential interpreter, I necessarily proceed from a state of anxiety, for this is the distinctive state of mind enabling one to define "the totality of Dasein's structural whole" (mood, understanding, discourse, falling) in a phenomenologically unified manner. This is not to found a reading of *Being and Time* on a psychologization of Heidegger, which would be like attempting to dismantle a theorist's misogynistic thinking on the premise that it emanates from his insecurities about "the woman inside him" (reproducing, in effect, the logic of psychological "projection"). Rather, my much more modest point is that anxiety's privileged position in Heidegger's phenomenology, as a form of projective logic reaffirming the distinction between "here" and "yonder," proceeds from his claiming an initial position of "consignment" or passivity. The individualizing freedom of "projecting

upon possibilities" ultimately remains grounded in one's initial surrender to being "thrown," just as in *Vertigo* the recovery of masculine agency seems predicated on initially being in a corset. And in
both accounts of anxiety, the image of thrownness guarantees the
subject an auratic distance from worldly or feminine sites of asignificance or negativity, even when these sites lack the definite, unchanging coordinates from which the relations of nearness and far-
ness are typically gauged.

The Metaphysical Novelist

If anxiety thus takes on similar configurations in one analyst's attempt to solve the mystery of feminine projection and regain his
equilibrium as a "free man," and in another's attempt to rescue Being from fallenness in a discursive world, the spatial organization
of anxiety in Melville's *Pierre; or, The Ambiguities* (1844) interestingly complicates these accounts by showing their concerns with
gender and discourse to be intimately related.[37] For in Melville's
novel-length study of his intellectual protagonist's "moody organization," the problem of recuperating *masculine* agency raised in
Vertigo, and the problem of recuperating Dasein's *self-interpretive*
agency raised in *Being and Time,* converge in a spatial metaphor
that encompasses both Pierre's destabilizing relations with women
and his equally vertiginous struggles with texts and textuality. In
effecting this convergence, *Pierre* reminds us that the nothingness
or asignificance featured in Hitchcock's and Heidegger's accounts
of anxiety is by no means a pure sort of nothingness, but one assigned to sites at once specific and yet by definition unfixed: it is assigned to femininity in *Vertigo,* and to the sinking "world" in *Being
and Time.*

Though *Pierre*'s two main plot lines begin in contrasting settings,
the story of his increasingly complicated and emotionally fraught
involvements with women and the account of his similarly fraught
efforts to fashion himself as an American intellectual eventually

twist together toward the end of the novel. This convergence comes to the fore in the important Book 25 (containing the triple sections "Lucy, Pierre and Isabel"—"Pierre at His Book"—"Enceladus"), when, in the middle of trying to write his own philosophical novel, Pierre's already unconventional domestic arrangement with one woman becomes newly recomplicated by the arrival of another. Here the protagonist's vexed relations with women and with philosophical language become similarly spatialized, coinciding in an experience of bodily disorientation. Oscillating between an illegitimate sister masquerading as a wife (Isabel) and an abandoned fiancée who masquerades as a cousin and nun (Lucy), just as Scottie oscillates between Judy and "Madeleine," Pierre grows increasingly agitated as a writer, and his agitation becomes inextricably linked to his conflicted allegiances to women whose social and symbolic roles are made increasingly difficult to categorize or define.[38] Thus, upon hearing a sailor call out, "Steer small, my lad; 'tis a narrow strait thou art in!" referring to the sight of Pierre "with both Isabel and Lucy bodily touching his sides as he walked" (*P,* 349, 353), Pierre experiences a "sudden tremble" exactly mirroring the convulsions accompanying the "terrible vertigo" he feels while attempting to write his metaphysical novel. That effort is similarly characterized, in nautical terms, as a precariously constricted passage: "His soul's ship foresaw the inevitable rocks, but resolved to sail on, and make a courageous wreck" (*P,* 339). Like the corridor in which Pierre dramatically pauses "between the two outer doors of Isabel and Lucy" (358), a "narrow strait" confines him when he attempts to write. Authorship is likened to claustrophobia: "Through [his] lashes he peered upon the paper, which so seemed fretted with wires." Here the narrow straits are produced by Pierre's own body, and by the transformations it undergoes as a result of his agitated efforts at writing—a negative encounter with language that turns him into a "most unwilling states-prisoner of letters" (*P,* 340). Just as *Moby-Dick* stages the "unlettering" of "unlettered Ishmael" through his hermeneutic obsession with the whale

as text, Pierre's unhappy efforts at philosophical writing and reading lead to entanglement and exhaustion.[39]

The "terrible vertigo" Pierre encounters in writing and women
is consolidated in the figure of Isabel as a site of textual negativity:
"So perfect to Pierre had long seemed the illuminated scroll of his
life so far, that only one hiatus was discoverable by him in that
sweetly-written manuscript. *A sister had been omitted from the text.*
He had mourned that so delicious a feeling as fraternal love had
been denied him. Nor could the fictitious title, which he so often
lavished on his mother, at all supply the absent reality" (*P,* 7). As
Priscilla Wald notes, citing this passage, Isabel's status as textual
lack or nothingness places her as an "alternative discourse" to Pierre: "Devoid of primary [social] relationships, she is unformed humanity, the exact opposite of her pampered brother."[40] Accordingly,
throughout *Pierre* the adult Isabel speaks an excruciatingly infantile language not far from the "two childish languages" she describes herself "chattering" as an child (*P,* 117). Since the story of
her socialization occupies three chapters and extends almost to adolescence, infantile Isabel's unusually protracted entry into the symbolic order also highlights a relation to language strikingly different from that of Pierre, though similar in its affective tonality.
Whereas Pierre finds himself confused by "speechless thoughts" or
an inability to translate preexisting cognitions into words, Isabel attributes her own "bewilderings" to a form of thoughtless speech, or
to the fact that, for her, language precedes all conscious activity: "I
never affect any thoughts . . . but when I speak, think forth from
the tongue, speech being sometimes before the thought; so often,
my own tongue teaches me new things" (*P,* 123). Seeming to in-
habit an entirely different signifying register, Isabel's socialization
"from the tongue" is significantly facilitated by a face-to-face encounter with an actual infant, an event which Isabel describes as
endowing her with "the power of being sensible of myself as something human" (122), and which thus becomes a crucial phase in her
development as a linguistic being. In a scene of identification not

unlike Lacan's mirror phase, Isabel's interaction with the baby inaugurates a sense of herself as a bounded self, and enables her to acquire the capacity for differentiating self from others. This capacity is strangely described in terms of the ability to differentiate persons from *rocks*. As Isabel puts it, "This beautiful infant first brought me to my own mind, as it were; first made me sensible that I was different from stones . . . first undid in me the fancy that all people were as stones" (*P,* 122).

Wald suggests that "Isabel points to a world *beyond* language, a chaotic world that lacks coherence and meaning in general" ("HNV," 111, emphasis added). Given that Isabel's own "singular infantileness" (*P,* 140) does seem to set her apart from the highly cultured and socially privileged Pierre, who is, as Wald observes, fully indoctrinated into the symbolic order of language and patriarchal law, it is tempting to describe her "alternative discourse" as a version of Julia Kristeva's feminine semiotic, and, accordingly, to associate Isabel's initial inability to distinguish humans from stones with the primordial signifying dimension she seems to embody. Yet since *pierre* is French for "stone," and since *Pierre*'s eponymous protagonist is later compared to an anthropomorphic boulder thrown off the side of a patriarchal mountain and a marble statue rotating on a pedestal, Isabel's original "fancy that all people were as stone" is less naïve and incongruous than it may at first seem. Far from being incoherent or meaningless, Isabel's "presymbolic" tendency to conflate stones with humans anticipates her hyperliterary brother's own fantasy about *being* a stone—a fantasy that, like Scottie's dream in *Vertigo,* becomes central to the novel's spatialized representation of Pierre's intellectual anxiety.

Melville's general fascination with sites of nothingness—evinced not only in Isabel's characterization as a textual absence, but in descriptions of the whale as the "naught beyond" a wall *(Moby-Dick),* in the fantasy of an enclosed hollow within the hollow of a central chimney ("I and My Chimney"), and in the "deadly space between" an office and a closet containing a corpse *(Billy Budd)*—is brought to the fore in *Pierre* during the eponymous protagonist's encounter with a "horrible interspace" formed by a massive and precariously hanging rock:

> Somewhere near the middle of its under side, there was a lateral ridge; and an obscure point of this ridge rested on a second lengthwise-sharpened rock, slightly protruding from the ground. Beside that one obscure and minute point of contact, the whole enormous and most ponderous mass touched not another object in the wide terraqueous world. It was a breathless sight to see. One broad haunched end hovered within an inch of the soil, all along to the point of teetering contact; but yet touched not the soil. Many feet from that . . . the vacancy was considerably larger, so as to make it not only possible, but convenient to admit a crawling man. (*P,* 132)

As an "enormous and most ponderous mass" under continual threat of collapse, the patriarchal rock points to its own status as a ponderous yet teetering masculine *symbol.* Claiming to have discovered the rock, which he originally names the Memnon Stone (after the king of Egypt), Pierre ends up consulting a "white haired old kinsman" as to the source of its enigmatic initialing: "Who,—who in Methuselah's name,—who might have been this 'S. ye W.?'" The paternal scholar informs him that the writer was most likely "[King] Solomon the Wise" (*P,* 133). The stone is also linked to male authority-figures associated with the New World and its "discovery": Columbus and Captain Kidd. Given this superabundance of mythic patriarchs, an explicit congruence is established between the "ponderous mass" Pierre apostrophizes and the massive rock formation to which Melville dedicates his novel: "The majestic mountain Greylock—my own more immediate sovereign lord and king." In a mirroring of Melville's comically overserious, rhetorical prostration before the Pittsfield, Massachusetts rock, also called Saddleback Mountain ("I here devoutly kneel, and render up my gratitude, whether, thereto, The Most Excellent Purple Majesty of

Greylock benignantly incline his hoary crown or no"), Pierre invokes and addresses, with similarly overblown rhetoric, the "Mute
Massiveness" of the rock in Saddle Meadows:

> Eyeing the mass unfalteringly . . . he threw himself prone
> upon the wood's last year's leaves, and slid himself straight into
> the horrible interspace, and lay there as dead. He spoke not,
> for speechless thoughts were in him. These gave place at last to
> things less and less unspeakable; till at last, from the very brow
> of the beetlings and the menacings of the Terror Stone came
> the audible words of Pierre:—
>
> "If the miseries of the undisclosable things in me, *shall ever
> unhorse me from my manhood's seat,* if to vow myself all Virtue's
> and all Truth's, be but to make a trembling, distrusted slave of
> me; if Life is to prove a burden I can not bear without igno-
> minious cringings . . . *then do thou, Mute Massiveness, fall on
> me!* Ages thou hast waited; and if these things be thus, then
> wait no more; for whom better canst thou crush than him who
> now lies here invoking thee?" (134–135, italics added)

Though Pierre's sense of menace initially derives from the "horrible interspace" *within* the structure he encounters, his soliloquy displaces this menace onto the material structure itself—a shift prefig-
ured by Pierre's act of renaming the Memnon Stone the "Terror
Stone." "Terror" thus becomes a property of the stone itself, rather
than an emotion triggered by Pierre's relation to a negative space
inside it. Reformulated as the terror posed by a ponderous *substance*
("do thou, Mute Massiveness, fall on me"), rather than as the original danger posed by a nothingness or void, anxiety now hinges on
Pierre's act of making *himself* the object of the substance's potentially crushing force. Much like Scottie's encounter with the open
grave in his dream, which immediately triggers his fantasy of being
hurled in space, Pierre's rhetorical self-transformation into an entity potentially crushed, crumbled, or "unhorsed" takes place as an
aversive turn from negativity. In the face of the objectlessness that

originally confronts him, Pierre's substitution of himself as "object" mirrors the numerous passive constructions used to characterize him as a victim of his moods (Wald, "HNV," 109, 116): "A sudden, unwonted, and all-pervading sensation *seized him*"; "a temporary mood . . . *invaded [his] heart*"; "the specializing emotion . . . *seized the possession of his thoughts,* and waved [a thousand forms] into his visions" (*P,* 341, 205, 50, italics added). Significantly, it is the process in which Pierre makes himself this "object" (through the act of apostrophizing the stone) that precipitates his fantasy of himself as being violently displaced or hurled from "manhood's seat."

Pierre's reconceptualization of threat in his Terror Stone address thus culminates in a new definition of anxiety, as a form of *masculine* dispositioning based on being "unhorsed" or thrown. This shift is brought to the fore in the novel's famous Enceladus fantasy, a dream which follows one of Pierre's failed attempts to write. Here the event of becoming a thrown "stone," as the imaginary act anticipated during the Terror Stone encounter, becomes realized in a fantasy caused by a state of disorientation similar to the "terrible vertigo" elsewhere associated with the novel's other main site of negativity: the "unknown, foreign feminineness" embodied in Isabel. "A sudden, unwonted, and all-pervading sensation seized him. He knew not where he was; he did not have any ordinary life-feeling at all. He could not see; through instinctively putting his hand to his eyes, he seemed to feel that the lids were open. Then he was sensible of a combined blindness, and vertigo, and staggering; before his eyes a million green meteors danced; he felt his foot tottering. . . . He put out his hands, and knew no more for the time" (*P,* 341). The similarity between this state of mind and the "whirlingness" Isabel describes in her own account of acquiring language is brought forth in Melville's description of the psychic conditions informing the act of writing under which Pierre nevertheless persists: "Against the breaking heart, and the bursting head; against all the dismal lassitude, and deathful faintness and sleeplessness, and the whirlingness, and craziness, still like a demigod he bore up" (339). If "the very termination *-ness*" marks "the projection of feeling into an object," as I. A. Richards notes in an excursus on "aesthetic or 'projectile' adjectives and their corresponding abstract substantives" (i.e., prettiness, loveliness, ugliness, et cetera), "anxiety" in *Pierre* might be described as the meta-affect or feeling tone *of* this affective projection—the "atmosphere" produced by the novel's overarching and, one might even say, slightly icky reliance on what Richards calls "aesthetic or 'projectile'" language as a whole.[41]

Pierre's vertigo is thus characterized by a cloud of phenomenological or Heideggerian substantives ("projectile" substantives) almost directly corresponding to Isabel's experience of "the stupor, and the torpor, and the blankness, and the dimness, and the vacant whirlingness of the bewilderingness" (*P*, 122). In the face of this vertigo, Pierre's acts of writing become acts of *aversion,* much the way his encounter with the "horrible interspace" does—as if language itself were an analogous site of negativity. This turning away is reinforced by Pierre's physical gesture of averting his gaze: "Sometimes he blindly wrote with his eyes turned away from the page . . . He had abused them so recklessly, that now they absolutely refused to look on paper. He turned them on paper, and they blinked and shut. The pupils of his eyes rolled away from him in their own orbits" (340, 341).

It is precisely this state of mind, one defined by an aversive trajectory arising specifically from a struggle between male subject and text, that engenders the Enceladus fantasy: "Again the pupils of his eyes rolled away from him in their orbits: and now a general and nameless torpor . . . seemed stealing upon him." The narrator continues:

> During this state of semi-unconsciousness, or rather trance, a
> remarkable dream or vision came to him. The actual artificial
> objects around him slid from him, and were replaced by a
> baseless yet most imposing spectacle of natural scenery. But

though a baseless vision in itself, this airy spectacle assumed very familiar features to Pierre. It was the phantasmagoria of the Mount of the Titans, a singular height standing quite detached in a wide solitude not far from the grand range of dark blue hills encircling his ancestral manor. (342)

In this hallucinatory return to the pastoral setting of Saddle Meadows and its rocky patriarchal ruins, the "baseless yet most imposing" configuration of Pierre's fantasy recalls the teetering yet ponderous structure of the Terror Stone—the mass that eventually supplants the negative space it surrounds as locus of Pierre's anxiety or dread. Within the dream, Pierre explicitly identifies himself with Enceladus, another anthropomorphic stone named after the mythological son of Titan. This stone is described as being hurled from the sides of the patriarchal mountain and lying "shamefully recumbent at its base" (*P,* 346). Scattered among other "recumbent sphinx-like shapes thrown off the rocky steep," the "American Enceladus" that Pierre confronts in his trance becomes a mirror image of himself: "'Enceladus! it is Enceladus!'—Pierre cried out in his sleep. That moment the phantom faced him; and Pierre saw Enceladus no more; but on the Titan's [dismembered] trunk, his own duplicate face and features magnifiedly gleamed upon him with prophetic discomfiture and woe. With trembling frame he started from his chair, and woke from that ideal horror to all his actual grief" (346).

Here the two "stones" from Saddle Meadows, the American Enceladus and the anxious *pierre,* are explicitly conflated. By the end of the fantasy, however, the object "wrested" and hurled from the precipice is eventually depicted as an object that *hurls itself back* at the paternal mass with a force comparable to that with which it was initially torn away: "No longer petrified in all their ignominious attitudes, the herded Titans now sprung to their feet; flung themselves up the slope; and anew battered at the precipice's unresounding wall. Foremost among them all, [Pierre] saw a moss-turbaned, armless giant, who despairing of any other mode of wreaking his immitigable hate, turned his vast trunk into a battering-ram, and hurled his own arched-out ribs again and yet again against the invulnerable steep" (346).

In shifting the American Enceladus from an object "thrown *off from* the rocky steep" to a "no longer petrified" entity capable of throwing itself *against* this steep, Pierre's dream performs a redoubling of "projection" that culminates in the phantasmatic restoration of masculine agency, much as the corseted and thrown analyst in *Vertigo* eventually regains his status as free man and active thrower of projections. In both cases, the male subject's anxiety assumes this projective character in the act of aversively turning away from "horrible interspaces" or sites of radical asignificance or negativity. Like the grave that marks an area Scottie's gaze cannot fully fix itself upon or actually reach, and from which it finally turns away, or like the "nothing-and-nowhere" in Heidegger's analysis of anxiety that occasions Dasein's fleeing or the aversive turning of its "sight," the absence of a "there" to orient Melville's male intellectual in the woman-dominated world around him provides the occasion for a displacement that subsequently *delivers* him over to this "there" as thrown. Thus, the redoubling or projection of projection in the Enceladus fantasy, as in Scottie's dream and Heidegger's philosophy, counters the directionless oscillation Pierre initially experiences in face of the "unknown, foreign feminineness" embodied by Isabel and later Lucy, with a trajectory enabling him to regain some form of situatedness in the world, albeit in the form of a transient dream, and in the form of a projectile object consigned to its being in the throw.

While doing so, however, the projective character Pierre's anxiety comes to assume, as a form of displacement marked by an implicit movement from agent to object, or center to periphery, performs a more conservative function as well. For, as is the case in Heidegger's and Hitchcock's similarly spatialized renderings of the male analyst's distinctive mood, the externalizing trajectory that anxiety becomes secures this disposition as a form of self-liberation (albeit only as fantasy in Melville's text) based partly on the claim to peripheral status which this movement makes available. The way to freedom via projection, like Scottie's pathway to becoming a free man, or the way Dasein is freed for its authentic possibilities through its disclosure in anxiety as thrown projection, occurs only in the claim of an initial "surrender" to thrownness that registers in the form of impotence or passivity. In each case, the projective character assigned to anxiety enables it to function as a way of recovering the subject's agency by propelling him up and away from the "horrible interspaces" that subject him to directionless oscillation, sites already placed in abeyance by being characterized as "nothing and nowhere." As the focus shifts from the specific occasions of this negativity—femininity in *Vertigo* and *Pierre*, forms of discursive asignifyingness in *Pierre* and *Being and Time*—and as the threat relocates to "nothingness" itself, which sheds its status as a property fixed to a specific structure or entity and becomes a substantive, anxiety acquires a strangely "basic" status as an affect without determinate object or target, as reflected in descriptions of its lack of "directedness" or intentionality. Greimas and Fontanille go so far as to suggest that anxiety presents a case of pure "phoria" prior to its polarization into euphoria and dysphoria, as a neutral "protensivity" or "soft chaos of nonarticulated tensions."[42] Yet contrary to being an "indefinite flatness" that suspends the assignation of values,[43] anxiety in Melville's, Hitchcock's, and Heidegger's formulations is object-directed but solely in a negative sense, involving an aversive turning *away from* rather than a philic movement *toward.*

Anxiety nonetheless comes to assume its prominent role in structuring the "philosophically stylized" quests for truth, knowledge, and masculine agency featured in *Pierre, Vertigo,* and *Being and Time* precisely as a way of rescuing the intellectual from his potential absorption in sites of asignificance or negativity. Moreover, the fantasy of thrownness central to each representation of anxiety enables the intellectual to achieve a strategic form of *distance* without the fixed or constant positions on which our concept of distance ordinarily depends, since the sites from which the intellectual flees are either revealed as nonplaces lacking positive coordinates, or as feminine or discursive sites already subject to projection and displacement—sinking, retreating, or in the throw. Yet in each topology, whether created by the throwing of corsets, of projections, or of stones, anxiety emerges as a form of dispositioning that paradoxically relocates, reorients, or repositions the subject thrown—performing an "individualization" (as Heidegger puts it) that restores and ultimately validates the trajectory of the analyzing subject's inquiry. In other words, there is a form of "revolutionary uplift" which anxiety's projective character makes available to these intellectual subjects and which directs attention away from the questions of "sinking" worlds, "horrible interspace[s]," and "unknown, foreign feminineness[es]" as quickly as it raises them, such that this moody organization might be described as an aversive turn from the very occasions of the subject's aversion. If the question of aversiveness *to* these embodiments of negativity is precisely what anxiety veers away from or postpones, it may be that this form of distanciation plays some role in the affect's general prominence in cultural narratives of intellectual life, and more specifically in its codification as the male knowledge-seeker's distinctive yet basic state of mind.

6 stuplimity

Less best. No. Naught best. Best worse. No. Not best worse.
Naught not best worse. Less best worse. No. Least. Least
best worst. Least never to be naught. Never to naught be
brought. Never by naught be nulled. Unnullable least. Say
that best worst. With leastening words say least best worst.
For want of worser worst.

    — SAMUEL BECKETT, *Worstward Ho* (1983)

Sorry. Sorry. I'm sorry. I regret it. Please accept my apology.
I'm extremely sorry. I regret my mistake. Pardon me. Pardon me. I hope you'll forgive me. I'm deeply apologetic. Do
forgive me. Pardon me. Accept my apology. Do forgive me.
I'm deeply apologetic. Excuse me. Excuse me. It was my
own fault. Do forgive me. I'm so sorry.

    — JANET ZWEIG, *Her Recursive Apology* (1993)

There is stupid being in every one. There is stupid being in
every one in their living. Stupid being in one is often not

stupid thinking or stupid acting. It very often is hard to
know it in knowing any one. Sometimes one has to know of
some one the whole history in them, the whole history of
their living to know the stupid being of them.
— GERTRUDE STEIN, *The Making of Americans*
(1906–1908)

Thick Language

"Gertrude and I are just the contrary," writes Leo Stein in *Journey into the Self* (1950). "She's basically stupid and I'm basically intelligent."[1] What Leo finds "stupid" about Gertrude Stein and her writing, which he abhorred, is perhaps similar to what Tod finds "thick" about Homer Simpson's use of words in Nathanael West's *Day of the Locust* (1939).[2] When Tod coaxes the sluggish, almost comatose Homer to talk about the departure of Faye, Homer's speech is at first incomprehensible to him. "Language leaped out of Homer in a muddy, twisting torrent. . . . The lake behind the dam replenished itself too fast. The more he talked the greater the pressure grew because the flood was circular and ran back behind the dam again" (*DL,* 143–144). Yet Homer's "muddy, twisting torrent" has a logic of its own, eventually enabling Tod to understand his back-flowing discourse on its own terms: "A lot of it wasn't jumbled so much as timeless. The words went behind each other instead of after. What [Tod] had taken for long strings were really one thick word and not a sentence. In the same way sentences were simultaneous and not a paragraph. Using this key he was able to arrange a part of what he had heard so that it made the usual kind of sense" (144). Homer's dull stupor in the wake of unexpected loss produces its own "thick" language—one that initially suggests an inability to respond or speak at all—by eroding formal distinctions between word, sentence, and paragraph. To use terms Gilles Deleuze adapts from John Duns Scotus, the thirteenth-century philosopher whose name gave rise to the word "dunce," these formal differences of quality or kind are exchanged for modal differences based on variations in intensity or degree.[3] Modal differences could thus be described as moody differences—unqualified, temperamental, and constantly shifting. Moreover, in West's novel the encounter with thick language, which is based on modal and as yet unqualified differences rather than on formal ones, produces a mimetic effect: Tod finds himself temporarily stupefied by the language generated by Homer's stupor. Which is to say he discovers that it challenges his own capacity to interpret or respond to it in conventional ways.

Radically altering the temporal order dictated by normative syntax ("the words went behind each other instead of after") and blurring the distinction between syntactic units (words, sentences, paragraphs), the thick or grammatically moody language that West describes can also encompass the signifying logic at work in Stein's dense *Making of Americans,* where words are deliberately presented in "long strings" rather than conventional sentences and where the repetition of particular words and clauses produces a layered or "simultaneous" effect.[4] As Stein puts it in "Poetry and Grammar,"

> Sentences and paragraphs. Sentences are not emotional but paragraphs are. . . . When I wrote *The Making of Americans* I tried to break down this essential combination by making enormously long sentences that would be as long as the longest paragraph and so to see if there was really and truly this essential difference between paragraphs and sentences, if one went far enough with this thing with making the sentences long enough to be as long as any paragraph and so producing in them the balance of a paragraph not a balance of a sentence, because of course the balance of a paragraph is not the same balance as the balance of a sentence.[5]

Stein's attempt to erode the formal difference—referred to above as "essential" difference—between sentences and paragraphs (a dif-

ference in kind or quality) by bringing into play the modal difference between long and "enormously long" sentences (a difference
in intensity or degree) poses a challenge to dominant systems of
sense-making, a challenge that she would pursue throughout her
career. In *The Making of Americans,* the strategy is also an agglutinative one, where the simple material buildup of language, turning
already long sentences into longer ones, is invested with the potential for altering the "balance," or equilibrium, of normative syntax
and prose structure.

The sense of urgency that inflects Stein's struggle to make sentences "simultaneous and not a paragraph" in *The Making of Americans* becomes amplified in *How to Write* (1928), whose opening
piece, "Saving the Sentence," bears a title suggesting that language,
like an occupied territory in time of war, is in need of rescue.[6] In
another section from *How to Write,* called "Sentences," Stein makes
a similar effort to explore the relation between different units of
sense: "*What* is the difference between words and a sentence and
a sentence and sentences" (*HTW,* 181, emphasis added). At first
glance, her statement seems to inquire about the element that enables us to distinguish one linguistic kind from another (words
from sentence), as well as single instances from plural instances of a
particular kind (sentence from sentences). It also seems to ask about
the difference that lies *between* the two kinds of difference exemplified by two sets of paired terms: formal difference (words and a
sentence) and modal difference (sentence and sentences). But, in
addition, we can read it as a statement that names the term "what"
as precisely this difference. What is "what"? Several things at once.
It is an interrogative adjective, as well as a relative pronoun equally
applicable to single and plural objects. As a word capable of standing alone to form its own sentence, "what" can also function as a
demand for repetition, or an expletive conveying a negative emotion such as disbelief, stupefaction, or incomprehension. Thus, in
locating "the difference between words and a sentence and a sentence and sentences" in "what," Stein suggests that the difference is

at once interrogative, relative, affective, and one that oddly compels or solicits repetition. Like the relationship between sentences and paragraphs in *The Making of Americans,* or between "one thick word" and a sentence in Homer's muddy discourse, difference as "what" could be described as difference without a determinate value or "difference without a concept"—which is one of the ways Deleuze defines repetition in *Difference and Repetition.*

The fact that "what" can become a demand for repetition also recalls Deleuze's counterintuitive thesis that repetition is what lies between two differences. If configured as "what," the "difference between words and sentences or a sentence and sentences" could be described as a demand for repetition that also poses a question: "What is a sentence. A sentence is something that is or is not followed" (*HTW,* 213). As Stein notes here, the word "what" is a sentence, or becomes its own free-standing sentence ("What?") when it becomes a question that solicits but may or may not be followed by a reply. "Now the whole question of questions and not answer is very interesting" (*HTW,* 32). Hence, the response that difference in the form of "what" solicits, as when encountered by Tod in Homer's thick speech, seems likely to take the form of a blocked or obstructed response—when the ability to "answer" the question posed by a specific kind of linguistic difference is frustrated or delayed. The negative experience of stupefaction arising from a relationship to language founded on a not-yet-qualified or -conceptualized difference (as in Tod's relationship to Homer's "muddy" discourse) raises the significant question of how we might respond to what we recognize as "the different" before a value has been assigned to it or before it becomes qualified—as "sexual" or "racial" difference, for instance. We are used to encountering and recognizing differences assigned concepts or values; Stein's writing asks us to ask how we negotiate our encounters with difference when these qualifications have not yet been made. The explosion of modal differences in Beckett's *Worstward Ho* poses a similar question: we may have a concept for the difference between "best" and "worst"—but what about the difference that Beckett insists lies between "worst" and "worser worst," or between "Best worse" and "Least best worse"?[7]

Hence, in Stein's effort to "break down the essential combination" of sentences and paragraphs and suggest that "what" is the difference between "words and a sentence and a sentence and sentences," her agenda is not to be confused with an attempt to level or neutralize difference by repetition; rather, it is an effort to reconfigure one's relationship *to* difference through repetition and grammatical play. If a specific emotional quality emerges through this new relationship to difference, it seems important to understand how the former might organize and inform strategies of reading made possible by the latter. Throughout Stein's career—beginning around 1906, when she began developing what Marianne DeKoven calls her "insistent" style based on repetition[8]—fixed or "essential" distinctions are replaced with as yet unqualified ones to generate new frameworks of sense-making: standards of continuity, order, and "balance" alternative to the symbolic status quo. What this requires from the writer, Stein suggests, as well as from her readers, is an experiment in both duration and endurance, testing whether one can go "far enough with this thing." As anyone who has read *The Making of Americans* in its entirety can attest, this astonishing 922-page narrative inevitably induces an exhaustion bound up with its taxonomic analysis and differentiation of human types. Stein's interest in how astonishment and fatigue, when activated in tandem, come to organize and inform a particular kind of relationship between subjects and language (or between subjects and difference, via language) can be further explored by examining how this peculiar amalgam of seemingly antithetical affects comes to bear on our contemporary engagements with radically "different" forms in American poetry.

Poetic Fatigue and Hermeneutic Stupor

In *Journey into the Self,* what Leo Stein implicitly defines as "stupid" language, in his characterization of his sister the writer, is language that threatens the limits of the self by challenging its ability to respond—temporarily immobilizing the addressee, as in situations of extreme shock or boredom. In the case of Homer's muddy and twisting torrent of words, the subject no longer seems to be the agent producing or controlling his speech; rather, language "leaps out" with its own force and stupefies the listener. Yet as West's scene of interpretation demonstrates, Homer's emotional speech becomes intelligible once Tod recognizes that it constitutes its own system of sense-making and that it requires the addressee to readjust his sense of linguistic "balance." Like the affectively charged, insistent language that Gertrude Stein uses in *The Making of Americans* to *unbalance* conventional syntax and create a vast combinatory of "bottom natures," Homer's "thick" and "muddy" speech invites a critical journey not into the self, but into the more complex problem of the self's relationship to a particular kind of linguistic difference that does not yet have a concept assigned to it.

"The words went behind each other instead of after. What he had taken for long strings were really one thick word and not a sentence. In the same way sentences were simultaneous and not a paragraph" (West, *DL,* 144). Deviating from conventional syntax and its standard way of organizing signs, Homer's gush, like Stein's prose, produces a simultaneousness or thickness that recalls the cause of the cryptanalyst Legrand's stupefaction in Poe's tale "The Gold-Bug" (1843). Trying to analyze the image of a scarabaeus he has sketched on a piece of parchment, Legrand is surprised to discover a skull on the reverse side, superimposed immediately beneath his drawing: "I say the singularity of this coincidence absolutely stupified me for a time. This is the usual effect of such coincidences. The mind struggles to establish a connection—a sequence of cause and effect—and, being unable to do so, suffers a species of temporary paralysis. But, when I recovered from the stupor, there dawned upon me gradually a conviction which startled me even far more than the coincidence."[9] In the scenes of analytical stupor staged by both West and Poe, the obstacle posed to the interpreter involves a superimposition of forms. Homer's words are placed "behind each other instead of after," and so are Legrand's glyphs, creating a layered simultaneity of signs. In West's narrative, the thickening of Homer's language is explicitly figured as an effect of this behindness—that of discursive flow "[running] back behind the dam again" (*DL*, 144). The backward slippage dramatized in Tod's description of Homer's language is likewise a feature of Stein's prose in *The Making of Americans*, where narration is repeatedly forced to "begin again," and it is an aspect of the style that dominates Beckett's later prose and poetry. In "Stirrings Still" (1988), a prose poem that deals specifically with a subject's experience of stupefying loss, the overlapping accretion of phrases and clauses within the boundaries of a severely limited diction results in a language that is paradoxically both ascetic and congested, "thickening" even as it progresses into a narrative of not-progressing:

> One night or day then as he sat at his table head on hands he saw himself rise and go. First rise and stand clinging to the table. Then sit again. Then rise again and stand clinging to the table again. Then go. Start to go. On unseen feet start to go. So slow that only change of place to show he went. As when he disappeared only to reappear later at another place. Then disappeared again only to reappear again later at another place again. So again and again disappeared again only to reappear again later at another place again. Another place in the place where he sat at his table head on hands.[10]

The theme of survival and endurance in the wake of a traumatic loss is conveyed here through a drastic slowdown of language, a rhetorical enactment of its fatigue—in which the duration of relatively simple actions is uncomfortably prolonged through a proliferation of precise inexactitudes. This process occurs not only through repetition but through a series of constative exhaustions staged through the corrective dynamics of retraction and restatement, of statements partially undoing the completion of preceding statements by breaking the movements they describe into smaller intervals. The undoing paradoxically relies on a process of material buildup, where words are slowly added rather than subtracted. The finitude of a simple action such as "He saw himself rise and go" is disrupted by being made increasingly specific in degree. "He saw himself rise and go." Not exactly: first he rises and stands, then sits again, then rises again. Then he goes. Not exactly: then he *started* to go. No again: then *on unseen feet* he started to go. The interstitial *no*'s that are unstated but implied in "Stirrings Still" are actually filled in for us in *Worstward Ho,* which attempts to exhaust all combinations of the values we assign to difference: "Less best. No. Naught best. Best worse. No. Not best worse. Naught not best worse. Less best worse. No. Least. Least best worst" (106). In both cases, the logic of progression from statement to statement is paradoxically propelled by a series of implicit or explicit objections continually jerking us backward, resulting in writing that continually calls attention to itself as lacking, even as it steadily accumulates. Because units of meaning are constantly shifting behind one another, Beckett's use of language performs a stacking of multiple temporalities, an overlapping of instantaneities and durations rather than a linear progression in time.

Like Stein's style in the period of *Making of Americans,* "Stirrings Still" becomes syntactically dense and complex while remaining minimalist in diction. As in the case of Homer's "simultaneous" or "timeless" language (West, *DL,* 144), its language is marked by the same absence of a "sequence of cause and effect" that stupefies Legrand, producing the effect of delay, fatigue, or "temporary paralysis" (Poe, "*GB,*" 305). This discontinuity is generated within the speech or text itself, as well as experienced by its interpreter as an interruption of understanding. What Poe, West, and Beckett suggest in different ways is that when language thickens, it suffers a "retardation by weak links," slowed down by the absence of causal connectives that would propel the work forward.[11] It is this change in temporal organization that in turn slows down the interpreter—as if the loss of strong links in the text paradoxically strengthens an affective link between text and reader, transferring the text's "stupor" to him or her.

To acknowledge and attempt to understand one's experience of being stupefied by a "thick" or "muddy" text, as Legrand and Tod do—an effort which enables them to go on as interpreters in spite of their "temporary paralysis"—is not the same as projecting stupidity onto the text that instigates the experience of stupefaction, as Leo Stein does when he displaces his emotional response to Gertrude Stein's writing onto the writing itself. Attempting to pinpoint the linguistic attributes that inform their stupefaction, rather than dismissing the stupefying text as senseless, Tod and Legrand perceive a breakdown of formal differences and a proliferation of modal ones, as well as a thick or "simultaneous" layering of elements in place of linear sequencing. A similar logic prevails in Dan Farrell's prose poem *366, 1996,* which was published in 1997 and which bears some stylistic allegiance to the "thick" uses of language in Beckett and Stein:

> Monday, Tuesday, Wednesday, Thursday, Friday, Saturday, Sunday, Monday, Tuesday, Wednesday, Thursday, Friday, Saturday, going into the woods, Sunday, Monday, typical trees, Tuesday, typical grass traces, Wednesday, Thursday, typical excitations, Friday, typical regional sounds, Saturday, Sunday, why slow rather than slowest, Monday, clouded height, Tuesday, some same ground, Wednesday, Thursday, Friday, Saturday, left and possible, Sunday, right and possible, Monday, Tuesday, could what there is not to be believed be asked, Wednesday, Thursday . . .[12]

Consider also this passage from Kenneth Goldsmith's FIDGET, a poem and conceptual-art piece transformed into a live performance at the Whitney Museum in 1997:

> Tongue and saliva roll in mouth. Swallow. Tongue emerges through teeth and lips. Tongue lies on lower lip. Teeth click tongue. Lower jaw drops away from upper. Flesh folds be-

neath chin. Repeats. Upper lip sucks. Rubs against lower. Swallow. Saliva gathers under tongue. Teeth tuck inside jaw. Gather saliva. Swallow. Left hand, grasping with three fingers, moves toward mouth. Swallow. Arm drops. Arm lifts. Swallow. Arm drops. Swallow. Arm lifts. Arm drops. Eyes move to left. Left hand hits. Arm lifts. Swallow. Arm drops. Right leg crosses left . . .[13]

Just as Beckett's poem stylistically enacts a form of discursive exhaustion or fatigue, Farrell's and Goldsmith's poems relentlessly focus on the tedium of the ordinary: the monotony of routines ("typical excitations") organized by calendar headings, the movements of a body not doing anything in particular. Simultaneously astonishing and boring, the experiment in "duration" is pushed in each text to a structural extreme: Farrell's poem incorporates every single day of the week of the year named in its title (366 days in all); Goldsmith's documents the writer's impossible project of recording every single bodily movement made in a twenty-four-hour period (Bloomsday, June 16). Using a similar conceptual framework, Judith Goldman's poem "dicktée" (2001), described by the author as "a study in the logic of paranoia" and its strategies of negation, is composed of every single word in Melville's *Moby-Dick* that begins with the letters *un-*, in the exact order in which those words appear:

> under, unite, unless, unpleasant, universal, uncomfortable, unaccountable, under, unbiased, undeliverable, under, underneath, universe, unequal, understanding, unaccountable, unwarranted, unimaginable, unnatural, unoccupied, undress, unobserved, unknown, unwarrantable, unknown, unaccountable, understand, uncomfortable, unsay, unaccountable, uncommonly, undressed, unearthly, undressing, unnatural, unceremoniously, uncomfortableness, unmethodically, undressed, unendurable, unimaginable, unlock, unbecomingness, understand, under, unusual, under, under, undergraduate, under,

unsheathes, undivided, unknown, unholy, unholy, unheeded, unrecorded, unceasing, unhealing, unbidden, universal, unstirring, unspeakable, unnecessary, unseen, unassuming, unheeded, unknown, until, uncheered, unreluctantly, unto, unwelcome, unto, unearthly, uncouthness, unbiddenly, unite, unite, unite, . . .[14]

In a dramatization of the way in which modal differences usurp formal ones, the poet converts *Moby-Dick* into Moby-dictation, producing a hyperbolic version of the collage of quotations compiled by the Sub-Sub-Librarian in Melville's novel. If for Melville the Sub-Sub is always already a small subject encompassed, like Ishmael, by an enormous system, Goldman comically positions herself as an even smaller one. This exaggeration of language's citability is similarly enacted in an encyclopedic work by Goldsmith entitled *No. 111 2.7.93–10.20.96.* Created in 1997, this is a collection of verbal materials that he compiled from February 7, 1993, to October 20, 1996—lists, phrases, conversations, found passages, and entire pieces of fiction, all ending on the sound of the letter *r* or schwa (his rhyme)—and that he laboriously ordered by syllable count, from a series of one-syllable entries to a piece containing precisely 7,228 (his meter).[15] Taking a more traditional versifier's attention to prosodic constraints to an extreme, and persistently subordinating content to the ruthless demands of its self-imposed rhyming pattern and metrical structure, Goldsmith's Sub-Subish work also results in what Raphael Rubinstein calls "a weirdly constructed Baedeker to late Twentieth-Century American society."[16] In chapter MDCLXXXVI (the titles of Goldsmith's chapters reflect the number of syllables they contain, which in turn determine their order in the volume), constative fatigue is hilariously performed through an overdetermined self-referentiality and the use of "literary devices" as clichés. That particular chapter, which self-referentially appropriates a text that could be described as prototypically postmodern in its own parody of postmodern appropria-

tion and self-referentiality, seems designed to exhaust the parody-
ing of these devices, as well as the devices themselves:

> This is the first sentence of the story. This is the second sen-
> tence. This is the title of the story which is also found several
> times in the story itself. This sentence is questioning the intrin-
> sic value of the first two sentences. This sentence is to inform
> you in case you haven't already realized it that this is a self-
> referential story containing sentences that refer to their own
> structure and function. This is a sentence that provides an
> ending to the first paragraph. This is the first sentence of a
> new paragraph in a self-referential story. This sentence com-
> ments on the awkward nature of the self-narrative form while
> recognizing the strange and playful detachment it affords the
> writer. Introduces in this paragraph the device of sentence
> fragments. A sentence fragment. Another. Good device. Will
> be used more later. This is actually the last sentence of the
> story but has been placed here by mistake. This sentence over-
> rides the preceding sentence by informing the reader . . . that
> this piece of literature is actually the Declaration of Indepen-
> dence but that the author in a show of extreme negligence (if
> not malicious sabotage) has so far failed to include even ONE
> SINGLE SENTENCE from that stirring document although
> he has condescended to use a small sentence FRAGMENT
> namely "When in the course of human events" embedded in
> quotation marks near the end of the sentence . . . (*No. 111*,
> 565–566)[17]

In extremely different ways, the conceptual work of Farrell, Goldsmith, and Goldman continues a tradition of poetic experimentalism grounded in the work of Stein—including her interest in
affectively reorganizing the subject's relationship to language
through stylistic innovation. Though such diverse texts should not
be reduced to a common equation, each could be described as simultaneously astonishing and deliberately fatiguing—much like

Beckett's late fiction, or the experience of reading *The Making of Americans.* Through hyperbolic uses of repetition, reflexivity, citation, and cliché, the poems perform a doubling-over of language that actively interferes with the temporal organization dictated by conventional syntax. When words or glyphs are placed "behind" each other, instead of after, "the mind struggles to establish a connection—a sequence of cause and effect—and, being unable to do so, suffers a species of temporary paralysis" (Poe, *"GB,"* 305). Yet "temporary paralysis" is not merely a state of passivity; rather, it bears some resemblance to what Stein calls "open feeling," a condition of utter receptivity in which difference is perceived (and perhaps even "felt") prior to its qualification or conceptualization. In what ways do contemporary artists engender this affective dynamic through their work?

From Stupefaction to Stuplime Aesthetics

Modern art, according to Susan Sontag, "raises two complaints about language. Words are too crude. And words are also too busy—inviting a hyperactivity of consciousness that is not only dysfunctional, in terms of human capacities of feeling and acting, but actively deadens the mind and blunts the senses."[18]

Though Sontag's conjunction of "hyperactivity" with what "deadens" already hints otherwise, the excessive, if abrupt and fleeting excitation of shock, and the prolonged *lack* of excitement we associate with boredom, would seem to give rise to mutually exclusive aesthetics. As Silvan Tomkins might put it, the two affects have diametrically opposite "profile[s] of activation, maintenance, and decay." Sudden in onset, brief in duration, and disappearing quickly, astonishment involves high levels and steep gradients of neural firing; whereas boredom, slow or gradual in onset and long in duration, involves low and continuous levels of neural firing.[19] Yet even as the temporalities of shock and boredom are inarguably antithetical, both are responses that confront us with the limitations of our capacity for responding in general. As Ernst Bloch notes, in classic taxonomies of feeling both tend to be placed in the category of "asthenic" versus "sthenic" emotions, "i.e. those which paralyze [rather than strengthen] heart innervation."[20] Both "paralyzing" affects consequently inform aesthetic responses that tend to be written off as unsophisticated: from this point of view, only a philistine would be bored by the later Beckett's fatiguing repetitions; only a naïf would be shocked by Jeff Koons's pornographic sculptures. By pointing to what obstructs aesthetic or critical response, however, astonishment and boredom ask us to ask what ways of responding our culture makes available to us, and under what conditions. The shocking and the boring prompt us to look for new strategies of affective engagement and to extend the circumstances under which engagement becomes possible. Here we will explore the peculiar phenomenon of the *intersection* of these affects, in innovative artistic and literary production, as a way of expanding our concept of aesthetic experience in general.

As Stein acknowledges in *The Making of Americans,* "Listening to repeating is often irritating, listening to repeating can be dulling" (302). Yet in that book, which presents a taxonomy or system for the making of human "kinds," repeating is also the dynamic force by which new beginnings, histories, and genres are produced and organized. As Lacan similarly suggests, "repetition demands the new," including new ways of understanding its dulling and irritating effects.[21] It thus comes as no surprise that many of the most "shocking," innovative, and transformative cultural productions in history have also been deliberately tedious ones. In the twentieth century, systematically recursive works by Andy Warhol, Robert Ryman, Jasper Johns, John Cage, and Philip Glass bear witness to the prominence of tedium as an aesthetic strategy in avant-garde practices; one also thinks of the "fatiguing repetitiveness of Sade's books"[22] and the permutative logics at work in the writings of Beckett, Raymond Roussel, Georges Perec, Alain Robbe-Grillet, Jackson Mac Low, and of course Stein. This strange partnership between enervation and shock in the invention of new genres is not limited to the avant-garde. It can likewise be found in the contemporary slasher film, which by continually using a limited number of trademark motifs replicates the serial logic of the serial killer (while also, of course, producing thrills), and in the pulsating, highly energized, yet exhaustively durational electronic music known as techno, which generated new musical subcultures in the 1980s.

Though repetition, permutation, and seriality figure prominently as devices in aesthetic uses of tedium, practitioners have achieved the same effect through a strategy of agglutination—the mass adhesion or coagulation of data particles or signifying units. Here tedium resides not so much in the syntactic overdetermination of a minimalist lexicon, as in Robert Ryman's white paintings, but in the stupendous proliferation of discrete quanta held together by a fairly simple syntax or organizing principle. This logic, less mosaic than congealaic, is frequently emphasized by sculptor Ann Hamilton in her installations, which have included 16,000 teeth arranged on an examination table, 750,000 pennies immobilized in honey, 800 men's shirts pressed into a thick wedge, and floors covered by vast spreads of linotype pieces and animal hair.[23] A similar effect is achieved by Gerhard Richter's installation *Atlas* (1997), which confronts the spectator with 643 sheets displaying more than 7,000 items—snapshots, newspaper cuttings, sketches, color fields—arranged on white rectangular panels.[24] While here the organization of material is primarily taxonomic rather than compressive, like Hamilton's, the accumulation of visual "data" induces a similar strain on the observer's capacities for conceptually synthesizing or metabolizing information. The fatigue of the viewer's responsivity approaches the kind of exhaustion involved in the attempt to read a dictionary.

This mode of tedium is specifically foregrounded in Janet Zweig's computer/printer installations, where rhetorical bits and scraps are automatically produced in enormous quantities, then stacked, piled, enumerated, weighed on scales, or otherwise quantified. To make *Her Recursive Apology* (1993), for example, four computers, each hooked up to a dot-matrix printer, were programmed to randomly generate apologies "in the smallest possible type" on continuously fed paper. As Zweig notes, "The printer apologized for two weeks, day and night. Whenever a box of paper ran out, the computer displayed the number of times it had apologized. Because the apologies were randomly chosen by the computer, no two sheets of paper are alike. I arranged the pages in a recursive spiral structure, each stack one sheet larger than the next."[25] Pushing the boundary between the emotive and the mechanical, and ironically commenting on the feminization of apologetic speech acts, *Her Recursive Apology* stages the convergence of gendered subject and machine not via a fashionable cyborg figure but through a surprisingly "flat" or boring display of text, its materiality and iterability foregrounded by the piles of its consolidation. Zweig's work calls attention to language as the site where subject and system intersect, as Stein similarly demonstrates through her own vast combinatory of human types—a text in which new "kinds" or models of humans are made through the rhetorically staged acts of enumerating, "grouping," "mixing," and above all repeating. For both Stein and Zweig, where system and subject converge is more specifically where language piles up and becomes "dense."

Like the massive *Making of Americans,* the large-scale installations of Zweig, Hamilton, and Richter register as at once exciting and enervating, astonishing yet tedious. Inviting further comparison with Stein's human taxonomy is the fact that each of these installations functions as an information-processing system—a way of classifying and ordering seemingly banal bits of stuff: newspaper clippings, snapshots, teeth, words and phrases, repetitions. To encounter the vastness of Stein's system is to encounter the vast combinatory of language, where particulars "thicken" to produce new individualities. As an ordering of visual data on a similar scale, what Richter's *Atlas* suggests through its staggering agglomeration of material is not so much the sublimity of information, but the sublimity of its ability to thicken and heap up.

But sublimity does not really seem the right concept to use here, despite its early role in making emotion—negative emotion, in particular—central to aesthetic experience. As noted in this book's introduction, the sublime might be thought of as the first "ugly feeling," in the sense of being explicitly contrasted with the feelings or qualities associated with the beautiful. It thus comes as no surprise that the sublime, conscripted to theorize an observer's response to things in nature of great or infinite magnitude (what Kant calls the mathematically sublime) or of terrifying might (Kant's dynamical sublime),[26] has had a revitalized cachet in what Arthur C. Danto describes as the twentieth-century avant-garde's attempt to separate the concepts of art and beauty.[27] Though the dynamical sublime is characterized in particular by "astonishment that borders upon terror" or by a kind of "holy awe" coupled with "dread" (Kant, *CJ*, 109), both sublimes involve an initial experience of being overwhelmed in a confrontation with totality that makes the observer painfully aware of her limitations—or at least at first. There is a sense in which astonishingly massive and totalizing works like Goldsmith's *No. 111 2.7.93–10.20.96* and Richter's *Atlas,* which reveal the limited reach of our perceptual and cognitive faculties, would seem to do the same. But Kantian sublimity remains the wrong aesthetic concept, as well as the wrong concept of feeling, to appeal to in describing the effects of works like *No. 111, Atlas,* and *The Making of Americans* on the reader or viewer. And its *interesting* failure to account for the affects summoned by works like these stems from reasons more complex than the ones detailed explicitly within the *Critique of Judgement* (1790), such as the fact that Kant limits his concept of the sublime to "rude nature," and explicitly bars it from being applied to products of art "where human purpose determines the form and the size" (*CJ,* 91).

Although the sublime encounter with the infinitely vast or powerful object—mathematical infinity, raging oceans, massive mountains, or hurricanes (to draw from Kant's own examples)—is at the outset negative, involving a failure of the imagination that threatens the mind's sense of its own capabilities (as in the case of the mathematical sublime) or precipitates a sense of physical inferiority to nature that induces fear and pain in the observer (as in the case of the dynamical sublime), both encounters end by reversing these initial challenges to the self's autonomy, culminating in "inspiriting satisfaction" rather than unpleasure (*CJ,* 101). This happens to the extent that the original revelations of subjective limitation and inadequacy, whether in the form of "the inadequacy of the imagination for presenting the ideas of a whole" or in that of the impotence the self feels when confronted with natural power and magnificence, ultimately refer the self back to its capacity for reason as a *superior* faculty—one capable of grasping the totality or infinity that the imagination could not in the form of a noumenal or supersensible idea, and also of revealing the self's final superiority to nature, inasmuch as its rational faculty is revealed as lying outside nature and in fact encompassing it (*CJ,* 91, 108–109). Hence, one surprise for the contemporary reader of Kant's analysis, given the numerous popularizations and recirculations of his sublime in the two hundred years following the third *Critique,* is that for Kant sublimity applies only to a quality or state of the subject's mind, and not to the object that excites that state of mind. Though we continue, colloquially, to describe things like "the boundless ocean in a state of tumult" as sublime, what is properly sublime for Kant is not the object of great magnitude or power that awes the self, but rather the self's pleasurable and emotionally satisfying estimation of *itself*—its "inspiriting" feeling of being able to transcend the deficiencies of its own imagination through the faculty of reason ("whose superiority can be made intuitively evident only by the inadequacy of that [other] faculty"; *CJ,* 97), and its feeling of autonomy from nature (*CJ,* 101). The paradoxical way in which a dysphoric feeling of subjective inadequacy culminates in a euphoric confirmation of what Kant calls "subjective purposiveness" and self-sufficiency involves an uplifting transcendence: intimidating objects that initially "exhibit our faculty of resistance as insignificantly small in comparison with their might" ultimately "raise the energies of the soul above their accustomed height and discover in us a faculty of resistance of a quite different kind, which gives us the courage to measure ourselves against the apparent almightiness of nature" (*CJ,* 100–101). And just as the observer is "raised above the fear of such operations of nature" in the dynamical sublime, aesthetic judgment, when referred to reason, is itself "rais[ed] . . . out of empirical psychology, in which otherwise [it] would remain buried among the feelings of gratification and grief" (*CJ,* 106). This is why, in the end, as Alan Isaacs stresses, the Kantian sublime is emotionally disinterested as well as transcendent and universally valid, forsaking the realm of negative emotion from which it initially proceeds.[28]

Hence, in spite of popularized, more contemporary versions of the Kantian sublime (as filtered through and disseminated by Romanticism, in particular), which tend to emphasize the self's initial feeling of limitation or disempowerment and thus to formulate the sublime primarily as an experience of being astonished and overwhelmed by a vast or intimidating object, the term "sublime" remains an inapt characterization of astonishing works like Richter's *Atlas* or Stein's *Americans,* as well as of our affective response to them. For one thing, works like *Americans,* with its thick language, muddy and twisting repetitions, and obsessive taxonomy of what Stein calls "bottom natures," tend to draw us *down* into the sensual and material domain of language and its dulling and irritating iterability, rather than elevating us to a transcendent, supersensible, or spiritual plane. The same could be said for both the "quaqua" and scatological sludge in Beckett's *How It Is* (of which I will say more shortly), in which the subject is literally pulled face down. In a similar vein, the vast spreads of human hair or typographic rubble that the observer is forced to interact with in Ann Hamilton's installations seem deliberately to invite, yet ultimately veer away from, being characterized as "sublime." For in contrast to the in-spiriting uplift of sublimity, this immersive, downward pull into what Ben Watson calls the "common muck" of language (or, in the case of Hamilton, linotype pieces and hair) not only preserves the initial sense of subjective limitation that Kantian sublimity ulti-mately reverses (as well as its accompanying dysphoria), but elimi-nates the distance that is essential to the Kantian sublime.[29] The precondition for experiencing the sublime, and the dynamical sub-lime in particular, is that the observer feel safely removed from the object that inspires this emotion. Thus, while "the boundless ocean in a state of tumult, the lofty waterfall of a mighty river, and such like . . . exhibit our faculty of resistance as insignificantly small in comparison with their might," they can be said to excite the feeling of sublimity *"provided only that we are in security"* (*CJ,* 100, italics added).[30] But most of all, while both Kantian and popularized ver-sions of the sublime might be conscripted to account for the aston-ishment, awe, or "respect" that a massive, even stupefying text like *Americans* solicits from its reader, no theory of sublimity seems ade-quately equipped to account for its concomitantly solicited effect of boredom. As a state of emotional deficiency paradoxically invoked in tandem with the emotional excess of shock or intense astonish-ment, this boredom is absolutely central to Stein's quasi-scientific experiment with sentences and paragraphs in *Americans,* in con-junction with her endless acts of enumerating, classifying, and re-combining human types, as well as to Beckett's effort to "exhaust the possible" by running through, and asking the reader to follow, every single permutation of variables in a relatively humdrum situ-ation—from putting on socks and shoes *(Watt),* to eating biscuits *(Murphy),* to sucking on stones *(Molloy),* to sitting, standing, and leaving a house ("Stirrings Still").[31] Yet the passivity, duration, and ignoble status of boredom would seem to contradict nearly all as-pects of the sublime, not only in its initial effect of shocked surprise bordering on terror, an emotion that is sharp and fleeting, but also in the subsequent transformation of this terror "into a feeling of tranquil superiority"—the serene, self-ennobling admiration for the colossal object in which Kant's sublime culminates.[32]

Boredom's antithetical relation to both shock and serenity, the two *competing* affects of the Kantian sublime, actually underscores the oddly discrepant status of affective lack throughout Kant's writings on sublimity. As Paul de Man notes, whereas Kant in his *Observations on the Sentiment of the Beautiful and Sublime* (published in 1764, nearly thirty years before the third *Critique*) states that "the phlegmatic as loss or absence of affect [*Affektlosigkeit*]" has nothing whatsoever to do with the sublime, in the *Critique* this absence of emotion *does* qualify as aesthetically sublime, though Kant immediately acknowledges that the characterization may seem "strange." After describing the energetic, spirited state of enthusiasm as aesthetically sublime, he argues that enthusiasm's opposite is not only sublime, but sublime in a superior way: "But (which seems strange) the absence of affection (*apatheia, phlegma in significatu bono*) in a mind that vigorously follows its own principles is sublime, and in a far preferable way, because it has also on its side the satisfaction of pure reason. A mental state of this kind is alone called noble" (*CJ*, 113). Yet the *apatheia* that Kant finds ennobling involves a calmness and neutrality that ultimately distinguishes it from the dissatisfied (and often restless) mood of boredom. We could say that Kant's sublime *apatheia* involves a lack of affect that is itself reflexively felt by the subject as neither pleasurable nor unpleasurable (that is, an absence of affect that is approached apathetically in turn, a lack about which the subject *feels nothing*), whereas boredom involves a deficiency of affect that is reflexively felt to be dysphoric—stultifying, tedious, irritating, fatiguing, or dulling. Ultimately only a bit different in affective value from the "serenity," "tranquil satisfaction of superiority" (de Man, *AI*, 85), or "disinterested *pleasure*" in which the sublime ordinarily culminates (*CJ*, 92), Kant's *apatheia* is a more neutral state, reflexively yielding neither pleasure or discomfort, that "frees" the subject for other mental activities and thus finds an ally in reason. In contrast to

freeing the subject from the realm of affect in its entirety, boredom immobilizes and stupefies—and indicates the *inability* of other
mental activities, including reason, to overcome an affective state.
Given the *sluggishness* associated with boredom, the difference between the two kinds of affective deficiency becomes clearer when
Kant subsequently contrasts "affection[s] of the strenuous kind,"
which merit characterization as aesthetically sublime, with "affec-
tions of the languid kind," which are barred from the sublime and,
as Kant notes, "have nothing noble in themselves" (*CJ,* 113).

Hence, to return to Sontag's comment about language, though
words may induce a "hyperactivity of consciousness" that might be
conceived, like Kant's alert and energetic state of "enthusiasm," as
aesthetically sublime, sublimity still remains unable to account for
this hyperactivity's secondary effect of "deaden[ing] the mind and
senses," as the sluggishness of boredom (but *not* Kant's *apatheia* or
emotional disinterestedness) is wont to do. (Despite its more radical
neutrality, the special case of emotional disinterestedness produces
virtually the same effect as disinterested pleasure—both end in "the
satisfaction of pure reason.") More specifically, the sublime cannot
be properly mobilized to account for the affective response elicited
by enormous, agglutinative works like *Atlas* or *Americans,* since
here the initial experience of being aesthetically overwhelmed involves not terror or pain (eventually superseded by tranquility), but
something much closer to an ordinary fatigue—and one that cannot
be neutralized, like the sublime's terror, by a competing affect. In
the case of Stein's colossal novel, a dysphoric affect is similarly summoned in which the reader's or observer's faculties become strained
to their limits in the effort to comprehend the work as a whole, but
the revelation of this failure is conspicuously less dramatic—and
does not, in the end, confirm the self's sense of superiority over the
overwhelming or intimidating object.

Our encounters with astonishing but also fatiguing works like
Americans thus call for a different way of thinking what it means to
be aesthetically overpowered—a new way of characterizing an affective relationship to enormous, stupefying objects that may seem

similar to, but ultimately does not fall within the scope of, either the Kantian or the popular sublime. One strategy for calling attention to the difference between the mixture of shock and exhaustion produced and sustained by a text like *Americans,* and the "dread" and "holy awe" eventually superseded by disinterested pleasure that are particular to the sublime, is to refer to the aesthetic experience in which astonishment is paradoxically united with boredom as *stuplimity.* This term allows us to invoke the sublime—albeit negatively, since we infuse it with thickness or even stupidity— while detaching it from its spiritual and transcendent connotations and its close affiliation with Romanticism. For whereas contemporary criticism depends on and repeatedly returns to make use of older aesthetic categories, even in its engagement with radically different forms of cultural production, these different forms call for new modes of critical response and thus for new terms designating our ways of responding to them. What constitutes stuplimity will become increasingly clear below, but for now I will briefly describe it as a concatenation of boredom and astonishment—a bringing together of what "dulls" and what "irritates" or agitates; of sharp, sudden excitation and prolonged desensitization, exhaustion, or fatigue. While the Kantian sublime stages a competition between opposing affects, in which one eventually supersedes and *replaces* the other (as de Man notes, "The victory of the sublime over nature is the victory of one emotion [tranquillity] *over* another emotion, such as fear"; *AI,* 123), stuplimity is a tension that holds opposing affects together. And while the sublime traditionally finds a home in the serious modes of the lyrical, elegiac, or tragic, stuplimity could be said to belong more properly to the dirtier environments of what Stein calls "bottom humor."

Stuplimity reveals the limits of our ability to comprehend a vastly extended form as a totality, as does Kant's mathematical sublime, yet not through an encounter with the infinite but with finite bits and scraps of material in repetition. And as Deleuze reminds us, one of the best examples of the finite and discrete in repetition is words: "Words possess a comprehension which is necessarily finite, since they are by nature the objects of a merely nominal definition. We have here a reason why the comprehension of the concept *cannot* extend to infinity: we define a word by only a finite number of words. Nevertheless, speech and writing, from which words are inseparable, give them an existence *hic et nunc;* a genus thereby passes into existence as such; and here again extension is made up for in dispersion, in discreteness, under the sign of a repetition which forms the real power of language in speech and writing" (*DR,* 13). In Beckett's *How It Is,* this encounter with the finite but iterable seems no less daunting than the effort by the imagination to comprehend the infinitely extended object—but unlike Kant's mathematic sublime, the effort is also tedious and exhausting: "quaqua on all sides then in me bits and scraps try and hear a few scraps two or three each time per day and night string them together make phrases more phrases . . ."[33] Here "bits and scraps" that surround the narrator on all sides are "quaqua," the material stuff of a larger signifying system. As such, these repeated finite elements express what Deleuze describes as "a power peculiar to the existent, a stubbornness of the existent in intuition, which resists every specification by concepts no matter how far this is taken" (*DR,* 13–14). This power of the finite and iterable to resist formal concepts and categories recalls a similar claim Kierkegaard makes in *Repetition:* "Every general esthetic category runs aground on farce."[34] And there is often a comical and even farcical element to stuplimity. Inducing a series of fatigues or minor exhaustions, rather than a single, major blow to the imagination, stuplimity paradoxically forces the reader to *go on* in spite of its equal enticement to readers give up (as many readers of *The Making of Americans* inevitably do), pushing us to reformulate new tactics for reading. Confrontations with the stuplime thus bear more of a resemblance to the repetitive, minor exhaustions performed by Kierkegaard's Beckmann, Buster Keaton, or Pee-Wee Herman than to the instantaneous breakdown dramatized in the imagination's encounter with infinitude or natural grandeur. In the stuplimity of slapstick comedy, which frequently stages the confrontation of small subjects with the big systems that circumscribe them, one is made to fall down—often, as in the case of Keaton, with an exaggerated expression of inexpressiveness—only so as to get up again, counteracting the seriousness of one-time failure with an accumulation of comic fatigues.

In this manner, stuplimity drags us downward into the realm of words rather than transporting us upward toward an unrepresentable divine. Or to use terms from *How It Is,* which agglutinates bits and scraps of language transmitted through a narrator who is merely quoting what he receives from an external source ("I say it as I hear it"), the affect submerges us in quaqua rather than sending us "ABOVE . . . IN THE LIGHT." This quaqua resembles the mud in *How It Is,* the thick medium in which the arrivals and separations that are the main events of the novel's story take place, yet whose viscosity produces an inertial drag or resistance that renders each arrival and separation exhaustingly difficult or slow. To understand how this scenario works, let us look at Leo Bersani and Ulysse Dutoit's synopsis of Beckett's novel.

> Imagine two old men lying still, face down in the mud, separated from one another by, say, a quarter of a mile. Now imagine two other old men, also face down in the mud, each one approaching one of the other two. The former, mysteriously silent, but intent on communicating with their new companions, devise an elaborate semiotic system in two stages. In [the first stage] the men toward whom the others have crawled are taught to respond to a series of signals [which are also forms of physical torture] administered by their silent partner's right hand. . . . At the [second stage] the former traveler imprints questions, with his fingernails, on his companion's back. In responding to his tormentor's written injunctions to tell something about his life "ABOVE . . . IN THE LIGHT," the victimized partner recites scraps of "that life then said to have been his invented remembered a little of each no knowing." . . . Our two couples, however, are not fixed in their positions or roles. Imagine that the victim of each couple leaves his tor-

mentor and crawls towards the tormentor of the other couple. The mobile and immobile roles are now reversed: the two who had previously crawled toward an immobile partner are waiting for the arrival of the two others who had, in an earlier time, lain still awaiting *their* arrival. Except, of course, that the first time around B had awaited A, and D had awaited C; now A awaits D, and C awaits B. When the new couples are formed, the same exchanges are repeated, with the roles of tormentor and victim being determined not by the actor's individual identities but rather by their functions in this relational diagram.[35]

Unlike Kant's dynamical sublime, there is no "safe place" in the world of *How It Is*—only a thick, dense mud in which everything is mired. Each old man's act of "journeying" and "abandoning" thus involves a laborious and "peristaltic" crawl,[36] leading us through "vast tracts of time" (Beckett, *HII,* 39). While Beckett's mud obstructs or slows the physical movements of individual characters toward and away from one another, it also seems to enable a process of cohesion, by which the discrete extensions of Pims, Boms and Bems, "one and all from the unthinkable first to the no less unthinkable last," come to be "glued together in a vast imbrication of flesh without breach or fissure" (*HII,* 140). The social community it creates is thus one of agglutination, as also suggested visually on the page through the absence of punctuation.

Here, large but finite numbers take the place of the infinity we associate with Kant's mathematical sublime, yet the effect of these enumerations is similarly to call attention to representational or conceptual fatigue, if not collapse. Such tiredness results even when the narrator subdivides the enormity of what we are asked to imagine into more manageable increments: "a million then if a million strong a million Pims now motionless agglutinated two by two in the interests of torment too strong five hundred thousand little heaps color of mud and a thousand thousand nameless solitaries half abandoned half abandoning" (*HII,* 115–116). Though the narrator often resorts to calculations in attempts to comprehend the "natural order" or organizing principle of the total system he lives in—one presided over by its "justice" or by the disembodied "voice of us all," from which he receives the words of his narration—these acts of enumerating, grouping, and subdividing only produce further fatigues; thus the wry double meaning of "I always loved arithmetic it has paid me back in full" (*HII, 37*). Attempting to make sense of his situation by finding smaller, more easily manipulated methods of ordering within his larger "natural order," the narrator finds these strategies of sense-making ultimately subsumed and thwarted by what encompasses them. We see this in his attempt to describe how information is exchanged in the world he inhabits. To understand the ordering principle behind this, we are asked to take twenty consecutive numbers, "no matter which no matter which it is irrelevant":

814326 to 814345

number 814327 may speak misnomer the tormentors being mute as we have seen part two may speak of number 814326 to number 814328 who may speak of him to number 814329 who may speak of him to number 814330 and so on to number 814345 who in this way may know number 814326 by repute

similarly number 814326 may know by repute number 814345 number 814344 having spoken of him to number 814343 and this last to number 814342 and this last to number 814341 and so back to number 814326 who in this way may know number 814345 by repute

. . . but question to what purpose

for when number 814336 describes number 814337 to number 814335 and number 814335 to number 814337 for example he is merely in fact describing himself to two lifelong acquaintances so to what purpose (*HII, 119–120*)

As in the case of the repeated pratfalls of the slapstick comedian, stuplimity emerges in the performance of such fatigue-inducing strategies, in which the gradual accumulation of errors often leads to the repetition of a refrain: "too strong" or "something wrong there." In this manner, every attempt by the narrator to comprehend the "natural order" or "logic" of the encompassing system (and the patterns of movement and violently forced acts of communication organized by this larger logic) by means of a smaller, more graspable, and more concrete way of thinking further blocks understanding of the wider principle and culminates in a kind of collapse ("so to what purpose"). The narrator makes many such attempts to explain the way his world works—for example, the use of Euclidean geometry (based on a circle and its division into chords "AB" and "BA") to map the trajectories of the travelers toward their destinations, and simple arithmetic to calculate the durations, distances, and velocities involved:

> allowing then I quote twenty years for the journey and knowing furthermore from having heard so that the four phases and knowing furthermore from having heard so that the four phases through which we pass the two kinds of solitude the two kinds of company through which tormentors abandoned victims travelers we all pass and pass again being regulated thus are of equal duration knowing furthermore by the same courtesy that the journey is accomplished in stages ten yards fifteen yards at the rate of say its reasonable to say one stage per month this word these words months years I murmur them (*HII*, 125)

We are thus brought to a series of calculations which in this case lead to a finite solution—if our fatigue permits us to follow them. Despite its arithmetical precision, on the page the accumulation of figures visually suggests babble: "four by twenty eighty twelve and a half by twelve one hundred and fifty by twenty three thousand divided by eighty thirty-seven and a half thirty-seven to thirty-eight say forty yards a year we advance" (*HII,* 125). The narrator's repeated arithmetical calculations suggest that whereas experiencing the sublime entails confronting the infinite and elemental (and from a safe distance), in stuplimity one confronts the mechanical operations of a finite system, whose taxonomy or combinatory incorporates oneself. *How It Is* also points to the temporal specificity of the stuplime text, as marked by extended cycles of exhaustion and recovery (in the effort to manipulate finite but repeated bits of material or information) rather than by an abrupt, instantaneous defeat of comprehension (in the face of a singularly vast or infinite object). If the temporality of stuplimity radically differs, in its slowness and duration, from the temporality of the sublime (as well as the temporality of other emotions or emotional states), this may have something to do with the laborious nature of processing the finite but iterated. One senses that the slowness of time in *How It Is* may also have something to do with the agglutinated landscape of the novel. Recalling Stein's fascination with "mushy masses" and "bottom natures" in *Americans* (a text which, according to Lisa Ruddick, operates through a similarly anal dynamic of "pressing" and "straining"),[37] the "agglutinated two by two" world of *How It Is* is a surprisingly cluttered and *dirty* world, marked by discarded "cultural" waste (torn sacks, empty food tins, dropped can openers) and by the mud in which all inhabitants find themselves partially submerged and limited in movement to a "peristaltic crawl" and in which all acts of socialization and communication take place. The only acts of sense-making allowed by this "thick" medium, the basis of all relationships and social organization, are exhausting ones that tend to culminate in gasps, pants, murmurs, or more quaqua: enumeration, permutation, retraction and emendation, measurement and taxonomic classification, and rudimentary arithmetical and algebraic operations (grouping, subdividing, multiplying).

Since the forms of stuplime exhaustion described above are related to tedium in a highly specific way, Beckett's novel shows us that there are different kinds and uses of tedium, and suggests the importance of distinguishing between them. What stuplimity does *not* seem to involve is the kind of mesmerizing, hypnotic tedium aimed at the achievement of higher states of consciousness or selfhood, as engendered by metaphysical plays of absence against presence in the work of, say, the painter Brice Marden. In this case, tedium assumes a seriousness and facilitates a transcendence more proper to the sublime than the stuplime, to an absorptive rather than anti-absorptive agenda. Stuplimity also evades the kind of wholly anti-absorptive, cynical tedium often used to reflect the flattening effects of cultural simulacra, as in the work of Andy Warhol or Jeff Koons—and I am thinking here of Koons's vacuum cleaners and basketballs, rather than his sex sculptures. Whereas the first type of tedium is auratic or hypnotic, the effect of works utilizing tedium in this manner could be described as glossy and euphoric.

What stuplimity relies on is an anti-auratic, anti-cynical tedium that at times deliberately risks seeming obtuse, as opposed to making claims for spiritual transcendence or ironic distance. Instead of emerging from existential or phenomenological questions or acts of exaggerating the banality of consumer culture and its larger-than-life icons, this boredom resides in relentless attention to the finite and small, the bits and scraps floating in the "common muck" of language (Watson, *ACC,* 223). As Beckett writes in *Murphy,* "What more vigorous fillip could be given to the wallows of one bogged in the big world than the example of life to all appearances inalienably realised in the little?"[38] Stuplimity arises in the relationship between these little materials and the operations of repetition and agglutination. As *How It Is* shows in particular, absurdity and black humor play significant roles in this use of tedium to facilitate linguistic questioning, even when such inquiry leads to direct confrontations with questions of violence and suffering, as evinced in much post–World War II writing. The particular use of "obtuse" boredom as a means of engaging in linguistic inquiry is also demonstrated in the following anecdote, told by Lacan in his 1959 seminar to introduce a definition of *das Ding* as "that which in the real suffers from the signifier":

> During that great period of penitence that our country went through under Pétain, in the time of "Work, Family, Homeland" and of belt-tightening, I once went to visit my friend Jacques Prévert in Saint-Paul-de-Vence. And I saw there a collection of match boxes. It was the kind of collection that it was easy to afford at that time; it was perhaps the only kind of collection possible. Only the match boxes appeared as follows: they were all the same and were laid out in an extremely agreeable way that involved each being so close to the one next to it that the little drawer was slightly displaced. As a result, they were all threaded together so as to form a continuous ribbon that ran along the mantelpiece, climbed the wall, extended to the molding, and climbed down again next to a door. I don't say that it went on to infinity, but it was extremely satisfying from an ornamental point of view. Yet I don't think that that was the be all and end all of what was surprising in this "collectionism," nor the source of the satisfaction that the collector himself found there. I believe that the shock of novelty of the effect realized by this collection of empty match boxes— and this is the essential point—was to reveal something that we do not perhaps pay enough attention to, namely, that a box of matches is not simply an object, but that, in the form of an Erscheinung, as it appeared in its truly imposing multiplicity, it may be a Thing. In other words, this arrangement demonstrated that a match box isn't simply something that has a certain utility, that it isn't even a type in the Platonic sense, an abstract match box, that the match box all by itself is a thing with all its coherence of being. The wholly gratuitous, proliferating, superfluous, and quasi absurd character of this collection pointed to its thingness as match box. Thus the collector found

his motive in this form of apprehension that concerns less the
match box than the Thing that subsists in a match box.[39]

Lacan uses this "fable" to illustrate his formula for sublimation
("[the raising] of an object to the dignity of the Thing"), but it
works equally well as an example of stuplimation, as the synthesis
of awe (evoked by "the truly imposing") with what *refuses* awe (the
"wholly gratuitous, proliferating, superfluous, and quasi absurd";
Seminar, 112). The description of the array of matchboxes and their
internal voids seems playfully meant to recall an earlier moment in
the seminar, where Lacan claims that the Thing, *das Ding,* "has to
be identified with the *Wieder zu finden,* the impulse to find again
that for Freud establishes the orientation of the human subject to
[a lost/absent] object" (*Seminar,* 58). The impulse to find again is an
impulse toward repetition, one centered around and organized by
negativity. In the fable above, the repetition which Lacan finds simultaneously imposing and ridiculous, threatening and nonthreat-
ening, leads him straight to this Thing, enabling "the sudden elevation of the match box to a dignity that it did not possess before"
(*Seminar,* 118). Yet this elevation is paradoxically achieved through
a lowering or debasement—an emphasis on the undignified or
"wholly gratuitous, . . . superfluous, and quasi absurd" status of the
collection through the proliferation of bits and scraps. As the producer of "multiplicities," repetition seems to do opposite things simultaneously in this anecdote: elevate *and* absurdify. In conjoining
these divergent dynamics (trajectory upward and trajectory downward), the repetition in the fable recalls a similar conjunction of rising and falling in the stuplime, through its syncretism of excitation
and enervation, its extreme "selected attentiveness," and its equally
conspicuous deficit of the same. Lacan's stuplime array also recalls the structure of a typical sentence from *The Making of Americans,* in which the tension created by slightly overlapping phrases
results in gap and disjunction (as figured in Lacan's image of "the

little drawer . . . displaced") as well as in what Peter Brooks calls the "binding" action of repetition (the agglutination expressed in Lacan's "threaded together").[40] And as in the case of Stein, its particular kind of tedium also seems willing to risk a certain degree of "shock value," unlike metaphysical boredom, which risks none whatsoever, and cynical boredom, which often demands more than we are willing to give.

In addition to highlighting the fact that not all boredoms are alike, the aesthetic differences between sublimity and stuplimity also call attention to the fact that not all *repetitions* are alike, which is a point Kierkegaard foregrounds in *Repetition*. When the young man on a quest for "real repetition" in Kierkegaard's narrative euphorically believes he has found it in the final outcome of his unconsummated love, his "perhaps disturbing enthusiasm is expressed in terms that only a little earlier in aesthetic history were standard when describing the sublime: 'spume with elemental fury,' 'waves that hide me in the abyss, . . . that fling me up above the stars.'"[41] Significantly, these prototypical invocations of Kantian sublimity highlight the effect of elevation, situating the young man's relationship to the ocean providing his "vortex of the infinite" as an experience of verticality and depth (Kierkegaard, *R,* 222). In contrast, having chosen to pursue repetition in a comic/materialist rather than tragic/Romantic arena, Constantin Constantius' description of farce as a "frothing foam of words that sound without resonance" ironically references this sublime imagery only to flatten or deflate it, reconfiguring the experience of genuine repetition as one of a superficial and almost abject horizontality (*R,* 156). "Thus did I lie in my theater box, discarded like a swimmer's clothing, stretched out by the stream of laughter and unrestraint and applause that ceaselessly foamed by me. I could see nothing but the expanse of theater, hear nothing but the noise in which I resided. Only at intervals did I rise up, look at Beckmann, and laugh so hard that I sank back again in exhaustion alongside the foaming stream" (*R,* 166). In a satirical twist of the young man's invocation of the sublime, Constantin's description of his stuplime encounter with farce places him not in the elemental fury of a vast and abyssal ocean, but rather horizontally alongside a mild and insipidly picturesque stream; it depicts him not as a mortal body engulfed by nature, but as a pile of garments discarded by an absent body. Instead of the roaring or crashing of oceanic waves in which one becomes lost, we have the "plaintive purling" of a small brook on the site of the family farm (*R,* 166). As a "frothing foam of words that sound without resonance," farce finds its structural counterpart in the mode of its reception: laughter. This laughter foams and flows past a self with no substantive content or body. Much like the "mushy mass," "flabby mass," or "lax condition" Stein attributes to "the being all independent dependent being in possibility of formation" in *The Making of Americans* (386), the self that experiences farce is described as a body's outline gone flaccid, having lost its original form. In laughter, the self becomes "stretched out" like the Steinian sentence itself, which would seem to generate a linguistic foam of its own through the cumulative buildup of repeated phrases and the repeated abutment and overlapping of clauses.

Unlike the upheaval of waves that fling the young man toward the sky, linguistic "foam" would seem to cling by cohesion to the ground, often in accumulated lumps. It is the vast sea's slaver or waste product: the dross of the sublime. Since to froth is to produce foam and foam is what froths, Constantin Constantius' phrase "frothing foam" is itself a repetition (like his own name)—one accordingly used by him to characterize the form of comedy he finds most repetition-friendly. Repetition is evident in what foams or bubbles; thus, the comic genius Beckmann is described as a "yeasty ingredient" (*R,* 165). The environment of farce in which Constantin pursues repetition might here recall the importance of "foaming" language to Stein's comic taxonomy of human types in *The Making of Americans,* as exemplified in this description of "bottom nature"—where "bottom" is literally "ground," in the sense of "dirt":

> The way I feel natures in men and women is this way then. To begin then with one general kind of them, this a resisting earthy slow kind of them, anything entering into them as a sensation must emerge again from through the slow resisting bottom of them to be an emotion in them. This is a kind of them. This bottom in them then in some can be solid, in some frozen, in some dried and cracked, in some muddy and engulfing, in some thicker, in some thinner, slimier, drier, very dry and not so dry and in some a stimulation entering into the surface that is them to make an emotion does not get into it, the mass then that is them, to be swallowed up in it to be emerging, in some it is swallowed up and never then is emerging. (*MA,* 343)

If Constantin seeks repetition not in the vast sea, but on a ground covered by its dross, Stein pursues it in the "slow resisting bottom" of language: a relentlessly materialist environment of words which similarly summons, yet ultimately deflates, the traditional Romanticism of the sublime.

Since for Stein, as for Deleuze, all repetition is repetition with an internal difference—"a feeling for all changing" (*MA,* 301)—people intent on "getting completed understanding must have in them *an open feeling,* a sense for all the slightest variations in repeating, must never lose themselves so in the solid steadiness of all repeating that they do not hear the slightest variation" (*MA,* 294, emphasis added). "Open feeling," which is a prerequisite for what Stein calls "loving repeating being" (*MA,* 295), could be described as a state of undifferentiated alertness or responsiveness—a kind of affective static, or noise, that Stein also finds particular to "that kind of being that has resisting as its natural way of fighting rather than . . . that kind of being that has attacking as its natural way of fighting" (*MA,* 296). In contrast to the sublime's dramatic terrors and awes, the paradox of open feeling is that the state of receptiveness fostered by it actually depends on slowing down other emotional reactions, much the way states of extreme excitation or enervation do:

> Resisting being then as I was saying is to me a kind of being, one kind of men and women have it as being that emotion is not poignant in them as sensation. This is my meaning, this is resisting being. Generally speaking then resisting being is a kind of being where, taking bottom nature to be a substance like earth to some one's feeling, *this needs time for penetrating to get reaction*. . . . Generally speaking those having resisting being in them have a slow way of responding, they may be nervous and quick and all that but it is in them, nervousness is in them as the effect of slow-moving going too fast . . . (*MA* 347–348, emphasis added)

Though stuplimity begins with the dysphoria of shock and boredom, it might be said to culminate in something like the "open feeling" of "resisting being"—an indeterminate affective state that lacks the punctuating "point" of an individuated emotion. In other words, the negative affect of stuplimity might be said to produce another affective state in its wake, a secondary feeling that seems strangely neutral, unqualified, "open." Though this new kind of unqualified feeling should not be confused with a lack of affect, the state remains difficult to imagine, since, as Greimas and Fontanille point out, our tendency to "reiterate uncritically the notion that living beings are structures of attractions and repulsions" limits how "phoria [might be] thought of prior to the euphoria/dysphoria split."[42] Yet in generating a form of "open feeling" in its wake, stuplimity leaves us precisely in a place to do so. Like difference without a concept, "open feeling" could described as stupefying. Yet, as Stein suggests, this final outcome of stuplimity—the echo or afterimage produced by it, as it were—makes possible a kind of resistance.

Mushy Masses and Linguistic Heaps

Consider the following, oft-cited passage from Fredric Jameson's *Postmodernism, or, The Cultural Logic of Late Capitalism:*

> The liberation, in contemporary society, from the older *anomie*
> of the centered subject may also mean not merely a liberation
> from anxiety but a liberation from every other kind of feeling
> as well, since there is no longer a self present to do the feeling.
> This is not to say that the cultural products of the postmodern
> era are utterly devoid of feeling, but rather that such feelings
> . . . are now free-floating and impersonal and tend to be domi-
> nated by a peculiar kind of euphoria, a matter to which we
> will want to return later on.[43]

The loss of affect—negative affect, in particular—that Jameson attributes above to "the end of the bourgeois ego" signaled by postmodernism (*PM,* 15) is closely tied to his definition of the latter as
an aesthetic situation engendered by a relentless spatialization that
disables our capacity for temporal organization, and thus our relationship to "real history" (21). The "waning of affect" that accompanies "the disappearance of the individual subject"—to a degree
that "concepts like anxiety or alienation (and the experiences to
which they correspond . . .) are no longer appropriate in the world
of the postmodern"—is thus characterized also as "the waning of
the great high modernist thematics of time and temporality" (14,
16). Just as the "alienation of the subject is displaced by the former's
fragmentation" in postmodernism, categories of time are displaced
by categories of space (14). Moreover, our sense of the here and now
is replaced by the aura of the simulacrum, which "endows present
reality and the openness of present history with the spell and distance of a glossy image" (21). Jameson continues: "Yet this mesmerizing new aesthetic mode itself emerged as an elaborated symptom
of the waning of our historicity, of our living possibility to experience history in some active way. It cannot therefore be said to pro-

duce this strange occultation of the present by its own formal power, but rather merely to demonstrate, through these inner contradictions, the enormity of a situation in which we seem increasingly incapable of fashioning representations of our own current experience" (21). Postmodernism seems to suggest a kind of sublimity here, insofar as it reveals a cognitive as well as emotional inadequacy on the part of the subject in the face of nothing less than history itself, revealing "the enormity of a situation in which we seem increasingly incapable of fashioning representations of our own current experience." More specifically, the subject's impotence in the face of this situation (an impotence which, as in the case of the Kantian sublime, ends not in dysphoria but in "a peculiar kind of euphoria") is revealed in his or her inability to "organize . . . past and future into *coherent* experience" (16, 25, emphasis added).

Since this loss of coherence, like the waning of negative affect, is central to Jameson's understanding of postmodernism (as an "aesthetic situation engendered by the absence of the historical referent"), we should take a closer look at how the breakdown in coherence is understood and described (*PM,* 25). A good place to do so is where Jameson begins to delineate a common feature of the "schizophrenic" writing he associates with Cage, Beckett, Ashbery, and language poetry. This is where he also, significantly, locates the "peculiar kind of euphoria" he introduces and promises to return to in the extract above:

> If, indeed, the subject has lost its capacity actively to extend its pro-tensions and re-tensions across the temporal manifold and to organize its past and future into coherent experience, *it becomes difficult to see how the cultural productions of such a subject could result in anything but "heaps of fragments" and in a practice of the randomly heterogeneous and fragmentary and the aleatory.* These are, however, very precisely some of the privileged terms in which postmodernist cultural production has been

analyzed (and even defended, by its own apologists). They are,
however, still privative features. (*PM,* 25, emphasis added)

The language of this passage clarifies Jameson's understanding of
what a coherent representation of experience might be, by giving
an example of what it is not: a heap of fragments. Jameson's essay
rests rather heavily on this heap, as a seemingly formless form used
to embody and exemplify nearly all of the privative features he ascribes to postmodernism: the loss of historicity, the loss of negative
affect, the loss of coherence. And since so much depends on this
heap of fragments, which strikingly *lacks* the slick and unifying
glaze of most of Jameson's other examples, it is interesting to note
that in the slippage from "heaps of fragments" to "the fragmentary" (a slippage in which Jameson shifts his emphasis from a specific form to the kind of aesthetic practice that gives rise to it), what
gets eclipsed from the sentence—and eventually from the analysis—is the *heap.*

Though the hypothesis of a contemporary waning of negative
affect is something my own book contests, my aim is not to defend
the cultural logic of postmodernism against Jameson's compelling
critique (which I think is more or less right). The much more
modest point I want to make here is that while half of Jameson's
examples of this hegemonic aesthetic—significantly the *visual* ones,
from Andy Warhol's *Diamond Dust Shoes* and Duane Hanson's
lifelike sculptures of tourists, to the monolithic "great free-standing
wall" of the Wells Fargo Court in Los Angeles—do seem to illustrate a replacement of "the older affects of anxiety and alienation" with "the positive terms of euphoria, a high, an intoxicatory
or hallucinogenic intensity" (*PM,* 28), resulting in what Jameson
calls a "camp or 'hysterical' sublime" (34), these examples are not
fragmentary or "heaps of fragments" at all. They are rather slick
wholes, held tightly and *seamlessly* together, as Jameson himself
notes, by a "glossy skin." These visual productions work perfectly,

moreover, as examples of euphoric postmodernism and of Jameson's camp sublime. But oddly, Jameson's *literary* examples—the only examples to which the description "heap of fragments" can really be said to apply—do not suggest this sublimity or exhilaration at all; in fact, nothing seems to run more counter to a glossy monolith than a pile of rubble or fragments. Moreover, when represented primarily by Beckett's dark prose and language poetry (works in which the evacuation of negative affect seems far more difficult to demonstrate than, say, in Warhol's work), these "heaps of fragments" would seem to be forms in which "the older affects of anxiety and alienation" are actually preserved.

So some of Jameson's examples seem to illustrate his argument better than others—but some also seem to generate aesthetic and affective effects that his larger argument, and his notion of the postmodern sublime in particular, cannot account for entirely. If there is a sense in which the heap of linguistic fragments functions differently from the high-gloss postmodernist object (which leads us either to a "camp" or "technological" sublime), we are still left with the task of understanding its exceptionality. We are also left with the fact that the "heap" in Jameson's "heap of fragments"— the form that emerges from an accumulation or accrual of fragments—vanishes from the prose, leaving us with just "the fragmentary," or with the privative concept of *fragmentation*. Effaced perhaps in the desire to emphasize the process in which wholes break down into parts, rather than the ways in which parts might be made to cohere or agglutinate, this heap disappears from Jameson's critique of postmodernity, just as the historical referent is said to do within the aesthetic situation it engenders. If what postmodernism lacks is a capacity to "organize" elements into "coherent experience," the heaping involved in making "heaps of fragments" does not appear to be a valid means of organization. Yet insofar as "to cohere" means "to hold together firmly as parts of the same mass; broadly: STICK, ADHERE," a heap *does* seem to be a coherence of some sort.[44] The only difference would seem to be the degree of "firmness" involved in the adhesion. Hence, even a less than firm sticking-together of parts would still be a form of coherence. We might think here of the "slowly wobbling," "flabby mass of independent dependent being" that is Stein's Martha Hersland, or the "slimy, gelatinous, gluey" substance that is "attacking being" disguised as "resisting being" (*MA,* 349). As Stein insists, "Some are always whole ones though the being in them is all a mushy mass." Thus, Jameson seems to have a more specific definition of "coherence" in mind when he cites "heaps of fragments" as examples of an *incapacity* to organize discrete elements into a coherent form. Insofar as "coherence" does not seem to include methods of adhesion that result in loosely organized or unstable forms like heaps or "mushy masses," what constitutes a legitimate form of coherence here would seem to be the process of making parts "fit or stick together in *a suitable or orderly way,*" implying "logical consistency" and systematic connection," especially in "logical discourse."[45] This more specific definition of the term would seem to disavow "wobbling" or "flabby" masses as equally viable organizations of matter.

Thus, if we follow the logic of Jameson's passage, "coherence" refers primarily to a preexisting concept or idea of order, dictating in advance how particles might be shaped or molded, rather than the activity by which particles are brought together in the first place. Yet if "coherence" implies only a cultural standard of suitability and orderliness, and not the activity or process of adhesion, then what word can we use for the way "little lumps" of matter come to be "stuck together to make a whole one cemented together" in *The Making of Americans,* or the way "bits and scraps" of language are strung together into phrases in *How It Is?* In stressing coherence as an aesthetic or formal ideal, rather than the actual act of *making* things "stick together," Jameson's use of the term is in many ways the opposite of Stein's. Stein's notion of coherence is, perhaps, more sticky.

In this sense, Jameson's and Stein's approaches to the concept also seem to diverge around the question of "consistency"—a key term in the standard definition of "coherence." Whereas for Jameson "consistency" would seem to imply regularity or conformity to a particular ideal, consistency for Stein is primarily a matter of matter:

> There must now then be more description of the way each one is made of a substance common to their kind of them, thicker, thinner, harder, softer, all of one consistency, all of one lump, or little lumps stuck together to make a whole one cemented together sometimes by the same kind of being sometimes by the other kind of being in them, some with a lump hard at the centre liquid at the surface, some with the lump vegetablish or wooden or metallic in them. Always then the kind of substance, the kind of way when it is a mediumly fluid solid fructifying reacting substance, the way it acts then makes one kind of them of the resisting kind of them, the way another substance acts makes another kind of them the attacking kind of them. It and the state it is in each kind of them, the mixing of it with the other way of being that makes many kinds of these two kinds of them, sometime all this will have meaning. (*MA*, 345)

Comic in its stuplimity, Stein's description approaches "coherence" as a *process* of creating form, rather than a value or ideal imposed on things made. As such, it involves possibility—pointing to the creation not just of new "kinds," but of as yet unforeseen kinds in the future. Moreover, for Stein the work of coherence complexifies and diversifies—becoming as varied in its process as the forms that it generates. In other words, coherence operates as a vast combinatory, in which new "consistencies" are produced through the "mixing" of others.

We can also see that different kinds of material consistency are emphasized in Stein's and Jameson's notions of coherence: firmly held-together versus mushy or gelatinous; graspable versus slimy. Generally speaking, Jameson's notion of coherence seems a lot less messy than Stein's; it excludes heaps, masses, and lumps. The disappearance of the "heap" seems related to the fact that Jameson very much wants to see the heaping of fragments as indicative of privation rather than accrual—perhaps because the accrual implied is so, well, unsightly. Yet as anyone with agricultural, office, laundry, or postal experience can attest, a heap *is* an organization, though perhaps not a particularly organized-looking one. "This *coming together in them to be a whole* one is a strange thing in men and women. Sometimes some one is very interesting to some one, very, very interesting to some one and then that one comes together to be a whole one and then that one is not any more, at all, interesting to the one knowing that one" (Stein, *MA,* 382, italics added). This passage suggests that the process of *how* things cohere or come together is of interest to Stein, more so than the entities produced through this process. Following her lead, we might similarly ask: How do the fragments in Jameson's "heap of fragments" get heaped? "Practices of the randomly heterogeneous and fragmentary and the aleatory" would seem to account for the fragments themselves, but this leaves the method of their agglutination unexplained. To further elucidate this characterization of late twentieth-century experimental writing, Jameson refers to what he calls Lacan's "schizophrenic" theory of language; it is, he says, a "linguistic malfunction" or breakdown of the relationships between signifiers in the signifying chain that ultimately results in "the form of a rubble" (*PM,* 26). While this reference to Lacan seems to elaborate causes for the fragmentation discussed above, it nevertheless continues to evade deeper inquiry into the particular structure or organization these fragments assume. Just as the heap in "heap of fragments" disappears from critical scrutiny, so does the form in "form of rubble." Are there not, as Stein suggests, multiple and various ways of heaping and cohering? As well as different kinds of linguistic or semiotic rubble? An isolated fragment may be an "inert passivity," as Jameson notes (*PM,* 31), but a *heap* of fragments is perhaps better described as a *constituent* passivity or a "passive *synthesis*"—a term Deleuze applies to the work of repetition for itself (*DR,* 72).

As noted above, Jameson finds the waning of historicity endemic to postmodernism (as reflected in its aesthetic productions), concomitant with a waning of negative affect, and of affects like anxiety and alienation in particular. Yet anxiety and alienation in their most hyperbolic manifestations—shock and boredom—converge in Beckett's and Stein's fairly explicit attempts to negotiate time and history—Beckett and Stein being writers Jameson considers "outright postmodernists" (*PM,* 4). *The Making of Americans* is, after all, nothing other than the fantasy that "sometime then there will be a complete history of every one who ever was or is or will be living" (*MA,* 283). For Stein, the work of "telling" or "making" history is inseparable from the labor of making subjects ("kinds of men and women"), which itself entails the tedious labor of enumerating, differentiating, describing, dividing and sorting, and mixing within the chosen limits of a particular system. Such making does have its moments of exhilaration, but more generally takes place as a painstakingly slow, tiring, and seemingly endless "puzzling" over differences and resemblances. Temporal and taxonomic "organization" becomes marked primarily by a series of minor exhaustions and fatigues, rather than by euphoric highs; hence, Stein makes history not transcendent or sublime, but *stuplime.* Stein accordingly acknowledges the number of failures occurring in this struggle for coherence (which she also describes as a process of "learning" or "studying"), as well as the alienation and anxiety it induces: "Mostly every one dislikes to hear it" (*MA,* 289). With this projection of a less than receptive audience, writing seems to become an isolating enterprise for the taxonomist-poet, who finds herself forced to announce: "I am writing for myself and strangers. This is the only way I can do it" (*MA,* 289). Yet this address can be read as an inclusive rather than exclusive formulation of audience if we understand Stein's writing as an active process of "strangering" its readers.

According to her constructivist worldview, everyone for Stein is a type or "kind of," and thus strangered by repetition. Yet the anxiety-producing and alienating effects of this subjection are themselves perceived as valuable subjects for study: "Mostly always then when any one tells it to any one there is much discussing often very much irritation. This is then very interesting" (*MA*, 338). The narrator thus finds herself able to continue even at moments where she finds herself "all unhappy in this writing . . . nervous and driving and unhappy" (*MA*, 348). For above all, the making of "completed history"—which is the self-consciously impossible (and thus unhappy) fantasy of *The Making of Americans* and which depends, even more impossibly, on the consolidation of the completed histories of every *single* subject—is absolutely synonymous with repeating: "Often as I was saying repeating is very irritating to listen to from them and then slowly it settles into a completed history of them. . . . Sometimes it takes many years of knowing some one before the repeating in that one comes to be a clear history of such a one. Sometimes many years of knowing some one pass before repeating of all being in such a one comes out clearly from them. . . . This is now more description of the way repeating slowly comes to make in each one a completed history of them" (*MA*, 292). Stein's comment that "sometimes many years pass" before the act of repeating slowly comes to make a "completed history" finds contemporary realization in *One Million Years (Past),* a work created by the Japanese artist On Kawara in 1970–1972. It comprises a series of ten black, official-looking ledgers, each containing 2,000 pages listing 500 years per page, from 998031 B.C. to 1969 A.D.[46] The sublimity of such a vast amount of time is trumped by its organization into bureaucratic blandness; our comprehension of a million years is rendered manageable, if also tedious, when consolidated in a set of ring binders bearing some resemblance to a completed report by the Senate Finance Committee. Yet this tedium turns back into astonishment when we come to realize the amount of time and labor it has taken (two years' worth) to make such a severely minimal product. Dedicated to "All those who have lived and died," this piece records not so much a completed "history," though it certainly speaks to the fantasy of or desire for this, but the time spent in the attempt to organize one even in the most stark and reductive way. The *hic et nunc* postmodernism of Kawara may be very different from Stein's *avant la lettre* variety, yet the comparison points to how *The Making of Americans* deliberately stages its own failures by setting itself against an impossible fantasy of absolute historical coherence or explicitness, usually imagined as an incipient future: "Sometime there will be here every way there can be of seeing kinds of men and women. Sometime there will be then a complete history of each one"; "Sometime then there will be a complete history of every one who ever was or is or will be living" (*MA*, 290, 283). Or even more hyperbolically: "Sometime there will be a description of every kind of way any one can know anything, any one can know any one"; "sometime there will be a completed system of kinds of men and women, of kinds of men and kinds of women" (311, 334).

While stuplimity offers no transcendence, it does provide small subjects with what Stein calls "a little resistance" in their confrontations with larger systems. The fatigues generated by the system which is *The Making of Americans* may be "nervous and driving and unhappy," but such fatigues can also be darkly funny, as Beckett's Molloy, Buster Keaton, Harpo Marx, and Pee-Wee Herman remind us by their exhausting routines: running endless laps around a battleship, trying to come through a doorway, falling down and getting up again, collapsing in heaps. Significantly, the humor of these local situations usually occurs in the context of a confrontation staged between the small subject and powerful institutions or machines: thus, we have Chaplin versus the assembly line; Keaton versus military engines such as the *Navigator* (a supply ship) and the *General* (a locomotive); Lucille Ball versus domesticity. And here we might add: Stein versus her own vast human taxonomy. Critics have suggested that Stein's refusal of linear time for cyclical time signals a rejection of official history for an alternative temporality grounded in the body. Yet this preference for the cycle, an endless round of driving excitations and fatigues, could equally well suggest the temporality of slapstick, or Stein in Chaplin drag.

Just as in Kierkegaard's *Repetition,* where Constantin Constantius describes himself, while consumed by laughter at Beckmann's stuplimity, as a pile of discarded clothes, the "kinds" of subjects produced in *The Making of Americans* function like garments without bodies—heaplike outlines, as it were, waiting to be "filled up" with the repeating that makes them "whole ones." Whole, yes—but mushy as opposed to firm. In *The Autobiography of Alice B. Toklas,* Stein similarly calls attention to Charlie Chaplin's use of misshapen clothes that "were all the delight of Picasso and all his friends"—and this is an allusion to Stein herself, well known for her loose and flapping garments.[47] We see here again the role of limpnesses or "flabby masses" in counteracting an oppressive system's fantasies of phallic virility: the clothes worn by Chaplin so admired by Stein are, of course, always falling down. Here, slackness is underscored by slacklessness. As if in anticipation of Oldenburg's soft and puffy typewriters and other machines, or Yayoi Kusama's squishy penis-shaped pillows covered with polkadots, Stein's love of the wobbling heap or mushy mass similarly recalls the fascination with flabby substances in Chaplin's *Dough and Dynamite* (1914), where he shapes dough into handcuffs and missiles. Perhaps he's asking us to imagine: What might happen to a machine when the exaggeratedly obedient cog within it, while continuing to maintain its function, goes limp? As when the characters played by Chaplin or Keaton, continually in confrontation with the larger systems enclosing them, repeatedly fall into heaps? Here we might also imagine the incontinent Molloy, collapsed under his bicycle or defeated by his stuplime "combinatorial" of sucking stones, or Murphy, overcome by the "total permutability" of his assortment of five biscuits when no preference for a particular flavor limits the order in which they might be eaten—"a hundred and twenty ways!" (Deleuze, "E," 153). This astonishing figure, of course, leads Murphy to collapse in exhaustion: "Overcome by these perspectives Murphy fell forward with his face in the grass, besides those biscuits of which it could be said as truly of the stars, that one differed from another, but of which he could not partake in their fullness until he had learned not to prefer any one to any other."[48]

In the tradition of Beckett's and Stein's reliance on "exhaustive series" of objects which lack a privileged term or referent, formulating a materialist poetic response to the "total permutability" of language is perhaps what is most at stake for poets like Farrell, Goldman, and Goldsmith, as well as visual artists like Zweig (Deleuze, "E," 154). For these contemporary practitioners, the staging of "accidental concretions" (Constantin Constantius' term for the way comic characters are built in farce; *R,* 163) strategically enables us to find new forms of "coherence" in an incoherent world—such as the form we see in Alice Notley's feminist epic *The Descent of Alette:* "'When the train' 'goes under water' 'the close tunnel' 'is transparent' 'Murky water' 'full of papery' 'full of shapelessness' 'Some fish' 'but also things' 'Are they made by humans?' 'Have no shape,' 'like rags' 'like soggy papers' 'like frayed thrown-away wash cloths' . . ."[49] Each phrase, presented as a citation, becomes "thick" and carries with it a contextual behindness—creating a series of halts or delays in the narrative produced through their accumulation. There's clearly nothing accidental about this concretion of language, yet the poem seeks to look accidental. Like the massive accumulations of hair or type pieces in Hamilton's installations, Stein's mushy masses, and the lumps formed by comic actors in their continual collapses and falls, such concretions challenge existing notions of form and aesthetic order. We can see how unsightly heaping offers a strategy of what Stein might call a "little resistance" for the postmodern subject, always already a linguistic being, hence always a small subject enmeshed in large systems. As Deleuze suggests,

There are two known ways to overturn moral law. One is by ascending towards the principles: challenging the law as secondary, derived, borrowed, or "general"; denouncing it as involving a second-hand principle which diverts an original force or usurps an original power. The other way, by contrast, is to overturn the law by descending towards the consequences, *to which one submits with a too-perfect attention to detail.* By adopting the law, a falsely submissive soul manages to evade it and to taste pleasures it was supposed to forbid. We can see this in demonstration by absurdity and working to rule, but also in some forms of masochistic behaviour which mock by submission. (*DR,* 5, emphasis added)

This "too-perfect attention to detail" is the main strategy used by Notley, Goldsmith, and Farrell, all of whom exaggeratedly submit to structural laws in their work: Farrell, to the days of the calendar ("Monday, Tuesday, Wednesday . . ."); Goldsmith, to the mechanisms of the body ("Swallow. Arm lifts. Arm drops . . ."). Exhausting as well as astonishing, this "too-perfect attention" is also the main strategy used by Stein's endlessly classifying and subdividing narrator in *The Making of Americans,* and by nearly all of Beckett's "combiners" or "exhausted persons [exhausting] the whole of the possible": Pim, Molloy, Murphy, Watt (Deleuze, "E," 152). For as Deleuze also notes, though one can oppose the law by trying to ascend above it, one can also do so by means of humor, "which is an art of consequences and descents, of suspensions and falls" (*DR,* 5, emphasis added). Like other "falsely submissive souls" before them, a significant group of contemporary American poets have followed this stuplime path in their confrontations with the systems encompassing them, formulating a resistant stance by going limp or falling down, among the bits and scraps of linguistic matter.

7. paranoia

Was "conspiracy theory" quietly claimed as a masculine prerogative in the last decades of the twentieth century? Consider the
TV show *X-Files*. Its pairing of Mulder and Scully, a speculative
paranoiac and a rational empiricist, was a prime example of how
the sexual polarity of a traditional Enlightenment dualism seemed
to have been reversed—though with the male term, even if re-
aligned with intuition rather than science, remaining privileged.[1]
Of the pair of agent-intellectuals, "Fox" Mulder (who seemed
to have inherited the name of his parent network) was not only
the one more nobly committed to identifying and pitting himself
against wide-ranging, even transglobal technological and political
structures; unlike his pragmatic, positivistic, and more locally oriented female partner, he was always right in his analyses. We find a
similar pattern in the conspiracy films that Fredric Jameson, in
The Geopolitical Aesthetic, reads as allegories for the attempt—and,
more significantly, failure—on the part of subjects to grasp global
capitalism's social totality in formal or representational terms.[2] The
films forefronting this dilemma center on the knowledge-seeking
trajectories of male protagonists who, like the conventional film

noir detective, belatedly find that they are small subjects caught in larger systems extending beyond their comprehension and control. Though such a situation has equal import for everyone (and Jameson sees the political necessity of describing it so), it is difficult to avoid seeing that the narrative tradition which most powerfully highlights the problem is a gendered one—as if "conspiracy theory" itself, an epistemology underpinned by the affective category of fear, becomes safeguarded *through* the genre of the political thriller as a distinctively male form of knowledge production. As Jameson himself suggests in using the conspiracy film's knowledge-seeking protagonists as figures for the postmodern intellectual, and the conspiratorial plot these protagonists attempt to analyze and expose as an allegory for the "potentially infinite network" of relations constituting our present social order (*GA,* 9), the male conspiracy theorist seems to have become an exemplary model for the late twentieth-century theorist in general, and conspiracy theory a viable synecdoche for "theory" itself.

The disposition to theorize thus finds itself aligned with paranoia, defined here not as mental illness but as a species of fear based on the dysphoric apprehension of a holistic and all-encompassing system.[3] This coupling of paranoia with theory seems summoned for tactical purposes in another work by Jameson, "The Theoretical Hesitation":

> Ours is an antitheoretical time, which is to say an anti-intellectual time; and the reasons for this are not far to seek. The system has always understood that ideas and analysis, along with the intellectuals who practice them, are its enemies and has evolved various ways of dealing with the situation, most notably—in the academic world—by railing against what it likes to call grand theory or master narratives at the same time it fosters more comfortable and local positivisms and empiricisms in the various disciplines.[4]

This passage raises provocative and one might say strategically "paranoid" questions about the "bad timing" of systematic critique.

Why is it that at the "same time" capital grows more virtual and abstract in its daily operations, cultural critique grows increasingly positivistic and empirical, veering away from the methods best suited for the analysis of its proliferation? In order to drive home his criticism of academic discourse's growing allergy to the level of abstraction increasingly necessary for the critical analysis of late capitalist culture (as Gayatri Spivak has often noted, "Capital . . . is the abstract *as such*"), Jameson uses what might be described as a conspiracy-theory rhetoric: one hinging on a reference not only to suspicious timing and holistic systems, but also to "the system."[5] And not just a singular and unified system, but one anthropomorphized into a subject capable of "understanding" its enemies and "dealing" with them accordingly. Not unlike the deceiving god in the first of Descartes' *Meditations,* "the system" in Jameson's essay conspires against the contemporary intellectual, transformed into an agent who counterplots against him. Clearly "the system" is a totalizing abstraction, but to criticize Jameson's argument on this basis puts one in the position of appearing to confirm the phobia he is discussing—the current fear of theoretical abstraction in academic discourse. In fact, it seems as if Jameson cannily uses the language of conspiracy theory in anticipation of such objections, and as a style reinforcing the content of an essay that raises provocative questions about the current *state* of academic discourse. For the feminist critic, however, it remains important simply to recognize the way in which conspiracy theory seems intimately tied to the hermeneutic quests of male agent-intellectuals, in contexts ranging from *Critical Inquiry* to Fox Television.

All the same, critics like Naomi Schor have found it politically strategic to claim paranoia as an equally viable model for *feminist* theorizing.[6] In her essay "Female Paranoia," Schor argues that the close affinities Freud noted between paranoia and theory, particularly in his "oft-cited comparison of paranoiacs and philosophers,"[7] make the one instance of female paranoia Freud examines (in "A Case of Paranoia Running Counter to the Psychoanalytic Theory of the Disease") not only a potential exception to his rule—a "contradictory case . . . which seems at first to call seriously into question the universal validity of the theory of paranoia derived from the analysis of a male paranoiac"—but a potential threat to "theory itself" ("FP," 206). For Schor, the need to define and argue on behalf of a specifically female paranoia resides in the fact that the question of whether such a clinical category even exists poses the more urgent question of whether females are capable of theorizing at all, "albeit in the caricatural mode of the mad" (206). Citing the distinction made by Freudian disciple Ruth Mack Brunswick between a masculine persecutory form of paranoia marked by "elaborate ideation, . . . excessive intellectuality, . . . occurrence in individuals with a high power of sublimation," and a jealous form that is "par excellence the paranoia of women," Schor points out that "the tremendous difficulties and dangers inherent in defining a specifically female form of paranoia" are in fact the same difficulties and dangers involved in defining a specifically female form of theorizing (207).[8]

Given the "systemization and theorizing" characteristic of the paranoiac, "which led many commentators to associate paranoia with knowledge and knowledge-producing systems *per se,*"[9] the effort to claim paranoia for feminist thought and cultural production does not really seem outlandish in a world where any analysis of power at the transindividual level increasingly requires a language capable of dealing with "the system" as an abstract and holistic entity, as the word "patriarchy" has done in feminist writing for several decades. Though increasingly a source of embarrassment to academics in today's newly repositivized intellectual climate, terms like "patriarchy" and "patriarchy-capitalism," which refer to monolithic yet amorphously delimited and fundamentally abstract systems, remain crucial for a critical language that in our antitheoretical time not only seems fated to ring with the debased rhetoric of "conspiracy theory," but seems capable of demonstrating how paranoia has become a normative state of affairs. This is not to say that feminists should claim paranoia merely because it has become an everyday structure of feeling. Nor should paranoia be claimed for feminism simply because of "the prestigious intellectual (hyper)activity associated with the male model" (Schor, "FP," 206). The link between them simply increases the importance of noting that paranoia can be denied the *status* of epistemology when claimed by some subjects, while valorized for precisely that status when claimed by others. In the former case, a mode of knowledge structured by an affective orientation already involving the cognition that power operates systemically will be reduced to its subjective implications alone (an ignoble "emotionalism"); in the latter, paranoia's cognitive dimensions will be emphasized as an enabling condition for knowledge.

Even if recuperated for feminist theory, however, paranoia will obviously have something equivocal about it, particularly when it cannot be neatly separated from the "everyday fear" that sustains existing forms of compliancy and subjection.[10] This is particularly the case if fear is part of the process of subject formation, as suggested by psychoanalytic accounts of an ego constituted through a central fantasy of persecution.[11] Both Klein and Lacan view the standard course of ego formation as a paranoiac process (Klein, more precisely, sees it as a paranoiac-schizoid process); for Lacan in particular, the central role which persecution fantasy plays in the constitution of subjects reveals that "taking one's place in the Symbolic Order means living in a paranoiac system which is culturally sanctioned."[12] Thus, as Brian Massumi notes, "if we are unable to separate our selves from our fear, and if fear is a power mechanism for the perpetuation of domination, . . . our unavoidable participation in the capitalist culture of fear [may be] a complicity with our own and other's oppression." And in situations where there is no purely external or even clearly identifiable nemesis but rather "the enemy is *us,*" "analysis, however necessary, is not enough to found a practice of resistance. Fear, under conditions of complicity, can be neither analyzed nor opposed without at the same time being *enacted.*"[13]

Such an analysis-enactment becomes particularly significant to a "late" body of writing by American women poets associated with the avant-garde, defined here as a social formation based on the collective activity fostered by specific material conditions and relations of production, and embodied in the rhizomatic network created by independent and nonprofit presses, small-press distribution centers, reading series, poet talks, and listserve discussions. In dystopic works ranging from Juliana Spahr's *Response* (1995), a collection including a poem in which alien-abduction testimonials provide a way of exploring "the claims of truth in the age of cover-up and misinformation," to Heather Fuller's *perhaps this is a rescue fantasy* (1997), whose cover features a diagram for building a book bomb, the conspiratorial imagination traditionally associated with an intellectually valorized masculine paranoia is not only reclaimed but reformulated for feminist inquiry as the highly specific problem of complicity.[14] Spahr takes this situation to nightmarish extremes in "thrashing seem crazy," a poem drawing on a segment from the TV show *Oprah*. The poem concerns a woman with "dissociative personality disorder" who is physically and psychologically assaulted by a male version of herself.

> these are things people can do to themselves
> they are:
> leave molotov cocktail on own yard
> set fire to own house
> leave a glass of urine on own porch
> leave an envelope of feces outside own door
> send a butcher knife to self at work
> send letter to health department that self is spreading VD
> stab own back

In Spahr's writing in particular, fear of unintended collusion with a system in which one is already inscribed—a fear that might be described as specific to a class of intellectuals—becomes the primary focus of investigations into the more general structure of fear and its implications for the politicization of aesthetics. Here, bad or suspicious timing, a question that is central to conspiracy theory ("why is it that at the same time . . . ?"), plays a prominent role as it resurfaces in a poetry that unapologetically aims for what Spivak has described as "the agential grasping *of* the spectral [entity]" that is patriarchy-capitalism.[15] The motif of bad timing will bring us to the question of the vexed relationship *between* poetry and theory—a relationship that not only played an incisive role in the historical development of late twentieth-century, language-centered avantgarde writing, but remains of pressing concern to feminist writers in this cohort, in their efforts both to theorize their own work and to assert their contemporaneity. For as Gertrude Stein noted, what it means to be "contemporary" is by no means self-evident or something to be taken for granted: "It is so very much more exciting and satisfactory for everybody if one can have contemporaries, if all one's contemporaries could be one's contemporaries."[16]

The Problem with the Timing Is That It Is Always Off While It Cannot Be Off at All

We can see some of these questions about gender, fear, and timing converge in "Memnoir" (2000), a short poem by Joan Retallack:

> . . . it might be necessary to replace all
> vowels with x mxgxcxlly txrnxg prxmxtxrx txrrxr xntx pxst-pxst
> xrxny.

> . . . it is that that is the problem with
> the timing that it is always off while it cannot be off at all that is
> the he to be sure that the she did not choose the wrong
> thing . . .[17]

The "always off" timing seems to reside in an oscillation between the excessively early (the "prxmxtxrx") and the excessively late ("pxst-pxst"). This timing clearly has affective consequences, since the transition from precipitateness to belatedness involves a shift from terror ("txrrxr") to irony ("xrxny"), while at the same time producing an illegibility undermining the transformation itself. The surplus of x's that attends the shift from one emotional tonality of late capitalism to another—premature fear ("prxmxtxrx txrrxr") to doubly-belated irony ("pxst-pxst xrxny")—recalls an analogous moment from Diane Ward's long poem "Imaginary Movie," in which a similar excess of signification coalesces around the issue of timing:

> as a center
> meanwhile & and
> at the same time
> refusing to be
> favored by fear
> and wage labor
>
> as fractions of dislocation
> the center
> family life
> moves to the screen
> where the cast mouths
> our thoughts[18]

In Ward's first stanza, the semantically unnecessary repetition of the conjunction, "& and," links two terms that independently signify the temporal coexistence of events: "meanwhile" and "at the same time." This overdetermined expression of simultaneity calls attention to another temporal relationship expressed in the image of "simulcast" figures mouthing the thoughts of the poem's collective subject. But in this case, the relation is one of *belatedness:* the subjects watching the screen find themselves spoken for in advance. These two relationships to time—a sense of overdetermined simultaneity or contemporaneousness ("meanwhile & and / at the same time") and a sense of redundancy or belatedness (the tempo-

rality characteristically associated with postmodern aesthetics)—
bring us face to face with a historically specific crux in feminist literary criticism that continues to have special relevance for the way
we read works by contemporary female poets associated with the
avant-garde.

This crux is best arrived at through a series of general observations which may initially seem to have little to do with gender per
se. We can start by merely noting that the linguistic paradigms developed in late twentieth-century theoretical writing that seem to
speak most directly to and about difficult poetry have been derived
and elaborated primarily through readings of canonically traditional and often "readerly" texts.[19] This ironic situation reveals the
drawbacks of excessive reliance on concepts like "writerliness" to
account for the qualitative differences between works produced
under the material conditions that give rise to an avant-garde and
those that sustain an official verse culture. If *S/Z* demonstrates that
even the classic realist novel can be read as a site marked by "the
infinite play of the word [before it becomes stopped] by some singular system" and thus as an occasion for readers to observe "the
plurality of entrances, the opening of networks, [and] the infinity of
languages" Barthes associates with the writerly, then these linguistic attributes cannot be solely relied upon to make arguments for
avant-garde distinctiveness, much less transgressiveness.[20] Even if
the writerly is, as Susan Suleiman notes, "playful, fluid, open, tri-
umphantly plural, and in its plurality impervious to the repressive
rule of structure, grammar or logic" (*SI,* 6), the fact that these qualities seem to describe twentieth-century avant-garde literature in its
diverse entirety still does not mean that concepts like writerliness
can be used as criteria for distinguishing work produced in this
cultural context from work that is not.

One strange and indirect consequence of this is that the now academically routinized notion of the open, polysemous, and endlessly
self-differing text, as initially developed in post-1968 poststruc-

turalist readings of canonical literature, often feels belated when with post-1968, language-centered writing—despite the fact that the initial developments of the two practices coincided historically.[21] Accordingly, the "belatedness" I am describing is not one related to an actual time difference between the emergence of language-centered theory and that of language-centered writing. The erroneous claim of historical belatedness has in fact been an argument used by some detractors of language-centered writing in order to dismiss avant-garde writing of the 1970s and '80s as a bad hybrid of poetry either simply wedded to or overeagerly trying to imitate the genre of theory.[22] Rather, the belatedness is one that exists for the literary critic *now*—which is one reason it is a belatedness oddly specific to our own contemporaneity with the literary works being produced. For what makes criticism or any other cultural production "contemporary" is not so much its rupture with work of the past, but rather its relation to other cultural developments (like poetry) happening "meanwhile & and / at the same time." Ironically, then, the very fact that language-centered writing and poststructuralist language theory followed parallel and concurrent trajectories in their historical development seems responsible for the way in which *current* articulations of these continuing projects with one another always seem to carry the sensation of a temporal lag or delay. As Retallack might put it, the problem with such timing is that it seems "off" while it cannot be "off" at all.

For the contemporary critic, an already unsettling experience— the emergence of this belatedness in the relationship between temporally coinciding discourses, avant-garde language theory and avant-garde language-centered poetry—is exacerbated by their conceptual attunement. From Julia Kristeva's theory of the semiotic as a rhythmic, polysemous dimension of language with the potential to disrupt a phallocentric symbolic discourse, to Deleuze and Guattari's notion of the rhizome as an acentered network capable of undermining rigid and hierarchical structures, poststructural models of textuality emphasizing heterogeneity and invested in a politics of form do seem to demonstrate (as the writers of the collaborative avant-garde manifesto "Aesthetic Tendency and the Politics of Poetry" argued in 1988) not only that the developments of theory and poetry in the late twentieth century have been complementary but that "theoretical models based on language . . . find *a uniquely proper object* in poetry."[23]

To generalize broadly (at the risk, of course, of flattening out the significant differences between various theorists and poets), the striking consonance between approaches to language in late twentieth-century theoretical writing and avant-garde poetry *would* seem to place each in a special, even privileged relation with respect to illuminating and extending the scope of the other, setting the stage for a productive cross-fertilization. Both practices share a basic commitment to the idea of "textual politics" and to the critique of liberal humanism; both emphasize and privilege difference over self-sameness and internal consistency, multiplicity over univocality, flux over stability, and ambiguity and slippage over rigid correspondences between words and meanings. Each would *seem* to be the other's "uniquely proper object." Yet this presumably ideal situation for the literary critic reading late twentieth-century avant-garde poetry (the theory and the poetry already seem to be "speaking" to each other, and doing so "meanwhile & and / at the same time") leads to what can only be described as a certain redundancy or obviousness when the two discourses are placed in dialogue with each other *now.* In other words, the paradoxical combination of the two factors characterizing the relation between late twentieth-century language theory and language-centered poetry (philosophical attunement and historical alignment) ensures that for the critic today, most attempts to articulate a poetics based on foregrounding connections between the literary text and poststructuralist theory will end up seeming, well, predictable or descriptive—a rather undesirable outcome from the standpoint of both discourses, in their mutual privileging and politicization of difficulty and defamiliar-

ization. Interestingly, the problem here is not one of a gap, dissonance, or contradiction (the negative terrain on which avant-garde
theorists and poets have traditionally found themselves most comfortable working) but rather one of a fit that seems too close. I
could say: "In its privileging of the letter and constant deferral of
stabilized meanings, Lyn Hejinian's *Writing Is an Aid to Memory*
produces a heterogeneous flow of matter and signs in order to
break down normative frameworks of reference and sense-making." And you might well respond: "Tell me something I don't already know!"

For contemporary readers of contemporary writing, this unusual
situation becomes even further intensified in the attempt to define
a *feminist* poetics within the literary avant-garde along similarly
theoretical lines. For the models of language advanced by the theoretical avant-garde in the 1970s and '80s that seemed in greatest
attunement with poetic explorations of language happening "meanwhile & and / at the same time" have, more frequently than not,
been models relying on abstract notions of the "feminine" to claim
their political efficacy or oppositionality to traditional humanist
values. As Rosi Braidotti notes, "From . . . Derrida's injunction that
in so far as it cannot be said the 'feminine' functions as the most
pervasive signifier, [to] Foucault's bland assertion that the absence
of women from the philosophical scene is constitutive of the rules
of the philosophical game, to Deleuze's notion of the 'becoming-
woman' marking a qualitative transformation in human consciousness—the feminization of thought seems to be prescribed as a fundamental step in the general program of anti-humanism that marks
our era."[24] Braidotti views the role the "feminine" comes to assume
in the discourse of male theorists in the late twentieth-century—
that of "a powerful vehicle for conveying critical attempts to define
human subjectivity"—as a dubious if not sinister development,
insofar as she finds this "advocating the 'feminine' or 'becoming-
woman' of theoretical discourse, [using] woman as the figure of
modernity," as coinciding with and reinforcing the waning of the

rational subject. More precisely, she questions the "deconstructing, dismissing, or displacing the notion of the rational subject *at the very historical moment* when women are beginning to have access to the use of discourse, power, and pleasure" (*NS,* 140, italics added).

The concept of bad timing thus reemerges as central to Braidotti's position, which follows the pattern of what Pamela Moore and Devoney Looser have critically (but not altogether disparagingly) described as the "conspiracy theory" version of feminist critiques of poststructuralism: "In this type of critique, feminists lament that poststructuralisms came into vogue just as women and people of color came into a voice."[25] Andrew Ross, in an essay using Nicolas Roeg's film *Bad Timing* as an allegory for late twentieth-century feminist theory's linguistic turn, similarly emphasizes the concept.[26] Whereas Braidotti singles out the privileging of "becoming-woman" in the work of male theorists as the object of skepticism (at one point describing theory's strangely timed feminization as an expression of male envy for women's enunciative position: "Envious[ness] of a history of oppression that the political will of the women's movement has turned into a major critical stance for women to use to their best advantage"; *NS,* 141), Ross points out that the privileging of the "feminine" predominantly takes place in the work of female theorists, particularly in what he refers to as the "language feminism" of Kristeva, Hélène Cixous, and Luce Irigaray, where "the feminine" is yoked to an explicitly antisexist and not just "antihumanist" approach to language and subjectivity. In this sense, Ross complicates the implication in Braidotti's critique that the valorization (or fetishization) of "becoming-woman" in avant-garde language theory can only amount to an afeminist position at best, and an antifeminist position at worst. Yet Ross's use of "bad timing" in his own account of language feminism not only reinforces the notion of antifeminist conspiracy reflected in Braidotti's critique of the "becoming-woman" of poststructuralist theory, but turns on a principle of belatedness similar to the kind I have described above. Summarizing how the category of the feminine enables theorists like Irigaray and Kristeva to define and advocate a specifically antiphallocentric language, Ross writes:

> Language is taken up as an instrument for changing subjectivity, rather than accepted as a given medium. In assuming this (by now) conventional role, the idea of a "woman's language" inherits the modernist taste for more natural forms of expression. Perhaps the language feminism movement is the last serious manifestation of the modernist tendency. If that is the case, then its *lateness* as a cultural phenomenon is open to question. What are the political consequences, for example, of taking up the cause of anti-rationalism—the traditional mark of oppression for women—as a liberationary style *after* the rationality of a feminist politics had begun to be acknowledged and respected? ("VW," 76)

Framed as a question with emphasis on the temporal preposition "after," Ross's way of discerning "bad timing" clearly echoes the rhetoric used by Braidotti and other, more stringent feminist critics of poststructuralism such as Nancy Hartsock ("Why is it just at the moment when so many of us who have been silenced begin to demand the right to name ourselves, to act as subjects rather than objects of history, that just then the concept of subjecthood becomes problematic?") and Somer Brodribb ("What is the meaning of this particular ideology of masculine domination? Strange timing: the subject is now annulled by . . . white western wizards while women's, black and Third World liberation movements are claiming their voices").[27] Yet after raising the issue of belatedness in this feminist "conspiracy theory" context, Ross immediately pushes the question further: "In whose political interests is it for that lateness not only to be ideologically produced, *but also to be produced as such a distinctive and vulnerable political target?* Above all, it would be in the interests of those for whom 'women don't know what they're talking about' anyway [Ross is alluding to Lacan], and many of those are not even modernists yet ("VW," 76, italics added).

While Ross thus describes language feminism in terms of a problematic belatedness, and then turns around provocatively to question the very construction of this belatedness *as* a problem (since it is an assessment open to exploitation by those wanting to dismiss the feminist project in its entirety), he nonetheless remains skeptical about the political efficacy of using the category of the feminine as a basis for claiming a *feminist* language or aesthetic. Here Ross comes to share a position put forward by Silvia Bovenschen as early as 1976 and reasserted in subsequent decades by numerous feminists, including Domna Stanton, Monique Wittig, and Teresa de Lauretis.[28] The point is perhaps argued most extensively from a Marxian perspective by Rita Felski, who questions not only the automatic equation of a recently countervalorized "feminine" discourse with feminist cultural production in the work of female theorists, but also the way this equation is often facilitated through an uncritical use or valorization of the term "avant-garde." In *Beyond Feminist Aesthetics,* Felski singles out Cixous' *écriture féminine* and Kristeva's use of the semiotic as "attempt[s] to argue a necessary connection between feminism and experimental form"—attempts that, "when not grounded in a biologistic thinking which affirms a spontaneous link between a 'feminine' textuality and the female body, rel[y] on a theoretical sleight-of-hand that associates or equates the avant-garde and the 'feminine' as forms of marginalized dissidence vis-à-vis a monolithic and vaguely defined 'patriarchal bourgeois humanism' which is said to permeate the structures of symbolic discourse."[29] Similarly, while acknowledging the extent to which psychoanalysis productively enables the critique of phallocentrism for numerous feminist thinkers, Ross argues that "the credentials offered by a 'feminine discourse' promise little more than to recycle those archaic sexual oppositions which modern psychoanalytical theory sought to render obsolete, and formulate them anew in terms of a set of linguistic characteristics—concrete/abstract, content/form, intuition/intelligence, parataxis/syntax, mass/outline, fluidity/consistency. Within this logic of identity, the materiality of language is asserted as the natural grain of the woman's voice, and is posited as a counterthrust to the rational "masculine" discourse of science power and knowledge." More disturbingly, according to Ross, in language feminism's appeal to female anatomy as an index of this different language, "the history lessons of psychoanalysis are freely ignored, bribed off by the more heady promise of self-determination from a position outside history, symbolic meaning, syntax, in short, a desertion of the logic of everyday social commerce" ("VW," 74).

As Ross's critique of language feminism progresses, however, the "lateness" that he is careful to problematize quickly, but nonetheless winds up emphasizing in his initial characterization of the "appeal for a different feminine speech" as a belated modernism, is eventually redefined as a temporal condition specific to postmodernity. For according to Ross, postmodern discourse—in contrast to "the modernist rage for new languages" that language feminism represents—demonstrates a "paradoxical concern with its own lateness, as a culture of secondarity, and not at all with its unified contribution to a linear history" ("VW," 77, 76). Postmodern feminist reading, according to Ross, is thus "especially tolerant of bad timing, since it sets out, as Lyotard has noted, to look for the rules which govern its own discourse only to find them too late to act upon, or else (the same thing), realizes that they have been acting all along" ("VW," 77). Setting aside the striking resemblance between this characterization of a "good" postmodern feminist reading and any one of the paranoid thrillers or conspiracy films discussed by Jameson (where the rules of the game are always discovered "too late," and this belated discovery provides the climax of every narrative), the notion of belatedness as simply an expression of the critical state of the postmodern condition leaves open the question of whether Ross views language feminism's "lateness" as specific to its own dubious status as a late modernism, or as specific to the sensibility of the postmodern viewpoint from which language feminism is currently perceived—in which case, it seems to lose its status *as* a problem for Ross, becoming instead, *in* its bad timing, temporally apropos.

In any case, the bad timing Ross attributes yet seems to back away from attributing to language feminism can usefully shed light on the paradoxical belatedness informing contemporary attempts to place avant-garde language theory and language-centered poetry in a continuing and productive dialogue. Carrying the inflection of paranoid rhetoric, this "bad timing" becomes all the more pronounced for critics attempting to articulate an explicitly *feminist* avant-garde poetics via the outmoded arguments of language feminism, or even via the afeminist yet feminine-embracing language theory that according to Braidotti constitutes the majority of late twentieth-century theoretical writing as a whole. The already overdetermined consonance between art and theory becomes even more explicit in this case, since both feminist avant-gardes tend to approach language as inflected by gender and gender differentiation as an effect of language, opening the possibility for a sexual politics grounded in, or at the very least intimately connected to, a politics of form. In other words, the already existing "dilemma" of an unusual affinity between the antihumanist stances, values, and tactics of two contemporaneous avant-gardes, artistic and theoretical, becomes heightened once feminism enters both pictures, particularly since one of the most significant things "language feminism" does, from the standpoint of avant-garde writers in general and female avant-gardists in particular, is to make explicit claims for avant-garde writing's political agency, as well as claims for a special relationship between "the feminine" and formally innovative writing.

As interlinked tensions exacerbated by feminism's intervention in both discourses, the belatedness or "always already" that has become the *sine qua non* of late twentieth-century theory, with its focus on the linguistically and retroactively determined subject, and the overdetermined contemporaneousness or "at the same time" informing this discourse's relationship to language-centered poetry quite understandably come to a particular head in avant-garde writing by women that is explicitly and unapologetically engaged with theoretical or philosophical work, from Joan Retallack's sustained interface with ordinary language philosophy in *How to Do Things with Words* (1999) to Diane Ward's oblique but running dialogue with feminist film theory in *Imaginary Movie* (1992). These texts and others equally committed from the very start to the premise of political form continue to raise questions that initially surfaced in feminist debates over the viability of a feminist aesthetic based on the concept of a feminine language. Though in academia this debate has waned to the point of obsolescence over the past decade, due in part to powerful critiques of language feminism (critiques such as Felski's) and in part to the general shifting of feminist criticism from the terrain of speculative theory to more locally grounded and historically based arenas of inquiry, the questions raised by it have had a much more lingering impact on feminists from the literary avant-garde, who for obvious reasons have found it more difficult to dismiss attempts to strategically align the avant-garde with feminism as entirely valueless, or as representing an embarrassing and ideally soon-forgotten "French phase" in feminist theory. For it is not difficult to see how arguments for "a necessary connection between feminism and experimental form," however faulty, belated, or strangely timed, might continue to have political and practical importance for female avant-gardists, since efforts to create new alliances between the "feminine" and the avant-garde offer strategic challenges to the condescending perspective from which women are viewed as earnestly striving but failing to make truly radical art (for reasons now ascribed to social factors instead of biological ones: the idea that women cannot politically afford to abandon more conventional means of expression for formally radical ones),[30] as well as the disabling notion that there is a fundamental incompatibility between the avant-garde (conceived as a "masculinist" cultural formation) and feminism's past and ongoing role in the critique of masculinist privilege.[31]

Moreover, in the case of the feminist avant-garde writer, the classic avant-gardist position that form is political leads to an all too familiar impasse between two standpoints, neither of which seems wholly secure or satisfying. For the feminist writer, the stance that form is political implies that there is no politically neutral language and, by extension, no language uninflected by gender and its ideological codes. From this standpoint, it makes sense to claim that there indeed are "masculine" and "feminine" languages, much in the same way there are masculine and feminine garments, as poet Harryette Mullen has observed.[32] Ultimately, this standpoint asks the feminist poet to accept the idea of feminine form, as a construction designating an "open and receptive, materially and contextually inventive" tradition dominated by male modernists and valorized by afeminist poststructuralist theorists; but, more important, it also asks her to join other women writers in a strategic *reappropriation* of "feminine" form, as Retallack argues in ":RE:THINKING: LITERARY:FEMINISM." As Retallack notes through a persona named Genre Tallique, a presumably French theorist onto whom Retallack places the burden of articulating her essay's more polemical claims (and who occasionally reappears, in the form of epigraphs and bibliographic references, in Retallack's poetry), "Men, like Joyce, Pound, and Duchamp, could be feminine in their art, but not their life. Women could be feminine in their life, but not their art (note the conspicuous absence of names here)."[33] The feminist challenge faced by the contemporary female avant-gardist, in the face of "a 'feminine' [aesthetic] tradition dominated by males," is thus to take advantage of the fact that "women have not until very recently been in a situation to *exercise* the power of the feminine," with "the feminine" now designating "aesthetic behavior" rather than an "expression of female experience" (365, 374). The premise (and promise) of textual politics thus underwrites the possibility of feminist agency Retallack finds available in the act of women reclaiming "the experimental feminine" for themselves (372). As Tallique states much more bluntly, "Feminist writing occurs *only* when female writers use feminine forms" (359, emphasis added).

But the same emphasis on the politics of form can also lead to an opposing feminist position: that the attachment, even the critical attachment of gender codes to language promotes the restriction of women to certain kinds of expression and in fact perpetuates binary gender divisions and the hierarchies inevitably accompanying them. This position culminates in a feminist need to insist that linguistic categories should not be gendered, even in aesthetic or critical efforts to challenge past ways in which forms and genres certainly *have* been gendered. It therefore calls on feminist practitioners to do away with the concept of "feminine form" altogether, however much political promise has been theoretically ascribed to it. Thus, if one adheres too strongly to either of the positions circumscribed by the "politics of form" position, one runs the risk of asserting "no language is code-free" to a degree that leaves one stuck with the task of constantly negotiating between "masculine" and "feminine" categories, inadvertently strengthening them; or one runs the risk of dangerously underestimating the pervasiveness of gender ideology in all cultural forms. As Judith Butler and others have asked: How does one develop a critique of sexual difference without referring to the binary terms whose reiteration would seem to affirm and reinforce the system of sexual difference itself? Since the feminist critic—or poet—constantly faces a situation in which the basic presuppositions of the sex-gender system are potentially reentrenched "by the practical context of [her own] intervention in them,"[34] the enterprise of critique threatens to become a paranoid economy with the question of complicity at its very center.

Poet Juliana Spahr has consistently explored these questions throughout her work. If paranoia forefronts the question of how to adequately distinguish our own constructions from those which construct us,[35] the poem entitled "responding," from Spahr's book *Response* (1995), deliberately occupies the boundary between these possibilities by using the "generic" phrasing we might associate with an institutional fill-in-the-blank form, diagnostic, or question-naire. By foregrounding the slots or positions in a predetermined arrangement over the particular objects which occupy them, Spahr's writing repeatedly raises the question of what forms of "re-sponding" are ultimately available to subjects when they heed the call to respond properly:

> we know we respond resistantly as faked children's books of realist
> adventure tales have turned into military instruction manuals

> or [name of major historical figure] hails a cab, [generic possessive
> human pronoun] hand raised here, beckoning as the red flag
> with [name of fast food chain] waves behind [generic human
> pronoun] and the red star on top of the [name of cultural
> landmark in major city] twinkles.

> many people raise their hands for different purposes all day long
> (19)

Spahr's use of administrative rhetoric here recalls Lacan's figure for the subject of paranoid knowledge, the "notary in his function," who is, as David Kazanjian notes, "a petty bureaucrat, an impover-ished figure through whom the state performs its functions without his or her conscious or willful consent."[36]

This Bartlebyan aesthetic recurs in Spahr's long poem *LIVE,* which begins with no less than three sections titled "INTRODUC-TION." One explains in fairly straightforward, first-person narra-tive the poem's connection to its author's "typical entry level job" at a state-run "psychiatric institution doing desktop publishing, slide production, and transcription." The "INTRODUCTION" preced-ing this, however, unfolds as follows:

> It begins like this: a man or woman speaks memo after memo
> with numbered and lettered items. Then a man or woman
> transcribes these memos into consecutively numbered or let-

tered items, correcting the speaker's mistakes in consecutivity. A man or woman cleans up after this original man or woman, the one who spoke the memos. Another watches his or her children. One answers his or her phone. In work a person is hired to do something for another person. In this language of hierarchy, the man or woman is called boss; the other man or woman is called secretary, maid, nanny, or receptionist. The person who does something may or may not do this thing if they were not paid. It is more common to not want to do this thing. This person who does something often feels oppressed by their job, by their relation to the monetary system which makes them work, by the continual tension between managers and workers. Figure that I or you have been looking for work for three or six or some amount of years and cannot find such work. As in theories of capital, realize this situation and see it as the beginning place for all current thinking or escaping.

The relentless splitting of the subject between "man or woman" and "I and you" in this passage is a situation both anticipated and rendered disturbingly literal in Spahr's earlier poem "thrashing seems crazy," the account of the woman stalked by a male version of herself. In "thrashing," the bifurcation is explored as a form of violence that cannot be properly understood as coming from either within or without—a situation that Spahr continues to foreground in *LIVE*.[37] "THE MAN OR WOMAN SAID TO THE TWO MEN OR WOMEN DRESSED IN SILK AND LACE AND SHOWING LOTS OF THEIR OR OUR BODIES ESPECIALLY ITS FORBIDDEN OR EXPOSED PARTS, HE OR SHE SAID 'YOU OR I ARE KILLING ME OR YOU, JUST KILLING ME OR YOU.'" In both "thrashing seems crazy" and *LIVE,* the subject's splitting demonstrates how "the uncertainty of paranoia—the uncertain demarcation of the subject" might function as "a way of understanding a set of controlling technologies, practices, and ideas that are responsible for one's persecution and yet a vital part of one's identity" (Melley, "SBL," 95). Yet there is a considerable difference between the way the "uncertain demarcation of the subject" associated with paranoia functions in these two poems. In "thrashing seems crazy," the "uncertain demarcation" operates at a thematic level to highlight explicitly gendered forms of persecution/identity. In *LIVE,* it operates at a grammatical level to highlight what seems to be a form of *generic* identity, in an exploration of "controlling technologies, practices, and ideas" that are ostensibly related less to the sex-gender system than to capitalism. But while producing an effect similar to that produced by Spahr's device of substituting abstract grammatical categories ("[gendered pronoun]," "[name of nation used as an adjective]") for concrete particulars in the poem "responding," the "OR" phrases in *LIVE* paradoxically call attention to the persistence of sexual difference in the very phrasing of "generic" identity. *LIVE*'s "irresolution" about gender specificity ("HE OR SHE") might be said to testify more to sexual difference's ideological tenacity as a binary system— and to its inseparability from the questions of labor, time, and money that are the poem's more overt concerns—than any statement made from a resolutely feminine or masculine position. We can see this situation dramatized by Spahr in the sentence, "The man or woman is called secretary, maid, nanny, or receptionist," where the predication of the noun phrase "man or woman" ironically relies on occupational classifications continuing to bear a decidedly gendered inflection.

This paradox is perhaps best captured in the following passage from the poem's central column of continuously running text: "WHILE MEN OR WOMEN ARE ATTRACTED TO SHORT PHRASAL UNITS, MEN OR WOMEN PREFER MORE ROLLING SENTENCES. THIS IS CALLED GENDER OR SEXUAL DETERMINISM. HIS OR HER POEMS SEEM TO DEMONSTRATE, DESPITE THEIR DISCONNECTED-NESS, THE CONNECTEDNESS OF EXPERIENCE RATHER THAN FREEDOM. THIS IS CONTRARY TO HIS

OR HER DESIRES YET IT IS WHAT MAKES US OR THEY APPRECIATE THE BALLSY ATTITUDE OF HIS OR HER WORK." Calling attention to the fact that *LIVE* itself deploys "short phrasal units" as well as "rolling sentences" in its analysis-enactment of everyday fear ("A MAN OR WOMAN WALKED ACROSS THE STREET WITH A PLASTIC MEDICAL APRON CAUGHT ON HIS OR HER ANKLE. THE CITY WAS SO DENSE THAT TOUCHING AND BEING TOUCHED WAS A PART OF EVERYDAY LIFE OR DEATH"), Spahr's generic-paranoid phrasing appears to neutralize the assignation of gender values to language even as the claim to gender specificity *in* language is being made. Yet the poem stages the resurfacing of this specificity in the lingo of aesthetic evaluation, once again demonstrating the persistence of sex and gender ("BALLSY ATTITUDE") in the very assertion of generic syntax and subjectivity. In doing so, this moment also seems to highlight the traditional masculinization of paranoid knowledge, given that the belief in an absolute "CONNECTEDNESS OF EXPERI-ENCE" fundamental to paranoia and conspiracy theory is precisely where the gender specificity of language resurfaces.

Elsewhere in *LIVE,* the logic of hyperconnectivity on which paranoid knowledge relies becomes a metaphor for communicative exchange, while also being presented as a possible threat or source of fear in itself. "A MAN OR WOMAN HAS A VACUUM TUBE UP TO HIS OR HER MOUTH AND HOLDS OUT THE OTHER END OF THE TUBE TO ME OR YOU OR ANYONE PASSING BY. I OR YOU SAY NO THANK YOU BUT PONDER REQUEST. IS IT COMMUNICATION OR MANSLAUGHTER? THE CLIPBOARDS AT PLANNED PARENTHOOD ARE COVERED WITH DECLARATIONS OF LOVE: SES AND JEFF 4 EVER; KIM LIKES JIM; KK + BK. TOO MANY TO WRITE DOWN." In the image of the MAN OR WOMAN offering to physically attach himself/herself to the speaker/reader by means of a familiar household or laboratory device, "CONNECTEDNESS OF EXPERIENCE" suggests the possibility of social bonding and violence at the same time. Yet the fearfulness implicit in this encounter does not seem securely anchored to a particular self, since the potential threat posed by the MAN OR WOMAN's ambiguous invitation (nothing less than "manslaughter") is being not only posed to a "generic" subject, but articulated in a language that is strikingly aloof or detached: "I OR YOU SAY NO THANK YOU BUT PONDER REQUEST."

In conjunction with its reliance on both concrete and abstract language, as well as first- and third-person narration ("I worked a year at a psychiatric institute doing desktop publishing, slide production and transcription" versus "A man or woman transcribes these memos into consecutively numbered or lettered items"), *LIVE*'s simultaneous insistence on "generic" and "gendered" phrasings of subjectivity renders the poem, like nearly all of Spahr's work, at once highly impersonal and personal. Conveyed with the insistence yet the typographic uniformity of all-capitalized text, a stylistic device reinforcing the seeming affectlessness and neutrality of Spahr's characteristic "zero-level writing," the generic/gendered delineation of the subject persists throughout *LIVE* as it explores the inextricably linked issues of time and labor:[38]

> THE MAN OR WOMAN SAYS I OR WE WILL TELL
> YOU OR THEY ONE THING, EVERYTHING THAT
> HAPPENS HAPPENS RIGHT ON TIME. RIGHT ON
> TIME, DID YOU OR ME HEAR ME OR YOU? RIGHT
> ON TIME. HE OR SHE KEPT THINKING OF GOOD
> THINGS THAT WOULD HAPPEN IF HE OR SHE
> WOULD GET A JOB; THINGS LIKE HEALTH INSUR-
> ANCE OR A FEELING OF USEFULNESS. WE OR YOU
> ARE INFLUENCED BY FORCES BEYOND OUR CON-
> TROL. PAULIE SHORE TALKS ABOUT AIDS ON THE
> TELEVISION IN A SILLY VOICE. CNN REPLACED
> THE WORD FOREIGN WITH THE WORD INTERNA-

TIONAL AND HE OR SHE WONDERED IF HE OR SHE SHOULD FEEL FUNNY WHEN HE OR SHE USES THAT WORD IN CONVERSATION.

The MAN OR WOMAN's emphatic, even somewhat hysterical insistence on the absolute synchronization or perfect timing of events ("RIGHT ON TIME") results in echolalia, ironically undermining the very concept of synchronization put forward by the speaker, as well as the speaker's ability to communicate his or her confidence in perfect timing in a temporally precise way. Despite the speaker's obstinate assertion that "EVERYTHING THAT HAPPENS"—including ordinary speech acts like the one being performed—"HAPPENS RIGHT ON TIME," the echolalic repetition of the phrase "RIGHT ON TIME" suggests a missed beat, or an unintended pause or delay, induced in his or her own communicative act by the implied silence or nonresponsiveness of the listener. "RIGHT ON TIME, DID YOU OR ME HEAR ME OR YOU? RIGHT ON TIME." In other words, the "generic" speaker, for all his or her insistence on perfect timing, fails to achieve the goal of being RIGHT ON TIME in his or her delivery of a proposition *about* perfect timing—a situation analogous to the temporal "stutter" or paradoxically redundant expression of synchronicity in Ward's "meanwhile & and / at the same time."

In the context of the poem's shift from this moment of badly timed communication ("DID YOU OR ME HEAR ME OR YOU?") to communicative events taking place on television (in particular, broadcast events with the capacity to induce changes in the American vernacular), *LIVE*'s preoccupation with synchronicity and the timely delivery of communications comes to connect with the ideals of simultaneity and flow associated with the medium of television itself. In addition to the poem's concern with the RIGHT ON TIME, through its absence of page numbers and continuous streaming of parallel texts, *LIVE*'s formal structure calls attention to television's own governing ideology of liveness, "the promise of presence and immediacy made available by video technology's capacity to record and transmit images simultaneously."[39] It is telling that simultaneity, immediacy, and "an equivalence between time of event and time of transmission"[40] have played crucial roles in arguments for a distinctly feminine language based on appeals to the female body as a site of temporal alterity, such as in Kristeva's theory of a nonlinear, nonconsecutive "women's time." It is almost as if *LIVE* takes up the tropes of flow and immediacy central to avant-garde language theory's concepts of feminine language and deliberately relocates them from the gendered body to the disembodied realm of mass media. More precisely, *LIVE* relocates these tropes of immediacy and presence (which are elsewhere associated with the female body) to the commodified activity of *transcription,* a form of employment made possible by the very liveness of visual or audial communications technologies, given the demand this "promise of immediacy and presence" introduces when the information originally recorded and transmitted "live" must be *rerecorded* or committed to memory in the decidedly nonlive technology of writing—an activity that, in late twentieth-century theoretical writing, is repeatedly associated with death. If the ideology of liveness explicitly counteracts the work of memory through its emphasis on the RIGHT ON TIME, on the now and the present, and on a simultaneity between time of event and time of transmission, the work of transcription enacts the very opposite temporality, *widening* the gap between time of event and time of transmission (or, more precisely, between the time of transmission and the time of recording). In fact, the work of transcription, which can *only* take place between these moments, presumes and requires that such a temporal gap exists.

The function of the transcriber, like that of Lacan's notary, thus entails a secondary, mechanical reprocessing of language which would seem completely at odds with standard notions of poetic practice. The transcriber writes down not only language that is not his or her own, but language which has been already put forth—in this case, by a state-run psychiatric institution. Transcription thus involves a relationship to language that is *inherently* one of belatedness or redundancy. The relationship between transcription and language is also one of labor, and in a form few would describe as intellectually or aesthetically "rewarding." In working on or reprocessing the language of the state, the transcriber, like Lacan's figure for the subject of paranoid knowledge, does seem to become "an impoverished figure through whom the state performs its functions without his or her conscious or willful consent" (Kazanjian, "NK," 129). Yet while dramatizing the contrast between the belatedness intrinsic to the labor of transcription and the RIGHT ON TIME or synchronization of communicative events insisted upon by its "generic" speaker, *LIVE* nonetheless uses the "impoverished figure" of the transcriber as a figure for the poet, deliberately blurring the difference between the decidedly unromantic labor of reprocessing the language of others and the work of poetic construction.

This conflation of poetry and transcription takes place partly at the level of composition itself, as we see from the author's statement about her writing process in the first-person introduction. Here *LIVE* is described as a "mimetic" poem, representing the author's attempt to "write work" while performing a type of commodified labor which would seem to preclude it: "I tried during my job to do my other work, that without an economy, only to realize that there was little hope. This [the poem] was my attempt to get around this problem." Yet according to Spahr's personal statement, the attempt "to get around the problem" seems to have involved nothing other than the activity of transcription itself, though in a form incapable of generating a wage: "I collected phrases from my day as they came to me on a notebook that I kept to the side. I collected notes from my boss's memos, things I had seen on the way to or from work, stories overheard. I collected them into one long stream of day/text and barely edited them."

At a certain level, this statement seems to suggest a self-conscious abdication of writing as a mode of personal expression. The poet claims not to have "written" during her tenure as a state-employed transcriber, but, in lieu of this activity, to have collected, catalogued, and recorded language in the form of unmediated information. In this sense, Spahr's statement suggests an attempt to write herself out of the poem, or, more precisely, to construct the poem as a deliberate elision of *self outside its economically imposed function as transcriber*. According to the statement, none of the language in *LIVE* is actually "live," in the sense of being uttered and recorded simultaneously, and none of it seems to be the speaker's "own"; all of it is language that has been *rewritten* or simply "inserted," in an act of labor ironically equivalent to the form of paid labor initially posited as obstructing poetic practice. Indeed, much of *LIVE*'s central column of text consists of editorial commands that presumably come from the speaker's employer: "CHANGE 'THE MOST DANGEROUS STUDIES ARE THOSE THAT COME WITH THE TRAPPING OF AN ELABORATE METHOD AND AUTHORITATIVE CONCLUSION THAT ARE BASED ON FLAWED SAMPLES OR INAPPROPRIATE DESIGN' TO 'THE PAPERS THAT UNDERMINE THE REPUTATION OF THE JOURNAL ARE THOSE THAT COME WITH THE TRAPPINGS OF ELABORATE METHOD AND AUTHORITATIVE CONCLUSIONS BUT ARE BASED ON FLAWED SAMPLES OR INAPPROPRIATE DESIGN.'"

But *LIVE* also consists of two other continuously running texts positioned on top and to the right of its central column: sentences from Gertrude Stein's essays "All about Money" and "Money," and, as Spahr informs us, "questions from a diagnostic instrument used to determine mental illness in children that I worked on over and over again." Spahr also tells the reader that these diagnostic questions were taken from "sections on Conduct Disorder and Oppositional Defiance Disorder," which she "found especially problematic in that they diagnosed any kind of potential protest about one's surroundings as deviant." Thus, at the bottom right-hand margin of the page alongside centered passages like this one:

THREE MEN OR WOMEN SURROUND ANOTHER
MAN OR WOMAN WALKING BESIDE THEM. THEY
OR YOU FLEX THEIR STUFF AND SAY QUIETLY TO
THE MAN OR WOMAN, "DON'T BE SCARED MAMA
OR PAPA, WE OR ONE AIN'T GOING TO HURT YOU
OR HE OR SHE." IT IS A THREAT WRAPPED IN A
CARESS. IN THE DREAM I OR YOU HELD HIM OR
HER AND AFTERWARDS I OR YOU FELT AFRAID
OF WHAT I OR YOU HAD EMBRACED. CHOOSE
CHOICE OR ANGER. HE OR SHE USED THE EX-
PRESSION ITS SO PROZAC NATION A LOT BEFORE
HE OR SHE WENT ON PROZAC. THE STONED MAN
OR WOMAN STUMBLES OR PASSES EFFORTLESSLY
DOWN THE CROWDED STREET AS I OR YOU OR
THE CROWD PART AROUND THEM OR US TO
MAKE ROOM

we find the question: "In the last year (that is, since [NAME
EVENT / NAME CURRENT MONTH of last year]), have you
been mad at people or things?" This juxtaposition explicitly foregrounds the connection between the clinical diagnosis of anger, in
which the transcriber employed by the state psychiatric institute indirectly participates, and the quotidian feelings of fear described in
the "THREAT WRAPPED IN A CARESS," or the dream-caress
that later leads to apprehensiveness. At other moments, the link
between the instrumental rhetoric used to identify "Oppositional
Defiance Disorder" and the central column of text seems less clear,
particularly as the questions initially unfold. All of the questions,
however, call attention to the manner in which the generic categories inscribed within the language of psychiatric diagnosis echo the
"generic" phrasings of subjectivity in which binarized sexual specificity paradoxically persists:

Now I am going to ask you some questions about getting angry or doing things that could get you in trouble.

> In the last year, that is, since [NAME EVENT / NAME CUR-RENT MONTH of last year], have you lost your temper?

> In the last year *(that is, since* [NAME EVENT / NAME CUR-RENT MONTH of last year]), have you argued with or talked back to your [CARETAKERS] (or [teacher/boss])?

Creating the possibility of actually producing the emotion it would seem to merely quantify and evaluate, the second meaning in the diagnostician's initial statement ("Now I am going to ask you some questions about getting angry or doing things *that could get you in trouble*") suggests that the questionnaire's neutral rhetoric nonetheless poses a certain threat to the subject who complies by responding. Spahr's adaptation of a format that characteristically produces kinds of persons in the process of individually assessing them (soliciting "responses" when the possibilities for responding have been predetermined by an existing generic grid) turns the poetic text into a phobic organization in which it becomes impossible to separate the interpretations the subject generates from those that generate the subject. Yet this aesthetic outcome speaks less to paranoia's "dual ability to objectify or realize a reality and yet to proclaim the 'subject's' innocence of its formation," than to an arrangement in which a threatening social reality is realized with the outcome of disclosing the subject's *participation* in its formation.[41] While also suggesting a displacement of anger from/to the speaker's own experience to/from the clinical tools used to assess it, the striking similarity between the generic language of the diagnostic instrument and the equally generic, neutral-sounding language used by *LIVE*'s speaker to describe her ordinary workday highlights this complicity to an extent that it becomes one of the poem's dominant themes.

Indeed, in the poem's claim to a certain passivity, it is possible to see how a cynical reader might interpret Spahr's relinquishment of poetic authority in her introduction ("I collected [all my phrases] into one long stream of day/text and barely edited them") as a capitulation to the demands of the wage-labor system. It does seem accurate to say that in *LIVE* the writer's self often seems reduced to the functions of gathering and recording language for which she is monetarily compensated, not unlike the way *Modern Times* depicts merging of a factory worker's subjective boundaries into the wrenching function he is paid to repetitively perform (as we saw in Chapter 2). But like Chaplin, the transcriber/poet/speaker in *LIVE* is an employee within the system who performs her function too well, generating an excess of activity that finally cannot be instrumentalized or assimilated into surplus value. Like Chaplin, the transcriber's subjection is revealed to have an aggressive component unleashed by a hyperbolic exaggeration or redoubling of the activity that the system demands. In this sense, in *LIVE* the speaker writes work—and "works" writing—in more ways than one.

In its inherent or structural belatedness, and as the site of connection between the speaker's work as state employee and her work "without an economy," transcription thus becomes the paradigm through which *LIVE* simultaneously analyzes and enacts everyday fear under its conditions of complicity. It also functions as the paradigm enabling *LIVE* to stage the reintegration of "art" and "life praxis," with the intent of organizing new forms of the latter, which Peter Bürger has described as central to the project of the historical avant-garde.[42] "HE OR SHE SAID THAT THE THEORY OF LIFE SHOULD BE THE THEORY OF POETRY, OR WAS IT THAT THE THEORY OF POETRY SHOULD BE THE THEORY OF LIFE? AND WHAT DOES EITHER OF THOSE MEAN? HE OR SHE WAS DISTURBED TO SEE HIM OR HER NAKED FIRST THING IN THE MORNING. IMAGINE THE QUESTION AS THE MOMENT OF COMPLEXITY AS IT LEAVES A NUMBER OF DIFFERENT ANSWERS POSSIBLE."

As part of this endeavor to integrate "day" and "text," or artistic production with the daily routines revolving entirely around one's wage labor, *LIVE* not only foregrounds "THE CONNECTED-NESS OF EXPERIENCE" historically privileged in avant-garde efforts to synthesize art and everyday life, but calls attention to the kind of articulating logic central to paranoid knowledge, which insists that there must always be a link or at the very least an "and" (maybe even an "& and") between situations and events—even ones as disparate as transcribing responses to "Oppositional Defiance Disorder" questionnaires and being offered a vacuum tube to suck on by a stranger in the street. Though the exact nature of the connections among *LIVE*'s social particulars always remains unexplained, their very aggregation suggests a social imagination—the desire and effort to think "a system," or at the very least to think gender and capital, "meanwhile & and/at the same time." Granted, like the "monolithic and vaguely-defined 'patriarchal bourgeois humanism' said to permeate the structures of symbolic discourse" that Felski sees "language feminism" defining itself against,[43] the social totality *LIVE* hints at through its exploration of fear under conditions of complicity is amorphously bounded. Yet this amorphousness of definition can be viewed as precisely the political point, as Timothy Melley demonstrates in his reading of women's stalking fiction, which argues that the characteristic amorphousness of the genre's persecutory figures strategically enables female authors to depict these shadowy and vaguely defined perpetrators as "deindividuated stand-ins of a more general cultural pattern" and to "construe male violence as if it were 'intentional *and* nonsubjective,'" thus "mak[ing] visible the violence involved in the production of 'normal' heterosexual relations" ("SBL," 94, 96, emphasis added). Moreover, while the vague or amorphous definition of a "total system" suggests a certain failure on the part of the subject to *conceptualize* a social whole, one could argue that it is only in such failures—or in failure in general, which Robyn Wiegman describes as "the unavoidable consequence of imagining political transformation"—that a *conceivable* totality manifests itself.[44] Far from presupposing or proceeding "hand in hand with . . . fantasies of subjective coherence, plentitude, and autonomy," the effort to "partake of and help constitute a familiar occidental epistemological category which is that of the conceivable whole" (Smith, *DS,* 88) might be viewed as an effort uniquely fostered within the negative, self-dislocating space created by belated and dysphoric disclosures of complicity.

By "writing work" that insistently foregrounds the subject's inscription within the system she opposes, but also assumes this situation as the beginning point rather than an obstruction to critical intervention, Spahr stages the poet's encounter with social totality as negative affect per se. In doing so, the minor, seemingly politically effete role of the state-employed transcriber comes to take on new cultural meanings, contributing to the effort to think how the small subject's inevitable complicity (or perhaps even her "paranoia") might eventually become "the condition of agency rather than its destruction."[45] For as Spahr herself suggests, while paranoid logic always offers "escaping" as one option, it offers "thinking" as the other: *As in theories of capital, realize this situation and see it as the beginning place for all current thinking or escaping.*

afterword: on disgust

Theories, poetics, and ethics of "desire" abound, but something about disgust seems to have resisted engendering these forms of attention.[1] Though Barthes's *jouissance*—the hyperbolic endpoint of desire, if not a form of desire per se—and all of its variants have energized critical writing on literature for decades, disgust has no keywords associated with it and has largely remained outside the range of any organized critical practice or school. Even the theory of abjection at the heart of Julie Kristeva's *Powers of Horror,* a theory initially formulated in a scene of "loathing an item of food, a piece of filth, waste or dung," is eventually reconceptualized in the libidinal terms of "want," "primal repression," and self-shattering *jouissance;* in fact, Kristeva argues, "*jouissance* alone causes the abject to exist as such."[2] To be sure, from the depiction of Marcel's first encounter with Gilberte in Proust's *Swann's Way* ("I thought her so beautiful that I should have liked to be able to retrace my steps so as to shake my fist at her and shout, 'I think you are hideous, grotesque; how I loathe you!'") to the films of John Waters, artists as well as philosophers have demonstrated that desire and disgust are dialectically conjoined.[3] As William Miller notes, "the disgusting itself has the power to allure," particularly as an object created by social taboos and prohibitions.[4] The allure is not even solely a matter of repression, for "fascination with the disgusting is something we are often quite conscious of even as we turn away" (Miller, *AD,* 110). Yet the striking asymmetry between the careers of disgust and desire in literary and cultural theory raises the broader question of why repulsion has such a long history of being overshadowed by attraction as a theoretical concern, even as we can plausibly assert that the late capitalist lifeworld is one in which there are at least as many things to turn away from—the strong centripetal pull of consumer culture notwithstanding—as things to be drawn toward.

This turning away is arguably the most polemical as well as the most passive gesture of the copyist in "Bartleby," who disturbs also in his closely related refusal to consume anything. Conversely, the principle of "charity," which we have seen Melville interrogate extensively in *The Confidence-Man,* is not only breezily acknowledged by the Lawyer as a practical attitude founded on "self-interest," but summoned in high professional-managerial fashion as an affective prophylactic against the repugnance he seems noticeably reluctant to admit that Bartleby produces—a repugnance which of course includes a great deal of fascination. Significantly, in keeping with his convivial "Wall-Street spirit" (and with no small amount of self-congratulation), it is the prudent suppression of his aversion that enables the Lawyer to tolerate his employee's discomforting presence. For what seems intolerable about Bartleby is how paradoxically visible he makes his social invisibility, even from behind the screen that literally conceals him from view, thwarting what Erving Goffman calls the "civil inattention" on which the routines of public life in an affluent democracy depend.[5] If the disgusting is always that which is insistent and intolerable, Melville suggests that tolerance is always, in some fundamental way, a negation of disgust. Benevolent tolerance is in fact presented in this story as a barely disguised euphemism for a pity that at times seems to verge on contempt: "I strove to drown my exasperated feelings toward the scrivener by benevolently construing his conduct. Poor fellow, poor fellow! thought I, he don't mean anything; and besides, he has seen hard times, and ought to be indulged."[6] Is Bartleby aware that the Lawyer secretly finds him repulsive? More interestingly, is he making use of the Lawyer's attempt to manage this repulsion, mobilizing "charity" to downgrade his unproductive disgust to the more socially acceptable, friendly contempt one has for someone perceived as inferior but basically harmless—that is, a person who "don't mean anything"?

It thus seems fitting to close this book with a few remarks on some implications of the asymmetrical fates, in late twentieth-century literary theory, of "desire" and this ugly feeling par excellence, which Kant highlights in the *Critique of Judgement* as the single exception to representational art's otherwise unlimited power to beautify things which are ugly or displeasing in real life, such as "The Furies, diseases, [and] the devastations of war."[7] As Kant notes, "There is only one kind of ugliness which cannot be represented in accordance with nature without destroying all aesthetical satisfaction, and consequently artificial beauty, viz. that which excites *disgust*. For in this singular sensation, which rests on mere imagination, the object is represented as it were obtruding itself for our enjoyment while we strive against it with all our might. And the artistic representation of the object is no longer distinguished from the nature of the object itself in our sensation, and thus it is impossible that it can be regarded as beautiful" (*CJ*, 155). As a negation of beauty that anticipates the modernist avant-garde's critical assault on art's identification *with* beauty,[8] there is a sense in which the disgusting is "the true Kantian sublime"—more sublime than the sublime itself, or, as Derrida suggests, the absolute "other" of the system of taste.[9] This is implicit in Kant's comment, in his earlier work *Observations on the Feeling of the Beautiful and the Sub-*

lime, that "nothing is so much set against the beautiful as disgust."[10] In the *Critique of Judgement,* what makes the object abhorrent is precisely its outrageous claim for desirability. The disgusting seems to say, "You want me," imposing itself on the subject as something to be mingled with and perhaps even enjoyed. The split between disgust and desire thus seems paradoxically internal to Kantian disgust. Disgust both includes and attacks the very opposition between itself and desire, and, in doing so, destroys not only "aesthetical satisfaction" but the disinterestedness on which it depends.

Yet there is always a certain asymmetry in the pairing of disgust and desire, since disgust is a structured and agonistic emotion carrying a strong and unmistakable signal, while desire is often noisy and amorphous. Like animatedness, desire almost seems pre- or sub-affective. There is thus a sense in which disgust is the ugliest of "ugly feelings," yet an interesting exception. For disgust is never ambivalent about its object. More specifically, it is never prone to producing the confusions between subject and object that are integral to most of the feelings discussed in this book. Whereas the obscuring of the subjective-objective boundary becomes internal to the nature of feelings like animatedness and paranoia, disgust strengthens and polices this boundary. Even if disgust is boiled down to its kernel of repulsion, repulsion itself tends to be a fairly definite response, whereas the parameters of attraction are notoriously difficult to determine and fix. Put simply, desire seems capable of being vague, amorphous, and even idiosyncratic in ways that disgust cannot. Moreover, as Miller notes, "the avowal of disgust expects concurrence" (*AD,* 194), whereas we tend not to ask for supplementary ratification of our desired object's desirability, or demand that others share our affective relation to it or our valuation of it, once that object has actually been established.[11]

Hence, while disgust explicitly blocks the path of sympathy in Adam Smith's theory of moral sentiment, and is closely linked to his "unsocial" passions of resentment and hatred, there is a sense in which it seeks to include or draw others *into* its exclusion of its object, enabling a strange kind of sociability.[12] Disgust's "expectation of concurrence" also distinguishes it from a particular kind of contempt characterized predominantly by indifference, as brought out most clearly in its definition by Hobbes: "Those things which we neither desire, nor hate, we are said to *contemn:* CONTEMPT being nothing else but an immobility, or contumacy [obstinacy] of the heart, in resisting the action of certain things."[13] The indifference of Hobbesian contempt (which, as Miller notes, looks more like "the contempt of complacency, of never doubting your superiority or rank," than like the contempt we associate with active dislike; *AD,* 215) surprisingly draws it closer to the very antithesis of disgust—tolerance—than to the aversive emotion it would seem much more to resemble. For unlike the disgusting, which is perceived as dangerous and contaminating and thus something to which one cannot possibly remain indifferent, the object of Hobbesian contempt, like that of its close relations, pity and disdain, is relatively harmless. Too weak or insignificant to pose any sort of danger, the object of contempt is perceived as inferior in a manner that allows it to be dismissed or ignored. Hence, contempt is part of the nexus of affects, in Nietzsche's *Genealogy of Morals,* that distinguishes the morality of the happy and self-secure "noble man" from the morality of the "slave." As Nietzsche writes, "There is indeed too much carelessness, too much taking lightly, too much looking away and impatience involved in contempt, even too much joyfulness, for it to be able to transform its object into a real . . . monster."[14] One could say that the object is perceived as inferior in a manner that permits it to be tolerated (if only barely). Contempt might be described as the negative boundary of the affective spectrum of tolerance, which includes affable versions as well. This is not to say that tolerance and contempt are the same thing, only that contemptuous tolerance is possible in a way that disgusted tolerance is not. If desire says "Yes" and disgust says "No," the contempt described by Nietzsche and Hobbes says, "Whatever." Disgust finds its object intolerable and demands its exclusion, while the objects of contempt "simply do not merit strong affect; they are noticed only sufficiently so as to know that they are not noticeworthy" (Miller, *AD,* 215). As Miller also notes, "One can condescend to treat them decently, one may, in rare circumstances, even pity them, but they are mostly invisible or utterly and safely *disattendable*" (*AD,* 215, italics added). This disattendability is the principle which Bartleby conspicuously and even stuplimely violates by adhering to it too well; in not eating, not striving, nor seeming to desire anything, Bartleby even seems to take *himself* as disattendable. Indeed, the aversion that Bartleby elicits from the Lawyer, which the Lawyer is then compelled to manage with the affects of conviviality and charity, involves a disattendability so exaggerated that the disattendability itself comes to demand attention. We might say that for all his passivity, Bartleby is finding a way to make to make himself intolerable: someone who can no longer properly fit into the slot of the object of Hobbesian contempt, and precisely by embodying the immobility that defines it. The unsettling proximity between Hobbesian contempt and the more benign notion of tolerance—disclosed precisely through the managerial suppression of disgust in Melville's story—is a topic to which we will shortly return.

Disgust is urgent and specific; desire can be ambivalent and vague. The former expects concurrence; the latter does not. I should clarify that in what follows, the word "desire" refers not to sexuality or sexual practices, or to psychoanalysis' highly exacting concept of drive or libido, but rather to the vaguely affective idiom broadly used as an "index of [literary] heterogeneity" by late twentieth-century literary theorists across methods and affiliations.[15] That is, I mean the "desire" associated with images of fluidity, slippage, and semantic multiplicity—what Kristeva in *Desire in Language* (111) calls *polynomia* or "the pluralization of meaning by different means (polyglottism, polysemia, etc.)"—which has become technical shorthand for virtually any perceived transgression of the symbolic status quo. Inclusive, pluralistic, and often eclectic, literary theory's "desire" is admittedly appealing, especially when positioned as "a mobile system of free signifying devices" in explicit contrast to the rigid hierarchies of the symbolic order (Kristeva, *DL,* 116). Its very attractiveness suggests that an explanation for the divergent fates of attraction and repulsion in critical discourse is not hard to seek; in fact, we do not have to begin in this narrowly circumscribed arena to do so. For in a consumer society in which the public sphere has become increasingly coextensive with the marketplace, the spectrum of desires is simply broader than that of disgust, offering a rich multiplicity of ways to define and express all sorts of attraction. At the same time, the language of repulsion is much more narrow and restricted, such that we tend to find a rhetoric of disgust supplanted by weaker but categorically different styles of indignation or complaint (as Miller points out, weak disgust is no longer really disgust). As the French writer Bernard Noël worries, "Revolt acts; indignation seeks to speak. From the start of my childhood, only reasons for becoming indignant: the war, the deportation, the Indochinese War, the Korean war, the Algerian war." But as Noël notes, "There's no language [to describe this] because we live in a bourgeois world, where the vocabulary of indignation is exclusively moral."[16] The moralization of aversive rhetoric, already present in the effort to depolemicize class envy which we examined in Chapter 3, puts a further constraint on what Noël acknowledges to be its already limited force: unlike revolt, which acts, revoltedness merely tries to speak. Indeed, a moralizing tone inadvertently seeps into the indignant language which Noël uses to problematize the moralization of indignation, though in a manner that provides a perfect illustration of his point. But perhaps the more obvious explanation for the asymmetrical attention to desire and disgust in literary and cultural theory is the latter's more spectacular appropriation by the political right throughout history, as a means of reinforcing the boundaries between self and "contaminating" others that has perpetuated racism, anti-Semitism, homophobia, and misogyny. Miller suggests that the worst aspects of disgust's awful political past can be traced to the relatively late arrival of democracy, which he provocatively describes as a society defined not so much by a more equitable distribution of rights or respects as by a more equitable distribution of contempts. This democracy of "mutual contempt" would theoretically make the low's repugnance for the high expressible in previously unsuspected ways—though Miller is careful to say that its primary and more equivocal effect has been to make possible the low's contemptuous *indifference* to the high. Here, the putative democratization of aversive emotion, in the milder form that is no longer truly disgust but contempt, curtails rather than fosters historical possibilities of revolt, culminating in the fundamentally indifferent tolerance (however negatively inflected) that true disgust, which perceives its object as harmful and infectious rather than "safely ignorable," cannot allow (Miller, *AD,* 181).

While the question of whether disgust is or behaves like a "moral sentiment" is debatable, the agonistic emotion certainly has no moral cachet. Even if one accepts Miller's argument that disgust "ranks and orders us in hierarchies" by making assessments of inferiority and superiority, and, in particular, by doing the moral work of disapprobation or blame (we will soon see a fault-line in this argument), few would argue that any of these actions (blaming, ranking, demarcating status) constitutes a virtue in itself. Moreover, like envy, paranoia, and other feelings that are more likely to be objects of moral disapprobation rather than ways of expressing it, disgust is neither of the left or of the right and has the capacity to be summoned in either direction. The fact that the political right has more visibly and unhesitatingly instrumentalized its disgust throughout history does not mean, however, that the left lacks or should suppress its own—particularly if the harmful and contaminating qualities it identifies as intolerable are those of racism, misogyny, or the militarism of a political administration. Perhaps it is awareness of the right's more flagrant conscription of disgust as a powerful political tool that steers Martha Nussbaum into making the rather strange claim that, regardless of its object, disgust is *inherently* immoral: "If no emotion is per se morally good, there may be some that are per se morally suspect, whose cognitive content is more likely than not to be false or distorted, and linked with self-deception. Such is the argument I have made for disgust. . . . We might make related arguments about envy."[17] But is there something morally suspect about one's disgust for feces or rotting meat? Given disgust's urgency that its object be rejected, is there even time to make a judgment about one's "superiority" over the feces or meat? It seems just as odd to claim there is something "false" or "self-deceptive" about the envy that the poor might have for the rich, or that the amputated might have for those able to walk. However irrational, Nussbaum's claims about the immorality "per se" of envy and disgust are ultimately consistent with her effort to build an "ethical theory" of emotion whose fundaments are sympathy, identification, and compassion.[18] Disgust and envy, which are not immoral but *a*moral—and thus inevitably prone to uglification by moralists—*block* sympathetic identification, as the third chapter of this book has shown. In any case, the moralization of the language of indignation that troubles Noël cannot register as a potential problem for Nussbaum, since it is an act in which her own account of emotions willingly participates.

In fixing its object as "intolerable," disgust undeniably has been and will continue to be instrumentalized in oppressive and violent ways. Yet its identification of its object as intolerable can also be mobilized against what Herbert Marcuse calls "repressive tolerance": the "pure," "indiscriminate," or nonpartisan tolerance that maintains the existing class structure of capitalist democracy.[19] As an important corollary to his concept of "repressive desublimation," which warns against a false understanding of desire as liberatory per se, Marcuse's critique of "pure" tolerance does not amount to a rejection of tolerance altogether.[20] In eliminating social conflict and violence, tolerance is a political necessity, Marcuse argues, but can become "an end in itself" only in a "truly humane" society that does not yet exist. Though in its historical origins tolerance was "a partisan goal, a subversive liberating notion and practice," in the later twentieth century "the political locus of tolerance has changed: while it is more or less quietly and constitutionally withdrawn from the opposition, it is made compulsory behavior with respect to established policies" ("RT," 82). Highlighting the political equivocality of the indifferent tolerance of the low for the high that Miller describes as uniquely achieved in our democracy of "mutual contempt," Marcuse writes, "Tolerance is turned from an active into a passive state, from practice to non-practice: laissez faire the constituted authorities. It is the people who tolerate the government, which in turn tolerates opposition within the framework determined by the constituted authorities. Tolerance toward that which is radically evil now appears as good because it serves the cohesion of the whole on the road to affluence or more affluence" ("RT," 82–83). Arguing against an "equality of tolerance [that] becomes abstract, spurious" and that can therefore be justified only "in harmless debates, in conversation, [and] in academic discussion," Marcuse claims that in "a society of total administration . . . the conditions under which tolerance can again become a liberating and humanizing force still have to be created" ("RT," 111). This calls for "discriminatory tolerance," however oxymoronic the term may sound.

It is crucial to note that "Repressive Tolerance" is a leftist critique of pluralism in the political state and not in culture per se; Marcuse explicitly states that he will discuss this question "only with reference to political movements, attitudes, schools of thought, philosophies which are 'political' in the widest sense" ("RT," 91). Although my much more delimited concern here is with the asymmetrical fates of disgust and desire in literary theory, there are two aspects of his argument that I wish to draw out in particular. The first is that the object of tolerance in any affluent, market-centered democracy is perceived to be harmless or relatively unthreatening. Its ability to be tolerated in this sociopolitical context thus becomes an index of its sociopolitical *ineffectuality*—in particular, its ineffectuality as a mechanism for dissent and change. From the vantage point of this market society, the best example of such a feckless thing—a thing taken as so ineffectual, harmless, and "safely disattendable" that it can be absently or even benevolently tolerated—is art. Which is why even in a critique expressly restricted to the domain of politics proper, art becomes the privileged illustration of what Marcuse perceives as one of the most antiprogressive consequences of indiscriminate tolerance or pluralism: its conversion of multiplicity into commensurability.[21]

> The danger of "destructive tolerance" (Baudelaire), of "benevolent neutrality" toward *art* has been recognized: the market, which absorbs equally well (although with often quite sudden fluctuations) art, anti-art, and non-art, all possibly conflicting styles, schools, forms, provides a "complacent receptacle, a friendly abyss" [Edward Wind, *Art and Anarchy*] in which the radical impact of art, the protest of art against the established reality is swallowed up. ("RT," 88)

Aesthetic pluralism, in its immediate relationship to the market, thus provides Marcuse with a useful analogy for the limitations of political pluralism. Nowhere is this conjoining of aesthetic and political pluralism more visible than in postmodern culture as a whole. If—as Ellen Rooney points out—pluralism, more than any political theory currently in circulation, dominates our way of understanding democracy to such an extent that "democracy" and "political pluralism" tend to be perceived as identical (*SR*, 17–18), commentators from disciplines across the humanities have increasingly used "pluralism" and "postmodernity" as synonyms for each other. Andreas Huyssen defines "postmodernism," for example, as "cultural eclecticism or pluralism," and Alex Callinicos characterizes it as a situation in which "cultural life becomes more fragmented or pluralistic."[22] And pluralism or eclecticism, as Hal Foster notes, has become a defining attribute not only of contemporary artistic practice, but of the theory and criticism of artistic practice as well.

> Art exists today in a state of pluralism: no style or even mode of art is dominant and no critical position is orthodox. Yet this state is also a position, and this position is also an alibi. As a general condition pluralism tends to absorb argument—which is not to say that it does not promote antagonism of all sorts. One can only begin out of a discontent with this status quo: for in a pluralist state art and criticism tend to be dispersed and so rendered impotent. Minor deviation is allowed only in order to resist radical change, and it is this subtle conformism that one must challenge.[23]

Perhaps here is a good place to offer one last explanation for the disproportionate amount of attention paid to configurations of attraction and repulsion in the past several decades of literary and cultural criticism, though an explanation that may seem less self-evident than the others previously discussed. There is a sense in which it is hardly surprising that desire is theoretically attractive and that the affective idiom of disgust disgusts, in a manner that recalls the autoreferentiality of Silvan Tomkins' affect system. Yet we might suspect that both the academic attraction to the "desire" associated with a polysemous fluidity starkly opposed to and privileged over semantic fixation, and, correspondingly, our relative inattention to aversion, have something also to do with the fact that the former seems especially consonant with critical or aesthetic pluralism in ways that the fundamentally exclusionary idiom of disgust is not. For the hegemonic pluralism of both the academy and the larger society is (as Rooney argues) a mode of "seductive reasoning" that conscripts the appealing rhetoric of inclusivity to *exclude critical discourses of exclusion*—in particular, those which take "the process of exclusion to be necessary to the production of meaning or community" (Rooney, *SR,* 5).

My point is not that the idiom of disgust is inherently more "radical" than a desire taken as a metaphor for "the pluralization of meaning by different means," or that the agonistic emotion has better rather than simply different theoretical possibilities to offer. It is rather that with its tropes of semantic multiplicity, slippage, and flow, with its general logic of inclusivity and strong centripetal pull, the academically routinized concept of "desire" is simply more concordant, ideologically as well as aesthetically, with the aesthetic, cultural, and political pluralisms that have come to define the postmodern than an emotional idiom defined by its vehement exclusion of the intolerable. If, in the context of a hegemonic pluralism that willfully misidentifies multiplicity with commensurability, the risk of "desire" is that of devolving into a "convenient receptacle" or "friendly abyss" for any form of "literary heterogeneity" or perceived transgression of the symbolic status quo, disgust's vulnerability as a poetics would seem to derive in part from pluralism's ability to manipulate the rhetoric of consensus and inclusivity in order to reduce oppositional and exclusionary formations to "monolithic totalitarianism[s]" (Rooney, *SR,* 27). This has been the fate of Marxism in particular, Rooney points out, in the American public sphere, where the mainstream media repeatedly marshal the language of "consensus" to caricaturize late twentieth-century socialist movements as *betrayals* of pluralism. Hence, "political pluralism, 'American-style,' is nothing but the exclusion of marxisms, both in domestic politics and abroad" (Rooney, *SR,* 27). As Hal Foster similarly points out, "Somehow, to be an advocate of pluralism is to be democratic—is to resist the dominance of any one faction (nation, class or style). But this is no more true than the converse: that to be a critic of pluralism is to be authoritarian" ("AP," 30).

If the poetics of desire that has dominated literary theory thus seems compatible with aesthetic, critical, and even political pluralism in ways that disgust is not, the argument can be reversed to suggest that a poetics of disgust would seem incompatible with pluralism, and with the ethic of indiscriminate tolerance that subtends it, in ways that *desire* is not. If tolerance itself is an emotional continuum, we can think of it as having positive and negative borders—the former consisting in what Marcuse calls "benevolent neutrality" (as exemplified in the market's friendly attitude toward art), and the latter in something akin to Hobbes's indifferent contempt. In a somewhat surprising fashion, given our common understanding of disgust and contempt as cousins rather than antagonists, there is a sense in which disgust does the work of blocking both. For if benevolence or pity can be a way of managing aversion to an object perceived as socially inferior (in order to maintain what Miller calls its "disattendability"), disgust can be a prophylactic against the contempt that marks the negative limit of that disattendability—one that already assumes its object to be relatively unthreatening, only mildly offensive if offensive at all.

Let us simply say, then, that in its centrifugality, agonism, urgency, and above all refusal of the indifferently tolerable, disgust offers an entirely different set of aesthetic and critical possibilities from the one offered by desire. It also, of course, offers a different set of limitations. Since we have already discussed these limitations (which have tended to be fairly self-evident), I would like to conclude by briefly examining some of the possibilities, using two late twentieth-century works that make use of the emotional idiom most associated with the question of what can and cannot be "swallowed up" (that is, what can and cannot be tolerated, benevolently *or* contemptuously) in ways that enable them to reflect upon the limited agency of art itself in a commodified society. As Bartlebyan allegories of how literature itself might respond to the market's disarmingly friendly *tolerance* of art—a tolerance that assumes its social ineffectuality or innocuousness—both can be taken as final demonstrations of the unique role ugly feelings can play, not only as interpretations of the predicament of blocked or suspended agency, but also as interpretations of art's suspended sociopolitical agency in particular.

Brazilian writer Clarice Lispector's *Passion According to G.H.* (1964), which could be read either as a philosophical meditation or a religious parody, is fundamentally the story of a woman smashing—and finally eating—a cockroach.[24] It is also the story of how the experience leads to the narrator's "depersonalization," which she describes as "the greatest externalization one can attain" (*PGH,* 168). This "externalization," which allows G.H. to discover that "the world interdepended with me," parallels the fate of the cockroach in the story, pointing to a striking identification between the disgusted (human) and the disgusting (object).

> The pulp started slowly to come out of the cockroach I had smashed, like out of a tube.
>
> The cockroach's pulp, which was its insides, raw matter that was whitish and thick and slow, was piling up on it as though it were toothpaste coming out of the tube.
>
> Before my nauseated, attracted eyes, the cockroach's form, as it grew on the outside, kept slowly changing. The white matter was slowly spreading across its back, like a load set for it to carry. Pinched in place, it was increasingly carrying on its dusty back a load that was in fact its own body.
>
> "Scream," I silently commanded myself. (*PGH,* 54)

In a hyperbolic version of the Lawyer's effort to manage his aversion to Bartleby with "charity," G.H. desires to reverse the "sin" of her repugnance by committing an "anti-sin": "putting into my own mouth the white paste from the cockroach" (157). As hilarious as it is awful, G.H.'s effort to spiritually redeem her disgust by the self-martyring act of ingesting the intolerable highlights the ludicrousness of the moralization of disgust in the first place: If there is something "per se morally suspect" about vehement repugnance, as Nussbaum argues, why not attempt to absolve oneself of this "sin" in the comically "logical" way G.H. does above? G.H.'s passion might also be read as a particularly horrible take on Kant's definition of the disgusting as something "represented as it were obtruding itself for our enjoyment." For in its comparison to toothpaste, the "raw matter" obtrudes as if it were intended for *cleaning* the very orifice in which it is to be consumed. It therefore offers "redemption" for both the sin of disgust and the self-contamination resulting from the effort to absolve that sin by ingesting the intolerable.

> For redemption must be in the thing itself. And redemption in the thing itself would be my putting into my own mouth the white paste from the cockroach.
>
> At just the idea I closed my eyes with the force of someone locking her jaws, and I clenched my teeth so tight that any more and they would break right out of my mouth. My insides said no, my mass rejected the cockroach's mass.
>
> . . . I tried to reason with my disgust. Why should I be disgusted by the mass that came out of the cockroach? had I not drunk of the white milk that is the liquid maternal mass? . . . But reason didn't get me anywhere, except to keep my teeth clenched together. (*PGH,* 157)

Despite her rational attitude that "disgust contradicts me, contradicts the matter in me," the protagonist's attempt to neutralize this disgust—first with reason, then with the perhaps all too rational act of attempting to ingest the matter she finds intolerable—fails (*PGH,* 156). Fueled by the desire to spiritualize or beautify, if not (as in the case of the Lawyer) professionally manage her disgust, G.H. eventually does eat the cockroach. Yet her body rejects it in spite of herself: "I dug my fingernails into the wall: now I tasted the bad taste [vomit] in my mouth, and then I began to spit, to spit out furiously that taste of nothing at all [the cockroach]. . . . I spit myself out, never reaching the point of feeling that I had finally spit out my whole soul. . . . I spat and spat and it kept on being me"

(160). However "externalizing," the self-transcendence G.H. hopes to attain from her passion is finally denied.

If *The Passion According to G.H.* can be read as an allegory of the failure of a reverent effort to absorb the intolerable from the perspective of the disgusted, the American poet Bruce Andrews, in his collection *I Don't Have Any Paper So Shut Up, or Social Romanticism* (1992), might be said to explore the limits of "pure" tolerance from the perspective of the disgus*ting*. This is not done by narrativizing disgust, as Lispector does in *The Passion,* but through a poetry unusually crowded with the linguistic equivalents of what Lispector calls "raw matter"—expletives, onomatopoeia, and proper names. Here, for instance, is the beginning of "It's Time to Stop Glorifying the White Army," a poem fairly representative of *Shut Up* as a whole:

> It's time to stop glorifying the white army. Swollen household
> clouds complain, guts galore Victorian
> nephews recolonize Brazil; I decided to serve Lipton tea to the
> chaingang. It's fun
> to raise pet sea-monkeys!—coin-operated
> vaginal nutrition—my borders are vulnerable, my borders
> are vulnerable! Find body of CIA witness silky legs stapled to
> parquet floors.
> Forget the Alamo: may your happiness be as deep as Loch
> Ness, and your troubles be swallowed by the Monster. The
> fender has to fit the car.[25]

As violently comical as Melville's "Bartleby," though it is hard to imagine two works that seem less alike, *Shut Up* is also insistently ugly. Indeed, most readers would agree that no contemporary American poet has continued the modernist avant-garde's project of decoupling art from beauty, or developed the negative aesthetic already latent in Kant's definition of the disgusting as the endpoint of mimetic art, as consistently or aggressively as Andrews. In a market society whose dominant attitude to art is one of "benevolent neutrality," as Marcuse argues, one could say that the desire of this poetry is to become intolerable—in particular, intolerable to the extent that it cannot be absorbed by the pluralist economy of an aesthetic eclecticism, whose inclusive pull is as strong as the externalizing tow of G.H.'s disgust. There is a sense, then, in which *Shut Up* and "Bartleby"—despite the fact that they are worlds apart—share a common goal: both activate an ugly feeling to disclose the limits of the "social disattendability" that enables friendly as well as disdainful tolerance for an object perceived as so unthreatening in its inferiority as to be barely perceptible at all. While the strategy of Bartleby is to exaggerate this disattendability by turning it on himself, as evinced most in his refusal to eat, the agenda of *Shut Up* is to occupy more aggressively the position of the disgusting and unconsumable (if not exactly, as its intransigent tone indicates, the abject)—of that which can no longer be the object of the indifference that is Hobbesian contempt, because it so insistently *obtrudes*. In a text as committed as Melville's to disclosing the political ambiguities of social disattendability, though by creating the semblance of something that looks more like Tourette's syndrome—the socially stigmatizing affliction defined by the uncontrolled expression of socially stigmatized content (obscenities, expletives, and so forth)—than like the "depression" we are often tempted to attribute to the emotionally unreadable scrivener, it seems telling that virtually every statement in Andrews' *Shut Up* has the insistence or rhetorical effect of an expletive or onomatopoeia, or is an expletive or onomatopoeia per se. Significantly, both noisy intensities are forms which Saussure bracketed as potential threats to his theory of the arbitrary and unmotivated sign, and whose exceptionality he quickly neutralized with qualifications: "*Onomatopoeia* might be used to prove that the choice of the signifier is not always arbitrary. But onomatopoeic formations are never organic elements of a linguistic system. Besides, their number is much smaller than is generally supposed. . . . *Interjections,* closely related to onomatopoeia, can be attacked on the same grounds and come no closer to refuting our thesis."[26] Interjections figure prominently also in Wittgenstein's discussion of aspects of language that run counter to its perceived primary use in naming or describing objects, "whereas in fact we do the most various things with our sentences." As Wittgenstein notes, "Think of exclamations alone, with their completely different functions: Water! Away! Ow! Help! Fine! No!"[27] To which Andrews might add: "It's fun to raise pet sea-monkeys!" We could say that the predominant function of the linguistic raw matter in Andrews' poetry is that of *insisting;* and that its agency—to reuse a pun Lacan plants in the title of his essay, "L'Instance de la lettre dans l'inconscient, ou La Raison depuis Freud" ("The Agency of the Letter")—resides precisely in this insistence *(l'instance).* This is the case for "Ow!" and "Help!"—utterances whose expressive power paradoxically lies in their *inability* to describe or refer, particularly in the urgent situations in which they tend to be used. In *Shut Up,* variations of the last exclamation in Wittgenstein's list abound in particular: "Scrape me off!"; "Gestalt me out!"; "Cream on my righteousness!"; "Whip my multiples!"; "My roots, no thanks"; "Do I have a receptacle for you!"—all forms of disgust's unambiguous "No!" to its object.

In their negative insistence, there is a sense in which the linguistic materials privileged in *Shut Up* resemble what Lyotard calls "tensors," referring to the "tension" in a sign that exceeds any semiotic dialectic of vertical fixation and horizontal displacement, including the "interminable metonymy" of slippage from word to word we have seen privileged in the use of "desire" as a figurative catch-all for any kind of literary polyvalency or multiplicity.[28] Lyotard's favorite example of the tensor is the proper name, a form that reminds us that while all signs are prone to semantic pluralization and slippage, not all are prone to this equally; some, like *Alamo* or *Lipton Tea,* have an "intensity" that makes them more resistant—if only slightly—to polysemous voyages. Because the proper name "refers in principle to a single reference" (think of "Harvey

Milk" or "Beirut") and is therefore *less* capable, however small the increment of difference, of being "exchangeable against other terms in the logico-linguistic structure," Lyotard argues that "there is no intra-systemic equivalent of the proper name, it points towards the outside like a deictic, it has no connotation, nor it is interminable."[29] Hence, while subject to resignification like any other sign, the proper name is always in some fashion more difficult to budge, countering the principle of infinite transferability that underlies the polysemous slippage routinely preferred but often too starkly opposed to semantic fixation in poetics of "desire." It comes as no surprise, then, that *Shut Up* is glutted with proper names— those of media figures, political figures, and commodities in particular: "I came dressed as a Pearl Buck novel" ("Tuck in Your Chains"); "Fassbinder was sucking the Hegel out of Habermas" ("Blab Mind Blab Body"); "Brezhnev / dies / from Tidy-Bowl injections" ("Everything You Didn't Know Is Wrong"); "Riot Act is new name for cops" ("Gesalt Me Out!"). If Whitman, America's first self-professed materialist poet and speaker of "blab," was also its first writer to produce poems filled with these insistently obtruding signs (*Kanuck, Tuckahoe, Congressman, Cuff; Hoosier, Badger, Buckeye; Kentuckian, Louisianian, Georgian; Vermont, Maine, Texas*), to read *Shut Up* is to encounter the intensities of *Mao, Santa Claus, Darwin, Mary Poppins, Joe Worker, Ku Klux Klan, Snow White, Moonies, Davy Crockett, Hardy Boys, Arafat, King Kong, Reagan, Liz Taylor, Billy Graham, Nixon, Trotsky, John Quincy Adams, Svengali, Calvin Coolidge, Yoko Ono, Allende, Marie Antoinette; Porsche, Marlboro, Saran Wrap, Mr. Clean, Harley Davidson, Ladies Home Journal, Jimmy Crack Corn, Motown, The Love Boat, Donald Duck, Felony Augmentation Program, Girl Scout, MIRV, Cold War, CIA, PLO, Lotto, Christian Science, Republicanos, Hi Hi Whoopee; Korean, Sioux, Marine, Catholic, Palestinian, Black Nationalist; El Salvador, West Bank, Laos, Beirut, Honduras, Nigeria, Iran, Vietnam,* and *Nebraska.* That is, to be crammed full with nothing less than the pluralist American public sphere itself and the culture industries in which all of the intensities above are so easily and eclectically mingled.

Yet of course the centrifugal aesthetic of Andrews could not distance him further from Whitman—the American poet of pluralist desire and libidinalized mingling par excellence. This is not to imply, however, that the matter of pleasure or libidinal attraction, particularly to all the things that clamor "eat me" or "have me" in consumer culture, is either missing or expunged from *Shut Up*—nothing could be further from the case. For what is at stake in the work's mobilization of disgust (or, more precisely, in the work's *desire* to be disgusting, contaminating, unignorable, intolerable) is precisely revulsion's dialectical relation to the fascination we can glimpse even in a work as unambiguously critical of consumer society as Horkheimer and Adorno's essay "The Culture Industry" (1944). From the striking relish with which the proper names of individual products are uttered, one gets the sense that the authors are indeed fascinated, if not exactly amused, by *Lone Ranger, Mrs. Miniver, Chesterfield Cigarettes, Greta Garbo, Life Magazine, Warner Brothers, General Motors, Guy Lombardo, Dagwood, Enrico Caruso, and Life with Father,* even as these products and their claim to the aesthetic are emphatically denounced as examples of "Enlightenment as mass deception" (which is the subtitle of "The Culture Industry"). Like G.H. in front of her raw matter, the two critics seem "nauseated, attracted." But while the dialectic of repugnance and attraction is disclosed here through what Miller calls "the disgust of reaction formation," where it is precisely the turning of *Mrs. Miniver* into a bad object that increases its allure, in *Shut Up* it is revealed through what Miller calls, in contrast, "the disgust of surfeit" (*AD*, 114). Whereas the former makes the disgusting alluring, in the latter the once-alluring is made disgusting—precisely by being that on which the subject deliberately gorges himself. As in the case of the binge smoker or eater who finds something about cigarettes or chocolates repulsive after consuming far too many in one sitting, the disgust of surfeiting desire, which also has the power to make the one who is disgus*ted* disgust*ing* (if only to himself or her-self), "pays us back for getting us just what we thought we wanted" (Miller, *AD*, 119). This is precisely the strategy of Andrews' comical text in its complex relationship to a public sphere virtually coeval with the marketplace, the inclusive pull of whose attractions the poet cannot repress or deny even when they become objects of his individual aversion. We could say that whereas G.H. eats the intol-erable in an unsuccessful effort to keep it down, *Shut Up* gorges on the alluring in order to throw it up. Both texts thus model two of art's possible responses to a pluralist consumer society's neutral or even friendly tolerance of it. In one, art becomes disgusted, staging its refusal or inability to ingest what consumer culture proclaims all should want or desire to take in (and what aesthetic pluralism pro-claims all are *capable* of taking in). In the other, art crams itself with what has been officially deemed desirable to a point at which it crosses a line from being disgusted to being *disgusting*—that is, an object that we ourselves as readers can no longer easily consume without disclosing the limits of the "pure" tolerance that signals the curtailed agency of all art in the public sphere in general. For while it may be the case, as Adorno argues in *Aesthetic Theory,* that "art is objectively intolerant even of the socially dictated pluralism of peacefully coexisting spheres, which ever and again provides ideologues with excuses," he also notes that "the shadow of art's autarchic radicalism is its harmlessness"—the same harmlessness that casts a political shadow over the refusals, however consistent and uncompromising, of Melville's emotionally illegible scrivener.[30]

We thus return, full circle, to the Bartlebyan predicament of sus-pended or curtailed agency that each of the minor affective idioms in this book has been summoned to interpret. Like animatedness, irritation, envy, anxiety, stuplimity, and paranoia—nonstrategic affects characterized by weak intentionality and characteristic of the situation of scriveners—disgust does not so much solve the di-lemma of social powerlessness as diagnose it powerfully. But while all of the negative affects we have discussed call attention to this problem, the poetics of disgust seems to have drawn us closer to the domain of political theory, perhaps even of political commitment, than these others. In its intense and unambivalent negativity, disgust thus seems to represent an outer limit or threshold of what I have called ugly feelings, preparing us for more instrumental or politically efficacious emotions. It therefore brings us to the edge of this project on the aesthetics of minor affects, marking the furthest it can go.

notes

index

notes

introduction

1. Theodor W. Adorno, *Aesthetic Theory,* ed. and trans. Robert Hullot-Kentor (Minneapolis: University of Minnesota Press, 1997), 31. Hereafter designated *AT.*
2. Hannah Arendt, *On Violence* (New York: Harcourt Brace, 1969), 82. Baruch Spinoza, *Ethics,* as translated and cited in Cheshire Calhoun and Robert C. Solomon, eds., *What Is an Emotion? Classic Readings in Philosophical Psychology* (New York: Oxford University Press, 1984), 85.
3. Rei Terada, *Feeling in Theory: Emotion after the "Death of the Subject"* (Cambridge, Mass.: Harvard University Press, 2001), 57.
4. Paolo Virno, "The Ambivalence of Disenchantment," in Paolo Virno and Michael Hardt, eds., *Radical Thought in Italy* (Minneapolis: University of Minnesota Press, 1996), 17, italics added. Hereafter designated "AD."
5. Fredric Jameson, *Postmodernism, or, The Cultural Logic of Late Capitalism* (Durham: Duke University Press, 1991), 15.
6. In fact, according to Virno, nothing currently unites "the software technician, the autoworker, and the illegal laborer" more than a process of socialization that, in teaching "habitual mobility, the ability to keep pace with extremely rapid conversions, adaptability in every enterprise, [and] flexibility in moving from one group of rules to another" ("Ambivalence of Disenchantment," 14), effectively runs on the affects of fear (which prompts mobility in the form of flight), opportunism (which relies on flexibility and adaptability), and cynicism (which arises from a particular intimacy with rules).
7. Philip Fisher, *The Vehement Passions* (Princeton: Princeton University Press, 2001), 137. Hereafter designated *VP.*
8. Fredric Jameson, *The Political Unconscious: Narrative as a Socially Symbolic Act* (Ithaca: Cornell University Press, 1981), 115. Jameson also refers to the ideologeme as the "world-view" or "spirit" of a text, and as the "minimal 'unit'" of ideological analysis. Ideological analysis is in turn defined as a task in which individual cultural products are read as "complex work[s] of transformation on that ultimate raw material which is the ideologeme in question" (87).

9. Barbara Johnson, *The Feminist Difference: Literature, Psychoanalysis, Race, and Gender* (Cambridge, Mass.: Harvard University Press, 1998), 13.

10. Herbert Marcuse, "A Note on Dialectic," in Andrew Arato and Eike Gebhardt, eds., *The Essential Frankfurt School Reader* (New York: Continuum, 1993), 445.

11. Max Horkheimer and Theodor W. Adorno, "The Culture Industry: Enlightenment as Mass Deception," in idem, *Dialectic of Enlightenment,* trans. John Cumming (New York: Continuum, 1994), 142.

12. Thomas Hobbes, *Leviathan* (New York: Oxford University Press, 1998), 94.

13. While Lincoln's oft-cited description of Stowe as a cause of the American Civil War has promulgated the idea of a direct connection between sentimental aesthetics and political action, Philip Fisher, in his book *Hard Facts,* argues that emotions in the sentimental novel are most intense at moments "where the capacity to act has been suspended." Yet what Fisher discloses as the hidden lie of the sentimental novel's strongest claim to political efficacy (the case of *Uncle Tom's Cabin*) can hardly be scandalous in the case of ugly feelings, which are explicitly and openly "about" suspended agency from the start. The myth about the direct link between high emotion and political effects that *Uncle Tom's Cabin* has come to stand for may or may not be true in the case of that particular novel, but such a myth is simply not available in the case of the affects I discuss here. See Fisher, *Hard Facts: Setting and Form in the American Novel* (New York: Oxford University Press, 1985), 22, cited in Michael Szalay, *New Deal Modernism: American Literature and the Invention of the Welfare State* (Durham: Duke University Press, 2000), 167.

14. Linda Hutcheon, *Irony's Edge: The Theory and Politics of Irony* (New York: Routledge, 1994).

15. Susan L. Feagin, "The Pleasures of Tragedy," *American Philosophical Quarterly,* 20 (1983), cited in Susan Feagin and Patrick Maynard, eds., *Aesthetics* (Oxford: Oxford University Press, 1997), 305–313.

16. Herman Melville, *Moby-Dick, or The Whale* (New York: Penguin, 1992), xxxix.

17. Sue Campbell, *Interpreting the Personal: Expression and the Formation of Feelings* (Ithaca: Cornell University Press, 1997), 4.

18. René Spitz, *No and Yes: On the Genesis of Human Communication* (New York: International Universities Press, 1957), 50.

19. Aristotle, *Poetics,* trans. Ingram Bywater, in *The Basic Works of Aristotle,* ed. Richard McKeon (New York: Random House, 1941), 1466–68. Cited in Feagin and Maynard, *Aesthetics,* 298. While the relationship between "story" and "discourse"—that is, between the fictional events we abstract from a narrative and their presentation in the narrative itself—is a key part of any analysis of narrative, the fullest treatment of the temporal implica-

tions of this relationship can be found in Gérard Genette, *Narrative Discourse: An Essay in Method,* trans. Jane E. Levin (Ithaca: Cornell University Press, 1980). See especially the chapters on "Order," "Duration," and "Frequency," 33–160. See also Seymour Chatman's application of the above for cinema in *Story and Discourse: Narrative Structure in Fiction and Film* (Ithaca: Cornell University Press, 1978), 64–84.

20. Chatman, *Story and Discourse,* 69; Fisher, *The Vehement Passions,* 137.

21. Fredric Jameson, "Totality as Conspiracy," in *The Geopolitical Aesthetic: Cinema and Space in the World System* (Bloomington: Indiana University Press, 1995), 9–86.

22. Rom Harré, "An Outline of the Social Constructionist Viewpoint," in Rom Harré, ed., *The Social Construction of Emotions* (Oxford: Blackwell, 1986), 12, italics added.

23. For a useful summary of the *katharsin* debate, as staged between the interpretations offered by Gerard F. Else in *Aristotle's Poetics: The Argument* (Cambridge, 1957) and those put forward by S. H. Butcher in *Aristotle's Theory of Poetry and Fine Art* (London, 1923), see Monroe C. Beardsley, *Aesthetics from Classical Greece to the Present* (Tuscaloosa: University of Alabama Press, 1966), 64–67. John Dewey, *Art as Experience* (New York: Perigee Books, 1980), 64, 78. T. S. Eliot, "Tradition and the Individual Talent," in *The Norton Anthology of Theory and Criticism* (New York: Norton, 2000), 1097. Gérard Genette, *The Aesthetic Relation,* trans. G. M. Goshgarian (Ithaca: Cornell University Press, 1999), 71, hereafter designated *AR.*

24. I. A. Richards, *Practical Criticism: A Study of Literary Judgement* (New York: Harcourt Brace Jovanovich, 1929), 336–340.

25. See Brian Massumi, "The Autonomy of Affect," in idem, *Parables for the Virtual* (Durham: Duke University Press, 2002), 23–45, hereafter designated *PV;* and Lawrence Grossberg, "Mapping Popular Culture," in *we gotta get out of this place: Popular Conservatism and Postmodern Culture* (New York: Routledge, 1992), 69–87.

26. On the psychoanalytical origins of the emotion/affect taxonomy, see Donna M. Orange, "Affect and Emotional Life" in *Emotional Understanding: Studies in Psychoanalytic Epistemology* (New York: Guilford, 1995), 90.

27. Grossberg, *we gotta get out of this place,* 81.

28. Raymond Williams, "Structures of Feeling," in idem, *Marxism and Literature* (Oxford: Oxford University Press, 1977), 128. Hereafter designated *ML.* It should be clarified that in "Structures of Feeling" Williams is not really talking about emotions or even affects. For while "structures of feeling" do designate "affective elements of consciousness and relationships" or "social content . . . of [a] present and affective kind" (132, 133), Williams defines them more broadly (and at the same time much more precisely) as "structured formation[s] . . . at the very edge of semantic availability" (132). His term thus represents a "cultural hypothesis" derived from efforts to un-

derstand "a social experience which is still *in process*" (132), and thus has "many of the characteristics of a pre-formation, until specific articulations—new semantic figures—are discovered in material practice" (134). Hence, Williams' "structures of feeling" cannot be equated with what we ordinarily think of as emotional qualities, since the former are defined as formations that are still in process and barely semanticized, while the latter have distinct histories and come heavily saturated with cultural meanings and value. It is easy to understand the impulse to conflate these two terms, for Williams presents us not only with a concept which is strikingly broad and inclusive ("structures of feeling" designating nothing less than "all the known complexities, the experienced tensions, shifts, and uncertainties, [and] intricate forms of unevenness and confusion" which "do not have to await definition, classification, or rationalization before they exert palpable pressures and set effective limits on experience and action"), but also with a concept adduced primarily in negative fashion. A "structure of feeling" is precisely that which "*escapes* . . . from the fixed and the explicit and the known"; it is a social experience which is *not* fully semanticized, yet *does not require* this semanticization in order to exert palpable pressures and generate concrete effects. Yet Williams is not analyzing emotion or affect, but, rather, strategically mobilizing an entire register of felt phenomena in order to expand the existing domain and methods of social critique. This is a subtle yet crucial distinction which Williams foregrounds in his own writing. Having spoken of changes in "qualit[ies] of social relationship" traditionally misperceived as "'personal' experience or as the merely superficial or incidental 'small change' of society" (131), and then defining these changes as "structures of feeling," Williams acknowledges: "The term is difficult, but 'feeling' is chosen to emphasize a distinction from more formal concepts of 'world-view' or 'ideology'" (132). While a structure of feeling thus cannot be reduced to "'personal' experience," it comes to represent something equally irreducible to ideology. Once again using a negative definition, Williams writes that the term designates social content "which cannot *without loss* be reduced to belief-systems, institutions, or explicit relationships" (133, italics added). It is clear, however, that structures of feeling remain inextricably intertwined with belief systems, institutions, and explicit social relationships; in fact, Williams describes all of the latter as encompassed by the former, though in a "lived and experienced" manner. Yet when he clearly states his methodological reasons for introducing his concept—to find a way of grasping social formations distinct from "more formal" concepts of ideology—it becomes clear that his primary aim is to mobilize an entire affective register, *in* its entirety, and *as* a register, in order to enlarge the scope and definition of materialist analysis. This is something quite different from the goal of offering "a materialist analysis" of affect itself.

29. Martha Nussbaum, *Upheavals of Thought: The Intelligence of Emotions* (Cambridge: Cambridge University Press: 2001), 135.

30. Dewey, *Art as Experience,* 16.

31. Jameson, *Postmodernism,* 15. Walter Benjamin, "Left-Wing Melancholy," in Benjamin, *Selected Writings, Volume 2: 1927–1932,* trans. Rodney Livingstone et al., ed. Michael W. Jennings, Howard Eiland, and Gary Smith (Cambridge: Harvard University Press, 1999), 423–427, 425. See also Wendy Brown, "Resisting Left Melancholia," *boundary 2,* 26, no. 3 (Fall 1999): 19–27.

32. Steve Evans, "The Dynamics of Literary Change," *Impercipient Lecture Series,* 1, no. 1 (February 1997): 8.

33. Jameson, *Postmodernism,* 29.

34. I owe these formulations to Mark McGurl.

35. See Friedrich Nietzsche, *On the Genealogy of Morals,* trans. Walter Kaufmann and R. J. Hollingdale, in idem, *"On the Genealogy of Morals" and "Ecce Homo,"* ed. Walter Kaufmann (New York: Vintage, 1967). Hereafter designated *GM.*

36. Wendy Brown, *States of Injury: Power and Freedom in Late Modernity* (Princeton: Princeton University Press, 1995), 44.

37. As Adorno puts it while writing on the guilty intellectual's moral beatification of the "simple folk": "In the end, the glorification of splendid underdogs is nothing other than glorification of the splendid system that makes them." See Adorno, *Minima Moralia: Reflections from Damaged Life,* trans. E. F. N. Jephcott (London: Verso, 1974), 28.

38. Indeed, given Nietzsche's unambiguous fear and hatred of "the mob," it is something of an understatement when Brown notes his "remove" from the "transformative possibilities of collective political action" (*States of Injury,* 74).

39. Jameson, *The Political Unconscious,* 202. I have replaced Jameson's example of Gissing's *Demos* ("Gissing resents Richard, and what he resents most is the latter's *ressentiment*") with a more generic scenario.

40. Brown, *States of Injury,* 47.

41. Jameson, *The Political Unconscious,* 202.

1. tone

1. All quotations are from Herman Melville, *The Confidence-Man: His Masquerade,* foreword by Toby Tanner (Oxford: Oxford University Press, 1989). Hereafter designated *CM.*

2. Thomas Hobbes, *Leviathan,* ed. J. C. A. Gaskin (Oxford: Oxford University Press, 1996), 38.

3. Hershel Parker, *Herman Melville: A Biography, Volume 2: 1851–1891* (Baltimore: Johns Hopkins University Press, 2002), 603.

4. Herman Melville, *Pierre, or, The Ambiguities* (New York: Penguin, 1996), 356. On the racial implications of the appeal to benevolence in particular, see Susan M. Ryan, "Misgivings: Melville, Race, and the Ambiguities of Benevolence," *American Literary History* (2000): 685–712.

5. On "affective investments," see Lawrence Grossberg, *we gotta get out of this place: Popular Conservatism and Postmodern Culture* (New York: Routledge, 1992). Hereafter *OTP*. Herman Melville, "Bartleby," in *Great Short Works of Herman Melville,* ed. Warner Berthoff (New York: Harper and Row, 1969), 64.

6. For analysts of modernity from Simmel to Giddens, this relocation of "trust" from known individuals to anonymous others, or from persons with whom transactions are carried out to the symbolic tokens transacted, not only changes the tenor of the role of trust in private life, but gives rise to new forms of social interaction in the public sphere—including one marked by a curious intersection of estrangement and familiarity which Mark Seltzer (drawing on Simmel's work) calls "stranger-intimacy." See Anthony Giddens, *The Consequences of Modernity* (Stanford: Stanford University Press, 1990), especially 112–150; Georg Simmel, *The Sociology of Georg Simmel,* trans. and ed. Kurt H. Wolff (Glencoe Ill.: Free Press, 1950). On "stranger-intimacy," see Mark Seltzer, *Serial Killers: Death and Life in America's Wound Culture* (New York: Routledge, 1998), 41–45. See also Erving Goffman's closely related analyses of "civil inattention" in *Relations in Public: Micro Studies of the Public Order* (New York: Harper and Row, 1971).

7. Martin Heidegger, *Sein und Zeit* (Tübingen: Niemeyer, 1972), as translated and cited by Charles Guignon in "Moods in Heidegger's Being and Time," in Cheshire Calhoun and Robert C. Solomon, eds., *What Is an Emotion? Classic Readings in Philosophical Psychology* (New York: Oxford University Press, 1984), 239.

8. Stephen Matterson, introduction, in Herman Melville, *The Confidence-Man: His Masquerade* (New York: Penguin, 1990), xxvii.

9. See Brian Massumi, "The Autonomy of Affect," in idem, *Parables for the Virtual* (Durham: Duke University Press, 2002), 23–45, hereafter designated *PV*; and Grossberg, "Mapping Popular Culture," in *we gotta get out of this place,* 69–87.

10. "He chooses or arranges his words differently as his audience varies, in automatic or deliberate *recognition of his relation to them.* The tone of his utterance reflects his awareness of this relation, his sense of how he stands towards those he is addressing" (175, original italics). I. A. Richards, *Practical Criticism: A Study of Literary Judgement* (New York: Harcourt Brace Jovanovich, 1929). Hereafter *PC*.

11. Tellingly, it is only in a footnote that Richards feels compelled to add: "Under 'Feeling' I group for convenience the whole conative-affective aspect of

life—emotions, emotional attitudes, the will, desire, pleasure-unpleasure, and the rest. 'Feeling' is shorthand for any or all of this" (ibid., 175). In the body of his text, the dominant description of "Feeling" remains that of "attitude."

12. William Empson, "Feelings in Words," in idem, *The Structure of Complex Words,* foreword by Jonathan Culler (Cambridge, Mass.: Harvard University Press, 1989), 17; Reuben Arthur Brower, *The Fields of Light: An Experiment in Critical Reading* (New York: Oxford University Press, 1951), 22. Brower was one of Richards' students.

13. Gérard Genette, *Narrative Discourse: An Essay on Method,* trans. Jane E. Lewin, foreword by Jonathan Culler (Ithaca: Cornell University Press, 1980), 214–215.

14. Immanuel Kant, *The Critique of Judgement,* trans. J. H. Bernard (New York: Hafner, 1951), 38–39. Roger Fry, *Vision and Design* (London: Chatto and Windus, 1925), cited in Susanne Langer, *Feeling and Form* (New York: Scribner, 1953), 37; *Feeling and Form* is hereafter designated *FF.* William K. Wimsatt Jr. and Monroe C. Beardsley, "The Affective Fallacy," in Vincent B. Leitch et al., eds., *The Norton Anthology of Theory and Criticism* (New York: Norton, 2001), 1387–1403.

15. Guignon, "Moods," 240. It is precisely this totalized notion of "public" or "world" that the New Critical definitions of tone seem to reach for but stop short of invoking. For even when tone is pared down to a "dramatic situation," defined as "the implied social relationship of the speaker to his auditor" in conjunction with "the manner he adopts in addressing his auditor," Brower's definition suggests a total matrix of numerous relationships which obviously cannot be expressed or made explicit all at once, yet whose full presence *as* a totality must be imagined in order for one to speak of a "situation" at all. We can see how vulnerable "tone" is to charges of relativism and arbitrariness even when its emotional dimension is carefully put aside. Since our recognition of what counts as a manner "always depends on a silent reference to a known way of speaking and on our perceiving variations from it," Brower concedes that in fact "our finest perception of [this] norm and of variations from it lie beyond our powers of expression. To define even one level of speech precisely would require an elaborate excursion in literary and social history" (*Fields of Light,* 23, italics added). Ironically, the overcareful reduction of tone to a highly codified "manner" of expression thus leads the "practical critic" to make reference to a totality "*beyond* our powers of expression," in a maneuver similar to Lionel Trilling's appeal to "a culture's hum and buzz of implication" in his own definition of "manners." Hence, even when the trouble-causing matter of feeling is left out altogether, literary tone seems to slip from the grasp of formalist vocabularies even as its consequentiality is being emphasized. As Robert Scholes notes, Genette's consideration of voice "is the place . . . where the New Critics'

concern with 'tone' *might* have entered the system, and if there is a weakness here it is in Genette's failure to incorporate sufficiently this important dimension of narrative art." See Lionel Trilling, "Manners, Morals and the Novel," in idem, *The Liberal Imagination: Essays in Literature and Society* (Garden City: Doubleday, 1950), 200; and Robert Scholes, *Structuralism in Literature* (New Haven: Yale University Press, 1974), 166.

16. Walter Benjamin, "Left-Wing Melancholy," in *Walter Benjamin: Selected Writings, Volume 2: 1927–1934,* trans. Rodney Livingston, ed. Michael W. Jennings, Howard Eiland, and Gary Smith (Cambridge, Mass.: Harvard University Press, 1999), 425. Anne Anlin Cheng, *The Melancholy of Race: Psychoanalysis, Assimilation, and Hidden Grief* (Oxford: Oxford University Press, 2000).

17. Langer adapts the concept of "significant form" from Clive Bell, *Art* (London: Chatto and Windus, 1914); see Langer, *Feeling and Form,* 32. Mikel Dufrenne, *The Phenomenology of Aesthetic Experience,* trans. Edward S. Casey, Albert A. Anderson, Willis Domingo, and Leon Jacobson (Evanston: Northwestern University Press, 1973), hereafter designated *PAE.* Roman Ingarden, *The Literary Work of Art: An Investigation on the Borderlines of Ontology, Logic, and Theory of Literature,* trans. George B. Grabowicz (Evanston: Northwestern University Press, 1973).

18. Langer is equally impatient with the privileging of "imagination," "make-believe," or "experience" in other twentieth-century theories of art (such as those associated with Jean-Paul Sartre, Kendall Walton, and John Dewey, respectively).

19. Fredric Jameson, *Postmodernism, or, The Cultural Logic of Late Capitalism* (Durham: Duke University Press, 1991), 32–34.

20. In the process of applying her music-based, asignifying concept of "symbol" to art in general, Langer rejects a privileging of "medium" (associated most prominently with the work of Clement Greenberg) as the criterion for distinguishing the various arts (painting, music, dance, sculpture, poetry, fiction, architecture, etc.) by asserting that their specificity resides less in the nature of the materials or techniques "used" than in the nature of the "primary illusion" or semblance *(Schein)* that each art *creates:* "virtual time" in the case of music, "virtual memory" in the case of narrative fiction, and so on. Langer identifies this "semblance" with the "aesthetic object" itself, as an object constituted first and foremost in perception. It is in this sense that all art, for Langer, including "the most illustrative murals and most realistic plays," is fundamentally abstract (51). As entities that are essentially appearance, all aesthetic objects have a "virtual" character, which is also why they seem "strange" or "other."

21. Theodor W. Adorno, *Aesthetic Theory,* ed. and trans. Robert Hullot-Kentor (Minneapolis: University of Minnesota Press, 1997), 275. Hereafter designated *AT.*

22. The feeling (*le sentiment*) that reveals this unified and unifying affective quality is also not, Dufrenne explicitly makes clear, an emotion. Since it reveals or "gives birth to" a world, feeling is a kind of "knowledge" *(connaissance)*, and has "a noetic function" (Dufrenne, *Phenomenology of Aesthetic Experience,* 378). Emotion, on the other hand, is way of reacting to or interpreting a world already given, either in a Sartrean effort to evade responsibility and action by "magically transforming" it, or, in Paul Ricoeur's view, to prepare for action within it (ibid., 378). Hence, "the emotion of fear is not to be confused with the feeling of the horrible. It is, rather, a certain way of reacting in the face of the horrible when the horrible is taken as a characteristic of the world as it appears at the time, that is, a means of struggling within the world of the horrible. . . . Before Rouault's *Le Pendu* I experience all the misery of the world without that element of anguish or fear which, in the real world, leads me to flee or avert the misery" (ibid., 378–379). What Dufrenne calls "feeling"—"a certain way of *knowing* an affective quality as the structure of an object"—is thus always somewhat removed, "disinterested in spite of the sort of participation which it presupposes" (ibid., 441). One could say that like his Husserlian colleague Max Scheler's "feeling-functions"—which, unlike the "feeling-states" that are merely undergone, disclose values or qualities and thus play a significant role in intellectual life—Dufrenne's *sentiment* is a feeling with a particularly intimate relationship to an idea *about* feeling. Unlike emotion, it is "an immediacy that has undergone mediation" (ibid., 377).

23. Guignon, "Moods," 240.

24. Tomkins' writing has been brought within earshot of the humanities only recently through the interventions of Eve Kosofky Sedgwick and Adam Frank, who edited an anthology based on selections from the four volumes of *Affect, Imagery, Consciousness* in 1995. See *Shame and Its Sisters: A Silvan Tomkins Reader,* ed. Sedgwick and Frank (Durham: Duke University Press, 1995). I have chosen to quote primarily from *Exploring Affect: The Selected Writings of Silvan S. Tomkins* (Cambridge: Cambridge University Press, 1995), edited by psychologist E. Virginia Demos, which gathers the articles Tomkins published in psychology and behavioral science journals before he synthesized his theories in *Affect, Imagery, Consciousness.*

25. Silvan Tomkins, *Exploring Affect: The Selected Writings of Silvan S. Tomkins,* ed. E. Virginia Demos (Cambridge: Cambridge University Press, 1995), 110. Hereafter designated *EA.*

26. Alex Woloch, *The One versus the Many* (Princeton: Princeton University Press, 2004).

27. Cecilia Tichi, "Melville's Craft and Theme of Language Debased in *The Confidence-Man,*" *ELH,* 39, no. 4 (1972): 643, 641. Hereafter designated "MC."

28. See Alexander Gelley, "Parasitic Talk," in idem, *Narrative Crossings: Theory*

and Pragmatics of Prose Fiction (Baltimore: Johns Hopkins University Press, 1987), 79–100.

29. See Harrison Hayford, "Unnecessary Duplicates: A Key to the Writing of *Moby-Dick,*" in Faith Pullin, ed., *New Perspectives on Melville* (Edinburgh: Edinburgh University Press, 1978), 128–161.

30. Linda Hutcheon, *Irony's Edge: The Theory and Politics of Irony* (New York: Routledge, 1994), 37.

31. And yet, given that the conceptual difficulty that tone poses seems most powerfully exemplified in irony (always an admixture of affective attitude and meaning, as well as a dialectic between the said and unsaid that one perceives rather than feels), it seems important to note the Confidence-Man's resemblance to the Greek *eiron* as dissembler (Hutcheon, *Irony's Edge,* 51). Indeed, it is tempting to read the novel as a systematic exploration of all of irony's different and politically ambivalent functions, which, as Hutcheon usefully shows, can be mapped out along an axis of minimal to maximal affective charge or as "part of a tonal and emotive continuum" (ibid., 46). One could argue that irony's most basic role as a means of semantic emphasis or reinforcement, in conjunction with its ludic, distancing, and defensive or self-protective functions, is the focus of the crowded and whimsical first half of *The Confidence-Man,* whereas the darker second half, in which myriad "operators" are replaced by the single figure of the cosmopolitan, focuses on irony's more polemical, oppositional, or assailing functions. Yet in somewhat mechanically going through all of these operations, the novel seems to remain as ambivalent *about* irony as its own tone remains elusive.

32. Eve Sedgwick and Adam Frank, eds., *Shame and Its Sisters: A Silvan Tomkins Reader* (Durham: Duke University Press, 1995), 62.

33. Ibid., 3.

34. Brian Massumi, "The Autonomy of Affect," *Cultural Critique,* 31 (Fall 1995): 97.

35. Jean-Joseph Goux, "Monetary Economy and Idealist Philosophy," in idem, *Symbolic Economies: After Marx and Freud,* trans. Jennifer Curtiss Gage (Ithaca: Cornell University Press, 1990), 106.

36. Ibid., 107, quoting George Berkeley, *The Querist* (italics added).

37. While replicated in both the structure and content of Melville's book, the practice of "writing one man's name for another's" as a means of fiduciary exchange also had an everyday meaning in an era in which banknotes created the semblance of personal agreements, with bank cashiers and presidents making "promises" (backed by replicas of their signatures) to pay amounts of money to their bearers. As David Henkin notes, "Often, a note would identify by name the particular party to whom the promise was made, so that no matter how widely the bill circulated, any subsequent use would commemorate and draw upon the original transaction, much in the

manner of a personal check signed over to an unlimited number of third parties." Yet ultimately, paper money "registered personal absence; once bills changed hands, all access to and accountability of the individual who passed them disappeared as well." Like *The Confidence-Man* and its eponymous agents, "banknotes addressed their readers impersonally and indifferently. They spoke to the bearer, who in principle could be anyone and therefore was no one in particular." See David M. Henkin, *City Reading: Written Words and Public Spaces in Antebellum New York* (New York: Columbia University Press, 1998), 144, 143.

38. Ibid., 138.

39. John Wentworth, *Reminiscences of Early Chicago* (Chicago: Lakeside, 1912).

40. Tomkins, *Exploring Affect,* 52. See also Hayford, "Unnecessary Duplicates," 128–161.

41. Lendol Calder, *Financing the American Dream: A Cultural History of Consumer Credit* (Princeton: Princeton University Press, 1999), 78, 87. As Calder notes, "Benjamin Franklin, Henry Ward Beecher, and Orison Swett Marden, authors of the three best-selling guides on financial advice in the nineteenth century, all taught the lesson that 'character is the poor man's capital.' Character earned the confidence of the community, and confidence established character. Late in the century character became more of an end in itself, an internalized mental attitude of initiative, self-reliance, and usefulness. But the original association of character and credit never faded away completely" (ibid., 88).

42. Melville, *The Confidence-Man,* 173, 162, 164, 166. See Peggy Kamuf, "Melville's Credit Card," in idem, *The Division of Literature, or, The University in Deconstruction* (Chicago: University of Chicago Press, 1997), 167–222. For a similar analysis of how this scene dramatizes the incorporation of the future into the commodity, see Wai-Chee Dimock, "Personified Accounting," in idem, *Empire for Liberty: Melville and the Poetics of Individualism* (Princeton: Princeton University Press, 1991), 193.

43. Herman Melville, "Benito Cereno," in *Great Short Works of Herman Melville,* ed. Warner Berthoff (New York: Harper and Row, 1969), 239, 272, 266. For a more detailed account of this earlier work's relation to *The Confidence-Man,* see Kamuf, "Melville's Credit Card," 183–200.

44. As Massumi notes about Ronald Reagan, "It was commonly said that he ruled primarily by projecting an air of confidence. That was the emotional *tenor* of his political manner, . . . that of the supposedly sovereign individual within a supposedly great nature at whose helm idiocy and incoherence reigned. In other words, Reagan was a great many things to many people, but always within a general framework of affective jingoism. Confidence is the apotheosis of affective capture. Functionalized and nationalized, it feeds directly into prison construction and neocolonial adventure" (*Parables for the Virtual,* 41–42, italics added).

45. These observations about anaphora are indebted to the astute reading of Whitman's catalogs in Tenney Nathanson, *Whitman's Presence: Body, Voice, and Writing in "Leaves of Grass"* (New York: New York University Press, 1992), esp. 139–143. Hereafter designated *WP*.

46. Gilles Deleuze, *Difference and Repetition,* trans. Paul Patton (New York: Columbia University Press, 1995), 39.

47. Ibid., 5.

48. Arne Melburg might describe this same process as illustrating the capacity for *mimesis* to become *repetition.* See Melburg, *Theories of Mimesis* (Cambridge: Cambridge University Press, 1995). The dissolution of syntax in favor of sonorous patterning increases throughout the novel, so that although we begin with anaphora at a macro level, involving completely predicated lines of text ("Charity thinketh no evil . . . Charity suffereth long, and is kind," etc.) the anaphorization eventually extends to the level of isolated noun phrases or single words ("Confidence! . . . Confidence!"), syllables (the "fid-" of *"Fidèle,"* "fidelity," "fiduciary"), initials or letters, and even absent or unwritten entities: "A _____! . . . / A _____" (Melville, *The Confidence-Man,* 256). On letters in the novel, see Elizabeth Renker, "'A——!': Unreadability in *The Confidence-Man,"* in Robert S. Levine, ed., *The Cambridge Companion to Herman Melville* (Cambridge: Cambridge University Press, 1998), 114–134.

49. As Wai-Chee Dimock argues, the novel is entirely about the "production of 'persons' out of an economic practice" that she describes as "personified accounting" (*Empire for Liberty,* 179, 186).

50. Michael Paul Rogin, "Revolutionary Fathers and Confidence Men," in idem, *Subversive Genealogy: The Politics and Art of Herman Melville* (New York: Knopf, 1979). Reprinted in Myra Jehlen, ed., *Herman Melville: A Collection of Critical Essays* (Englewood Cliffs: Prentice-Hall, 199–216, 202).

51. Tomkins, *Exploring Affect,* 313.

52. Jacques Attali, *Noise: The Political Economy of Music,* trans. Brian Massumi (Minneapolis: University of Minnesota Press, 2002), 34.

53. Jean-Christophe Agnew, *Worlds Apart: The Market and the Theater in Anglo-American Thought, 1550–1750* (Cambridge: Cambridge University Press, 1989), 201.

54. Ibid., 201.

55. As Rogin points out, just as "the Republican party glorified the free market, in opposition to chattel slavery, Melville investigated the sort of freedom that actually resided there," amplifying the virtual feeling at the core of the antebellum economy for aesthetic ends ("Revolutionary Fathers," 203).

56. It is perhaps the "great noise," or the chaos it represents, that prompts Tomkins to amend his original interpretation of the face as a "communication mechanism." After the disappointing results of his photography exper-

iment, Tomkins turns from this idea to a reinterpretation of facial responses as "sources of motivating feedback" (*Exploring Affect,* 90). Though in earlier writings we already find Tomkins suggesting that "the awareness of the feedback of the facial response *is* the experience of affect" (ibid., 217), he still describes this feedback as a form of communication, "evolved in part . . . for the maximal transmission of information" (ibid., 218). By 1978, however, after the surprisingly "noisy" conclusion of his expensive study, Tomkins downgrades "the communication of affect" to "a secondary spin-off function rather than the primary function" of the affect system, once again mobilizing his analogy between affect and pain to illustrate the point: "The cry of pain does communicate, but the *feeling* of pain does not" (ibid., 91). At this point, Tomkins also changes the physical locus of "the critical feedback which is experienced as affect" from the muscles of the face to the skin. This revision is significant, I would argue, since as an autonomic response system, skin can play no role in voluntary communication and, as Tomkins notes, "is not . . . an 'expression' of internal dynamics" (ibid., 42).

57. My reading of this film is indebted to Chris Wagstaff, "Sexual Noise," *Sight and Sound,* 2, no. 5 (May 1992): 32–35. Wagstaff uses the noise-to-signal ratio to allegorize how sexuality (noise) disrupts the traditional love story (signal) promised but never delivered in *Blow-Up,* and refers to the same scenes of amplification to illustrate this connection.

58. Gelley, "Parasitic Talk," 100.

59. Spitz, *No and Yes: On the Genesis of Human Communication* (New York: International Universities Press, 1957), 7.

60. I have borrowed this term from N. Katherine Hayles, *Chaos Bound: Orderly Disorder in Contemporary Literature and Science* (Ithaca: Cornell University Press, 1990).

61. Gérard Genette, *The Aesthetic Relation,* trans. G. M. Goshgarian (Ithaca: Cornell University Press, 1999), 91.

62. See Theodor Lipps, "Empathy and Aesthetic Pleasure," trans. Karl Aschenbrenner, in Aschenbrenner and Arnold Isenberg, eds., *Aesthetic Theories: Studies in the Philosophy of Art* (Englewood Cliffs: Prentice-Hall, 1965), 403–414. Though Lipps tries to distinguish it from projection, his definition of empathy as the self "experiencing an activity or a kind of self-activity as an attribute of the object" reveals the two to be closely related.

63. Walter Benjamin, "The Work of Art in the Age of Mechanical Reproduction," in idem, *Illuminations: Essays and Reflections,* ed. Hannah Arendt, trans. Harry Zohn (New York: Schocken, 1968), 222.

2. animatedness

1. Frederick A. Talbot, *Moving Pictures: How They Are Made and Worked* (Philadelphia: Lippincott, 1912), 238, 235. Hereafter designated *MP.*

2. Given these early cinematic examples of work performed "without hands," the slew of horror films in later decades featuring animated disembodied hands—that is, hands endowed with a life of *their* own—might be said to constitute a return of the repressed.

3. As Miriam Hansen notes, "In the ideological division of labor between the two—rather unequal—genres" of animation and live-action film, "animation traditionally served the role of exemplifying the 'mechanical magic' of the cinematic apparatus as a whole so as to complement and uphold mainstream narrative film's claim to 'realism.'" See Hansen, "Of Mice and Ducks: Benjamin and Adorno on Disney," *South Atlantic Quarterly,* 92 (Winter 1993): 27–61.

4. John Yau, "Genghis Chan: Private Eye," in idem, *Radiant Silhouette: New and Selected Work, 1974–1988* (Santa Rosa: Black Sparrow, 1989), 189–195; hereafter designated *RS. Radiant Silhouette* contains "Genghis Chan: Private Eye I" to "VII." Yau continues the series in *Edificio Sayonara* (Santa Rosa: Black Sparrow, 1992), which contains "VIII" to "XX," and in *Forbidden Entries* (Santa Rosa: Black Sparrow, 1996), which contains "XXI" to "XXVIII."

5. Friedrich Nietzsche, *On the Genealogy of Morals,* trans. Walter Kaufmann and R. J. Hollingdale, in idem, *"On the Genealogy of Morals" and "Ecce Homo,"* ed. Walter Kaufmann (New York: Vintage, 1967), 57, italics in the original. Hereafter designated *GM.*

6. For more on the affective politics of civil "disattendability," see Erving Goffman, *Relations in Public: Microstudies of the Public Order* (New York: Harper and Row, 1971), as well as the discussion of Goffman's work in William Ian Miller, *The Anatomy of Disgust* (Cambridge, Mass.: Harvard University Press, 1997), 199.

7. For a cultural history of this "ubiquitous Latino mouse" and some of his more contemporary cousins, see William Anthony Nericcio, "Autopsy of a Rat: Odd, Sundry Parables of Freddy Lopez, Speedy Gonzales, and other Chicano/Latino Marionettes Prancing around Our First World Emporium," *camera obscura,* 37 (January 1996): 189–237. (Note how Nericcio's title cannily "deadens" the liveliness of this animated racial character.)

8. Herman Melville, *The Confidence-Man: His Masquerade,* foreword by Toby Tanner (Oxford: Oxford University Press, 1989), 31.

9. Ibid., 30.

10. Robert Stonum, "Surviving Figures," in Gary Shapiro and Alan Sica, eds., *Hermeneutics: Questions and Prospects* (Amherst: University of Massachusetts Press, 1984), 199, 204.

11. *Webster's Collegiate Dictionary,* 10th ed. (1995), s.v. "animate" and "animated."

12. William Lloyd Garrison, preface to Frederick Douglass, *Narrative of the Life of Frederick Douglass, an American Slave,* in Henry Louis Gates Jr., ed.,

The Classic Slave Narratives (New York: Mentor, 1987), 248 (emphasis added). Hereafter designated "P."

13. Harriet Beecher Stowe, *Uncle Tom's Cabin, or, Life among the Lowly* (New York: Penguin, 1981), 78. Hereafter designated *UTC.*

14. Jonathan Culler, "Apostrophe," in idem, *The Pursuit of Signs: Semiotics, Literature, Deconstruction* (Ithaca: Cornell University Press, 1981), 135.

15. Barbara Johnson, "Apostrophe, Animation, and Abortion," in idem, *A World of Difference* (Baltimore: Johns Hopkins University Press, 1987), 185.

16. Rey Chow, "Postmodern Automatons," in idem, *Writing Diaspora: Tactics of Intervention in Contemporary Cultural Studies* (Bloomington: Indiana University Press, 1993), 61. Hereafter designated "PA."

17. Rosalind Krauss, "'The Rock': William Kentridge's Drawings for Projection," *October,* 92 (Spring 2000): 11.

18. Ibid.

19. Sergei Eisenstein, "II," in *Eisenstein on Disney,* ed. Jay Leyda (Calcutta: Seagull Books, 1986), 35, cited in Krauss, "'The Rock,'" 16. On the cartoon world as animistic, see Stanley Cavell, "More of the World Viewed," in *The World Viewed: Reflections on the Ontology of Film* (Cambridge, Mass.: Harvard University Press, 1979), 169.

20. Sasha Torres, paraphrasing Jane Feuer. See Torres, "King TV," in Sasha Torres, ed., *Living Color: Race and Television in the United States* (Durham: Duke University Press, 1998), 141. See also Jane Feuer, "The Concept of Live Television: Ontology as Ideology," in E. Ann Kaplan, ed., *Regarding Television: Critical Approaches—An Anthology* (Frederick, Md.: University Publications of America, 1983), 12–21.

21. Torres, *Living Color,* 2–3 (introduction).

22. Ibid., 1.

23. Feuer, "Concept of Live Television," 14, cited in Torres, "King TV," 141.

24. The 1970s animation comedy *Fat Albert,* which featured African-Americans in the inner city, preceded *The PJs,* but it was not a prime-time evening program aimed at adult audiences. Canceled by Fox at the start of the 1999–2000 season, *The PJs* moved in the fall of 2000 to the Warner Brothers network, which during its inception in the late 1990s repeated Fox's effort at the beginning of the decade to establish itself as a major network through niche programming. The Warner Brothers network (WB) currently seems to be following Fox's pattern of dropping much of its African-American programming as the network gains an increasing foothold in the market. For a history of this marketing strategy, see Kristal Brent Zook, *Color by Fox: The Fox Network and the Revolution in Black Television* (Oxford: Oxford University Press, 1999). After a short-lived revival on WB, *The PJs* was cut from the fall 2001 season. Whether the show will be brought back to life on the cable network BET is currently uncertain.

25. Kweisi Mfume, keynote address, 90th annual NAACP convention, July

1999. Cited in Greg Braxton, "Is TV Diversity Drive Slowing? NAACP's New Drawn-Out Strategy Causes Concern among Some Supporters," *Los Angeles Times,* 5 November 1999, section F.

26. "Critics Accuse *The PJs* of Having Anti-Black Message," *CNN Showbiz Today,* narrated by Jim Moret, 16 February 1999 (Transcript 99021600V17). Also quoted in Jim Moret, "Despite Strong Ratings, Foes Still Protest *The PJs,*" 17 February 1999, *CNN Online,* Lexis-Nexis, 10 November 1999.

27. Spike Lee, quoted in Richard Huff, "Murphy Back in *PJs* Fold: Ends Rift after Fox Apologizes for Its Handling of the Series," *New York Daily News,* 2 July 1999, 120.

28. Philip Brian Harper, "Extra-Special Effects: Televisual Representation and the Claims of 'the Black Experience,'" in Torres, *Living Color,* 64. Harper also discusses the tension between mimetic and simulacral realism in "Around 1969: Televisual Representation and the Complication of the Black Subject," in Werner Sollers and Maria Diedrich, eds., *The Black Columbiad: Defining Moments in African American Literature and Culture* (Cambridge, Mass.: Harvard University Press, 1994) 265–274.

29. Harper, "Around 1969," 268.

30. Harper, "Extra-Special Effects," 71.

31. On producers Norman Lear and Bud Yorkin, and on issue-oriented racial situation comedy in the 1970s, see Daryl Hamamoto, *Nervous Laughter: Television Situation Comedy and Liberal Democratic Ideology* (New York: Praeger, 1989). See also Jannette L. Dates, "Commercial Television," in Jannette L. Dates and William Barlow, eds., *Split Image: African-Americans in the Mass Media* (Washington, D.C.: Howard University Press, 1993), 290–295; and J. Fred MacDonald, *Blacks and White TV: African Americans in Television since 1948* (Chicago: Nelson-Hall, 1992), 181–194.

32. Armond White, "*The PJs,* Conceived by Eddie Murphy," *New York Press,* 10–16 February 1999, 10. Hereafter designated "*TPJS.*"

33. See Zook, *Color by Fox.*

34. See Cavell, "Types: Cycles as Genres," in idem, *The World Viewed,* 33.

35. Recent critical reevaluations have usefully complicated the politics of blackface minstrelsy with analyses of gender and class, especially in light of postmodern theories of identity and performance (see Eric Lott's groundbreaking *Love and Theft: Blackface Minstrelsy and the American Working Class* [New York: Oxford University Press, 1993]). But the comedic representation of racialized subjects remains a vexed issue, impossible to detach from the ways these representations have been historically deployed in conjunction with actual acts of violence (institutional, symbolic, and physical) against racialized bodies. In the wake of nineteenth-century minstrelsy and the revitalization of its traditions in early radio and television (NBC's *Amos 'n' Andy* being the key example), the problematic relation that develops between the representation of blackness and comedy in general resurfaces in ongoing cultural debates over the conspicuous lack of dramatic roles for

black performers in mainstream entertainment today, as well as in recent critical studies of the black television sitcom. Zook thus identifies the "battle for drama" as a key element unifying black-produced television of the early 1990s (*Color by Fox,* 80). The idea of a deliberate move away from comedy as an act of ideological resistance is taken further in Robin R. Means Coleman's indictment of virtually all post–*Cosby Show* African American programs involving clownish figures or physical humor as "Neo-Minstrelsy" (Coleman, *African-American Viewers and the Black Situation Comedy: Situating Racial Humor* [New York: Garland, 1998], 69). For Coleman, this category includes *Martin, Living Single,* and *The Fresh Prince of Bel-Air,* shows that Zook views as challenging the notion of authentic African American identity by depicting blackness as a site of cultural contestation and struggle, rather than as a fixed or unitary subject position. In contrast, Coleman argues that these programs, including the numerous comedies now airing on UPN and WB (which copied Fox's now-abandoned project of targeting black audiences in the initial attempt to establish a niche in the television market), are merely revamped versions of *Amos 'n' Andy,* following the 1950s television series (which spun off from the radio show) in revitalizing minstrelsy stereotypes from the antebellum era, including Stepin Fetchit, Uncle Tom, Mammy, and Sapphire.

Much scholarship has been done on the relation between nineteenth-century minstrelsy and black situation comedy. In addition to MacDonald's *Blacks and White TV* and Zook's *Color by Fox,* see Herman Gray, *Watching Race: Television and the Struggle for "Blackness"* (Minneapolis: University of Minnesota Press, 1995); and Coleman, *African-American Viewers and the Black Situation Comedy.* For an informative cultural history of *Amos 'n' Andy,* see Martin Ely, *The Adventures of Amos 'n' Andy: A Social History of an American Phenomenon* (New York: Free Press, 1991).

36. See, for instance, Kristin Thompson, "Implications of the Cel Animation Technique," in Teresa de Lauretis and Stephen Heath, eds., *The Cinematic Apparatus* (New York: St. Martin's, 1980), 106–120. Hereafter designated "ICAT."

37. For an abbreviated history of racial stereotypes in major studio animation (Warner Bros, MGM, Paramount, etc.), see Karl F. Cohen, "Racism and Resistance: Stereotypes in Animation," in idem, *Forbidden Animation: Censored Cartoons and Blacklisted Animators in America* (Jefferson, N.C.: McFarland, 1997), 49–76.

38. Ralph Ellison, *Invisible Man* (New York: Random House, 1952; rpt. Vintage, 1972), 421–422 (final emphasis added). Hereafter designated *IM.*

39. My point here echoes and is indebted to an argument made by N. Katherine Hayles about humans' relationship to virtual creatures. See Hayles, "Simulating Narratives: What Virtual Creatures Can Teach Us," *Critical Inquiry,* 26 (Autumn 1999): 15.

40. As we think about how Ellison's animation scene might illuminate issues

raised by *The PJs* and its critical reception, it is interesting to note that when Eddie Murphy first conceived the idea for the show, his original intention was to use puppets rather than stop-motion cinematography to represent the characters (Sue Conklin [Will Vinton Studios], email to the author, 9 December 1999). The difference between characters animated in the form of marionettes pulled on strings, like Clifton's dancing doll, and characters animated by stop-motion photography seems to be a difference in their capacity to create an illusion of independence or autonomy. At a purely visual level, stop-motion characters seem less manipulated than puppets. As Sue Conklin informed me, convincing Murphy to use stop-motion in lieu of marionettes thus entailed persuading him that "it would be better than puppetry for making the characters one step closer to 'real.'" It may also be of interest here to note that one of the roles that contributed to Murphy's popularity in the early 1980s was his *Saturday Night Live* character "Grown-up Gumby"—a perverse live-action reproduction of television's most famous dimensional stop-motion character. In conjunction with this interest in puppets, Murphy's shift from playing "realistic," street-talking characters in his strictly live-action films from the 1980s (*Trading Places, Beverly Hills Cop, Beverly Hills Cop II and III, 48 Hours, Another 48 Hours*) to emphatically cartoonish characters in the late 1990s and in films that incorporated digital animation and numerous special effects to forefront the body's "plastmaticness" (*The Nutty Professor* [a remake of the Jerry Lewis original], *The Nutty Professor 2,* and of course *The PJs*) is a career turn worth thinking about in light of the issues this essay raises.

41. Bergson's essay on laughter is notorious for including, as part of its analysis, the question, "And why does one laugh at the Negro?" Bergson, "Laughter," in Wylie Sypher, ed., *Comedy* (New York: Doubleday Anchor, 1956), 86.

42. Sue Conklin (Will Vinton Studios), email to the author, 9 December 1999.

43. Peter Boyd (Will Vinton Studios), email to the author, 10 December 1999.

44. On this strategy of excessive submission, which will be discussed in further detail in Chapter 5, see Gilles Deleuze, *Difference and Repetition,* trans. Paul Patton (New York: Columbia University Press, 1994), 5.

45. As Cavell notes, "It can be *internal* to a character that he threaten his own limit" (*The World Viewed,* 159, emphasis added).

46. Tom Carson, "Darndest Things," *Village Voice,* 2 February 1999, 137.

3. envy

1. Cynthia Chase, "Desire and Identification in Lacan and Kristeva," in Richard Feldstein and Judith Roof, eds., *Feminism and Psychoanalysis* (Ithaca: Cornell University Press, 1989) 65, note 2.

2. Rey Chow, "Where Have All the Natives Gone?" in *Writing Diaspora: Tac-*

tics of Intervention in Contemporary Cultural Studies (Bloomington: Indiana University Press, 1993), 31–32. Chow cites Gayatri Chakravorty Spivak, "French Feminism in an International Frame," in idem, *In Other Worlds: Essays in Cultural Politics* (London: Methuen, 1987), 141 (Chow's emphasis). Spivak cites Julia Kristeva, *About Chinese Women,* trans. Anita Barrows (New York: Marion Boyars, 1977, rpt. 1986), 11.

3. Clayton Koelb suggests that feminized lack can itself be an object of envy. See Koelb, "Castration Envy: Nietzsche and the Figure of Woman," in Peter Burgard, ed., *Nietzsche and the Feminine* (Charlottesville: University of Virginia Press, 1994), 71–81.

4. Helmut Schoeck, *Envy: A Theory of Social Behavior,* trans. Michael Glenny and Betty Ross (New York: Harcourt, Brace and World, 1966), 172. Hereafter designated *E.*

5. Fredric Jameson, *The Political Unconscious: Narrative as a Socially Symbolic Act* (Ithaca: Cornell University Press, 1981), 268, 202.

6. Rom Harré, "An Outline of the Social Constructionist Viewpoint," in Rom Harré, ed., *The Social Construction of Emotions* (Oxford: Blackwell, 1986), 12 (italics added).

7. Peter Stearns, "Gender and Emotion," in David D. Franks and Viktor Gecas, eds., *Social Perspectives on Emotion, Volume 1* (Greenwich: JAI Press, 1992), 127–160, 135. Though obviously related, envy and jealousy are structurally different emotions: the first involves twosomes, the second involves threesomes. Melanie Klein usefully clarifies this: "Envy implies the subject's relation to one person only. . . . *Jealousy is based on envy,* but involves a relation to at least two people" (italics added). Moreover, while envy is associated with an "angry feeling," jealousy "is mainly concerned with love that the subject feels . . . is in danger of being taken away." Hence, as Klein notes, quoting Crabb's *English Synonyms,* "Jealousy fears to lose what it has; envy is pained at seeing another have that which it wants for itself." See Melanie Klein, "Envy and Gratitude," in *The Writings of Melanie Klein, Volume 3: "Envy and Gratitude" and Other Works, 1946–1963* (New York: Free Press, 1975), 181–182. Hereafter designated "EG." My essay will stress the connections rather than the differences between the two emotions.

8. George Stanley Hall, *Adolescence* (New York: Appleton, 1904), 357; E. B. Duffy, *What Every Woman Should Know* (Philadelphia: Lippincott, 1873); both cited in Stearns, "Gender and Emotion," 135.

9. Søren Kierkegaard, *The Sickness unto Death,* cited in Schoeck, *Envy,* 172.

10. Ellen Brinks, "Who's Been in My Closet? Mimetic Identification and the Psychosis of Class Transvestitism in *Single White Female,*" in Sue-Ellen Case, Philip Brett, and Susan Leigh Foster, eds., *Cruising the Performative: Interventions into the Representation of Ethnicity, Nationality, and Sexuality* (Bloomington: Indiana University Press, 1995), 3, hereafter designated

"MI." For additional comments on the film's reactionary attitudes toward race, see Lynda Hart, "Race and Reproduction: *Single* White *Female,*" in Hart, *Fatal Women: Lesbian Sexuality and the Mark of Aggression* (Princeton: Princeton University Press, 1994), 104–179, hereafter designated "RR." Hart's commentary on the film's racial ideologies usefully references Patricia Williams' critique of its segregationalism. See Williams, "Attack of the 50-Foot First Lady: The Demonization of Hillary Clinton," *Village Voice,* 26 January 1993, 35–39.

11. Karen Hollinger, "Backlash: The Anti-Female Friendship Film," in idem, *In the Company of Women: Contemporary Female Friendship Films* (Minneapolis: University of Minnesota Press, 1998), 207–235. Hereafter designated "B."

12. My question borrows its syntax from a question posed by Barbara Johnson in *The Feminist Difference: Literature, Psychoanalysis, Race, and Gender* (Cambridge, Mass.: Harvard University Press, 1998), 175. Hereafter designated *FD.*

13. Susan Gubar, "What Ails Feminist Criticism?" *Critical Inquiry,* 24, no. 4 (Summer 1998): 880, hereafter designated "WAFC." A later version of the essay appears in Gubar, *Critical Condition: Feminism at the Turn of the Century* (New York: Columbia University Press, 2000). I refer throughout to the original article.

14. This debate took place across the following texts: Gubar, "What Ails Feminist Criticism?"; and Robyn Wiegman, "What Ails Feminist Criticism? A Second Opinion," *Critical Inquiry,* 25, no. 2 (Winter 1999): 362–379, hereafter designated "SO." See also Susan Gubar, "Notations *in Medias Res,*" ibid., 380–396, for her response to Wiegman.

15. I am referring of course to Klein's essay "Envy and Gratitude"; see 176–235. Carolyn Heilbrun, "Letter to the Editor," *Critical Inquiry,* 25, no. 2 (Winter 1999): 397–400, hereafter designated "L."

16. Gubar, "What Ails Feminist Criticism?" 888, 889, 893 (italics added).

17. The examples of Judith Butler's prose cited by Gubar are taken from Butler, *Gender Trouble: Feminism and the Subversion of Identity* (New York: Routledge, 1990), 40, 45. See Gubar, "What Ails Feminist Criticism?" 896–897, original italics.

18. Teresa de Lauretis, *The Practice of Love: Lesbian Sexuality and Perverse Desire* (Bloomington: Indiana University Press, 1994), 120; Jackie Stacey, "Desperately Seeking Difference," in idem, *The Sexual Subject: A Screen Reader in Sexuality* (London: Routledge, 1992), 244–257. Drawing also on *All about Eve,* Blakey Vermeule similarly warns about enfolding lesbian identity into female homosociality in her critique of Eve Sedgwick's valorized concept of a female homosocial-homosexual continuum. See Vermeule, "Is There a Sedgwick School for Girls?" *Qui Parle,* 5, no. 1 (Fall–Winter 1991): 53–72. The "lesbian continuum" model referred to by Vermeule appears in Eve

Kosofsky Sedgwick, *Between Men: English Literature and Male Homosocial Desire* (New York: Columbia University Press, 1985), 5.

19. Scott Paulin, "Sex and the Singled Girl: Queer Representation and Containment in *Single White Female*," *Camera Obscura*, 37 (1996): 52. Hereafter designated "SSG."

20. For examples of the focus on identification versus desire in treatments of such woman-versus-woman "woman's films," see also Rhona J. Berenstein, "'I'm Not the Sort of Person Men Marry': Monsters, Queers and *Rebecca*," in Corey K. Creekmur and Alexander Doty, eds., *Out in Culture* (Durham: Duke University Press, 1995), 239–261; Mary Ann Doane, "*Caught* and *Rebecca*: The Inscription of Femininity as Absence," *enclitic*, 5, no. 2 (Fall 1981): 75–89; and Janet Harbord, "Between Identification and Desire: Re-reading *Rebecca*," *Feminist Review*, 52 (Summer 1996): 95–107.

21. Though critics have often argued that Freud's notion of innate drives *(Triebe)* is essentialist, for a persuasive argument that his understanding of drives actually undermines the opposition between constructionism and essentialism, see Teresa de Lauretis, "The Stubborn Drive," *Critical Inquiry*, 24, no. 4 (Summer 1998): 851–877.

22. On Klein as "high priestess of psychic negativity," see Jacqueline Rose, "Negativity in the Work of Melanie Klein," in John Phillips and Lyndsey Stonebridge, eds., *Reading Melanie Klein* (London: Routledge, 1998), 128. See also Jacqueline Rose, *Why War? Psychoanalysis, Politics, and the Return to Melanie Klein* (Oxford: Blackwell, 1993).

23. Paulin, "Sex and the Singled Girl," 51. It is clear, though, that Hedy perceives Allie's "look" as a generic and mass-produced one: "Where did *you guys* learn to dress like that? I mean, it's just so 'New York.'"

24. Judith Butler, "Phantasmatic Identification and the Assumption of Sex," in idem, *Bodies That Matter: On the Discursive Limits of "Sex"* (New York: Routledge, 1993), 105.

25. Sigmund Freud, *Group Psychology and the Analysis of the Ego*, trans. James Strachey (New York: Bantam, 1965), 79. Hereafter designated *GP*.

26. Diana Fuss, *Identification Papers* (New York: Routledge, 1995), 67. Hereafter designated *IP*.

Significantly, it is in this chapter that Freud also advances his notorious theory of homosexuality as narcissistic identification, defining the former as object-choice having "regressed" to the latter (*Group Psychology*, 48). This theory is inadvertently replicated by some antihomophobic critics in their readings of *Single White Female*, who use what seems to be Hedy's mimetic "love of the same" as *evidence* of her homosexual orientation. Thus Hart's characterization of Hedy as "seeking the same; indeed she is seeking the self-identical" occurs in tandem with her characterization of Hedy as a "pathological 'lesbian'" who "effects a disruption of Allie's heterosexuality" (Hart, "Race and Reproduction," 115, 114, 117). The tendency to conflate copying and identification seems often to subtend this equation ("seeking same" = "lesbian"), which is one of my other motivations for questioning it. For a detailed discussion of the troubling implications of reducing homosexuality to love of the same, see Michael Warner, "Homo-Narcissism; or, Heterosexuality," in Joseph A. Boone and Michael Cadden, eds., *Engendering Men: The Question of Male Feminist* Criticism (New York: Routledge, 1990), 190–206.

27. Butler, "Phantasmatic Identification," 105.

28. Ibid.

29. The change in the gender of Freud's exempla also occurs in tandem with a move away from the use of ingestion as a dominant metaphor for identification, and toward the metaphor of infection—a turn which, as Fuss notes in an excellent close reading of the same chapter, involves switching from "an *active* subject's conservation of the object of its idealization" to "a *passive* subject's infiltration by an object not of its choosing" (*Identification Papers*, 41, italics added).

30. *The Prime of Miss Jean Brodie* (a film based on the novel by Muriel Spark) also establishes this link, in order to associate homophilic idealization with political leader-worship (and by extension with fascism). When her prize student, Sandy (Pamela Franklin), "puts a stop" to the ability of Jean (Maggie Smith) to transmit or reproduce her theories of ideal femininity (puts a stop to her ability to copy as well as be copied), Jean equates this with "assassination"—hence linking the end of transmissibility with the death of a feminine ideal, but also with the death of the fascist political leaders Jean admires. The relation between the mimetic production of "compound" female subjectivity in this "woman's film" and Freud's postwar analysis of the "libidinal organization of groups" in *Group Psychology* is a worthy topic for an essay on its own.

31. Judith Butler, "Performative Acts and Gender Constitution: An Essay in Phenomenology and Feminist Theory," in Sue-Ellen Case, ed., *Performing Feminisms: Feminist Critical Theory and Theater* (Baltimore: Johns Hopkins University Press, 1990), 270–282.

32. Brinks makes a similar point; see "Who's Been in My Closet?" 4–5.

33. J. Laplanche and J.-B. Pontalis, *The Language of Psychoanalysis,* trans. Donald Nicholson-Smith (New York: Norton, 1973), 206. Hereafter designated *LP.*

34. Algirdas Julien Greimas and Jacques Fontanille, *The Semiotics of Passions: From States of Affairs to States of Feelings,* trans. Paul Perron and Frank Collins (Minneapolis: University of Minneapolis Press, 1993), 124.

35. In contrast, in Lutz's novel, the lack of "self-worth or identity" that drives Hedra's pathological impersonation of Allie is revealed as stemming from the fact that Hedra's father abused her when she was a child. There is a sense in which the novel relies on a much more stereotypical, more "Holly-

wood" explanation for Hedy's psychosis than the film does. See John Lutz, *SWF Seeks Same* (New York: St. Martin's, 1990), 250. Hereafter designated *SWF.*

36. *Webster's Collegiate Dictionary,* 10th edition, 1995, s.v. "borrow."

37. This is again a significant departure from Lutz's novel, where Allie explicitly encourages Hedra to borrow whatever she wants from her closet (*SWF Seeks Same,* 128).

38. This scene illustrates a pattern of relentlessly negative self-assertion in the film as a whole, a pattern in which both subjects interpret propositions puts forward by the other concerning the other as actually being propositions about the subject, and vice versa. For instance, when Hedy makes a statement concerning Allie's appearance ("Where did you learn to dress like that?"), Allie immediately reads this as Hedy making a statement about *Hedy's* appearance, and responds accordingly ("I think *you* look very comfortable"). Hedy similarly reads Allie's comment "I think *you* should get them," a statement about *Hedy's* desire for the shoes, as a statement about *Allie's* desire for the shoes.

39. The significant difference between the relationships Hedy and Allie have to feminine property is reflected in the contrast between Hedy's remark here ("Anything of mine you want is yours"), and what Allie says to a cab driver while in pursuit of Hedy dressed as Allie's double: "Don't lose her. She has something of mine."

40. Laplanche and Pontalis: "In Freud's work the concept of identification comes little by little to have the central importance which makes it not simply one psychical mechanism among others, but *the operation itself whereby the human subject is constituted*" (*The Language of Psychoanalysis,* 206).

41. Citing Lauren Berlant, "The Female Complaint" (*Social Text,* 19–20 [Fall 1988]), Gubar partly concedes this point in her response to Wiegman. See Gubar, "Notations *in Medias Res,*" 394.

42. Though envy bears much resemblance to sadism in its destructive aims, Judith Hughes reminds us that "what distinguished [Kleinian] envy from sadism was that envy constituted an attack upon the good *because it was good.*" See Hughes, *Reshaping the Psychoanalytic Domain* (Berkeley: University of California Press, 1989), 88.

43. Rather than seeking to "preserve and spare" the object, "envy is the angry feeling that another person possesses and enjoys something desirable—the envious impulse being to take it away or to spoil it" (Klein, "Envy and Gratitude," 181). In other words, envy is the impulse to change the *status* of the object with respect to its ownability, and thus alter one's relation to the thing originally admired and desired. Envying interferes with the subject's ability to accept, assimilate, possess, or internalize the "good object" (which it subsequently transforms by challenging its value), as well as with its ability to distinguish between objects "good" and "bad" (ibid., 185, 192).

44. Raymond Williams, "Structures of Feeling," in idem, *Marxism and Literature* (Oxford: Oxford University Press, 1977), 132.

45. This is to argue not that one has to go through envy to recognize persecution, but that envy in the Kleinian sense might provide a particular strategy for doing so—particularly when what is at stake is the ability to recognize an *idealized* object (what the dominant culture admires and strives toward) as persecutory.

46. Brian Massumi, *Parables for the Virtual: Movement, Affect, Sensation* (Durham: Duke University Press, 2002), 18.

47. J. Hillis Miller, *The Ethics of Reading* (Ithaca: Cornell University Press), 11.

48. Andrzej Warminski, *Readings in Interpretation* (Minneapolis: University of Minnesota Press, 1987), 110. Cited in Slavoj Zizek, *For They Know Not What They Do: Enjoyment as a Political Factor* (London: Verso, 1991), 40–42.

49. Wendy Brown, *States of Injury: Power and Freedom in Late Modernity* (Princeton: Princeton University Press, 1995), 38.

50. Hollinger, "Backlash," 207.

51. Jacques Derrida, "The Law of Genre," *Glyph: Textual Studies,* 7 (1988): 206. Cited in Alexander Gelley, "Introduction," in Gelley, ed., *Unruly Examples: On the Rhetoric of Exemplarity* (Stanford: Stanford University Press, 1995), 10.

52. As Lynda Hart notes, "The 'White' of the title appears to have dropped out of the picture entirely. It seems to be only an incidental remark, perhaps just a slip of the filmmaker's pen" ("Race and Reproduction," 115). In accordance with her essay, which focuses on "the making of the (modern) lesbian as white," Hart's explanation for why *Single White Female* produces, if only to rapidly erase, this evocation of race, is that it needs not only to construct Hedy as a lesbian but to construct all lesbians as white—so as to raise the threat of nonreproductive ("single") femininity historically posed by the figure of the lesbian as a threat about the annihilation of the white race in particular (ibid., 116).

53. One answer to this question is that by specifying her race in accordance with the conventions of "passion" ads, Allie finds an oblique way to *eroticize* the domestic homosocial from the very beginning. Note how race becomes a signifier for sexuality here. The emphasis on envious antagonism rather than desire in this chapter, however, will lead us to an alternative reading.

54. Allie *is* presented as explicitly homophobic in *SWF Seeks Same:* "I never doubted your sexual preference, Hedra, or I wouldn't have chosen you for a roommate" (55).

55. I am grateful to Gopal Balakrishnan for suggesting this comparison.

56. In Lutz's novel, Hedra is a temporary office worker who "fills in" for other female employees (receptionist, typist, executive secretary of a catering film)—a mode of labor that cannily parallels her larger role in the story as a

female shapeshifter and emulator. In contrast to these multiple jobs, Allie has only one—yet the novel similarly challenges her singularity on this front as well: "Work was scarce for computer programmers; colleges were churning them out by the thousands" (*SWF Seeks Same,* 129).

57. Slavoj Zizek, "Class Struggle or Postmodernism? Yes, Please!" in Judith Butler, Ernesto Laclau, and Slavoj Zizek, *Contingency, Hegemony, Universality: Contemporary Dialogues on the Left* (London: Verso, 2000), 90–135, 96.

4. irritation

1. Nella Larsen, *Quicksand and Passing,* ed. Deborah McDowell (New Brunswick: Rutgers University Press, 1989), 34, italics added.

2. Barbara Johnson, "The Quicksands of the Self," in *The Feminist Difference: Literature, Psychoanalysis, Race, and Gender* (Cambridge, Mass.: Harvard University Press, 1998), 37–60, 42.

3. Aristotle, *Nicomachean Ethics,* trans. Terence Irwin (Indianapolis: Hackett, 1985), 106.

4. I am grateful to Mark McGurl for suggesting this to me.

5. Beverly Haviland, "Passing from Paranoia to Plagiarism: The Abject Authorship of Nella Larsen," *Modern Fiction Studies,* 43, no. 2 (1997): 295–318, 296. Noting that "abjection is a kind of failure to represent ourselves to the world as authors of our own being," Haviland's thought-provoking essay suggests that "there is a psychological profile that sustains the construction of legitimate authorship—a profile that was impossible for Larsen to maintain." In the short story "Sanctuary," the only work in which Larsen makes use of black vernacular, Larsen appears to have taken a short story by a British writer (Sheila Kaye-Smith's "Mrs. Adis") and to have "made it black" by replacing Kaye-Smith's characters with African-Americans. Haviland links this act of plagiarism, which effectively ended Larsen's publishing career only months after she was awarded a Guggenheim Fellowship in 1930, to "an instability in the recognition and respect for boundaries between self and other" which similarly defines "paranoia" (as embodied by Irene in *Passing*). Ironically, both paranoia and plagiarism, as instances of this "disorder of the boundaries of subject/object relations," can be understood "as attempts by Larsen to imagine a more intimate relationship with her origins, familial and social" (ibid., 310, 296). As Haviland notes, it is precisely "a desire *to identify herself as an African-American writer* that self-destructs when Larsen takes an English story and recasts it with American blacks" (296)—a point which resonates in interesting ways with *Quicksand*'s treatment of the matter of identification in African-American artforms in general. Drawing on Larsen's biography, Haviland suggests that Larsen's plagiarism of "Mrs. Adis" can be read as both a phantasmatic identification with as well as an act of aggression toward the white mother who rejected

her—calling attention to a "convoluted play of identification and [aggression]" in Larsen's relation to the social profile of the autonomous author in general (296).

6. I am indebted to Mark McGurl for this observation.

7. See Thadious M. Davis, *Nella Larsen, Novelist of the Harlem Renaissance: A Woman's Life Unveiled* (Baton Rouge: Louisiana State University Press, 1994), 151.

8. Larsen's career as a writer can be charted in explicit counterpoint to these other labors; moreover, her relation to the words of others as a professional writer seems intimately bound up with her relation to them *as* a librarian. As Thadious Davis notes, Larsen's first published essay, a review of Kathleen Norris' novel *Certain People of Importance* (1922), was a direct result of her coursework in book selection at the Library School, for which she wrote a description of the novel as an assignment. And "perhaps not coincidentally," her first creative works, the short stories "The Wrong Man" and "Freedom," appeared in print immediately after she first left the library in 1926. *Quicksand* and *Passing* would be written and published in the enormously productive interval between this resignation and Larsen's resumption of the position in 1929, from which she resigned again after receiving her Guggenheim Fellowship in 1930. See Davis, *Nella Larsen, Novelist of the Harlem Renaissance,* 150, 170.

9. Michael North, *The Dialect of Modernism: Race, Language, and Twentieth-Century Literature* (Oxford: Oxford University Press, 1994).

10. W. E. B. Du Bois, "*Home to Harlem* and *Quicksand,*" *Crisis,* 35 (June 1928). Reprinted in Theodore G. Vincent, ed., *Voices of a Black Nation: Political Journalism in the Harlem Renaissance* (San Francisco: Ramparts, 1973), 359.

11. Van Vechten's remark is cited in Nathan Huggins, *Harlem Renaissance* (Oxford: Oxford University Press, 1971), 99. W. E. B. Du Bois, review of *Nigger Heaven,* by Carl Van Vechten, *Crisis,* 33 (December 1926): 81.

12. The following argument is usefully representative of the dominant, "repression"-centered reading to which I refer: "Nella Larsen's portrait of Helga Crane . . . criticizes the ways in which white racist constructions of black women's lasciviousness have cut black women off from experiencing their legitimate sexual desires. Helga fears her desires because they seem to confirm stereotypes about black people's 'primitivism' and 'savagery.'" See Kimberly Monda, "Self-Delusion and Self-Sacrifice in Nella Larsen's *Quicksand,*" *African American Review,* 31 (Spring 1997): 23. I would argue that far from being unacknowledged by Helga, or stifled by Larsen's prose, sexuality is overtly and even graphically displayed in the novel. There are repeated references to Helga's "*uncontrollable* fancies," "*irrepressible* longing," and "the *hardiness* of [her] insistent desire" (105, 106, 107, italics added). And though these explicit references to sexual longing are primar-

ily delayed until the second half of novel, the timing of their appearance does not change the fact of their explicitness:

"Desire welled up in her with . . . suddenness" (104).

"She was used to kisses. But none had been like that of last night. She lived over those brief seconds, thinking not so much of the man whose arms had held her as of the ecstasy which had flooded her. Even recollection brought a little onrush of emotion that made her sway a little" (105).

"For days, for weeks, voluptuous visions had haunted her. Desire had burned in her flesh with uncontrollable violence. The wish to give herself had been so intense that Dr. Anderson's surprising, trivial apology loomed as a direct refusal of that offering" (109).

"And night came at the end of every day. Emotional, palpitating, amorous, all that was living in her sprang like rank weeds at the tingling thought of night, with a vitality so strong that it devoured all shoots of reason" (122).

In addition to the anatomical reference to female erection at the very "tingling thought" of sex in this last passage, the "voluptuous visions," flooding ecstasy, and a "desire" that devours reason, makes the body sway with emotion, and burns in the flesh "with uncontrollable violence" seem to function as *anything* but signs of repression, either in the protagonist's "struggle to express her sensuality" (as Claudia Tate puts it in a paraphrase of Deborah McDowell's introduction to the Rutgers University Press reprint of the novel) or the text's "reluctance to utter" (as argued by Linda Dittmar). See Claudia Tate, "Desire and Death in *Quicksand,* by Nella Larsen," *American Literary History,* 7, no. 2 (Summer 1995): 240; Linda Dittmar, "When Privilege Is No Protection: The Woman Artist in *Quicksand* and *The House of Mirth,*" in Suzanne W. Jones, ed., *Writing the Woman Artist: Essays on Poetics, Politics, and Portraiture* (Philadelphia: University of Pennsylvania Press, 1991), 145, hereafter designated *WWA*.

13. Jeffrey Gray, "Essence and the Mulatto Traveler: Europe as Embodiment in Nella Larsen's *Quicksand,*" *Novel* (Spring 1994): 259.

14. Cheryl Wall, "Passing for What? Aspects of Identity in Nella Larsen's Novels," *Black American Literature Forum,* 20 (Spring–Summer 1986): 97.

15. As Stanley Cavell notes, "The wish for total intelligibility is a terrible thing." *The World Viewed: Reflections on the Ontology of Film* (Cambridge, Mass.: Harvard University Press, 1979), 159.

16. Annette Baier, "What Emotions Are About," *Philosophical Perspectives,* 4 (1990): 3.

17. Ibid.

18. "As portrayed, the character is not quite of one pattern. . . . If she was at all the young woman of the first of the book, she cannot be the older woman of the latter half. There is no continuity of development, no wholeness

here." Eda Lou Walton, review of *Quicksand,* by Nella Larsen, *Opportunity,* 6, no. 7 (July 1928): 212–213. Reprinted in Cary D. Wintz, ed., *The Harlem Renaissance, 1920–1940, Volume 4: The Critics and the Harlem Renaissance* (New York: Garland, 1996), 192.

19. See Tom Lutz, *American Nervousness, 1903: An Anecdotal History* (Ithaca: Cornell University Press, 1991).

20. Alain Locke to Carl Van Vechten, 9 February 1926, Carl Van Vechten Papers, cited in Kathleen Pfeiffer, introduction to Carl Van Vechten, *Nigger Heaven* (Urbana: University of Illinois Press, 2000), ix; W. E. B. Du Bois, "Criteria of Negro Art," *Crisis,* 32 (October 1926): 290–297, reprinted in Wintz, *The Harlem Renaissance,* 366–374.

21. Fisher, *The Vehement Passions* (Princeton: Princeton University Press, 2001), 175. Hereafter designated *VP.*

22. Audre Lorde, "The Uses of Anger: Women Responding to Racism," in idem, *Sister Outsider* (Freedom, Calif.: Crossing Press, 1984), 124–133. Thanks to Paula Moya for bringing this essay to my attention.

23. Aristotle, *Nicomachean Ethics,* 105. Cited in Fisher, *The Vehement Passions,* 173.

24. Johnson, "The Quicksands of the Self," 42.

25. For instance, Helga is so irritable that the affect is as easily provoked by her own states of mind as it is by external objects. She is "annoyed to find herself actually trembling" while waiting to be received by her white step-aunt in Chicago, and, similarly, "irritated at finding herself wondering just how she was going to tell [Robert Anderson] of her decision [to resign]" (Larsen, *Quicksand,* 28, 17). Yet the irritation that could be read, at first glance, as distracting Helga from the stronger emotions we are more likely to attribute to these moments (fear of familial rejection; nervousness about an impending confrontation with one's employer) is primarily used to reveal Helga's acute awareness of her own state of mind. As a reflexive affective response to other affective states, Helga's irritation actually suggests a *heightened* form of self-consciousness (in both examples above, she is irritated by recognizing or "finding herself" in state X or Y), rather than an effort to reject or keep something *out* of consciousness. In fact, the expressive reluctance Dittmar attributes both to the character of Helga and to the text of *Quicksand* is carried out with an overtness that suggests the exact opposite of repression, involving a flaunting of rupture, illegibility, and obfuscation of psychological "depth" that parallels Helga's love of surfaces and of ostentatious, flagrant acts of consumption.

26. *Microsoft Office Thesaurus* (1998 ed.), s.v. "irritation."

27. Frantz Fanon, *Black Skin, White Masks* (New York: Grove, 1967), 11. As another example of irritation's ability to blur the boundaries between psychic interiors and bodily exteriors, note the conversation with Robert An-

derson that precipitates Helga's flight to Chicago, in which Helga attempts to explain her reasons for leaving Naxos:

"Naxos! It's hardly a place at all. It's more like some loathsome, venomous disease. Ugh! Everybody spending his time in a malicious hunting for the weaknesses of others, spying, grudging, scratching."

"I see. And you don't think it might help to cure us, to have someone who doesn't approve of these things stay with us? Even just you, Miss Crane?"

". . . No, I don't! It doesn't do the disease any good. Only irritates it. And it makes me unhappy, dissatisfied." (19–20)

The introduction of irritation as a bodily or corporeal condition is immediately followed by a rhetorical twist that flips it back into the realm of emotion. While the black educational establishment initially constitutes the apparently cutaneous disease (since it promotes "scratching"), Helga describes her presence as an irritant *to* the disease, aggravating an assault on a body's epidermis already taking place. However, this intensification of a bodily phenomenon is described as precipitating an emotional state, Helga's unhappiness or dissatisfaction. The parallel between the unhappily aggravated disease and "unhappy, dissatisfied" Helga identifies the two as simultaneously irritated and irritating—much like Helga's perception of herself as a "obscene sore" exposed, without her volition, for all to see.

28. See Larsen, *Quicksand,* 21, 77, 29, emphasis added.

29. As Douglas Mao and Rebecca Walkowitz pointed out to me (email, January 15, 2003).

30. Ibid.

31. Stanley Cavell, "Opera and Film," course lecture, Harvard University, Cambridge, Mass., 1996.

32. As Derrida notes, "The overweening presumption from which *no response will ever be free* . . . has to do with the fact that the response claims to measure up to the discourse of the other, to situate it, understand it, indeed circumscribe it by responding thus *to* the other and *before* the other." See Jacques Derrida, *On the Name,* ed. Thomas Dutoit, trans. David Wood, John P. Leavey Jr., and Ian McLeod (Stanford: Stanford University Press, 1995), 20, italics in the original.

My argument is that irritation's persistent "offishness" in *Quicksand* is precisely what makes this affect so propitious for the novel's larger inquiry into race and aesthetics. Yet there is one racial context in which this minor affect actually seems "fitting": as a response to the casual or "low-level" racism one encounters on an everyday basis (the offhand remark, the exchanged look, the "kindly" racism of Helga's patron uncle), in contrast to its more overt, explicitly antagonistic, or vehement forms. To recall my earlier observation about how the novel's concept of irritation manages simultaneously to "put us off" and "rub us the wrong way," the minor feeling seems entirely "appropriate" as a response to the kind of racism with which one most repeatedly comes into contact, *and* which seems easiest to detach oneself from, to brush off or ignore. It is worth noting here that while Helga does find her Uncle Peter's racial attitudes irritating, her relations with her other relatives, whose attitudes are not tempered by his benevolence, are characterized, more strongly, by "antagonism" and "fear" (*Q,* 6; cited by Mark McGurl, email to author, March 7, 2004). Written in a decade marked by an escalation in organized violence toward African-Americans (and the intensified spectacularization of that violence across various media), the novel does seem to be calling our attention to differences between the daily varieties of racism foregrounded in *Quicksand,* to the much more vicious kinds (often culminating in terrorism and murder) represented in the works of James Weldon Johnson, Jean Toomer, and many other of Larsen's contemporaries. This raises new questions about the spitting incident on the train, which is perhaps the closest Larsen comes to evoking the latter. If Helga's emotional response to the white man's act is left unstated, as we have noted, it is key to note that his affect and motivations are left unstated as well. The white man's emotion thus constitutes yet *another* "blank spot" in the discourse, as if deliberately to raise the question of whether his spitting is in fact a vehement expression of racist passion or, instead, racism of a "superficial" or careless sort—that is, a more offhand, casual racism which Helga's low-level negative affect would very much seem to mirror. From the perspective of both Larsen and her fictional character, such expressions of racist sentiment might more likely be perceived as commonplaces (to be met with a relative and even hard-won indifference) than as shocking or unusual events. Indeed, we can imagine how Larsen and Helga might find them irritating precisely because of their status *as* ordinary (McGurl, ibid.). Yet to say that irritation seems "appropriate" in this racial context not only leaves the problem of affective proportionality intact, but exacerbates it further. For to say that the minor affect "fits" a "minor" or "ordinary" sort of racism requires disconnecting this racism from its "nonordinary" forms, a move which presents as many risks as the move of too quickly conflating them. To say this is also to imply the "insignificance" of everyday racism, which brings it into uncomfortable proximity to the matter of ugly teacups, along with the other "appropriately" trivial objects of irritation in the novel. Indeed, it is to risk implying that "ordinary" racism, in being something which one can more or less shrug off, is "tolerable"—that is, more or less acceptable. If from a perspective that emphasizes the differences (and not the continuity) between "casual" and "vehement" racism the problem of affective commensurability no longer seems as "intrinsic" to irritation as I have previously suggested, Larsen's novel nonetheless ensures that the problem is left to persist *around* the affect of irritation. For in a novel dominated by principles of excess and lack, and structured by the protagonist's erratic swerves from one extreme to another, it is clear that nothing in the racist modernity it represents is "balanced" in any way—and that the desire or quest for this aesthetically idealized proportionality may itself be the problem. The world that Larsen depicts is exactly one defined by a general inability to "balance" things, least of all the emotions inspired by the irrationality of racism. In this manner, the one racial context in which irritation might actually seem "appropriate" to its occasion in *Quicksand* is arguably where the novel most emphatically problematizes the idea of affective proportionality. And indeed the principle of proportionality, symmetry, or balance—as elevated in the aesthetics and moral philosophy of Aristotle and numerous others—*in general. Quicksand*'s "peculiar irritation" might be thought of as explicitly posed against this classical standard of beauty and/or virtue—indeed, as playing a crucial role in what I take to be its polemical assertion of the African-American artwork's *right to be ugly.*

33. As Fisher notes, one of the literary devices most commonly used to incite readers to volunteer unfelt emotion is character—in particular, the use of "naïve central figures such as a child," or the "more important, because more common," the use of "the ignorant or mistaken figure" (*The Vehement Passions,* 143). Fisher describes "the ignorant or mistaken figure" (who bears a striking similarity to both the "repressed" figure and the fool in the *Nicomachean Ethics*) as one "otherwise equal to us, who in this moment does not know what is happening, or misreads it, while we, *knowing better,* must supply the passion that his mistake or unawareness rules out" (ibid., italics added). Yet Larsen's irritated protagonist cannot be said to have any of these qualities. Given Helga's acute sense of irony and highly reflexive awareness of self and others, it does not seem right to describe her as naïve or childlike—even if at times her actions seem puzzling or opaque in the conspicuous absence of explicit causes. And while there is clearly something discomfortingly "inadequate" about Helga's response to the racist incident on the train, it cannot be said that she is unaware of the incident as it unfolds, or that she misreads or interprets the incident incorrectly, mistaking the white man's expression of racial hatred for something other than what it is. What Fisher's description of the "ignorant or mistaken figure" alerts us to is the role played by moral or epistemological superiority in cases of volunteered passion—the character may be unaware or mistaken about what is happening, but the reader, "knowing better," is able to fill the gap created by the missing emotion. Yet the emphasis on moral or epistemological superiority as a prerequisite for the reader's ability to volunteer passion helps us further understand why Helga's irritation blocks our efforts to

do so, since, as we have already seen, her aggressively off-key affect polemically questions the moralism that inflects our judgment of Helga's response to the racist's vehement expression *as* inadequate and inappropriate—exposing the very demand for emotional adequation or propriety in this context as politically problematic.

34. My thanks to Barrett Watten for calling my attention to the ugliness of the expression.

35. Yet the paradox is that the shame we are led to locate "inside" Helga, in contrast to her outward display of remove, is described as the outcome of an *externalizing* exposure to the same "pale pink and white people" watching the black performers. The vaguely defined yet racialized "something" in Helga is not only exposed to these spectators, but voraciously consumed by them. I would suggest that it is the spectacle of this European audience's consumption of Helga's involuntarily externalized *identification* with the African American entertainers (and not just their avid consumption of the entertainment per se) that pulls her back to the scene that initially repulses and mortifies her: "But she returned again and again to the Circus, always alone, gazing intently and solemnly at the gesticulating black figures, an ironical and silently speculative spectator" (Larsen, *Quicksand,* 83). Soliciting both Helga's fascination and her disgust, the minstrel show could in fact be described as yet another "obscene sore."

36. See Hortense E. Thornton, "Sexism as Quagmire," *CLA Journal,* 16 (1973): 285–301; and Tate, "Desire and Death," 246.

37. Ironically, it is Helga's failure to become a "pore los' sinner" that leads her to the church in the first place. Her newfound allegiance to the Baptists is thus based on a misrecognition of her sexual identity that she nevertheless accepts.

38. See Giorgio Agamben, "Bartleby," in idem, *The Coming Community,* trans. Michael Hardt (Minneapolis: University of Minnesota Press, 1993), 35–38.

39. Tate, "Desire and Death," 235; Dittmar, "When Privilege Is No Protection," 145.

40. Ann E. Hostetler, "The Aesthetics of Race and Gender in Nella Larsen's *Quicksand,*" *PMLA,* 105 (1990): 35.

41. Van Vechten, *Nigger Heaven,* 14, 12–13.

42. Claude McKay, *Home to Harlem* (Boston: Northeastern University Press, 1987), 32, 57–58.

43. Laura Kipnis, "Marx: The Video" (script), in *Ecstasy Unlimited: On Sex, Capital, Gender, and Aesthetics,* foreword by Paul Smith (Minneapolis: University of Minnesota Press, 1993), 289.

44. Ibid., 257.

45. Robyn Wiegman, *American Anatomies: Theorizing Race and Gender* (Durham: Duke University Press, 1995), 23.

46. Ibid., 21.

5. anxiety

1. This quotation, which I have been unable to locate in Althusser's works, is cited in Jeff Derksen's poem "Social Facts Are Vertical," *Sulphur,* 44 (Spring 1999): 65–72, issue titled *Anglophone Poetry and Poetics Outside the U.S. and U.K.,* ed. Jenny Penberthy and Marjorie Perloff.

2. Ernst Bloch, *The Principle of Hope, Volume I,* trans. Neville Plaice, Stephen Plaice, and Paul Knight (Cambridge, Mass.: MIT Press, 1995), 74–75.

3. Fredric Jameson, *Marxism and Form: Twentieth-Century Dialectical Theories of Literature* (Princeton: Princeton University Press, 1971), 127.

4. As Bloch puts it, "All emotions refer to the actually temporal aspect in time, i.e. to the mode of the future, but whereas the filled emotions only have an unreal feature, i.e. one in which objectively nothing new happens, the expectant emotions essentially imply a real future; in fact that of the Not-Yet, of what has objectively not yet been there" (*The Principle of Hope,* 74–75). In other words, while both kinds of feelings "ask something of the future . . . [since they] are at their very heart a type of wishing or desiring," the expectant feelings are more closely tied to futurity than filled ones. Jameson beautifully explains, "This is because filled emotions . . . ask for fulfillment in a world at all points identical to that of the present, save for the possession of the particular object desired and presently lacking. Such affects are primitive or infantile to the degree that they amount to magical incantations, a conjuring up of the object just exactly as we long for it, at the same time we hold the rest of the world, and our own desire, magically in suspension, arresting all change and the very passage of real time itself. As though everything in the world were not interrelated and interdependent in the most astonishing and imperceptible fashion! As though the very changes in the world required to bring about our ultimate possession of the longed-for object did not run the risk of transforming the very object itself to the point where it no longer strikes us as very desirable, or of transforming ourselves to the point where we no longer desire it! Such emotions or feelings therefore not only imply a kind of provincialism of the present, into which we are plunged so utterly that we lose the very possibility of imagining a future which might be radically and constitutionally *other;* their analysis also implies a kind of ethics, a keeping faith with the open character of the future, a life in time which holds to the prospect of the absolutely unexpected as the only expectation" (*Marxism and Form,* 126–127).

5. J. Laplanche and J.-B. Pontalis, *The Language of Psychoanalysis,* trans. Donald Nicholson-Smith (New York: Norton, 1973), 349. Hereafter designated *LP.*

6. Louis Althusser, *The Future Lasts a Long Time,* ed. Olivier Corpet and Yann Moulier Boutang, trans. Richard Veasey (London: Chatto and Windus, 1993), 274, italics added.

7. Sigmund Freud, *The Interpretation of Dreams,* trans. and ed. James Strachey (New York: Basic Books, 1965), 436, note 2.

8. Sigmund Freud, "On the Grounds for Detaching a Particular Syndrome from Neurasthenia under the Description 'Anxiety Neurosis,'" in idem, *Collected Papers,* ed. Joan Riviere, vol. 1 (London: Hogarth, 1959), 76, italics added.

9. Freud's analysis of phobia in terms of the spatial metaphors of "turning" and fleeing" lays the groundwork for approaching phobia and projection as one and the same thing. In his analysis of anxiety-hysteria in "The Unconscious," for instance, Freud writes: "The whole protective structure of the phobia corresponds to a 'salient' of unconscious influence of this kind. . . . By the whole defence-mechanism thus set in action *a projection outwards* of the menace from the instinct has been achieved. The ego behaves as if the danger of an outbreak of anxiety threatened it not from the direction of an instinct but from the direction of perception: this enables the ego to react against this external danger with the attempts at flight consisting of the avoidances characteristic of a phobia." Freud, "The Unconscious," in idem, *General Psychological Theory: Papers on Metapsychology,* ed. Philip Rieff (New York: Collier, 1963), 132, italics added.

10. See, for instance, the discussion of introjection and expulsion in Sigmund Freud, "Instincts and Their Vicissitudes," ibid., 83–103.

11. In discussing the paranoiac's outward deflection of his own fantasies and ideas, which return in inverted form as reproaches or threats, Freud emphasizes grammar or positionality rather than semantics: "*The subject-matter remains unaffected;* what is altered is something in the *placing* of the whole thing." Sigmund Freud, "Further Remarks on the Neuro-Psychoses of Defence," *Collected Papers,* vol. 1, 155, italics added. Cited in Laplanche and Pontalis, *The Language of Psychoanalysis,* 351.

12. This is the case study in which paranoia is infamously theorized not just in terms of a syntactic transformation, but as the outcome of the repression of male homosexuality.

13. "Here" and "yonder" are terms used by Heidegger in his discussion of anxiety and fear. See Martin Heidegger, *Being and Time,* trans. John MacQuarrie and Edward Robinson (San Francisco: Harper Collins, 1962), 231. Hereafter designated *BT.* In extracts from this book, all italics are Heidegger's unless otherwise noted.

14. I am indebted to Thalia Field for finding this point lurking in my larger argument.

15. Brian Massumi, "Preface" and "Everywhere You Want to Be: Introduction to Fear," in Massumi, ed., *The Politics of Everyday Fear* (Minneapolis: University of Minnesota Press, 1993), vii–x, 3–40.

16. Sigmund Freud, *Inhibitions, Symptoms, and Anxiety,* ed. James Strachey, trans. Alix Strachey (New York: Norton, 1989), 50.

17. Søren Kierkegaard, *Either/Or: Volume 1,* trans. Howard V. Hong and Edna H. Hong (Princeton: Princeton University Press, 1987), 129. The speaker here is the aesthetician Mr. A.

18. Richard Burton, *The Anatomy of Melancholy,* ed. Holbrook Jackson (New York: New York Review Books, 2001), 300–335.

19. On the centrality of "neurasthenia" to twentieth-century American literature and culture, and the uses made of its discourse by Theodore Dreiser, Theodore Roosevelt, William James, Hamlin Garland, and others, see Tom Lutz, *American Nervousness, 1903: An Anecdotal History* (Ithaca: Cornell University Press, 1991).

20. Stephen Rachman, "Melville's *Pierre* and Nervous Exhaustion; or, 'The Vacant Whirlingness of the Bewilderingness,'" *Literature and Medicine* 16, no. 2 (Fall 1997): 231.

21. Thomas Trotter, *A View of the Nervous Temperament* (Troy, N.Y., 1808), cited ibid.

22. See Lutz, *American Nervousness.*

23. The *American Heritage Dictionary,* 2nd college edition (1991), defines "cantilever" as "a projecting beam or other structure supported only at one end"; "a beam or other member projecting beyond a fulcrum and supported by a balancing member or a downward force behind the fulcrum."

24. Laura Mulvey, "Visual Pleasure and Narrative Cinema," in *Feminist Film Theory: A Reader,* ed. Sue Thornham (New York: New York University Press, 1999), 58–69.

25. Jonathan Lear, *Love and Its Place in Nature: A Philosophical Interpretation of Freudian Psychoanalysis* (New York: Farrar, Straus and Giroux, 1990), 38. Hereafter designated *LPN.*

26. Sue Campbell argues this thesis extensively in *Interpreting the Personal* (Ithaca: Cornell University Press, 1997); see especially "Expression and the Individuation of Feeling" (46–74). Jonathan Lear's study of Freudian catharsis suggests a similar point of view. In *Love and Its Place in Nature,* Lear reexamines Freud and Breuer's early papers on hysteria in order to put critical pressure on their early definition of catharsis as a type of emotional discharge, or as the expulsion of an individuated substance as foreign body. He stresses that the discharge or purgation of "psychic energy" typically ascribed to catharsis in early psychoanalytic theory is actually a *theoretical fantasy* of discharge or purgation—one described by the hysterical patient (Anna O) herself, though not explicitly conceptualized by her as such. Thus, "the case of Anna O shows us, right at the beginning of psychoanalysis, that . . . archaic mental life has a 'theory' of the mind's own workings. . . . Her 'theory' was expressed at the same archaic level of mental functioning as the rest of her fantasies: she experiences [psychoanalysis' therapeutic] catharsis as a corporealized discharge" (*Love and Its Place in Nature,* 36). Lear argues, however, that the phantasmatic nature of the "theory" does

not necessarily imply its invalidity. Since "even the most archaic unconscious mental process contains within it an implicit, fantasied 'theory' of that process" and this theory of the mental process "is part of the person's (perhaps unconscious) experience of that process," Lear notes that "the fantasied 'theory' becomes part and process of the mental process itself, and in altering the fantasy one alters the mental process itself." Though Lear does not make this point directly, his argument that in giving conscious, conceptualized expression to one's emotional life or "archaic fantasies of mental functioning" in language, "one is able to influence the fantasy and thus the mental functioning which embodies and expresses that fantasy" (ibid., 38), comes close to Campbell's suggestion that feelings, as forms of "mental functioning," are individuated by their expressions.

27. Scottie's anxiousness, *as* projective dis-positioning, thus becomes posited as an odd sort of symbolic homeopathy: as a subject previously disturbed by and unable to gaze at "thrown" images, he eventually becomes a normative viewer by acquiring the skill of throwing them—i.e., by reenacting the same externalizing principle underlying his original phobia. Here we should recall that Elster deliberately seeks to enlist Scottie, precisely in his role as anxious skeptic or observer, as part of his initial scheme. Foregrounding Scottie's unknowing collaboration *with* Elster in the act of constituting female subjects as "thrown," *Vertigo* presents a schematization of its male knowledge-seeker's dread that reveals one of the most perverse paradoxes of American capitalism's "do-it-yourself" ideology, whereby a subject's awareness of his inscription *within* a system of power becomes predicated on replicating its functions. Thus, the condition for the male subject's realization of himself as a subject *enmeshed in* the economic system Elster represents—one in which women can be, as the amateur historian notes, always already projected and then thrown away ("Men could do that in those days; they had the power, and the freedom")—is active participation in the production of self and others as projected projections. For Scottie's final understanding of his *collaborative* role in Elster's machinations (an arrival that coincides, significantly, with the "curing" of his anxious condition, as if as a psychological reward for this self-awareness) ultimately depends on subjecting Judy to the same acts of projection used by Elster to concoct the fiction of "Madeleine" needed to kill his wife—replicating what Elster does, down to sartorial details.

28. Pierre Bourdieu, *The Political Ontology of Martin Heidegger,* trans. Peter Collier (Stanford: Stanford University Press, 1991), 10.

29. Charles Guignon, "Moods in Heidegger's *Being and Time,*" in Cheshire Calhoun and Robert C. Solomon, eds., *What Is an Emotion?* (Oxford: Oxford University Press, 1984), 235. Guignon cites Heidegger, *Being and Time,* 390.

30. Heidegger, *Being and Time,* 176, cited in Guignon, "Moods in Heidegger's *Being and Time,*" 236, italics added.

31. Giorgio Agamben, *Language and Death: The Place of Negativity,* trans. Karen E. Pinkus with Michael Hardt (Minneapolis: University of Minnesota Press, 1991), 56.

32. Søren Kierkegaard, *The Concept of Anxiety: A Simple Psychologically Orienting Deliberation on the Dogmatic Issue of Hereditary Sin,* ed. and trans. Reidar Thomte and Albert B. Anderson (Princeton: Princeton University Press, 1980), 14n. Hereafter designated *CA.* Heidegger also claims that "ontologically mood is a primordial kind of Being for Dasein, in which Dasein is disclosed to itself *prior* to all cognition and volition, and *beyond* their range of disclosure" (*Being and Time,* 175).

33. Christopher Macann, "Heidegger's Kant Interpretation," in Macann, ed., *Critical Heidegger* (London: Routledge, 1996), 100.

34. Ibid.

35. The claim that anxiety, unlike fear, has no concrete thing or "entity within-the-world" as its object is by no means an original thesis; this particular point, like much of Heidegger's discussion of falling and ambiguity, comes straight from Kierkegaard: "I must point out that [anxiety] is altogether different from fear and similar concepts that refer to something definite. . . . The relation of anxiety to its object [is] to something that is nothing" (*The Concept of Anxiety,* 42, 43). Kierkegaard's distinction recurs in Freudian psychoanalysis—"[Anxiety] has a quality of *indefiniteness* and *lack of object.* In precise speech we use the word 'fear' [*Furcht*] rather than 'anxiety' [*Angst*] if it has found an object"—and in writings by existentialists as well: "Anxiety differs from fear in that the object of anxiety is 'nothingness,' and 'nothingness' is not an 'object.'" See Freud, "Supplementary Remarks on Anxiety," in idem, *Inhibitions, Symptoms, and Anxiety,* 100; and Paul Tillich, "Existential Philosophy," *Journal of the History of Ideas,* 5 (1944): 44, cited in Thomte, introduction to Kierkegaard, *The Concept of Anxiety,* xvi. Contemporary philosophers of affect have similarly been compelled to reassert this difference: Greimas and Fontanille, for example, write that "fear is real only in terms of a coming event, one that is in play here in terms of an object of knowledge that mobilizes expectations, . . . [whereas] worry by definition has no precise object." Algirdas Julien Greimas and Jacques Fontanille, *The Semiotics of Passions: From States of Affairs to States of Feelings,* trans. Paul Perron and Frank Collins (Minneapolis: University of Minneapolis Press, 1993), 138.

36. As many critics have noted, this is the same thesis Kierkegaard proposes in *The Concept of Anxiety.* See, for instance, Dam Magurshak, "The Concept of Anxiety: The Keystone of the Kierkegaard-Heidegger Relationship," in Robert L. Perkins, ed., *International Kierkegaard Commentary* (Macon, Ga.:

Mercer University Press, 1985), 174; and Gordon D. Marino, "Anxiety in *The Concept of Anxiety,*" in Alastair Hannay and Gordon D. Marino, eds., *The Cambridge Companion to Kierkegaard* (Cambridge: Cambridge University Press, 1998), 308–328.

37. Herman Melville, *Pierre; or, The Ambiguities,* ed. William C. Spengeman (New York: Penguin, 1996). Hereafter designated *P.*

38. Aside from the constant and deliberate blurring/reshifting of kinship relations that occurs early in the novel—crossing lines of exogamous and endogamous affiliation (mothers become sisters, sisters become wives, wives become nuns)—once Lucy moves to the city, the symbolic roles of Isabel and Lucy modulate and become increasingly difficult to fix. If one wants to read the novel as a sequence of generic shifts, Isabel as conventional Gothic figure (dark, nomadic, mysterious, a site of "unknown, foreign feminineness") appears to neatly supplant Lucy as classic heroine of the sentimental novel (blonde, bourgeois, virginal). Yet these roles seem to dissolve in the second half of the novel; the previously sublime Isabel becomes increasingly flattened into a caricature of a jealous wife, and Lucy seems to acquire a mystique—"a brilliant, supernatural whiteness" and "inscrutableness"—of her own (Melville, *Pierre,* 328).

39. See Rachman, "Melville's *Pierre,*" for a more extensive analysis of this exhaustion vis-à-vis American neurasthenia, and "as an image in which disease and literary understanding converge" (227).

40. Priscilla Wald, "Hearing Narrative Voices in Melville's *Pierre,*" *boundary 2,* 17, no. 1 (1990): 105. Hereafter designated "HNV."

41. I. A. Richards, *Practical Criticism: A Study of Literary Judgement* (New York: Harcourt Brace Jovanovich, 1929), 337, 336.

42. Greimas and Fontanille, *The Semiotics of Passions,* 6.

43. Ibid., 6.

6. stuplimity

1. Cited in Neil Schmitz, *Of Huck and Alice: Humorous Writing in American Literature* (Minneapolis: University of Minnesota Press, 1983), 100.

2. Nathanael West, *"Miss Lonelyhearts" and "The Day of the Locust"* (New York: New Directions, 1962), 169–247. Hereafter designated *DL.*

3. Gilles Deleuze, *Difference and Repetition,* trans. Paul Patton (New York: Columbia University Press, 1995), 39. Hereafter designated *DR.*

4. Gertrude Stein, *The Making of Americans* (Normal, Ill.: Dalkey Archive Press, 1995; orig. pub. 1906–1908)). Hereafter designated *MA.*

5. Gertrude Stein, *Writings and Lectures, 1909–1945,* ed. Patricia Meyerowitz (Baltimore: Johns Hopkins University Press, 1974), 142. Hereafter designated *WL.*

6. Gertrude Stein, *How to Write* (Los Angeles: Sun and Moon, 1995; orig. pub. 1928), 7–32. Hereafter designated *HTW.*

7. Samuel Beckett, *Worstward Ho* (1983), in idem., *Nohow On,* introduction by S. E. Gontarski (New York: Grove, 1996), 106.

8. Marianne DeKoven, *A Different Language: Gertrude Stein's Experimental Writing* (Madison: University of Wisconsin Press, 1983), 50. See all of ch. 3.

9. Edgar Allan Poe, "The Gold-Bug" (1843), in idem, *"The Fall of the House of Usher" and Other Writings* (New York: Penguin, 1986), 305. Hereafter designated "GB."

10. Samuel Beckett, "Stirrings Still," in idem, *The Complete Short Prose, 1929–1989,* ed. S. E. Gontarski (New York: Grove, 1995), 259–260.

11. See Jean-François Lyotard, *Duchamp's TRANS/formers,* trans. Ian McLeod (Venice, Calif.: Lapis Press, 1990), a study of Duchamp's *Large Glass.* Lyotard's analysis of Duchamp's aesthetics as underwritten by a logic of "inexact precision" and "intelligent stupidity" also pertains to and sheds light on the poetics of Stein.

12. Dan Farrell, *366, 1996* (New York: Iced Ink Press, 1997). Cited from Farrell's collection *Last Instance* (San Francisco: Krupskaya, 1998), 57.

13. Quotations are taken from the FIDGET website, which is sponsored by the Whitney Museum of American Art, Printed Matter, and Stadium, and is available at http://stadiumweb.com/fidget. FIDGET was originally commissioned by the Whitney Museum and was performed in collaboration with vocalist Theo Bleckmann on June 16, 1998, at the Whitney Museum in New York. A book and compact disc were issued by the Maryland Institute of Art in 1998.

14. Judith Goldman, *Vocoder* (New York: Roof Books, 2001), 50–54.

15. Kenneth Goldsmith, *No. 111 2.7.93–10.20.96* (Great Barrington, Mass.: The Figures, 1997). As Raphael Rubinstein notes on the volume's jacket, "Goldsmith's epic litanies and lists bring to the textual tradition of conceptual art not only an exploded frame of reference, but a hitherto absent sense of hypnotic beat. Under its deceptively bland title, *No. 111 2.7.93–10.20.96* attempts no less than a complete reordering of the things of the world."

16. Ibid.

17. The "self-referential" text Goldsmith appropriates and edits for incorporation into his own conceptual project was written by mathematician David Moser and cited in Douglas Hofstadter, *Metamagical Themas: Questing for the Essence of Mind and Pattern* (New York: Basic Books, 1985), 37–38. What ultimately determines this text's positioning between ch. MDCLXXXV and ch. MDCLXXXVII in Goldsmith's poem (encyclopedia? Baedeker?) is the fact that it contains the appropriate number of syllables, and, like the other rhymed "verses" in the volume, ends on the sound of the letter *r:* "Harder harder" (Goldsmith, *No. 111,* 568).

18. Susan Sontag, "The Aesthetics of Silence," in idem, *Styles of Radical Will* (New York: Doubleday, 1969), 22.

19. Silvan Tomkins, *Exploring Affect: The Selected Writings of Silvan S. Tomkins,* ed. Virginia Demos (Cambridge: Cambridge University Press, 1995), 88.

20. Ernst Bloch, *The Principle of Hope, Volume I,* trans. Neville Plaice, Stephen Plaice, and Paul Knight (Cambridge, Mass.: MIT Press, 1995), 73.

21. Jacques Lacan, *The Four Fundamental Concepts of Psycho-Analysis,* ed. Jacques-Alain Miller, trans. Alan Sheridan (New York: Norton, 1981), 61.

22. Susan Sontag, "The Pornographic Imagination," in idem, *Styles of Radical Will,* 62.

23. Neville Wakefield, "Ann Hamilton: Between Words and Things," *Ann Hamilton, Mneme* (Liverpool: Tate Gallery Liverpool, 1994), 10.

24. Gerhard Richter, *Atlas* (New York: Distributed Art Publishers, 1997).

25. Janet Zweig, *Her Recursive Apology,* 1993 (a work consisting of 4,386,375 apologies), paper, 2 ft. × 9 ft. × 9 ft. Collection of the artist, Brooklyn, New York. Janet Zweig, note on *Her Recursive Apology,* in *Chain,* 2 (1995): 248–249 (issue entitled *Documentary*).

26. Kant, *Critique of Judgement* (1790), trans. J. H. Bernard (New York: Hafner, 1951). Hereafter designated *CJ.*

27. Arthur C. Danto, *The Abuse of Beauty: Aesthetics and the Concept of Art* (Chicago: Open Court, 2003).

28. Alan J. Issacs, "The Ironic Sublime," diss., Stanford University, 1993, 40.

29. Ben Watson, *Art, Class and Cleavage* (London: Quartet, 1998), 233. Hereafter designated *ACC.*

30. Kant claims, "This estimation of ourselves loses nothing through the fact that we must regard ourselves as safe in order to feel this inspiriting satisfaction," and is careful to defend the seriousness of the sublime against the argument that "as there is no seriousness in the danger, there might be also (as might seem to be the case) just as little seriousness in the sublimity of our spiritual faculty" (*Critique of Judgement,* 101). But as Philip Fisher notes, there is a certain "sophistry" in this argument. For while "never denying that a safe place is a precondition of the feeling of the sublime," Kant "nonetheless requires us to believe that it is not this safe place but a subtle belief in our reason's location outside nature and encompassing nature that generates the feeling of the sublime. Fascinating as this subtle possibility might be, it is important to notice that Kant never leaves out the words "provided we are in a safe place." Fisher, *The Vehement Passions* (Princeton: Princeton University Press, 2001), 148–149.

31. Gilles Deleuze, "The Exhausted," in idem, *Essays Critical and Clinical,* trans. Daniel W. Smith and Michael A. Greco (Minneapolis: University of Minnesota Press, 2000), 152. Hereafter designated "E."

32. Paul de Man, "Phenomenality and Materiality in Kant," in idem, *Aesthetic*

Ideology, ed. Andrzej Warminski (Minneapolis: University of Minnesota, 1996), 84. Hereafter designated *AI.*

33. Samuel Beckett, *How It Is* (New York: Grove, 1964). Hereafter designated *HII.*

34. Søren Kierkegaard, *"Fear and Trembling" and "Repetition,"* ed. and trans. Howard V. Hong and Edna H. Hong (Princeton: Princeton University Press, 1983), 159. Hereafter designated *R.*

35. Leo Bersani and Ulysse Dutoit, "Beckett's Sociability," *Raritan,* 12, no. 1 (Summer 1992): 1–2.

36. William Hutchings, "'Shat into Grace,' or, A Tale of a Turd: Why It Is *How It Is* in Samuel Beckett's *How It Is,"* *Papers on Language and Literature,* 21 (1985): 65.

37. Lisa Ruddick, *Reading Gertrude Stein: Body, Text, Gnosis* (Ithaca: Cornell University Press, 1990), 81. Hereafter designated *RGS.* Ruddick's account of Stein's "anal voice" is developed in the chapter titled *"The Making of Americans:* Modernism and Patricide," 55–136.

38. Samuel Beckett, *Murphy* (New York: Grove, 1957), 181.

39. *The Seminar of Jacques Lacan, Book 7: The Ethics of Psychoanalysis,* trans. Dennis Porter (New York: Norton, 1992), 113–114. Hereafter designated *Seminar.*

40. Peter Brooks, "Freud's Masterplot," *Reading for the Plot: Design and Intention in Narrative* (Cambridge, Mass.: Harvard University Press, 1984), 101.

41. Arne Melberg, "'Repetition (in the Kierkegaardian Sense of the Term),'" *Diacritics,* 20, no. 3 (1990): 76.

42. Algirdas Julien Greimas and Jacques Fontanille, *The Semiotics of Passions: From States of Affairs to States of Feelings,* trans. Paul Perron and Frank Collins (Minneapolis: University of Minnesota Press, 1993), 3.

43. Fredric Jameson, *Postmodernism, or, The Cultural Logic of Late Capitalism* (Durham: Duke University Press, 1991), 15–16. Hereafter designated *PM.*

44. *Webster's Collegiate Dictionary,* 10th ed., 1995, s.v. "cohere," "coherence."

45. Ibid.

46. Displayed at the exhibition *Deep Storage,* P.S. 1, New York, 1998.

47. Cited in Linda Wagner-Martin, *Favored Strangers: Gertrude Stein and Her Family* (New Brunswick: Rutgers University Press, 1995), 75.

48. Beckett, *Murphy,* 97.

49. Alice Notley, *The Descent of Alette* (New York: Penguin, 1992), 16. In the Author's Note, Notley offers "a word about the quotation marks. People ask about them, in the beginning; in the process of reading the poem, they become comfortable with them, without necessarily thinking precisely about why they're there. But they're there, mostly, to measure the poem. The phrases they enclose are poetic feet. If I had simply left white spaces between the phrases, the phrases would be rushed by the reader—read too

fast for my musical intention. The quotation marks make the reader slow down and silently articulate—not slur over mentally—the phrases at the pace, and with the stresses, I intend. They also distance the narrative from myself, the author: I am not Alette. Finally they may remind the reader that each phrase is a thing said by a voice: this is not a thought, or a record of thought-process, this a story, told."

7. paranoia

1. One of the liabilities in making references to television in academic writing is the speed with which changes in programming take place, outpacing the timing of writing and publishing. After this chapter was first drafted, the gendered positions of paranoiac and empiricist flip-flopped once again: Agent Scully (Gillian Anderson) became the paranoiac when Agent Mulder (David Duchovny) was replaced by Agent Doggett (Robert Patrick).

2. Fredric Jameson, *The Geopolitical Aesthetic: Cinema and Space in the World System* (Bloomington: Indiana University Press, 1992), in particular the opening section, "Totality as Conspiracy," 9–84. Hereafter designated *GA*.

3. It is my hope that this definition of paranoia—as a specific subcategory of fear grounded in the apprehension of a "total system" encompassing the subject, and amenable to analysis from within despite the fact that its external boundaries cannot be securely delimited (a situation requiring that the system be "imagined" rather than "known")—provides an affirmative response to the question, put to me by Paula Moya, of whether or not a paranoia whose causes are real is, in fact, "paranoia" at all. One useful outcome of this distinction is that it accounts for the seemingly contradictory (though very familiar) position of being paranoid and correct.

4. Fredric Jameson, "The Theoretical Hesitation: Benjamin's Sociological Predecessor," *Critical Inquiry*, 25 (Winter 1999): 267. Hereafter designated "TH."

5. Gayatri Chakravorty Spivak, conversation with Ellen Rooney, quoted in Spivak, *Outside in the Teaching Machine* (New York: Routledge, 1993), 13. Cited in Alys Weinbaum, "Marx, Irigaray, and the Politics of Reproduction," in Emanuela Bianchi, ed., *Is Feminist Philosophy Philosophy?* (Evanston: University of Illinois Press, 1999), 133–134. As Weinbaum notes, Spivak makes the point that while capital opens up the abstraction necessary for antiessentialist thinking, it also makes instrumental use of essences to sustain itself: "Capital," says Spivak, "is antiessentializing because it is abstract as such, . . . [while essences] are deployed by capitalism for the political management of capital" (cited ibid., 133). In more recent writing, Spivak emphasizes the "spectralizing global sweep" of "'pure' finance capital—the abstract as such," while also pointing to the potential disruptions

of this sweep by resistance networks associated with a "partially spectralized 'rural.'" See Spivak, "From Haverstock Hill Flat to U.S. Classroom," in Judith Butler, John Guillory, and Kendall Thomas, eds., *What's Left of Theory?* (New York: Routledge, 2000), 1–39.

6. Naomi Schor, "Female Paranoia: The Case for Psychoanalytic Feminist Criticism," *Yale French Studies,* 62 (1981): 204–219. Hereafter designated "FP."

7. "The delusions of paranoiacs," says Freud, "have an unpalatable external similarity and internal kinship to the systems of our philosophers." *The Standard Edition of the Complete Psychological Works of Sigmund Freud,* ed. James Strachey, trans. James Strachey et al. (London: Hogarth Press, 1953–74), vol. 17, 261. Cited in Schor, "Female Paranoia," 206.

8. Through an appeal to Julia Kristeva's theory of the semiotic and a close reading of Freud's essay, Schor ultimately argues that the specifically female paranoia/theory she wants to adduce is a psychoanalytically informed theory "grounded in the body." For Schor, not only is "female theory" this "materialism riveted to the body, its throbbing, its pulsations, its rhythms"; "female theory is clitoral," with the clitoris viewed as coextensive with the concreteness of the detail ("Female Paranoia," 210–211).

9. Cyndy Hendershot, "Paranoia and the Delusion of the Total System," *American Imago,* 54, no. 1 (Spring 1997): 17.

10. Brian Massumi, "Preface," in Massumi, ed., *The Politics of Everyday Fear* (Minnesota: University of Minnesota Press, 1993), ix.

11. For a reading of these psychoanalytical theories that links constitutive paranoia to a globalized commodity culture, see Teresa Brennan, "The Age of Paranoia," *Paragraph,* 14 (1991): 20–45.

12. Hendershot, "Paranoia and the Delusion of the Total System," 17.

13. Massumi, "Preface."

14. Juliana Spahr, *Response* (Los Angeles: Sun and Moon, 1995); Heather Fuller, *perhaps this is a rescue fantasy* (Washington, D.C.: Edge Books, 1997). In an essay outlining some of the major conflicts arising from attempts by contemporary writers to define a feminist aesthetic, Sally Minogue repeatedly praises the "bravery" of those who address "the problem of [aesthetic] value outright." In doing so, Minogue calls attention to the "feminist writer's fear of being found politically suspect" and to the predominance of fear, on a more general level, in feminist criticism itself: "The more one reads feminist criticism the more one perceives the presence, either implicitly or explicitly stated, of fear." Sally Minogue, "Prescriptions and Proscriptions: Feminist Criticism and Contemporary Poetry," in Sally Minogue, ed., *Problems for Feminist Criticism* (London: Routledge, 1990), 193.

15. Spivak, "From Haverstock Hill Flat to U.S. Classroom," 9.

16. Gertrude Stein, "Composition as Explanation" (1926), in *Gertrude Stein:*

Writings, 1903–1932, ed. Catharine Stimpson and Harriet Chessman (New York: Library of America, 1998), 521.

17. Joan Retallack, "Memnoir," *Chain,* 7 (Summer 2000): 156–158.

18. Diane Ward, *Imaginary Movie* (Elmwood, Conn.: Potes and Poets Press, 1992).

19. See also Marjorie Perloff, *Poetic License: Essays on Modernist and Post-modernist Lyric* (Evanston: Northwestern University Press, 1990). In this text, as Hank Lazer notes, Perloff "expresses frustration with an academism that is receptive to poststructuralist criticism but that misapplies that reading to inapplicable strains of American poetry, 'the irony being that the poems of a Charles Bernstein or a Lyn Hejinian, not to speak of Leiris or Cage, are much more consonant with the theories of Derrida and de Man, Lacan and Lyotard, Barthes and Benjamin, than are the canonical texts that are currently ground through the poststructuralist mill.'" Hank Lazer, *Opposing Poetries, Volume 1: Issues and Institutions* (Evanston: Northwestern University Press, 1996), 69–70, citing Perloff, *Poetic License,* 23. While I would not claim that poststructuralist language theory is "misapplied" when used to read canonical writing (in fact, the readings always seem more potent when the texts are *not* "consonant" with the theory), I agree with Perloff's observation that there is something ironic about this situation.

20. As Susan Suleiman notes, one of the main paradoxes of *S/Z* "is that after formulating the difference between the readable and writable in such stark terms, Barthes appears to undermine those very differences by reading Balzac's *Sarrasine,* which he singles out as a readable text par excellence, *as if* (well, almost as if) it were a writable text." Suleiman, *Subversive Intent: Gender, Politics and the Avant-Garde* (Cambridge, Mass.: Harvard University Press, 1990), 38. Hereafter designated *SI.*

21. The contemporaneity of the two discourses is stressed by the poets Ron Silliman, Carla Harryman, Lyn Hejinian, Steve Benson, Bob Perelman, and Barrett Watten in their collective essay "Aesthetic Tendency and the Politics of Poetry," *Social Text,* 19–20 (1988): 261–275. As the authors note, "Beginning with Stein and Zukofsky, and significantly reinforced by the examples of the abstract poems of Frank O'Hara and John Ashbery and the aleatorical texts of Jackson Mac Low in the fifties, there has been a continuity of experimental work that foregrounds its status as written. Partly by virtue of its contributions to a critique of the self, this kind of writing became in the seventies and eighties a way to extend poetry into areas that had previously been closed to it. This development of experimental technique took place at the same time as the historic explosion of interest in language and linguistics resulting from the work of such authors as Barthes and Kristeva. In no sense did the theory precede the work; the early literary magazines of our movement were almost entirely concerned with pub-

lishing poems. It was only with the publication of the collaborative poem *Legend* (1978), the magazine *L-A-N-G-U-A-G-E* (ed. Bruce Andrews and Charles Bernstein from 1978) and the transcripts of some of the early talks in *Hills/Talks* (1978) that theory began to take its place alongside poetry as a matter of real concern" (268).

22. Interestingly, though similar arguments have been made about "theory art" in other media during the same period, particularly in the plastic and media arts, for the most part the marriage of art and theory in these cases was respected and even celebrated by critics, with practitioners like Martha Rosler, Cindy Sherman, Mary Kelley, and Laura Mulvey frequently cited as exemplars of visual art's theoretical turn. Moreover, in addition to increasing the market values of individual works, the "turn to theory" in visual arts from the 1970s and '80s increased the cultural cachet of "avant-garde experimentalism" itself—though ironically the theoretical turn lauded by art critics was in effect a *linguistic* turn. In one situation, a close relationship between theory and art was critically embraced; in the other, it provided grounds for critical dismissal.

23. Silliman et al., "Aesthetic Tendency and the Politics of Poetry," 268, emphasis added.

24. Rosi Braidotti, *Nomadic Subjects: Embodiment and Sexual Difference in Contemporary Feminist Theory* (New York: Columbia University Press, 1994), 140. Hereafter designated *NS.*

25. Pamela Moore and Devoney Looser, "Theoretical Feminisms: Subjectivity, Struggle, and the 'Conspiracy' of Poststructuralisms," *Style,* 27 (Winter 1993): 535.

26. Andrew T. I. Ross, "Viennese Waltzes," *enclitic,* 8 (Spring–Fall 1984): 71–83. Hereafter designated "VW."

27. Nancy Hartsock, "Foucault on Power: A Theory for Women?" in Linda Nicholson, ed., *Feminism/Postmodernism* (New York: Routledge, 1990), 163; Somer Brodribb, *Nothing Mat(t)ers: A Feminist Critique of Postmodernism* (North Melbourne, Australia: Spinifex, 1993), xvii. Both cited in Moore and Looser, "Theoretical Feminisms," 535.

28. Silvia Bovenschen, "Is There a Feminine Aesthetic?" *New German Critique,* 10 (1977): 111–137. The journal editors note that Bovenschen's article was first published in German in *Aesthetik und Kommunikation,* 25 (September 1976). See also Domna C. Stanton, "Difference on Trial: A Critique of the Maternal Metaphor in Cixous, Irigaray, and Kristeva," in Nancy K. Miller, ed., *The Poetics of Gender* (New York: Columbia University Press, 1986); and Monique Wittig, "The Point of View: Universal or Particular," in idem, *"The Straight Mind" and Other Essays* (Boston: Beacon, 1992), 59–67. Citing Bovenschen, Teresa de Lauretis similarly points to the limitations of a countervalorized "feminine" discourse, though in the context of

rethinking avant-garde "women's cinema" rather than literary practice. See de Lauretis, *Technologies of Gender* (Bloomington: Indiana University Press, 1987), 127–148.

29. Rita Felski, *Beyond Feminist Aesthetics: Feminist Literature and Social Change* (Cambridge, Mass.: Harvard University Press, 1989), 5.

30. A version of this position was put forward by Ron Silliman in his editorial introduction to the July–September issue of *Socialist Review* (1988), and later challenged by Leslie Scalapino in a critical exchange with Silliman in *Poetics Journal,* 9. In his introduction, Silliman writes: "Progressive poets who identify as members of groups that have been the subject of history—many white male heterosexuals, for example—are apt to challenge all that is supposedly 'natural' about the formation of their own subjectivity. That their writing today is apt to call into question, if not actually explode, such conventions as narrative, persona, and even reference can hardly be surprising. At the other end of this spectrum are people who do not identify as members of groups that have been the subject of history, for they instead have been its objects. The narrative of history has not led to their self-actualization, but to their exclusion and domination. These writers and readers—women, people of color, sexual minorities, the entire spectrum of the 'marginal'—have a manifest political need to have their stories told. That their writing should often appear much more conventional, with the notable difference as to who is the subject of these conventions, illuminates the relationship between form and audience." Cited in David Buuck, "Against Masculinist Privilege," *Tripwire: A Journal of Poetics,* 3 (Summer 1999): 27–28. Buuck's essay provides a useful overview of this debate, as well of more recent exemplary moments within the avant-garde writing community in which questions of gender and form have come to the fore.

31. This is still an important task for feminism—though, as Wiegman and others suggest (see Chapter 3), not necessarily its primary goal.

32. Harryette Mullen, *Trimmings* (New York: Tender Buttons, 1992), n.p. This quotation appears in an epilogue to the poems called "Off the Top."

33. Joan Retallack, ":RE:THINKING: LITERARY:FEMINISM: (three essays onto shaky grounds)," in Lynne Keller, ed., *Feminist Measures* (Ann Arbor: University of Michigan Press, 1994), 366.

34. See Judith Butler, "Competing Universalities," (159); and Slavoj Zizek, "Da capo senza fine" (229), in Judith Butler, Ernesto Laclau, and Slavoj Zizek, *Contingency, Hegemony, Universality: Contemporary Dialogues on the Left* (London: Verso, 2000).

35. On this problem as specific to a male humanist tradition, see Paul Smith, *Discerning the Subject,* foreword by John Mowitt (Minneapolis: University of Minnesota Press, 1988), 97. Hereafter called *DS.*

36. David Kazanjian, "Notarizing Knowledge: Paranoia and Civility in Freud and Lacan," *Qui Parle,* 7 (Fall–Winter 1993): 129. Hereafter designated "NK."

37. On this phenomenon as one specific to the representation of gender relations in stalking fictions, see Timothy Melley, "'Stalked by Love': Female Paranoia and the Stalker Novel," *differences,* 8, no. 2 (1996): 68–100, an essay reappearing as a chapter in Melley's book *Empire of Conspiracy: The Culture of Paranoia in Postwar America* (Ithaca: Cornell University Press, 2000), 107–132. Throughout, I refer to the version originally published in *differences.* Hereafter designated "SBL."

38. Spahr makes reference to her own "zero-level writing" in a poem titled "responding." See Spahr, *Response,* 28.

39. Sasha Torres, "King TV," in Torres, ed., *Living Color: Race and Television in the United States* (Durham: Duke University Press, 1998), 141.

40. Jane Feuer, "The Concept of Live Television: Ontology as Ideology," in E. Ann Kaplan, ed., *Regarding Television: Critical Approaches—An Anthology* (Frederick, Md.: University Publications of America, 1983), 14. Cited in Torres, "King TV," 141.

41. Smith, *Discerning the Subject,* 87.

42. Peter Bürger, *Theory of the Avant-Garde,* trans. Michael Shaw (Minneapolis: University of Minnesota Press), 49–50.

43. Felski, *Beyond Feminist Aesthetics,* 5.

44. Robyn Wiegman, "Feminism, Institutionalism, and the Idiom of Failure," *differences,* 11, no. 3 (1999): 130.

45. Judith Butler, "Dynamic Conclusions," in Butler, Laclau, and Zizek, *Contingency, Hegemony, Universality,* 277.

afterword

1. Jonathan Dollimore, "Sexual Disgust," paper presented at "Dirt: An Interdisciplinary Graduate Student Conference," Harvard University, March 1995. This afterword is inspired by Dollimore's observation, as well as by his following comment that he did not intend to propose a "theory of disgust." (Why not? I wondered.) Unlike Dollimore, when speaking of "desire" throughout this essay, I will be referring not to sexuality or sexual practices but to theories of textual production and reception based on libidinal metaphors.

2. Julia Kristeva, *The Powers of Horror: An Essay on Abjection,* trans. Leon S. Roudiez (New York: Columbia University Press, 1982), 2, 9.

3. Marcel Proust, *In Search of Lost Time,* Volume 1: *Swann's Way,* trans. C. K. Scott-Moncrieff and Terence Kilmartin, revised by D. J. Enright (New York: Modern Library, 1998), 200.

4. William Ian Miller, *The Anatomy of Disgust* (Cambridge, Mass.: Harvard University Press, 1997), 111. Hereafter designated *AD.*

5. Erving Goffman, *Behavior in Public Places: Notes on the Social Organization of Gatherings* (New York: Free Press, 1963), 83–88.

6. Herman Melville, "Bartleby," in *Great Short Works of Herman Melville,* ed. Warner Berthoff (New York: Harper and Row, 1969), 64.

7. Immanuel Kant, *The Critique of Judgement,* trans. J. H. Bernard (New York: Hafner, 1951), 155. Hereafter designated *CJ.*

8. Arthur C. Danto, *The Abuse of Beauty: Aesthetics and the Concept of Art* (Chicago: Open Court, 2003).

9. I am grateful to Omri Moses for this eloquent paraphrase of Derrida's thesis, and to Joshua Kates for helping me locate the actual reference. See Jacques Derrida, "Economimesis," in *Diacritics,* 11, no. 2 (Summer 1981): 3–25, esp. 21–25.

10. Cited in Danto, *The Abuse of Beauty,* 56.

11. The opinions of others obviously inform what counts as desirable to us in the first place; my point is that once the desirability of the object is established, we do not ask that others feel exactly what we feel toward it.

12. Adam Smith, *The Theory of Moral Sentiments,* ed. D. D. Raphael and A. L. Macfie (Oxford: Clarendon, 1976). Cited in Miller, *The Anatomy of Disgust,* 190–191.

13. Thomas Hobbes, *Leviathan,* ed. J. C. A. Gaskin (Oxford: Oxford University Press, 1996), 34–35.

14. Friedrich Nietzsche, *On the Genealogy of Morals,* trans. Walter Kaufmann and R. J. Hollingdale, in idem, *"On the Genealogy of Morals" and "Ecce Homo,"* ed. Walter Kaufmann (New York: Vintage, 1967), 37.

15. Julie Kristeva, *Desire in Language: A Semiotic Approach to Literature and Art,* ed. Leon S. Roudiez, trans. Thomas Gora, Alice Jardine, and Leon S. Roudiez (New York: Columbia University Press, 1980), 116. Hereafter designated *DL.*

16. Bernard Noël, "The Outrage against Words," in Bruce Andrews and Charles Bernstein, eds., *The L-A-N-G-U-A-G-E Book* (Carbondale: Southern Illinois University Press, 1984), 190.

17. Martha Nussbaum, *Upheavals of Thought: The Intelligence of Emotions* (Cambridge: Cambridge University Press, 2001), 453–454.

18. Even though Nussbaum's attempt to argue for an ethics of emotion is made in the domain of moral philosophy (and is directed, one suspects, at a minority holdout of analytical philosophers who have resisted acknowledging the evaluative or cognitive dimensions of emotion), a reader cannot help wondering if one really needs more than 750 pages to make the argument that love is a good thing.

19. Herbert Marcuse, "Repressive Tolerance," in Robert Paul Wolff, Barrington Moore Jr., and Herbert Marcuse, *A Critique of Pure Tolerance* (Boston: Beacon, 1965), 88. Hereafter designated "RT."

20. On repressive desublimation (also referred to as "institutionalized," "adjusted," and "controlled" desublimation), see Herbert Marcuse, *One-Dimensional Man: Studies in the Ideology of Advanced Industrial Society* (Boston:

Beacon Press, 1991), 72–80; see also Marcuse, *Eros and Civilization: A Philosophical Inquiry into Freud* (Boston: Beacon Press, 1966), 207–221.

21. Ellen Rooney, *Seductive Reasoning: Pluralism as the Problematic of Contemporary Literary Theory* (Ithaca: Cornell University Press, 1989), 5. Hereafter designated *SR*.

22. Andreas Huyssen, "Mapping the Postmodern," in Huyssen, ed., *A Postmodern Reader* (Albany: State University of New York Press, 1990), 130; Alex Callinicos, *Against Postmodernism: A Marxist Critique* (New York: St. Martin's, 1989), 134.

23. Hal Foster, "Against Pluralism," in idem, *Recodings* (Seattle: Bay Press, 1985), 13. Hereafter designated "AP."

24. Clarice Lispector, *The Passion According to G.H.*, trans. Ronald W. Sousa (Minneapolis: University of Minnesota Press, 1994). Hereafter designated *PGH*.

25. Bruce Andrews, *I Don't Have Any Paper So Shut Up, or Social Romanticism* (Los Angeles: Sun and Moon, 1992), 150.

26. Ferdinand de Saussure, *Course in General Linguistics,* ed. Charles Bally and Albert Sechehaye, trans. Wade Baskin (New York: McGraw-Hill, 1966), 69.

27. Ludwig Wittgenstein, *Philosophical Investigations,* trans. G. E. M. Anscombe (Oxford: Blackwell, 1958), para. 27, 13e.

28. Jean-François Lyotard, *Libidinal Economy,* trans. Iain Hamilton Grant (Bloomington: Indiana University Press, 1993), 43.

29. Ibid., 55.

30. Theodor W. Adorno, *Aesthetic Theory,* ed. and trans. Robert Hullot-Kentor (Minneapolis: University of Minnesota Press, 1997), 313, 29.

Index

Abjection, 332, 381n5

Abstraction, 45, 48, 53, 300, 301

Academia, 300, 301, 343, 344

Action, 2, 14, 17, 27, 128–129

Admiration, 129–130, 141–142

Adorno, Theodor W.: on autonomy, 2; art in, 2, 29, 36, 87–88; and audience, 29; mood in, 46; on aura, 87–88; "The Culture Industry," 352; *Aesthetic Theory,* 353; intolerance in, 353; pluralism in, 353

Aesthetic predicate (Richards), 23–24, 82

Aesthetics: and politics, 3, 399n14; and emotion, 6, 23; in Genette, 23; and object, 85; in *The PJs,* 119–120; in Yau, 122; in Larsen, 176, 189, 192, 195, 197, 198, 199–200, 201–208; in modernism, 177; and blackness, 177, 178; and race, 177, 206; and boredom, 261–262; in Spahr, 321, 328; and pluralism, 342; eclecticism in, 349. *See also* Art

Affect: equivocal, 1; and capitalism, 3, 4, 5; as interpretation, 3, 27; and emotion, 25–26, 27–28, 40, 42; intensity of, 26; and modal *vs.* formal aspects, 27; and tone, 28, 29; and animatedness, 31, 91; and stock market, 39; in Dufrenne, 44; in Grossberg, 46–47; as read by feeling, 47; in Tomkins, 49, 52–56, 59, 72–73, 343, 368n56; and ideology, 49, 72, 74, 77; autonomy of, 52, 53; in Melville, 52, 56, 57, 61, 68, 69, 243; in Massumi, 56, 61; exchange of, 62; perceived *vs.* experienced, 71; and mattering, 72; and amplification, 74, 81, 84; and communication, 79–80; and detachment, 86; in Fordist era, 91; and animation, 98; and feminism, 164; illegible, 175; and race, 175; in Larsen, 175, 183, 187, 188, 189; expectation, 209–210;

and concept, 228; in Kierkegaard, 228; and boredom, 269; in Kant, 269; and stuplimity, 271; negative, 285, 286, 287; loss of, 285, 287, 292; Jameson on, 285, 292; and timing, 304–305; lack of, 322; in Spahr, 322. *See also* Emotion; Feeling

Affective fallacy, 42

Affective investment, 40, 46, 49, 72

African-Americans, 32, 95–99, 101–122, 177, 179, 183, 185, 186, 191, 192, 200, 201, 372n35, 385n32, 388n35. *See also* Blackness; Race

Agamben, Giorgio, 200, 227

Agency/agent: suspended, 1–2, 12, 32–33, 35–36, 346, 358n13; restricted, 2; obstructed, 3, 14, 32; limited, 36; in Melville, 55, 236, 245, 246; in trick films, 90–91; and lump, 92; and *The PJs,* 92, 115, 117; in Yau, 94; in Ellison, 113, 114; in Heidegger, 236, 246; in Hitchcock, 246; in Stowe, 358n13

Agglutination, 251, 263, 270, 273, 274, 277, 278, 281, 288, 291

Aggression: and feminism, 33; in Ellison, 118, 119; in *Single White Female,* 131, 141, 142, 161, 162; in Heilbrun, 134; in Gubar, 135; and women, 139–140; in Freud, 140; and sexuality, 140; and emulation, 142; and compound subject, 143; and identification, 161; and envy, 162; in Larsen, 186; in Andrews, 348. *See also* Antagonism; Violence

Agitation, 31, 32, 35, 90, 91, 96, 214, 237

Agnew, Jean-Christophe, 76

Alienation, 13, 285, 287, 292, 293

All about Eve (Mankiewicz), 133, 139, 140

Althusser, Louis, 210

Ambivalence, 3